H. E. B

AN AUTOB

"Wonderful reading".

H. E. Bates was born in 1905 at Rushden, Northamptonshire and was educated at Kettering Grammar School. His first novel, *The Two Sisters,* was published when he was twenty and in the next fifteen years he acquired a distinguished reputation for his stories about English country life, the best of which are collected in *Country Tales* (1938).

During the Second World War he was commissioned to write short stories of RAF life by the Air Ministry. He produced two best-selling collections, *The Greatest People in the World* (1942) and *How Sleep the Brave* (1943), under the pseudonym 'Flying Officer X', and under his own name wrote the enormously successful *Fair Stood the Wind for France* (1944).

In the 1950's he began to write the popular Larkin family novels, starting with *The Darling Buds of May* (1958). His autobiography originally appeared in three parts: *The Vanished World* (1969) was followed by *The Blossoming World* in 1971 and *The World in Ripeness* in 1972.

H. E. Bates was awarded the C.B.E. in 1973 and died in January 1974. He married in 1931, had four children and lived most of his life in Kent.

Also available from Methuen

The Purple Plain
The Jacaranda Tree
The Feast of July

THE VANISHED
WORLD

Jill Ravey.
October 2008.

I

I was born under Taurus, the Bull, that supposedly most favoured of the signs of the Zodiac, and was further blessed, if Old Wives' tales are to be believed, by being born wrapped in a caul (from O. Eng. Calle, Fr. Cale, a cap), a membranous covering, a portion of the *amnion,* which is sometimes found still enveloping the head of a child after birth. Various superstitions have from earliest times been attached to this caul, called in Scotland *sely how,* a holy or lucky hood, among them being that a child so adorned is exceptionally blessed and gifted, that the caul itself is a sign of good luck and, when preserved, an infallible protection against drowning. For these reasons it was often sold by midwives, more especially to sailors. Indeed I am assured that cauls are still sold by hospital porters in seaports.

It is easy to see why a caul should be considered a protection against drowning, since an infant may well drown at birth with the breaking of its mother's water. It is also no doubt considered lucky because of its rarity. My own doctor in fact assures me he has never seen one in all the years of his practice, though I recently talked to a young district nurse who had seen two cauls in the first year of her practice, much to the envy of several doctors she knew.

In this matter of being born in a caul I was in celebrated company. David Copperfield was born in a caul, as also was Sigmund Freud, back in 1856, in Vienna. The account by Dickens' hero of his birth (the novel appeared six years before Freud was born) is vastly entertaining and vivid, the account of Freud's hardly less interesting. Both confirm what I have already said of the supposedly blessed nature of the phenomenon and this is how Dickens, through the mouth of Copperfield, describes it:

I was born in a caul, which was advertised for sale, in the newspapers, at the low price of fifteen guineas. Whether sea-going people were short of money at that time, or were short of faith and preferred cork-jackets, I don't know; all I know is, that there was but one solitary bidding, and that was from an attorney connected with the bill-broking business, who offered two pounds in cash, and the balance in sherry, but declined to be guaranteed from drowning on any higher bargain. Consequently the advertisement was withdrawn at a dead loss . . . and ten years afterwards the caul was put up in a raffle down in our part of the country, to fifty members at half a crown a head, the winner to spend five shillings. The caul was finally won by an old lady who paid all of her five shillings in halfpence and 'was never drowned, but died triumphantly in bed, at ninety-two.' Her caul was therefore remarkably cheap, especially in view of the fact that she was anyway tuppence ha'penny short in payment, though in fact the price of cauls had sunk as low as thirty shillings by the end of the century.

Paternal Grandfather

Jews in Russia and Poland maintain that it is lucky 'to be born in a little shirt', a belief that seems certainly to have been connected with Freud, himself a Jew, whose caul 'was believed to ensure him future happiness and fame', and certainly his mother was delighted when later told by an old woman in a pastry shop 'that she had brought a great man into the world', an idea that Freud himself discounted, though he was not unimpressed by a still later prophecy, made by an improvising poet in a restaurant, that 'I should probably one day become a "Minister".' This same prophecy, happily unfulfilled, was also made by my maternal grandfather about me and was probably one equally cherished by my father though in his case the wish related to the Church rather than to the Crown. Perhaps another prophecy, contending that those born in a caul are lucky in love, was nearer the mark. Swift, in *Polite Conversations* (1738), wrote 'I believe you were born with a caul on your head you are such a favourite among the ladies,' and a character in Thomas Randolph's *The Jealous Lover* (1632) declared 'Sure I was born with a caul on my head and wrapped in my mother's smock, the ladies do love me so.' There is still further proof of the just esteem in which cauls were held in the fact that there may still be found, in antique shops, heart-shaped lockets, of silver, in which a caul could be kept, the lockets apparently being worn around the neck like a crucifix.

Whether it is in fact lucky to be born in a caul, or as the French say, *être né coiffé*, or not, it is certain that I was born, in 1905, into a world of leather and shoemakers. My grandfather on my mother's side was a shoemaker; my father was also a shoemaker, though not in the sense my grandfather was; my grandfather on my father's side had his own boot and shoemaking business, from which he not infrequently slipped away to the smoother, easier, more seductive life of warmer climates, notably the Mediterranean and later, permanently, to Australia; my mother went to work as a half-timer, in the shoemaking industry at the tender age of ten, tying knots, for the princely sum of two shillings a week. If indeed I ever suffer from some ailment of the lungs it may well be because the distant pungent odours of leather and shoemakers' shops still linger tenaciously within me.

Of my two grandfathers I knew the paternal one scarcely at all, except by reputation. I have no personal visual recollection of him whatever, except from photographs, in which he looks remarkably like H. G. Wells, whose undeniable and fatal attraction for women he shared. Short and not particularly handsome, he may fairly be called a lady-killer, having caused my father's mother, a beautiful, proud, highly sensitive girl devoted to the world of nature, to die of a broken heart – literally – at the age of twenty-one. That he omitted to marry her was responsible for the fact that, in due course, twentieth-century English literature was spared the embarrassment of having yet another Herbert Lawrence on the scene. I think I saw him perhaps twice or three times in my life, so frequent and prolonged were his journeys about the world, and on neither occasion did he offer a word or sign of recognition. By contrast I grew up, as I shall presently explain in greater detail, in my maternal grandfather's pocket, bonded in a great warm mutual affection, neither of us able in the other's eyes to do the slightest wrong.

When I say that my maternal grandfather was a shoemaker I mean that he could, after the fashion and tradition of centuries, create a boot or shoe from the sole upwards, stabbing and stitching, with his own hands. The world in which he plied his craft – he used to recall for me an occasion when a messenger rode on a white horse into the little market square of his native Higham Ferrers to bring the news, weeks after the event, that the Crimean War was over – knew no machines for shoemaking, except perhaps treadle-machines for stitching uppers. Consequently I am able still to see him to perfection in the mind's eye: shoemaker's last between his knees, tossing handfuls of tacks and sprigs into his mouth, to my extreme consternation; his awls, thread, leather, files, hammers all about him.

Not only, however, was he a shoemaker, but a craftsman of the highest class: so much so that when very special orders came down from London it was almost always to George William Lucas that they were given. It used to be his proud boast – though boast is altogether too strong a word to apply to so self-effacing, modest a man – let us say therefore that he was proud to have made both the largest and the smallest shoes in the world – the largest being those flat comic seven-league boots worn by the Victorian comedian Little Tich, the smallest a pair of doll-like miniatures for a midget dancer.

Higham Ferrers is a pleasant little stone built town overlooking the serene pastures of the Nene Valley in Northamptonshire. In my boyhood some of its streets were still cobbled. It is not only very nearly plumb in the middle of England, but if you take a pair of compasses and draw a circle of fifty or sixty miles with the little borough as its centre you will find yourself enriched by a truly remarkable company of famous men. Henry V's famous archbishop – of whom more in a moment – was born in the town itself; Thomas Rudd, Charles the First's chief engineer in the Civil War, was also born there; seven or eight miles away the tiny village of Aldwinkle, which has two churches and therefore two rectories, produced within five years John Dryden from one rectory and Thomas Fuller, the historian, from the other; a dozen miles or so to the south, over into Bedfordshire John Bunyan wrote *Pilgrim's Progress* and occasionally came to preach at Higham Ferrers and also at the stone Baptist meeting house which still stands at the end of the street in Rushden where I grew up as a boy; another dozen miles over the border into Buckinghamshire lived the poet

William Cowper; Shakespeare and Milton just about squeeze into the perimeter; farther down the valley John Clare wrote his poems, later to die in the asylum at Northampton, farther up the valley. This indeed is the old Kingdom of Mercia, cradle of so much of our literature and of the Standard English we know.

At one time Higham Ferrers was to have been a university town. Indeed its main street is still called College Street, in which stand the partially restored buildings of the college itself, with its associations with All Souls College, Oxford. These buildings, half in decay, were part of a farm in my boyhood and it was here, from time to time, that my grandfather and I went through a mystical process known as 'tekking the old gal down.' This was the business of taking the sow to the boar, though my innocence never grasped what the process exactly consisted of. This sow was

a remarkable lady. Small and puny when a suckling – what is sometimes called a dillin – she grew up to be bountiful both in girth and fertility. Great pink belly swaying, her keyboard of teats swinging, her ponderous, passive mouth slightly slobbering, she would of necessity have to be coaxed, rather than driven, the two miles or so from sty to farm. The resulting fruitfulness of her life was truly prodigious. First she began with modest litters of ten or a dozen; then fourteen and fifteen; then seventeen and eighteen; then an incredible nineteen. With bated expectancy we awaited her crowning twenty. Alas, it never came and soon she was hanging in the form of salty pictures, vast, fatty, succulent sides of bacon, on the walls of my grandmother's kitchen.

My grandfather was greatly given to storytelling, in the pursuit of which he almost invariably began at the end of the story and worked backwards to the beginning, clearly on the assumption that you already knew what the beginning was. Until you were familiar with this method you were bound to be enmeshed in much confusion. Thus it was that occasionally, as we were driving the horse and trap along the motorless summer lanes outside the town, he would pull up the horse, point the whip across the fields and say with solemn and mysterious emphasis: 'Masterpiece of man. Ploughboy. Used to scare the crows down there.'

Who this masterpiece of a man was it was utterly impossible to tell until, perhaps half a mile further on, you were presented with the cryptic enlightenment of the single word 'Chichele', followed at about the same interval by 'Archbishop' and at a third pause by 'Ploughboy'. Now my grandfather had, in mid-Victorian times, also been a ploughboy, scaring crows and taking his place as a boy of six every morning at four o'clock in the big farm kitchen a stone's-throw from the house where he was born, there to be given, together with all other farm-hands, a pint of beer. He could never manage to drink this beer – pretty strong it must have been, brewed as it was in the farm's own brew 'us – though there was never any lack of willing lips and throats to help him out in that direction.

It thus became borne upon me that the masterpiece of a man, Henry V's great archbishop at the time of Agincourt, who also has a part in Shakespeare's play and whose tomb may now be seen in Canterbury Cathedral in company with the Black Prince and

Thomas a'Beckett, had served as ploughboy and crow-scarer side by side with my grandfather. It was not for some considerable time that I amazedly discovered that some six hundred years separated the two local ploughboys. Not that this had the remotest effect on the great, glowing fraternal pride with which my grandfather always spoke of Chichele, a pride he also devoted to the great Mr Gladstone, of whom he was also accustomed to speak as if Victoria's Prime Minister and himself were near relations.

Chichele was in fact born in 1364, the son of Thomas Chichele, a farmer and Mayor of the borough. There were two other sons, Robert, afterwards Sir Robert, who became prosperous in the city of London and a great friend of the famed Dick Whittington; and William, who became a Sheriff in the city in 1410 and later an Alderman. Distinguished though the brothers must have been it was Henry who caught the eye of no less a person than William de Wykeham, Bishop of Winchester, when on a visit to the town. As a result Henry was placed at Winchester School and his extraordinarily distinguished and fruitful career was launched. Promotion to the Archdeaconry of Salisbury came in 1408; a little later he was sent by Henry IV as ambassador to Pope Gregory and then to the council of Pisa in 1409. In 1413 he was made Archbishop of Canterbury and in 1414 Henry V sent him as ambassador to Charles I of France and John, Duke of Burgundy.

If the world of my childhood, like that of grandfather, is almost wholly a vanished one, it is pleasant to record that that of Chichele still survives today in the shape of two splendid buildings of his own creation, both in the shadow of the magnificent church of Higham Ferrers: first the delicate and enchanting little grammar school in Perpendicular style, secondly the larger and altogether heavier-looking Bede-House, created as an institution and almshouse – rather oddly, I always feel – for twelve men and one woman. The men selected for this benefaction were entitled to wear a scarlet star on their coats and it was, I think, the proudest day of my grandfather's life when, six hundred years after these two fine buildings were erected, he too could walk in his native town so star-adorned while I, from time to time, changed into my football kit in the empty, slightly sepulchral Bede-House itself.

But before this happened there fell on the craft of shoemaking, about 1910, a great blight. The day of the hand-craftsman was virtually over; the machine was inexorably advancing. As in the Swiss watchmaking industry so in the world of shoemaking almost all the work was done at home. There were no forty-hour weeks, no clocking in. For ever independent, shoemakers were a law unto themselves, mostly getting rousing drunk on Saturdays and Sundays, never by long tradition working on Mondays. Either out of duty to their patron saint St Crispin or in pursuit of a cure for mountainous hangovers, they sought solace in the surrounding countryside, rabbiting, coursing, mushrooming, following hounds, walking or riding miles by devious routes to secret hideouts where bare-fisted bruisers bloodily battered themselves to pulp before crowds of gentry and poor alike. With

Monday behind them, shoemakers returned to their lasts, madly stitching and hammering away until midnight and even into the small hours in pursuit of cash that would, when Saturday came again, be riotously squandered on booze and the 'blues'.

Into the hayfields of June and the harvest-fields of August they also went, to join 'you sunburnt sickle-men of August weary', mostly the great gangs of itinerant Irish labourers who had been seasonally invading England ever since Stuart times. They too were roughly, fiercely independent. The communal bargain struck with the local farmer for the reaping of wheat, oats and barley was based solely on beer and money and if the bargain had to be gilded in favour of the reaper it was always by means of more beer, potently home-brewed of course. Years later a smallish man of cunning appearance with the appropriate nickname of Smack used to lend my grandfather a hand at harvest time, a magnificent and devastating craftsman with the scythe who confessed that he and his father thought little or nothing of drinking, in hayfield or harvest-field, twenty-five pints a day. His thirst remaining undiminished, I therefore often found myself riding pony-back to the outdoor beer-house, to bring back a load of bottles in a nosebag in readiness for dinner-time.

All pubs and beer-houses also sold, in those days, small beer; which, though not strong enough for men, had body enough for boys or what in Northamptonshire were vividly described as 'bwoy-chaps', the word boy always being pronounced in that strong, special, earthy way. Old women also brewed, and were still brewing in my boyhood, a herb beer, confined solely to summer, made of nettles – I rather fancy the stingless, flowering kind – dandelions, root ginger and various other wild hedgerow plants, together with yeast and sugar. It had a mildly astringent taste, not unlike a watered-down vermouth, and was known, as near as it is possible to get the pronunciation into words, as diar-drink or dior-drink. This curious word, which I always imagined to be strictly local, has had me infinitely puzzled for a great many years and it was only recently that I discovered that the Welsh name for herb beer, the brew being composed of exactly the same ingredients as the Northamptonshire one, is *diod-dail*: hence, it would clearly seem, the diod-drink, or herb drink, of my boyhood. English dictionaries offer no clues as to the word *diod* and perhaps only some erudite modern Professor Higgins can explain for us how this Welsh word came to have common usage in Midland England.

I would gravely doubt if diod-drink is ever made today, or for that matter sloe-gin or blackberry-vinegar, a concoction of hideous, indeed almost brutal throat-searing flavour once made and kept by every Northamptonshire household as a sovereign remedy, like eucalyptus and camphorated oil, against the barking coughs of winter. I should doubt also if the milkman of today, in his sterilized world of huge dairy combines, ever delivers beastings or bustings or biznins, as we always called them: the first milk given by the cow after calving. But beastings, or biznins were, in our world, little short of a luxury. The extreme richness of the milk cooked quickly into a custard that was creamy, stiff and rich. It was always a red letter day when the biznins arrived and I loved it.

This world, in which hiring-fairs were still a common autumnal practice and *largesse* was still distributed as it had been from time immemorial, all of it I fancy little changed since Shakespeare's day, also belonged to the women. They too invaded the fields of hay at harvest, their children with them, the children to make bonds for the sheaves, the women to bond and stook them. I have heard my grandfather say of these women that it was no uncommon sight to see a woman suddenly unbutton her blouse in the harvest-field, take out a milky breast, and suckle a child old enough and tall enough to stand and reach the nipple. Later they fell on the stook-empty fields like flocks of human hens, in the guise of gleaners, gleaning frenziedly from dawn to dark, when the final gleaning bell sounded: a custom so rewarding that I have heard my paternal great-grandmother, who brought up her twelve children on twelve shillings a week supplemented by a further half-crown earned by her husband as town lamplighter, say that on one occasion she and her family gleaned enough corn to justify hiring a threshing machine.

If the world of the gleaner, a figure common to the summer scene ever since Ruth stood in tears among the alien corn, was to continue for some good few years yet, the old world of the hand-craft shoemaker was rapidly withering before the blight. The years about 1910 were a time of much distress. Whole families emigrated to Australia and the New World (you could then get a one-way passage for as little as £6); shoemakers went to London in marches of hunger and protest; there were empty houses everywhere. For the shoemaker, the hand craftsman, there was no future.

It was about this time that my grandfather decided to return to the land that had first nurtured him. Stimulated perhaps by that smooth slogan 'two acres and a cow' he decided, with two or three of his shopmates, to set up as a small-holder. From a chosen field of about twelve acres, overlooking the great pastoral width of the Nene valley, his share was five. Many years later I met a farmer who well remembered the choice. 'They chose it,' he said and sadly shook his head, 'because in the previous summer it had borne a splendid crop of wheat. They couldn't have chosen worse.' The land in fact was wickedly heavy, impossible to touch in winter, drying out to a surface of cracked concrete in summer, a devilish challenge, year in, year out, to a virtually single-handed man.

But if the choice almost meant a sentence of penal servitude for my grandfather for the rest of his life it afforded me the foundation on which all the joys of my childhood, together with all my feeling and love of the countryside, is based. There sprang up for me, out of this very ordinary, unprepossessing piece of Midland earth, a paradise that remains to this day utterly un-blemished, a joy for ever.

Shoes worn by John Clare when in St Andrew's Hospital

II

At first the tools my grandfather had for the tillage of this intractable piece of land were pathetically simple. He had neither horse nor stable to put one in. His only vehicle was a wheelbarrow, in which I can distinctly remember being wheeled to the land on spring and summer mornings.

But soon things began to improve and it was largely my father who brought about the improvement. One of the positively good things he had inherited from his recalcitrant father, and which in turn I have failed to inherit from him, was a near genius for doing anything with hammer, saw and nails. Accordingly he began, on Saturday afternoons, to build for my grandfather a few simple farm buildings: a stable, a hen-house, pigsties, a cart-shed, an outhouse for storing tools, seeds and bran for pigswill, a copper house for boiling potatoes for the pigs, and a privy. There was also a little shed containing a chaff-cutter, the big handle of which I sometimes used to turn on winter afternoons, when I also helped chop up mangel-wurzels (wezzles, as they were always called) for horsefeed. The resulting farmyard, later adorned with hay and straw ricks, became the hub of my world.

Soon a succession of horses, some of them no more than ponies, inhabited the stable. One by one, with disconcerting frequency, they fell down dead. Since their unremitting task was to draw plough, harrow, seed-drill, horse hoe, trap and a truck from which we sold vegetables, fruit and flowers from house to house two mornings a week, this was by no means surprising. It is in fact astounding that the tumbril from the knacker's yard didn't appear more frequently than it did, to take away its melancholy load of stiffening horseflesh.

What this continuing succession of tragedies meant to my grandfather, poor and single-handed as he was, I was too young to tell. Small wonder that his figure, once tall and upright, was now deeply bent, or that his hair, black in early manhood, was now completely snow-white. But if I was too young to understand it is equally certain that I was, to him, an intense source of joy and comfort. He had in fact greeted my birth with the words: 'Capital! We've had enough o' gals!' – this resounding comment referring not to the fact that he had fathered a whole regiment of women but merely to my mother and her sister, his only children, and even they separated by ten years or so. He had long wanted a son and this, at last, was what I virtually was to him.

If I was also a source of great irritation to him – and I am perfectly certain I was, constant as I was in my cajoling insistence that he take me fishing, birds' nesting, playing cricket or gathering water-cress – he never once revealed it. His sharpest rebuke, not often repeated at that, was a mere 'Drop it, boy,' though very occasionally he might go so far as to refer to me as 'that young gallus'. His constant reward for this great indulgence was to be told by my grandmother and aunt that 'you'd cut off your head and give it to him if he as much as asked for it,' an undoubted truth if ever there was one.

Apart from the main holding with its little farmyard my grandfather rented from time to time two other fields, both pasture and both of about five acres in area, one for the purpose of gathering a stack of hay, the other for grazing one of the unfortunate ponies; but it was really about the little farmyard, with its clucking hens and squealing pigs, that the horizon of my world extended. The crest of the valley here is quite high, wide and open to every searing, soaking wind. On a really clear fine day it was possible here to pick out no less than nine of the church spires for which Northamptonshire is justly famous. Few trees and no great woodlands were there to break the view. Ash, hawthorn and elm, with here and there a few small oaks, made up the general pattern of trees; the beeches, sweet chestnuts, turkey oaks and whitebeams which I now know and love in the south country were never to be seen.

Nevertheless, sparsely clothed as it was, the land in spring and summer was a great thrilling palpitation of bird song. I can see now huge droves of grey elephantine April cloud-shadows rushing across the valley before the western wind and feel the cut of ice in the air each time the sun went in. Along the headlands flowered yellow drifts of coltsfoot, doubly precious because this was a countryside with no primroses, no bluebells, no kingcups, none of Shakespeare's beloved lady-smocks, still to me one of the high aristocrats of England's spring flowers. Above it all a pee-witting chorus of plovers would beat strongly at the air, but never strongly enough to drown the celestial choirs of skylarks, for whose nests I was constantly going in diligent search along the plough furrows. Kestrels hovered above too, poised for the long darting kill, and the May hedgerows clinked with the pink-pink of chaffinches, not long since one of England's commonest birds but now, alas, almost a rarity. And then in summer the yellow-hammers, the endless drowsy repetition of 'a little bit of bread

and no cheese', and the occasional whistle of swan wings beating up from the river.

If my grandfather had no time to come with me birds'-nesting – and how he ever found the time I cannot think – I had perforce to go alone, at first tremulous of being found trespassing in other people's fields, then so lost in the search for nests and eggs that presently I even forgot my fears. The blue clutches of hedge-sparrow and thrush, the green-blue of blackbird, the peppered delicacies of the finches, the scribble of writing-larks, even some-times the thrill of a plover and the even greater thrill of that marvel among nests, the long-tailed tit, 'the pudden-bag': all were part of a nervous springtime miracle. And sometimes on early mornings, while I still slept, my grandfather would come back to the house, having been up since four o'clock, with a handful of partridge eggs for my breakfast. I can still see them dancing and bubbling, tiny, golden and white, among slices of home-cured bacon in the frying pan.

Of wider journeyings into the surrounding countryside, sometimes into Huntingdonshire, more often into Bedfordshire, to which I looked forward passionately, I shall have much to say later; but often we had shorter journeys to make, either in trap or truck, and the most frequent of these was into the village of Chelveston-cum-Caldicott down the hill, where a little tributary of the Nene twice made a watersplash across the road, white in summer with water ranunculus, green with brook-lime and cress and alive with gudgeon and sticklebacks. Here we always stopped to water the ponies and, in drought years, to fill barrels with water before going on to the village to find out if the cunning and redoubtable Smack could come and knock an acre or two of wheat down or to see some other man about something or other.

Thousands of American ex-servicemen will have no need to be told what and where Chelveston is. Here, after Pearl Harbour, came the bulldozers and bombers to carry out the necessary ruthless murder of part of my childhood countryside. Here, in place of woods where I had gathered violets and revelled in the heady perfume of crowds of cream-green butterfly orchids, there sprang up

a vast airfield, furnished with
what was probably the most
useless and vulnerable flying
machine ever sent, like a
ponderous duck, into combat:
the Flying Fortress. Over-
armoured, slow, unable to be
fitted with exhaust-cowlings
because of the extra weight, it
fell prey to Goering's Luftwaffe
fighters with an ease so fearful
that its first concerted daylight raid over Germany was
nothing but naked ruthless
murder itself, leaving strong
men weeping at Chelveston

and the air-field itself crushed and stunned in mourning.

But of course on those other mornings, as I turned the stones
of the brook for the sight of sticklebacks, I had no idea of these
things. Every morning was golden; even the First World War had
not begun. The hedgerows of spring were clothed with the cream
of may blossom; those of June and July with pink and white dog-
roses, meadowsweet and willowherb. If the paradise made by it all
was about to be shattered, not once but twice, I happily hadn't
even the remotest suspicion of the gathering cloud. Sticklebacks
were in the brook, cuckoos called from the elms, yellowhammers
swooned away long summer afternoons in lanes shimmering with
heat and virtually undefiled by the motor car, and consequently
all was right with the world.

At the boundary of Chelveston my grandfather would
frequently halt the trap to make another of his mysterious
'masterpiece of a man' pronouncements. As with Chichele this
followed a pattern of cryptic brevity, 'the masterpiece' opening
being succeeded, a minute or so later, by 'coalman', a little later
by 'musician', then by 'London' and finally by 'Britton'. As a
child I had not the faintest idea of what all this meant and it

took several years of adult detective work to discover that my grandfather was in fact referring to yet another celebrated son of Northamptonshire, namely Thomas Britton (1644-1714) coalman indeed, musician, book-collector, close acquaintance of nobility and friend of Handel.

The pronouncement on Britton was undoubtedly made at the parish boundary of Chelveston on the supposition that he was born there, almost every other family in the village being called, even in my time, Britton. In this my grandfather may or may not have been mistaken. *The Dictionary of National Biography* gives Britton's birthplace either as Wellingborough or Higham Ferrers; *Grove's Dictionary of Music* settles for my own birthplace, Rushden. Whichever is correct it is certain that Britton went to London at an early age, apprenticed himself to a coal-merchant in Clerkenwell for seven years and then set up in business for himself, hiring an old stable for the purpose.

This stable was evidently so small as to be described as 'not much higher than a Canary Pipe and the window of his State Room but very little bigger than the Bunghole of a Cask'. Nevertheless here, in 1678, Britton started his celebrated series of musical soirées. These attracted not only some of the most gifted musicians of the time, including the great Handel himself, who played the organ, but leaders of fashion and nobility. Coffee was served at a penny a cup and there were, it seems, 'many notable performances in the charming science of Musick'.

Music, however, was not the only science in which Britton was interested. He also took up chemistry, turning later to the occult sciences, on which he collected a large and distinguished library. In pursuit of this he was aided by a number of notable and titled bibliophiles, among them the Earl of Oxford, the Duke of Devonshire and the Earls of Pembroke, Winchelsea and Sunderland. All the time he continued to sell coal in the streets. The suspicion that a man of such humble origins could hardly move in elevated circles without nefarious purposes of some kind led to his being variously accused of being an atheist, a Jesuit, a Presbyterian and a magician. Grove declares all of this to be quite unfounded – 'Britton was a plain, simple, honest man.' But one thing seems to have been certain: he was highly superstitious, a fact that seems to have led, in 1714, to his death. To one of the concerts came a celebrated ventriloquist, a blacksmith named Honeyman, who proceeded to tease Britton by telling him that unless he at once fell on his knees and repeated the Lord's Prayer he would die within an hour or two. The wretched Britton immediately did as he was told but was apparently so frightened that he died a few days later. His collection of some fourteen hundred books was auctioned after his death and the catalogue of it is still, apparently, extant.

These 'masterpiece of a man' episodes are by no means irrelevant. Indeed they throw much light on my grandfather's considerable character. It must be remembered that the only schooling he ever received was a very brief period at a mid-Victorian Dame school, so that although he could read a little he could scarcely write his name. Yet he was a man of advanced and liberal views, constantly energetic in politics, perpetually scornful of and in opposition to all organised religion, a co-founder of the local co-operative society and above all a staunch and passionate Englishman. His face, bronzed by wind and sun, with its fine acquiline nose and pure white hair, had about it an indisputably aristocratic air. What even a smattering of education would have done for him is something I often ask myself and it is my friend David Garnett, I think, in the first volume of his own auto-biography, *The Golden Echo,* who touches on the answer.

'We have reason to believe,' he says, 'that every living creature is a fresh permutation of ancestral genes which determines its individuality. Half of the possible genes are passed on to the new individual from each parent, half are discarded. The hereditary constitution which results is infinitely more important than education or experience.'

Precisely; so with my grandfather.

III

The church of Higham Ferrers, thanks no doubt to the early influence of Chichele, has always been, and still is, very High; that at Rushden always has been, and still is, very Low. My grandfather would have no part of this High Church, nor indeed of any Low one. Scornfully he spoke of 'Popery and humbug, sciencing about with incense and singing in nightshirts'. My father, by contrast, was a deeply religious man, not merely devoted to the Methodist faith but positively locked in its uncompromising straitjacket. It is therefore time now to say something of him, the other great formative influence on my childhood.

He started life with several disadvantages, not to say misfortunes, the most grievous of which was the death of his broken-hearted mother when he was two, followed shortly afterwards by that of his grandmother, in whose care he had been left. The death of his mother was, I think, something that secretly grieved him for the rest of his life. In photographs she is shown as a proud, very beautiful girl in that pure mould for which the Midland valleys of England are justly famous. Not only are the people of these valleys, from Ouse to

Trent, the best looking in all England; they are probably some of the handsomest in all Europe. Both my father and mother were cast in this mould and if family gossip is to be accepted there was a succession, on the Lucas side, in Victorian times, of such beauties as to keep squires, doctors and young bloods constantly on the boil.

My father's mother, as I have already said, cared passionately for the countryside, as indeed all of that side of the family did. My father, and indeed I in turn, inherited this strong love of nature and in my father's case it was responsible for some interesting tricks on his part. Sent to the local board school, he quickly discovered that the nearby national school, or church school, was favoured with several more days' holiday, on such occasions for instance as Ascension Day, than his own. Apart from playing truant pretty often anyway, he therefore from time to time did a quick change act, removing his allegiance from board school to national, where he enjoyed the bonus holiday before going back again.

At the age of ten he went, like my mother, to work. Those were the days of half-timers, when children of ten went to school for one half of the day and to work for the other. The hand shoe-makers of the day also employed small boys – at, I should guess, about sixpence a week – as runners between their backyard shops and factories. They were known as sweaters. My father was never a sweater but I should guess that his starting wage was not more than three or four shillings a week. It is certain that my mother's was only two.

In spite of all this and in spite of much truancy and changes of scholastic scene, he had achieved such distinction at the age of thirteen, then the school-leaving age, that he was asked to stay on as a teacher. This invitation he declined. He had in fact an excellent and diligent brain. He could write a beautiful copper-plate hand, though for all ordinary purposes he used a sort of secondary copper-plate, quite excellent in itself. He was an extremely good mathematician; in all my experience I never knew him to make a spelling mistake; his grasp of general knowledge was wide and first class; he read a good deal and collected himself a tolerably good little library.

His other great passion was music. Orphaned, pitched into work at childhood in an industry he hated, virtually abandoned by a profligate father who gaily gave up his partnership in business to go to Australia, largely on the grounds of ill-health, though he lived to his mid-eighties, my father nevertheless applied his difficult adolescence first of all to teaching himself to read music, then to buying himself a piano. He himself was possessed of a very fine, strong bass voice, the rich warm depth of which I can still hear emerging from the tiers of the chapel choir, of which he was subsequently conductor, like a splendid diapason.

His was the age of male-voice choirs, male-voice quartettes and mixed quartettes and he threw himself into all this sort of thing with much conscientious and ardent activity. I do not wish to give the impression here that he was in any way a narrow-minded or bigoted man – this indeed was far from the case – but the strictness with which he devoted himself to the Methodist faith was, to say the least of it, pretty unyielding. It is hard to say whether pubs or clubs inspired him to greater contempt. Card-playing, gambling, horse-racing, drinking, dancing: all, in the true tradition of Wesley, were anathema to him, the only exception being that he enjoyed a game of cribbage. Even there the eye of the faith was for ever watchful, as I discovered some years after I had married when I remarked, after he had enjoyed a phenomenal run of luck on the crib board, that he was having the luck of the very devil himself. He at once fell upon me with righteous wrath, as if I were still a recalcitrant small boy who had done something phenomenally disgraceful. After the same fashion he would suddenly rise from his seat at a football match to deliver a loud and stern homily to some spectator who had just counselled the referee to keep 'his bleeding eyes open'. What he would have said about today's so-called permissive society, where tons of toilet paper are thrown at goalkeepers every season and the literary advisor of the National Theatre uses the language of gutter-snipes on television I simply dare not think.

One result of all this was that I grew up in an atmosphere of intense respectability in which, though we were never affluent, we knew nothing of the poverty and squalor so common to Edwardian working-class towns, where booze and the pawnshop dominated a great part of the population. My parents were never a farthing in debt; great was the pride they took, as my grand-parents did, in paying their way. Yet the margin left between one pay packet and another was often as low as sixpence, as manifested by a story of my mother's in which she tells of being left with exactly that sum of a Friday morning, faced with the problem of giving my father the hot midday meal a working man expected in those days. Quite undeterred, she crossed the road to the butcher's shop, bought a pennyworth of suet, two pennyworth of kidney and three pennyworth of steak and then went back to make a steak-and-kidney pudding, her purse empty.

My father pursued his passion for nature and the countryside, and incidentally fostered my own, by doing a vast amount of walking – oh! how we walked. Winter and summer we tramped, by Shanks's Pony, the bus-less, motor-less roads, the footpaths, the blackberry hedges, the river towpaths, the woodland ridings, mostly in Bedfordshire, my father striding out athletically, I desperately struggling to keep up. I vividly recall an occasion when – I was not more than five – we penetrated deep by footpath into the next county, lost our way and at last, after hours of wandering, came to a signpost indicating that it was still six miles to home. Even my father afterwards confessed to dismay.

To this day the joy of these walks remains. There is a certain woodland just over the Bedfordshire border that is crossed by a broad grass riding which is etched on my mind with such imperishable clarity that I can still see and smell the bluebells, the honeysuckle, the meadowsweet, the dog roses and the sheer concentrated fragrance of summer leaf and sap. If I have nothing else to thank my father for – and I have a very great deal – this in itself would be enough.

Not that we always walked. Quite often, mostly when my father's choir or quartette was off to keep an engagement to sing at some village fête or chapel or garden party or great house, we went by brake or wagonette. The scene is as remote as something

out of Pickwick or Hardy's *The Woodlanders:* the varnished brake itself, the gleaming brass and neats-foot oil of the harness, the odours of horse-flesh and horse-droppings, the summer dust, the harsh crunch of metal wheel rims on the rough stones of the road, the pantomime of half the passengers having to alight at the approach of every modest hill – and above all an air of unsophisticated, almost naïve enjoyment that our contemporary world of fast cars, planes, television and vast motorways never knows and will never know: a vanished world indeed.

It is undoubtedly from those summer journeyings that my adult preoccupation with great country houses, in terms of much of my fiction, stems. Rich though Northamptonshire is in great and lovely houses it is more the transition from red-brick, factory and chapel to the broad serenity and dignity of noble estates that, I fancy, has left so imperishable an impression on me. I still re-experience the feeling, fifty years later, that the start of these journeys was very like being let out of prison.

In structure Rushden is an odd town; in the lateness and rapidity of its development perhaps odder still. Unlike Higham Ferrers it has no ancient history worthy of the name. At the beginning of the 19th century it was still a mere village of a few hundred inhabitants; by the end of the century it had become an industrial town of 15,000 people. Its shape ill-suited to bear the scars of jerry-building and the Industrial Revolution, might well have been carved out by a madman gone slightly berserk with a giant bulldozer. It is impossible to get out of the town without going uphill. Hills rise and slant and dive in all directions, some so precipitously that one or two streets are closed to downhill traffic. The miserable little brook that runs through the entire length of it seems to be the central point of magnetism for these many steep streets and alleyways, which can be wickedly cold in winter and steamily, oppressively hot in summer. The only buildings of any architectural significance in the whole town are the church, with its famous Strainer arch, one of only three in England, and the Hall, which is the setting for a great deal of my novel, *Love for Lydia.* The rest is a palpably dreadful mess of that mixture of blue slate, factory, chapel and that harsh Midland red brick which equally oppresses heart, soul, eye and senses.

Just occasionally you find this dreary pattern relieved by corner facings of that deep beer-brown ironstone which lies near the surface of the Nene and Walland Valleys, and sometimes in the years of my boyhood you would find grapevines growing on the south walls of these older, softer houses of local stone. But the street in which I was born was wholly of brick, not all red but ranging from plain white at the southern, more respectable end to a shade of dreary dreadful puce-blue at the other. In it were two boot factories, and next to one of them I was born. In the street running in at right angles almost opposite to my parents' house stood the factory where my father worked, and immediately over the roof of the pork butcher's opposite us I could see, on winter evenings, the gaslights of another factory shining greasy-yellow until six o'clock. The geography of the town might indeed have been laid out by some shoemaking dictator who had insisted that for every hundred yards of dwelling houses there should be thirty or forty of factory sandwiched between and then had added the humanitarian proviso that a bakehouse and a chapel or two should somehow be tucked in among them. Immediately opposite us there were indeed two bakehouses, both absolutely identical. At the far end of the street was another, with a fourth fifty yards beyond. A fifth, again next door to a factory, and in this case an outdoor beerhouse as well as a bakery, stood at the far end of the street where my father worked. Here too, within a distance of a few hundred yards, were three chapels; and this pattern of house, factory, bakehouse and chapel, with here and there little front room sweet-shops, continued all over the town.

In photographs of these Midland streets taken in the first years of the century it is sometimes possible to see what the shoemakers of the day looked like. They were very often dressed in the sort of curly bowler now called Edwardian or in the flat almost peakless cap that is again, like the bowler, popular today. Their jackets were longish, black and cut away, often with those capacious pockets called poachers' pockets, and no man ever wore anything on his feet but boots, never shoes, or anything but a muffler round his neck, except of course on holidays and Sundays. I can just remember these men, not only hurrying to work in the morning but hurrying during the course of the day from factory or backyard work shop to the sewing and stitching shops, either carrying armfuls of boot uppers or wheeling them in big three-wheel basket trucks.

But what I really remember most vividly about these men are their aprons and mufflers. My father wore a muffler, the ends of which he crossed, folded over and tucked into his armpits exactly in the style of all other working men. He also wore an apron. This was of white cotton, with a white tape band to go over the head and two others to tie at the waist. It was more or less possible to tell the craft of a man from the degree of dirtiness on his apron. Clickers, the men who begin the whole process of shoemaking by cutting out from skins of leather the uppers, toecaps, tongues, facings and so on, could keep their aprons clean for a long time, but finishers, who give the soles of shoes their final blacking and polishing, could never be clean, either as to aprons or hands, and my impression is that sometimes they wore wholly black aprons. On Sundays I myself wore a little apron, white and cut exactly like my father's, in order that I should avoid spilling gravy and pudding down my best blue serge waistcoat. I was not, of course, allowed to sit at table with my jacket on; nor did my father and nor indeed any other shoemaker or his son.

There were times when I took my father's tea to him at the factory in a blue enamel can with a cup balanced on the top. The plan of those old factories, all built just before the turn of the century, was very much the same: three storeys of brick, windows of thick opaque glass, heavy wooden front door, widish wooden staircase, and a little matchwood office on the first floor where clerks dealt with wages, kept books and made use of the wall fixture telephone. I used to go to this dark, ugly, dreary, noisome, thunderous bedlam of industry with a sense of dread: not dread, I think, of its sheer drabness, its stench of leather and gaslight or its racket of presses and whining scream of machines, but a terrible

dread at the half-conscious notion that one day I too might have to work in it. I did not then know that my father, the gentlest of men, had vowed before God that I never should work in it; nor did I know, until far beyond these earliest years of childhood, that he had begun work in that same bedlam at the age of ten, as a half-timer, and that for almost all of another fifty years he was to detest it.

The impression I chiefly gain from the recollection of those shoemaking men is not exactly one of coarseness; they lack the sheer belted belching muscle and guts of what used to be known as labouring men; they do not exhibit the beery-spitting swagger I remember of navvies, bricklayers or those wild-eyed drovers of cattle I sometimes used to see, drunk and rosy-eyed, on Midland market days. Their roughness is of rather a different order, and I find it difficult to describe. If I use the word rude, in the sense of uncouth, the impression will be a shade too strong. Nor are they loud; nor, in Rupert Brooke's words, excessively 'black of mouth'. Nor are they as forthright, or as blunt or as self-opinionated as northern men. The impression I really get is of a dry, droll, unshaven independence and it is not at all an unlikeable quality.

This impression of unshaven men is a very real one and I think it springs largely from the fact that I saw these shoemakers so often in barbers' shops. There were two barbers' shops to which I went in my childhood and both inflicted on me so considerable an amount of torture that even now, nearly half a century later, I still intensely dislike having my hair cut. It was my penance to have to go to them on Saturdays, an ill-favoured day as far as boys were concerned, since both saloons would be crammed from eight-o'clock onwards with crowds of shag-smoking, snuff-taking, stubble-faced working men, mufflered and capped, most of them waiting to be shaved. The system by which customers would be taken in strict rotation was something that worked very well with men but broke down instantly it came to the turn of a boy. In consequence I used to sit for three or four or even five hours in ever increasing boredom and despair, exhausting one by one the tattered pink copies of *Chips* and the tattered white copies of *Comic Cuts,* turning in eventual desperation to the bewildering pages of *Sporting Life* or, as I grew older, to the terrors of the *Police Gazette*. All the time, all about me, a lather boy would be ceaselessly brushing soap into three-day beards, and the barber himself – in one saloon a gossiping idiot of brainless nosiness, in the other a dapper little jockey-like man of sporty instinct – would be clipping, snipping and scraping away with scissors and cut-throat. The smell of shag, after two or three hours, had the power to move mountains, and in one corner there burned, like some semi-evil fire out of a picture of an opium den, the three-forked flames of a gas-geyser heating water. Many customers kept their own shaving mugs at the saloons and these stood about on shelves between advertisements for navy-cut, Woodbines, plug, twist, the beloved shag and, most surprisingly, brands of cigars. And in odd corners there stood piles of umbrellas, that strange sideline of the provincial barbers' world, very much like piles of battered old rooks, brought in for repair.

I would say that the average shoemaker of those days, whether self-shaven or shop-shaven, had the razor on his face no more than twice or three times a week. My father shaved every day, but then my father was not an average shoemaker; whereas my grandfather, a man of an older, more rural, more home-spun generation, as I have described, shaved on Wednesdays and Saturdays unless some special mid-week evening took him out to political meetings or lectures, when he would again scrape off his beard and, in his own words, get himself titivated up. There were of course plenty of men who were great dandies in that generation – the moustache-waxers, the quiff-plasterers, the wearers of patent toecaps – and these were exceptions to the two-shaves-a-week system, just as they were far removed from the habit of smoking shag in short nose-warming clays.

I do not wish to give the impression here that I am speaking of a generation composed entirely of uncouth louts: very much the contrary. The shoemakers of the Midlands have long been noted for their pride, political acumen, sturdy independence of mind and an ability to talk sense under conditions where others often signally fail. It is in fact from this same generation, so many of whom were to be wiped out in the holocaust of Somme and Passchendaele, that there sprang, to their abiding credit, an industrial arbitration system that has virtually kept the boot and shoe industry in England free from any kind of serious dispute or stoppage for over half a century. When dockers, miners, car-workers, railway men and bus drivers use what they so charmingly call the strike-weapon to back industrial grievance I become very proud of my shoe-makers, the men who had the guts and sense to put an end to years of seemingly irremediable bitterness, hunger, lockouts, strikes and sheer destitution by a system built on simple commonsense, honour and a rejection of acrimony. These were my shag-smokers, the unshaven ones. They lived very largely on kippers, bloaters, tea, beer, cheese, potatoes and plenty of good bread from the coal-ovened bakehouses; and the lordly inevitable roast-beef on Sundays. They were the ones who ran to work in fear of losing farthings, waking me every morning in my waking years.

A few years earlier, just too far back for me to remember, at a time when the old hand shoemaker and his world were passing for ever, the life of these towns was very much a man's domain. There was much brawling, fighting, drinking and sheer squabbling squalor. There also existed two kinds of animosity which town-ships no longer know: that between street and street, when gangs of louts brawled in small possessive warfare, and that between township and township, when men out of crude bravado rolled from one town to another, beating up rival gangs, rough-housing outside ever-open pubs and inventing strange labels of contempt for rival towns. 'Hock-and-Dough' was a term still commonly used for Wellingborough, the market town with the public school on the Nene, when I was a child, the name deriving from some kind of poor man's dish of trotter and pastry said to be much favoured in that town but which the men of Rushden, the Evensford of my novels, held to be food beneath contempt. The men of Raunds, a rough little, tough little town with a rare church, had the jeer of Hair-and-Teeth thrown at them, and replied by calling the men of Irthlingborough Yow-Yows.

In that world, meanwhile, women drudged, slaved, pawned clothes, conceived, gave their children bread and scrat to eat and waited and wept. There was an extraordinary amount of tuberculosis in these valleys, both then and for many years later. Yellowish-blue faces, far gone in decline, peer at me through memory with haunting cadaverous thinness. The harrowing picture of Victorian industrial hunger has been too often painted for me to attempt it again, but there is no doubt that thousands of women of that masculine shoe-making world just before and perhaps even after my birth waited in desolation, Saturday after Saturday, for fools, braggarts, wasters and almost every other kind of husband to bring home the week's wages; and waited in vain. The Saturday drunken beat-up, when beer drowned every penny of a man's money, was as fixed a part of life as the Sunday morning parade to chapel and church; and women, dreading it, bled their hearts out.

If you care now to make a journey into this Midland shoe-making country I do not think that you will find, except for the factories themselves and the familiar brick street pattern, anything left of what I describe. A great number of the people of my native Evensford work, for example, in a factory designed by the late President of the Royal Academy, Sir Albert Richardson; and on Sundays enjoy music played in a bandstand, also designed by that eminent twentieth-century Georgian, standing in the park of the great house described in *Love for Lydia.* Men no longer wear aprons and mufflers or, I believe, run to work. Most of the old bakehouses are closed and I doubt very much if an old familiar cry, a great favourite of mine, the cry of the watercress man, is ever heard on Sunday afternoons. Women please themselves what time they arrive in factory closing rooms, going in to work at nine or nine-thirty or two or two-thirty as they wish and leaving in the same way. Just before Christmas they festoon the workrooms with decorations and, unless my relatives in the boot and shoe towns misinform me, hold parties, complete with wine. Every man is a collar-and-tie man now and the girls and women, always so handsome and conscious of their clothes, are among the prettiest and best-dressed in England – the daughters and granddaughters, many of them, of those same women who bled their hearts out at Victorian street corners and in summer gleaned the surrounding fields for a winter's bread.

IV

It has long been my impression that I went to school at the age of three, but my mother, now in her ninety-second year but happily possessed of all her faculties including a memory quite unimpaired, insists that I was four. In either case I remember the occasion vividly, having put on a gigantic-tantrum (what my grandfather sometimes used to call 'a mad' or 'a paddy'), in my determination not to go. I was thwarted in this purpose, however, by the opportune arrival of my step-grandmother, a formidable lady who promptly seized me by the ear, lugged me away and deposited me unceremoniously on the steps of the council infant school, two streets away.

Whether I had inherited from my father an antipathy towards school it is difficult to say; but that I viewed the prospect of attending it with as much dread as going to prison there is absolutely no doubt. Like my father I did not at all relish the prospect of confinement; already, even at that age, I had tasted the free range of fields, hedgerows, woods and streams to such an extent that I was constantly thirsting to get back to them. I was also, I am sure, mostly frightened by the very thought of school-teachers, whose habits of terror and whipping had already been fearfully etched on my mind by older children only too keen to exaggerate their experience of school-going and its pain.

The immediate district served by this, my first school, was almost wholly working class. It is true that on the very eastern edge of the town, where open country began, there were incongruously a few affluent properties, fairly large houses set in well timbered grounds where teacups tinkled on lawns on summer afternoons and the clock of croquet balls might sometimes be heard, but much in the surrounding streets was near

sordid, an adjective not inapplicable to some of my early class mates. 'They make me sit next to a boy who stinks,' I one day informed my mother and to this day the peculiar acrid stench of the unwashed lingers in my nostrils. Not only were many unwashed indeed – I suppose there was not more than one bathroom to a thousand houses in those days – but sometimes as I trailed to school a door in a row of terrace houses would open to give a swift and revolting picture of unmitigated squalor, of filthy rags spread about a carpetless floor, a gas-stove ghastly with grease, a packing case serving as a chair and as likely as not a chamberpot, unwashed too, on prominent display on a broken chair. Small wonder that many of the children from these homes were in a constant state of itch and scratch, so that it needed all my father's vigilance and industry with soap and tooth-comb to keep me, as he would say, free of livestock.

But not all were unwashed. I still have in my possession a faded photograph of my class in the year, probably, of 1910, and a highly interesting social document it is. Three significant things are at once to be noted about it: all the little girls are wearing rather long flouncy pinafores; nine-tenths of the boys are wearing large, almost flamboyant white lace collars over their jackets, sometimes so big as to stretch to the tips of their shoulders; the other tenth are, however, dressed in plain dark blue jerseys, buttoning at the neck. These jerseys are what would now be called status symbols. The boys wearing them are sons of fathers higher up the social ladder or, as the shoemakers themselves used to put it so aptly, of men who are 'notch above a tapper'. I am one of them.

My brain is a quick and receptive one and I learned to read at an early age. The influence of my father is again apparent here; being able to read is one thing, having something to read is another. Where so many fathers of the unwashed wasted their pitiful substance on booze and betting my father was putting much of his into his piano, music and books. The end of the nineteenth century was notable for a considerable revolution in the world of popular newspapers and magazines, a revolution largely instigated in Fleet Street by the Harmsworth brothers, and to several of these magazines my father became an avid subscriber. *The Strand, The Harmsworth, The Windsor* and a rather preachy affair called *Young England* were among them and these he would subsequently have bound up into fat, half-leather volumes.

The result of all this was that at quite an early age I began to have access to the work of Conan Doyle, Kipling, Barrie and a considerable number of other late Victorian and Edwardian writers. I revelled in Holmes and *The Speckled Band,* smelled the putrefying rats in *Stalky & Co* and even swallowed the Scottish treacle of Barrie, never my favourite writer, and the fine doings of Captain Kettle. As my father's library grew it also revealed most curious divisions of taste: on the one hand there were tomes of insufferable solemnity on subjects divine and theological, on the other hand were works by William le Queux, E. Phillips Oppenheim, Conan Doyle, Edgar Wallace and a now rather forgotten though excellent French writer of detective stories, Gaboriau, creator of what I suppose was a sort of French Holmes, *Arsène Lupin.*

Like Graham Greene, I am sure that as I devoured these writers I unconsciously assimilated something of their methods – by which I mean the way all of them had no time for wasting words but had to make their points economically and incisively, rejecting all highly descriptive padding: an assimilation which, though unconscious at the time, as I say, was later to emerge as a guiding principle when I myself began to handle the short story. Even now I can remember expressing sharp impatience if a story went on too long, an impatience that has probably led to my disposition to stop stories short, leaving the reader in a state of speculative suspense and wondering guesswork, rather than take him on to a well-ordered and boring end.

In all these things I was fully engrossed by the age of nine or ten; but some time before this, I suppose when I was seven or eight, an event of some scholastic significance occurred. I suddenly found myself removed from the main body of my class, given a separate and special desk of my own and there set down to pursue work much in advance of that done by other pupils. A rapid climb followed and soon I was soaring away to the top of the main school, a circumstance that in no way prevented my joining in the rough-and-tumble of playground, football field or the long-since lost arena of street games. I have never, thank God, been in danger of becoming a male blue stocking. The world of street games is not only far distant; it has slipped away for ever. The author of *South Wind,* Norman Douglas, writing some years before my time, published what is now a rare book, *London Street Games,* in which he recorded something like a thousand games. Though we played nothing like this formidable and fascinating number we nevertheless played a great many and were never short of a game for all seasons. Not the least curious feature of these games was the intensely guarded and parochial conditions under which they were played. Like jungle cocks jealously defending their territories or cock robins their patch of garden, each street rigorously repelled and rejected all others except perhaps its very nearest neighbour. Thus the children of Grove Street, in which my parents' house faced the gaslights of the pork-butcher's shop and the two bake-houses, never dreamed of consorting with Crabb Street, from which we might have been removed by a thousand miles, even though we were not more than two hundred yards apart.

The ritual of street games went on freely and unhampered, summer and winter, except in the very severest weather. There was no danger. A bicycle or two, a baker's cart trundling home with its golden candles trembling in the lamps, a late horse-drawn dray delivering a load of belly leather or packing cases to a factory before going back to the railway yards: these were about the only hazards we might expect to disturb us. The street was not only ours; we were expected, and ordered, to play there.

So, fortified in my case by hot tea, hot toast spread with home-made lard and salt – and how very good it was – we all went out, on early winter evenings, to the gas-lit street stage. I remember the winter evenings more vividly, I suppose, than the summer ones simply because of the gaslight: the one big street light round which we played

> Sally go round the moon
> Sally go round the stars
> Sally go round the chimneypot
> On a Sunday afternoon

and the lights of the three shops.

Almost always, I think, we first gathered round the window of one of the bakers shops to sort out preliminaries for play. Certain preliminaries had always to be gone through, among them the picking of teams, and also 'who was going to start it'. We always did this by rhymes. Thus, as we gathered in a circle, one of us went round, pointing to each in turn, reciting:

> Paddy on the railway, picking up stones,
> Down came the engine and broke Paddy's bones.
> Well, said Paddy, that isn't fair.
> Well, said the engine, I don't care.
> O – U – T spells
> 'Out Goes She'

or we varied it thus:

> Ink, Pink
> I think
> There is
> A stink
> And it comes from
> Y O U !
> O – U – T spells
> 'Out Goes She'

After this the teams divided up, one going to the far side of the street, the other remaining by the shop window, so to speak on

home ground. The main games in this category, in all probability
having origins going back for centuries, were 'I apprentice my son',
I spy, 'three old men come workhouse' and 'what's your trade?'
though the last two may well have been slightly different versions
of the same thing. Norman Douglas, I think, records all these as
London games. There were also various versions of tick or tag, one
with the odd name of 'chibby (or chivy) up the rat's hole', probably
the same game as Norman Douglas' 'Chivy Chase', another
cockerels, which he doesn't mention. In due season we played
whip-and-top, hopscotch and marbles – incredible now to think
we played marbles across the full width of the street, from gutter to
gutter, quite unhampered. There were also various versions of
hide-and-seek, one with the curious name of hi-acky or perhaps
hi-yacky, a name I thought for many years to be no more than
a piece of meaningless local childhood slang, until I discovered

it to be a corruption of the Latin *hic jacet* (here lies) – in other words the call you make when hidden, inviting others to come and find you.

Girls of course played some games which most boys considered to be cissy: hopscotch, buttons (you had a collection of old buttons which you picked up one by one from the pavement by wetting your thumb, pressing hard and hoping that the buttons would stick), skipping, and various ball games. There was also jackstones or five-stones, at which girls were at least as good as boys if not better (a certain girl I met much later was an absolute dabster at this and still isn't by any means a novice), but girls as far as I remember were never invited to play with us at cat-and-stick. For this you needed a stout stick and a second shortish stick, 'the cat', sharpened at both ends. You could draw a chalk ring on the pavement as your playing arena, but we mostly preferred to play on manhole covers. The loser of the toss first stood with eyes shut, feet at ten-past-ten on the perimeter of the manhole cover and head well back, with 'the cat' balanced on his forehead. 'The cat' was then allowed to roll off his forehead, down his nose and into the ring below. According to how 'the cat' fell, whether in the ring, out of it or touching the perimeter, so you were allowed a certain number of strikes with the stick. The technique was to strike 'the cat' smartly at the sharpened end so that it leapt in the air. As it leapt you hit it. If you were lucky enough to have three strikes you could end up by hitting it as much as thirty yards. Whatever length it was you had to 'offer it up', so to speak, to your opponent. Thus you guessed ten, or twenty or thirty yards and your opponent then either gave you the number or offered to 'measure you out'. This he did by striding out the yards from manhole cover to 'cat'. If he 'measured you out' it was then his turn, since his gamble had failed. Cat-and-stick I always loved; it was a great game for hand, leg and eye.

Of cat-and-stick I can find no mention in Douglas' *London Street Games,* a book that, incidentally, was rejected by a number of publishers before it finally appeared in the middle of the First World War, when its 'flurried accumulation' and apparently 'casual methods' irritated some critics and its contents may well have appeared to the general public as being of slight importance in comparison with the games being played in the company of blood, lice, rats, mud, shell-holes and other barbarous futilities on the fields of Flanders. But one critic at least had a remark of sage and indeed prophetic importance to say of it and after fifty years of social standardisation and reform its truth seems to have an even sharper significance: 'one marvels at the stupidity of the social reformer who desires to close to the children the world of adventure, to take from them their birthright of the streets, and coop them up in well-regulated and uninspiring playgrounds where, under the supervision of teachers, their imagination will decline, their originality wither.' To this Douglas himself added: 'The standardisation of youth proceeds relentlessly; it is part of what Richard Aldington calls the insane process of making great groups happy by destroying the personal happiness of every individual in that group; it is one of the many steps in the direction of that termite-ideal towards which we are trending.'

How many of these street games are still played? was Douglas' final question, and if the question even then had about it a note of despair it is one of utter futility today. The termites have taken over. In place of cat-and-stick youth plays at shoplifting; instead of the hurly-burly of mop-stick, an hilarious version of leapfrog which was my favourite of all street games, it stages protesting marches of babble and rabble against this and that; in the place of 'chibby up the rat's hole' it prefers to crawl up the devious rats' holes of drugs; in its new-found affluence it no longer kicks a football made of newspaper tied with string about streets and alleys but sings ballads licentious and malodorous at supposedly first-class matches; it prefers violence to marbles; it would rather wreck trains, public conveniences and shop windows than run off its energies at stag and cockerels. Termites, after all, can only be expected to behave like termites in a termite-world.

Searching for possible origins for these many street games Douglas treated with scorn the theorising notion of his fictitious Aunt Eliza that 'London Bridge is broken down' went 'back to bloodthirsty rites of foundation-sacrifice', that 'fie Sally, cry sally' originated in early water worship and that 'here we come gathering nuts in May' was 'a relic of marriage by capture'. More and more I fear that Douglas' scorn was misplaced. He had evidently forgotten that one form of water-worship, still calculated to have circus audiences rolling in the aisles, is one of the oldest pantomimic jokes in the world; that in the world of entertainment the fascination of 'marriage by capture' never palls; and that blood, whether on the sacrificial altars of a more ancient world, the arenas of bullfighting and foxhunting, or in the tribal warfare of football fields, still exercises and satisfies a remorseless universal taste.

We are all playing games, adults perhaps even more than children, and most of them are far far older than those Douglas collected so assiduously from London's streets or that I played on winter evenings under the long since departed gaslight of the baker's shop.

V

That the golden days with my grandfather must have been interspersed with dark and dismal ones I have no doubt; but I find it hard to recall them. The days in the hayfield were always hot, those in the harvest-field even hotter. Always the air in June seems to have been clotted with the intoxication of mown grass, of may blossom, of moon-daisies dying along the paling swathes. In August the great bearded, or horned wheat – surely another of my grandfather's mistakes – undoubtedly stood higher than a man, dark brown and rough indeed like a beard, the straw tough as reed and as difficult to mow, the sheaves correspondingly prodigious of weight. The heavy clay-land dried out to concrete, splitting under the heat into fissures wide enough to swallow the foot of a man, let alone of a boy. All, it must be remembered, was done by hand. Try as I would, and try though my grandfather did to teach me, I was never really able to make bonds for the great bearded sheaves. The bonds always slipped and broke; the sheaves collapsed as I manfully tried to bear them to the stooks, the beards and docks and drying thistles stabbing into my small bare arms.

Just before half past twelve we always started to look down the road for the little figure of my grandmother, bringing up the dinner baskets. She never failed to appear, nipping quickly along. Back in Victorian days my grandfather had gone over the Bedfordshire border, to the tiny village of Souldrop, on the edge of the valley of the Ouse, to court his bride. No one was ever better named than Priscilla Bird. She looked indeed for ever like

47

a bird: perhaps most aptly a wren, tiny, quick, bright-eyed, sharp, indefatigable. After the fashion of her day she went out, as a young girl, to service, one result of which was that she cooked superbly, another that her household was always scrupulously, miraculously clean. Whenever I remember her I smell baking bread, roasting beef, soapsuds, starch, beeswax and hot irons. Scarcely possible though it is to believe, she had a sister, Matilda, who kept the Chequers Inn over the Bedfordshire border at the village of Yelden, (well-known to many an American service man) who was even cleaner. Her pub tables were scrubbed until they looked like scoured stone; her bar gleamed like an altar.

Our dinner in the harvest-field was always hot; none of your makeshift lumps of dough with onions stuffed into them: a dish known as a Bedfordshire Clanger; no lumps of cold bacon and bread, no plain bread and cheese, no sandwiches. In one basket would repose a steak-and-kidney pie, perhaps a rabbit pie, or a beef pudding, together with basins of new potatoes, carrots, peas or beans: all wrapped in clean white napkins. In the other there would be, perhaps, an apple pie or, what I myself loved best of all, a pie of a small yellow local plum of extraordinarily good flavour and rather squarish in shape and touched with a faint blush of crimson, very like an apricot.

To eat all this we sat, on very hot days, in the shade of a vast ash tree, or if the weather were a little cooler, in the shelter of a wheat stook. All about us the deep summer silence spread in a vast hush broken only, though really accentuated, by the whirr of grasshoppers and occasionally, from down the hedgerows, the crooning song of yellow-hammers, deepening the silence too with their endless 'little bit of bread and cheese'. 'Pass the pepper and walt, boy,' my grandfather would say and eventually, replete, would fall into a doze, at which signal I crept away along the hedgerow to look for the first dew-berries, the sweet-sharp taste of which still bursts on my tongue as the true juice of full summer.

Always indefatigable, my grandmother was back at half past four, this time with one basket and a big blue can of tea. Now perhaps we sat in the stack-yard, under a haystack, out of the glare

of the western sun. My grandmother always baked her own bread, which I called 'mucky bread' because of its dark brown shade. My grandfather always ate this bread with its butter side down, insisting that only in this way could you really taste bread and butter. With it we ate dark red plum or damson jam and afterwards there was perhaps dough-cake, a bread with currants and sultanas in it, and another great favourite of mine, caraway cake, which my grandmother baked exquisitely. All about us, as we ate, sat a large bevy of cats and kittens, waiting for a saucer of tea and scraps of bread and butter, while in the pigsties the pigs worked up their own appetite, beginning to scream hungrily on the hot afternoon.

After tea my grandmother left us and soon a man with the redoubtable name of Smack arrived. Shoemaker by day, he turned into pure peasant countryman by evening, beery, cunning, masterly with whetstone and scythe. For so small a man he had a tireless and astonishing strength. The tall powerful stalks of horned wheat fell before his scythe-blade with a great crisp, crushing sound, the fallen swathes beautifully and perfectly laid, no stalk out of place. Sometimes a hare or a leveret would start up out of the corn and all tools were downed as we set off on the hunt, which more often than not was fruitless, and occasionally the scythe-blade would be dramatically stilled and poised in air and a whisper from Smack would tell us that he had stopped short, just in time, of a late nest of partridge eggs.

In those days, before the lavish use of weedkillers, which have now done so much to ravage the wildlife of the English countryside, birds, butterflies and flowers alike, the cornfield was flowery from end to end. Tiny red periwinkles, pink convolvulus, occasional corncockles, cinquefoil, camomile, blue cornflowers and endless scarlet poppies spread themselves everywhere. As the scythe bared the wheat down to stubble, the poppies, cornflowers and corncockles all laid low, a sort of creeping garden of all the prostrate, tiny things remained. They are indeed tiny things to remember for ever but they persist in my mind, with both joy and affection, long after greater things have faded. There also persists, in utter contrast, the sight of the great lines of stooks, at last set up like tents ready for camping in the evening sun. I sometimes crept into these tents, to be embalmed by that eternal, warm, friendly fragrance that only straw can give; and it was this fragrance, eternal indeed and as old as civilised man and his earth, that lingered with me as I went home at last in the deepening summer twilight, often so tired that I had to be carried, my face and hands and arms and legs scratched by stubble, bitten by harvest-bugs and as mucky in colour as my grandmother's 'mucky bread'.

Beyond Souldrop, in the larger village of Sharnbrook, my grandmother had another sister, Mary Ann. Here the wide pastoral view of the Ouse Valley opens up to its full breadth and beauty: the river itself white with waterlilies in summer, the woods rich in spring with primrose and oxlip, the pastures soft and luscious. If the villages today are no longer locked in the dreaminess I knew more than half a century ago their velvety, v-stitched, dreamy names remain: Turvey, Stevington, Odell, Felmersham, Lavendon, Newton Blossomville.

My grandmother's sister, also an excellent cook, especially as I remember it of potatoes, which she always served with a particularly delicious butter sauce, lived a short distance outside the village of Sharnbrook, in a tiny thatched cottage, at the top of a rough stony track, on the edge of a wood. This wood remains, for me, a paradise: crowded in spring with violets, both purple and white, primroses, anemones and later bluebells and pink campion. In high summer its fringes were red with wild straw-berries. In June, after the gold of cowslips had faded, the fields on all sides were white with moon daisies and deeply fragrant with red clover. Not far away the main railway line from London to the north runs up the long escarpment of the river valley and it is still the sound of the great double-engined steam expresses rushing magnificently past, shattering the woodland silence with a thousand echoes, that remains as vividly with me as the sight and sound of flowers and the song of thrush, blackbird and nightingale.

Even more vividly remains the picture of cottage and garden. The little low-ceilinged rooms are for ever steeped in the smell of

wood smoke; from the walls look down faded sepia portraits of Victorian relatives dressed in Sunday best; dried bulrushes, feathery brushes of pampas grass and the silvery coinage of dried honesty seed decorate the mantelpiece with its drapery of claret velvet. Outside the door, always open in summer, there grew a bush of that old enchantress of a rose, Maiden's Blush, surrounded by white Madonna lilies, double white pinks, larkspur, poppies, marigolds and cottage favourites of that sort. In the longish stretch of garden extending to the very edge of the wood there were gooseberry trees bearing fruit of such size that they might well have been inflated, like balloons, together with white and red currants and, unless my memory tricks me, a golden yellow raspberry of choicest flavour. Rows of peas, beans, sweetpeas rose from a soil black as only soil long-cultivated and long enriched can be. Most vivid of all a scarlet Turk's Cap lily flaunted a kingly head above the crowd of common cottage subjects, like a strange aristocrat from another world.

This scarlet lily is the key that unlocks the world of a certain Joseph Betts, husband of my grandmother's sister. Born in the Hungry Forties, reprobate, rapscallion, crafty as a monkey, liar, gardener of much cunning, drinker of infinite capacity, afflicted with one bloodshot eye that gave him a look of devilish fascination, he is the original of *My Uncle Silas*, the character whose alcoholic and womanising adventures I was to chronicle in a series of stories some twenty-five years later. Sitting propped by the kitchen door in corduroy trousers and a thick old broad-cloth waistcoat, he was, to a small boy, a figure both compelling and fearsome. An aura of positively Satanic secrecy surrounded his prowess in raising gooseberries big as golf balls, potatoes un-matched for earliness and flavour, peas of unrivalled succulence and most of all the presence of the Turk's Cap lily. As he supped at glasses of home-brewed cowslip and elderberry wine – in spring the kitchen floor would often be yellow with sheets of drying cowslips – I listened to him with ears cocked and eyes utterly hypnotised. Already he then seemed to me to be venerable, almost patriarchal, a figure from a past even more remote than Hardy's early novels. He was in fact still to ripen to an even greater age, living into his nineties, for ever growing more crafty, devilish and fearsome, so much so that one day when I much later took my future wife to meet him for the first time she was as near-terrified, poor girl, as if I had presented Old Nick himself.

From those golden days at the little cottage by the woodside there stands out one gilded with special splendour: a summer day when my mother, my grandmother, my aunt, my sister and myself arrived there for the wedding of Joe Betts' only son. By the generosity of the local squire a big white marquee had been put up in the little paddock; inside it long trestle tables were filled with cold meats and sandwiches and salads and cakes and beer and wine. Already by the time we arrived Joe was as merry as a boozy cricket; by afternoon he was rollicking; by evening he was prancing with the ladies; by dusk he was drunkenly bawling 'We won't go home till morning! – let 'em all come!', the leading jester on an uproarious summer stage. Such was the sharpness of the impression it all made on me that though it was a near quarter of a century before I put it down in a story called *The Wedding* the words practically wrote themselves.

Joe too belongs to a vanished world. His little thatched cottage, so a correspondent writes to tell me, has been pulled down. The world of television, jets and space craft dazzles our generation with new if sometimes near useless wonders, but for myself I would cheerfully exchange it all for that bloodshot eye, the smell of wood-smoke, the scent of bluebells, cowslips, primroses and the Maiden's Blush, the Turk's Cap lily and the voices of nightingales.

VI

My father was a diligent early riser. Indeed he always conveyed the impression that there was something slightly immoral about remaining in bed after seven o'clock. On Sundays it is true that he relaxed a little, though even then if you arrived a minute or two late for eight o'clock breakfast you were more than likely to get a look of some severity and a cryptic and admonishing 'You're last!' that might have been in itself a foretaste of the stern Sabbath pattern of the day to come.

A small sweetener, however, brightened the early morning before Sunday really claimed us body and soul. On the piano stood two white china swans. Miraculously, overnight, they had always laid eggs in the shape of little packets of chocolates wrapped in blue, green, scarlet and silver tinfoil and tied with narrow coloured ribbons, and I never failed to search for and discover them with a sensation of excitement, astonishment and joy.

At a quarter to nine Sunday began. Dressed in my best blue serge with a big white Eton collar, I made my way to Sunday school. The old chapel, now the school, was barely two streets away. My route to it took me by the factory next door, then past the Band Club, where much blowing and practising on silver wind instruments continually enlivened the summer evening air, past another factory and my father's factory next door, past a little farm where I often went to fetch a penny can of milk, and finally past a Baptist chapel and yet another factory.

If I was not oppressed by quite the same feeling of dread with which I went so long to day-school I was nevertheless always haunted on Sundays by a secret sensation of impending imprisonment. Rain, fog, frost, hail, snow: there was never the remotest chance of escaping. With me I took a sort of passport, a star-card, which I duly presented at the Sunday school door to have stamped with a violet star as proof of my punctual attendance. Once inside I was captured by an air that somehow yet remains with me as dusty musty, over-sanctified. I am

unfamiliar with what contemporary Methodism now produces in the way of its more dedicated adherents, but fifty years ago it was still dominated by stern and tyrannical believers who upheld the piety of silence, were convinced that even whispering among boys was a sin and had no compunction about boxing the ears of the recalcitrant with bible or hymn book as penalty for the minutest misdemeanour. Often the sternest of these mentors were men converted from the wickedness and evils of looser living, more often than not drink, and were now purified and on the narrow path of righteousness. Later, in chapel, inspired by some divine inner fervour, they would sometimes leap suddenly to their feet or drop down on bended knees and cry aloud to Heaven in the blessed name of the Lord, as if having seen a vision. 'Praise Him!' they would shout, 'Bless His name! Glory be and grant us mercy!'

No doubt on the principle that 'the devil finds work for idle hands to do' we were kept in close confinement at Sunday school for close on two hours, singing hymns, locked in prayer, listening to windy homilies, reading biblical chapter and verse. The pews were hard, the slow dragging minutes intolerable. This, however, was merely the beginning of our sanctified day. At a quarter to eleven we were shepherded into chapel, there to undergo a repeat adult performance of what we had already suffered. If anything the homilies were even windier, the pews harder, the silences longer and harder to bear. Methodism decrees that its preachers shall move on a three year circuit, so that at intervals a new face appeared in the pulpit. Sometimes we were harangued by humourless, impassioned Welshmen. Occasionally there appeared a local preacher, as often as not a half-literate from some remote village, burdened with strong country accent, unravelling a long tangled skein of biblical rhetoric ('Now what did our good Lord mean by them there words?' etc.) droning on and on until not only children became restless but even adults started fidgeting with watches, and hungry bellies rattled.

At last came the blessed relief of the anthem, the taking of the collection and then the last hymn. Sure enough it would have an intolerable number of verses, not one to be cut. Then all eyes closed for the final benediction. As often as not that too would be long drawn-out, developing sometimes into yet another homily. By this time it might well be half past twelve, the hour at which everybody except the beer-swillers at clubs and pubs ate their midday dinner. The sensation of being released into fresh open air was unbelievably sweet. Hungry, my bottom aching, I hurried home to meet a procession peculiar to the times: that of men hurrying from bakehouses, bearing Sunday dinners of roast meat and Yorkshire pudding, sizzling in baking tins and covered with cloths to keep them hot. After the nightly bread-baking, with the fires damped down, the big coal ovens were perfect for cooking pudding and meat: charge, a penny.

At home, as I have already said, I took off my Sunday jacket and put on my little white apron before sitting down to eat. Always, in the true Midland tradition, we ate pudding first and meat afterwards, a practice my father insistently continued all through

his life. (My grandfather maintained that in his day the pudding was eaten from the underside of the plate, after which the plate was turned right side up for the meat.) No drink, not even a glass of water, was allowed throughout the meal ('It'll only blow you up,' I was always told), but after dinner I was allowed the luxury of a bar or two of the chocolates the white swans had laid, before – yes, it isn't hard to guess – going yet again to Sunday school.

The devil, I fear, had a poor time of it on those Midland Sundays. For a third time we were imprisoned, this time for a mere hour, but often, as if this were still not enough, we were ushered yet again to chapel, to listen perhaps to a diatribe by some missionary home from China or to what was called a 'sacred concert' or an oratorio. Even then there loomed before us the prospect of a fifth term, that of evening chapel at six, though I must here be honest and admit that, in my early childhood at any rate, we were granted release from this either to visit my grandfather and his pigs or to walk tranquilly across footpaths in summer fields. Yet with the same honesty I must record that there often imposed itself upon us yet a sixth term, that of a late prayer meeting, where Methodist fervours, far from dwindling after the long day's devotions, gathered new life, so that the converted visionaries were once again inspired to leap to their feet, blessing and praising the Lord's Holy name and thanking Him for providential deliverance from the evil of their ways.

Truly the Methodists were iron shepherds to their sheep; yet if the Sundays of my childhood seem over-disciplined they compare quite favourably with those of my mother, who had to rise at a quarter to six every Sunday in order to attend a first service at half past and then had yet another session thrown in at five o'clock in the afternoon – little relaxation for a girl of eleven already working half-time.

VII

There's a Divinity that shapes our ends, Rough-hew them how we will. Shakespeare's words, as so often, vividly and succinctly enshrine truths which lesser men merely grope to discover. In the year 1916, rough-hewn though my young life might perhaps have been until that time, the first but by no means the last of several divinity-shapings imposed itself upon me.

But it is first necessary to go back a couple of years: to the Easter of 1914. In the spring of that year two events of importance occurred. First, my step-grandmother decided to join my paternal grandfather in Australia, to which he had emigrated some time before, largely on the grounds of poor health. A story arising from this does much to demonstrate that though my grandfather may have been something of a philanderer – which is perhaps putting it mildly – he was by no means lacking in shrewdness. It would appear that some time before these events he had become involved in some sort of business deal with a man who eventually either went bankrupt or welshed on him. As to the details I have never been clear, but when the resulting mess came to be sifted and straightened out the solicitors dealing with the affair offered my grandfather a modest lump sum out of the wreckage or, if he preferred it, two pounds a week for life, a not inconsiderable sum in the early years of the century. There seems little doubt that in making this attractive offer they were not uninfluenced by the state of my grandfather's health, no doubt reasoning that two pounds a week was the more advantageous settlement from their point of view. Wisely my grandfather accepted it and went on receiving the two pounds a week for the rest of his life, or for a good thirty-five years or more.

The first immediate result of my step-grandmother's decision to emigrate was that the villa my grandfather had built for himself in 1900 had become available for my father, profiting now from his early years of thrift and prudence, to buy. One of my grandfather's favourite winter resorts had been Menton, the name by which the villa was duly called. It is a house very typical of a time when boot manufacturers were making money fast and providing themselves with a higher status and new degrees of comfort: solid red brick with stone facings, quite spacious dining-room and drawing-room and the almost unbelievable luxury of a bathroom. In his determination to give the house a still further touch of class my grandfather had even called in Italian workmen to lay floors of multicoloured mosaic in hallway and passages. No doubt he had been impressed by all this in Italy and Menton but had neglected to question the entire unsuitability of cold mosaic floors for the English climate. In winter both hallway and passages were consequently more frigid than a tomb.

With the house, set in a street that incredibly had no factory, no bakehouse, no club, pub or chapel, though Bunyan's old meeting-house still stood and in fact still stands, just round the corner, went a reasonably spacious walled garden, complete with greenhouse and summerhouse. This my father had, with his usual aptitude for making good use of his hands, already planted up with fruit trees, on his father's behalf, some ten years before. Now the walls were furnished with maturing Doyenne du Comice and Williams Bon Chrétien pears, together with Victoria plums yielding fruit of incomparable size and succulence. There were many apple trees, most of them of Victorian and Edwardian varieties no longer grown or seen, though none the worse for that, and there was a positive forest of gooseberries, black-, white- and redcurrants and raspberry canes. To move into such a house and garden after the very modest terrace we had occupied, penned in on one side by the walls of a factory, from which came the eternal whine of machines and the thunder of presses, was a tremendous leap up the social ladder and I have no doubt that I, at the age of nine, was probably more than a little snobbish about it all. But equally there is no doubt that its acquisition reflects the very greatest credit on my father, whose own childhood years of misfortune, penury, truancy and unhappiness were not so very far behind him.

On the eve of Good Friday that year, 1914, my father and mother departed for London to say farewell and wish *Bon Voyage* to my step-grandmother at Tilbury Docks, leaving me behind. Quite why I didn't go to stay as usual with my other grandfather I cannot now remember, but what I do remember, and that most vividly, was that someone or other had come up with the inspired suggestion that I should briefly set up in business on Good Friday, for the purpose of selling hot cross buns. For some days beforehand I accordingly went about calling on neighbours with my little order book, recording orders for a dozen buns here, two dozen there and so on. On the eve of Good Friday I could hardly sleep for excitement. Next morning I must have been up at six o'clock and across the road, in the bakehouse, complete with large clothes basket and clean white cloth, by half past, ready to pick up my first load of fresh warm buns.

It is very natural that I should cherish a great fondness for that old bakehouse. I suppose I was in there, for some purpose or other, to fetch bread or flour or yeast or just to stare, almost every day. There was always a great heavenly embalming warmth about it, together with the even heavenlier fragrance of new-baked bread. The big low bread ovens, hung about with wooden peels for sliding dough in and loaves out, were dark and fascinating caverns. The baker, a thin, rather ill-looking, cadaverous man, always appeared to be saturated with ghostlike clouds of whiteness. In the little yard outside the bakery his horse and baker's cart were stabled. A pile of soddened dung always steamed on the air, the ammoniac sting of it powerful enough to kill even the aroma of baking. On winter nights a weary looking horse and an even wearier-looking baker came home at walking pace, journeyings done, the golden candle flames in the cart-lamps flabbily flickering in the dark air.

Good Friday, as far back as I can remember, has always been the most dismal, the most inaptly named day of the year. Only a few weeks ago, as I write this, I was in Switzerland on Good Friday; it was bitterly cold and raining; there was much fresh snow on the mountains. At my hotel the young lady receptionist hugged her shoulders and said: 'Always, always it is the same. Always on Good Friday.' So indeed it would appear to be: a day that seems always to be cursed with rain and cold and darkness at noon.

But at least one Good Friday in my life, that of 1914, is filled with light. My impression is that I was given the traditional Baker's dozen when I collected my buns, so that I was able to make a little extra profit. Another impression is that I was so keen and eager to get my orders delivered that I was too early for many customers, quite half of whom were not up when I first called, so that I was forced to call again, often to be greeted by sleepy-eyed, disgruntled ladies in curling pins. It was a tradition in those days – I doubt very greatly if it persists today – that the buns should be delivered hot and to that end I went back to the bakehouse several times for fresh hot supplies, always keeping them carefully covered with the clean white cloth. The weather too was true to its tradition, the early morning typically dismal and chill as I remember, but for once I never really felt it. My heart was as warm with excitement as the buns.

When war broke out in August of that year, although I was only nine, I was acutely conscious of a dark and enshrouding shadow. At least one part of the world that was about to be destroyed and to vanish for ever still seems to me like a delicate, decorated meringue. It was my parents' custom to take us, every August, to the seaside. For one week only, since these were the days long before paid holidays, when one week was the statutory holiday for the average worker, we moved into a world of sea and sunlight, sand and promenades, gentlemen in blazers and boaters, fishermen and jolly rowing in *The Skylark,* ladies in flowered hats and hobble skirts, military bands playing light music on piers and in bandstands, and the elegance of Sunday morning church parades.

When you live absolutely in the centre of a country, as we did in Northamptonshire, the sight of the sea on a shining summer's day can only be likened to the sudden sight of the Promised Land. It is yet another example of blessed escape from imprisonment. Several times we went north to Scarborough and pleasant though the memories of that agreeable watering place still are it is really to the south country that I find the mind's eye turning over and over again with greater pleasure. Indeed it is not too much to say that when the train rushed out of the first tunnel through the chalk of the North Downs, into the wide pastoral of Kent and Sussex, I never failed to get a strong impression that somehow this was my second home, this rich and varied cornucopia of fruit and corn and pasture and hops, of woodland and hills and oast-houses, that makes the Midland plain of grass and elm look about as appetising as a slice of stale bread. It was to be nearly another twenty years before the desire to live there became a fully conscious one but when at last it did come and was amply fulfilled the sense of escape from imprisonment was as powerful as ever.

Brighton, Hastings, St Leonards, Worthing, Eastbourne – we went to stay in all of them in turn and we were at a modest little boarding establishment at Eastbourne when war broke out. It is odd how the recollection of little things over and over again creates the most powerful impression: the smell of sea, of seaweed drying in the sun, of plaice being fried for breakfast, or horse dung and the whiff of vinegar from whelk-stalls. The memory of sea-side Sundays is strong and brilliant too. Here again, even on holiday, the hand of Methodism still took its stern grip on us. Even to set foot on the beach on the Sabbath Day was forbidden. Buckets and spades and balls and bathing drawers were put away as if they were devices of the devil. Others might trip down the steps of horse-drawn bathing cabins to disport themselves in the Sunday sea, but not us. Donkey rides, games, running, ice creams, pop: all were taboo. Circumspectly we strolled along the promenade at a pace unhurried and dignified, my father in straw boater and white buck-skin boots, my mother in mutton-leg sleeves and with the then fashionable band of black velvet round her neck. Like a scene from Monet or Renoir, the elegant church parade of straw hats, parasols and long sweeping ladies' skirts flowed towards and past us, while in the road the few blessed rich rode past in open Darracqs and Daimlers, Renaults and Rolls Royces with almost the grandeur of parading royalty, scornfully overtaking horse-drawn landaus and an occasional sight-seeing brake or wagonette. Perhaps memory cheats a little, perhaps it doesn't; perhaps the scene wasn't quite all elegance, all charm, all grace, all opulence, as the rose spectacles of fifty years appear to depict it, but one thing is quite certain: it was all about to be utterly shattered, for ever destroyed.

Before the sense of destruction made itself fully felt – even a child couldn't escape the eventual insufferable gloom of the holocaust that every morning was reflected in the long columns of the dead, wounded and missing that darkened every newspaper and still more intimately in the little mourning shrines set up in every street with their own lists of agonies and pitiful jam jars of flowers – I went through a period of martial excitement. War suddenly became glorified – or perhaps it would be truer to say that it merely became glamourised.

I am not now absolutely sure how long the war had been in progress when an advance party of billeting officers suddenly descended on the town, chalking what seemed to me to be meaningless sets of numbers and figures on the walls of houses. Soon the town was full of the sound of marching feet, the bang and blare of army bands and the voices of babbling Welshmen. The Royal Welch Fusiliers, disporting their famous black flash behind the tunic collar and their equally famous goat mascot at the head of their marching columns, were a proud regiment. But none of its soldiers could have been prouder than the small boy who positively worshipped at their parades, became a devout follower of route marches far out into the country and would have given his heart for the privilege of blowing a bugle or beating a drum. Mercifully he had never heard of the words cannon-fodder. All was glamour and glory, from the nodding head of the goat to the silvery jugglings of the magnificent drum major.

To our family fell the duty of billeting a young upper-class lieutenant, a great eighteen stone bag of a man, and his petite, pretty wife. Newly married, they too brought glamour to the house. Wining and dining with fellow officers in the dining-room they produced not only an atmosphere of opulence and aristocracy but also one that until that time had been as foreign to the household as, say, bad language or the smell of opium: the odours of strong drink. It was really a twilight world. While the young lieutenant painfully slogged it out with his men on long route marches, his tender feet unequal to the task of supporting so vast a frame, his attractive little wife sat at home and, after the fashion of the day, painted in water colours. And sometimes, when both were out, I used to creep into their room and lift the lid of the long black tin box and gaze down at the glittering grandeur of an officer's wardrobe, from the finery of mess kit to the flashing gleam of scabbard and sword.

Soon the obese young officer was to be killed in the filth that was Flanders and the babbling Welshmen were to be replaced as cannon-fodder disguised as symbols of glory by men of the Yorkshire and Lancashire Regiment, at whose feet I worshipped with renewed devotion. It was their lot to be massacred in due course in the holocaust of the Dardanelles, far from the pubs and fish-and-chip shops of home. Often I wonder now what the thoughts of the cannon-fodder were, though I knew of no such wondering then. All was still glory: blow, bugles, blow, swing, rifles, swing. As I listened to the music of marching feet I longed, always, to be a soldier.

Instead of which, in the spring of 1916, as I have already indicated, the 'Divinity that shapes our ends, rough-hew them how we will', decided to take another and decisive hand in my affairs.

VIII

I was now almost eleven and the time had come for me to take an examination for a scholarship. Not more than half a dozen of us were chosen for the privilege of sitting for this and it is notable that all these came from homes whose heads 'were notch above a tapper'. The unwashed were also, I fear, the unprivileged. Not that being deprived of the opportunity of sitting for a scholarship was necessarily a deterrent to progress and success. I can recall half a dozen of my 1916 contemporaries who, though leaving school at thirteen, later proceeded to set up successfully in business, often to make sizable fortunes. The mere acquisition of a little learning is not by any means all, dangerous though it may sometimes turn out to be.

Of the written part of the scholarship examination I now recall very little, except that it took place at Wellingborough, to whose celebrated public school I hoped later to go. My recollection of the oral part is much sharper. This took place at Northampton, to where, on a torrid summer day, my father and I went by train. After some delay and difficulty we managed to discover the place of appointment in a back street, by which time, perhaps because of the heat of the day, I felt nervous and flustered. In due course I found myself in an upstairs room, confronted by a bevy of solemn-looking gentlemen who proceeded to ask me a number of questions, all of which with one exception have faded from my mind. This solitary one demanded to know what would happen if a spray of blackberry flowers were covered, throughout the time of flowering, with a muslin bag. I replied that I thought there would be no blackberries because all means of fertilisation, such as bees, would be excluded, but whether this was the correct or expected answer I shall never know.

In due course the list of successful examinees was published and to my utter chagrin and bitter disappointment my name was not among them; I was the only one who had failed. Bang went my dream of going to a public school but far more difficult to bear was the bruising blow to my pride. I had sallied into the lists with a certain degree of confidence, duly supported by my teachers, and I now felt I had received a cruel and startling sock in the eye. My grandfather's old country adage that I had 'something in my head besides lice' now echoed about me like a piece of empty boasting. I believe that for many days I was very near to tears.

I had, however, reckoned without 'the divinity which shapes our ends'. Clearly it was not part of its plan either that I should win a scholarship or go to Wellingborough; another and far more influential pattern had been prepared for me. In due course this was revealed in a letter delivered on an August Sunday morning – even in the darkest hours of the war we still had a Sunday morning post – wherein the County Education Authorities were pleased to inform me that I had been granted something known as a 'Free Place' at the grammar school at Kettering. 'Free' meant free tuition and free railway fares. My pride was restored.

In 1934 Graham Greene got together about twenty celebrated young writers, most of them even more celebrated now, to contribute their impressions and recollections of school-days to an anthology called *The Old School*. The Schools ranged from Eton to a Salford Council School; Harrow to a Lancastrian school in Cork; Wellington to Cheltenham Ladies' College; Berkhamsted, Graham Greene's own school, to Kettering, my own. The writers included Auden, Spender, Harold Nicholson, Elizabeth Bowen, Anthony Powell, William Plomer and others of equal distinction. Looking back over these pieces today I observe that my own is largely a discourse on disillusion, a feeling to which I still subscribe, and that I attribute this largely to the war but equally to the fact that a certain romantic streak in my boyhood temperament had led me mistakenly to suppose that life at a grammar school would be as different from life at a local elementary school as life in Windsor Castle differs from life in a council house. In other words I had dreams of grandeur which were unfulfilled and it was without doubt this strong and early disillusionment that resulted in my new status being, for a time at any rate, frustrated and unhappy.

There were of course some singular differences between my old school and the new; but in one respect war had affected them equally. The destruction of cannon-fodder now being on the vast charnel-house scale that it was, killing and maiming men by the million, it was a natural consequence that there should be a great shortage of male teachers and a corresponding increase in the number of women occupying the teacher's desk. But whereas this was something that in no sense bothered me at the elementary school I was presently to find it a source of extreme irritation at Kettering. I am now disposed to think that this in all likelihood has something to do with puberty; up to the age of twelve or so it would seem not unlikely that a boy welcomes and indeed relishes a certain maternal touch in the attentions of a schoolmistress. But at fourteen he himself is about to become a man and it is to men that he then begins to look, in my opinion, for greater guidance. At Kettering, until 1919 at any rate, we looked in vain.

Again, in these early years, I was not only disillusioned; I was also the victim of extraordinary sensitivity and abysmal shyness. I was so shy that at first I could not face the communal dining-room; my mother packed me midday meals of sandwiches and pasties. Nor, for an agonised period, could I face morning prayers; with trembling and sweat I would hide myself in a classroom until the daily ritual was over. This is not to say that I was in any sense a namby-pamby. I was very fond of, and very good at, football, playing for my First XI at the age of fourteen and occasionally for my town XI at eighteen; I loved both cricket and tennis; I became a very fast sprinter, at one time collecting prizes in both the Open and Under-15 100 yards in one afternoon. It was simply that a great sensitivity of temperament was there and as yet there was no adult cloak to protect it. There was, however, an adult hand in readiness to bruise it and bruise it presently, indeed, it did.

The hand was that of Scott, the headmaster. I am fully aware that my comments on Kettering in Greene's anthology *The Old School* aroused consternation, ire and indeed wrath in certain devoted Kettering breasts when the book first appeared. I cannot help this; the experiences of others are not mine; my eyes and mind record for themselves, unaffected by the prejudices of others. (*Apropos* of this, my mentor Edward Garnett used to tell a story of D. H. Lawrence, whose sister came once to see E. G., begging him, 'Oh! Mr Garnett, could you *please* make D. H. write like other people?') I am, I am afraid, unable to observe like other people; I am content to observe in my own way. Others among my school-fellows may have been less sensitive, and perhaps for that very reason less observant, than I; they may also have been less prone to be victims of an acute sense of injustice. I do not know. What I do know is that one day when I was in the fourth form I was suddenly summoned to Scott's study, without being told why, there to be immediately and relentlessly whipped, also without being told why. Now I believe that children do not resent punishment, provided they are first told what the punishment is for and secondly that the cause of the punisher is at least reasonably just. Scott, who had neither the wit nor the perspicacity to grasp this elementary truth, accordingly behaved with dismal, orgiastic, lamentable stupidity. I was stunned and lacerated by a monumental sense of injustice; for some hours I actually lost my power of speech. It was only some considerable time later that I discovered that my heinous, hideous, impossible crime had been to allow a dumb, dull classroom neighbour to crib a single sentence from me at a weekly exam. By then, however, it was too late for reparation. The damage was done; the foundations of an implacable hate relationship with Scott had been laid.

Auden, in his piece on Gresham's School, then a very modern one, has something to say about schoolmasters. 'I have no wish to belittle a profession to which I have the honour to belong . . . At the same time if one were invited to dine with a company representing all trades and professions, the schoolmaster is the last person one would want to sit next to . . . far, far too many are silted-up old maids, earnest young scout-masters, or just generally dim.' Scott, in my view, should never have been a schoolmaster; Scottish himself and therefore prone to call us 'byes', he would have made a good civil servant. But the attributes that make good civil servants do not, alas, necesarily make good schoolmasters. Small, bald, fussy, interfering, a tireless busybody, he trotted about the school with what he no doubt hoped was headmasterly dignity, only to achieve precisely the opposite effect.

'If we owe regard to the memory of the dead,' said Dr Johnson, 'there is yet more respect to be paid to knowledge, to resolve and to truth', and I am aware of course, as I have already said, that Scott served in extremely difficult, not to say distressing, times. He had never more than two or three other male teachers to help him; other possible candidates in that direction were being shot. We were left with what my grandfather, with his usual truthful forthrightness, would have called females; and very female and formidable most of them were. We were either in the charge of tall, gangling, large-breasted women whose thoughts, I fear, were often on subjects far removed from geography; little bouncy ladies of whose virginity there was little question; stern angular mentors, some of them horse-women, of whom it was possible to doubt if they were, in fact, even female. It must be remembered here that men were not only becoming very scarce as schoolteachers; they were becoming very scarce, as one of the lady contributors to *The Old School* points out, for women too. The disturbing day of the low-necked dress had accordingly arrived and one of our female staff would often stand in front of us and, with what object I do not know, idly caress her large breasts backwards and forwards in her silk blouse, perhaps in gentle reference to the peaks of the Himalayas, the importance of whose dizzy heights she was trying to communicate to us from the blackboard. The ascent of high mountain peaks by men, is, as I understand it, of deep sexual significance; and I am not surprised.

One of our male teachers was a certain Mr Gaul. A York-shireman, already past sixty, brother of a composer named A. R. Gaul who had written a number of Oratorios, Mr Gaul had come out of retirement to teach us scripture and Latin. A short man, white-bearded, poor-sighted and slightly deaf, he was ripe prey for that particular brand of mischievous persecution that only schoolboys know how to administer. The result was that my Latin was atrocious and my Scripture about as bad. Indeed I have a strong impression that at this time – I am writing now of the last year or so of the war – I was not very good at anything, except perhaps painting and drawing, of which I had always been very fond. Subjects such as trigonometry, mechanics and chemistry were totally beyond my comprehension; I was hopeless at carpentry; I do not recall any particular interest in literature. I was filled in fact with a vast apathy, so much so that I was presently guilty of the unpardonable folly of cutting football, for which I was whipped again and this time justifiably.

How long all this might have gone on and where it might have ended it is impossible to say; but fortunately the hand of 'the Divinity which shapes our ends' had not finished with me. Indeed it was almost ready to play not one card in my favour, but two. One such stroke of fate in the year 1919 would have been miraculous; two were to provoke nothing short of a revolution.

But before I divulge these matters it is necessary to go back to my grandfather and his fields, to what was virtually the last golden phase of pure childhood.

IX

It was my grandfather's practice to buy up, every summer, a small orchard or two, and occasionally even a solitary tree of plums or pears from some private garden whose owner had neither the time nor inclination to pick the fruit for himself. Of the solitary trees I most vividly remember a tall conical-shaped tree of small honey pears, ripening in August, that grew in an old stone-walled garden side by side with Chichele's charming small grammar school, (see page 30), now used for sacred purposes rather than the secular ones for which it was intended six hundred years ago. The tree not only appeared to me very tall and the pears of a singular juicy sweetness, but the whole garden must have made on my young mind an impression at once permanent and endearing, for it is from this garden and its adjoining stone house that the tragic heroine of *The Sleepless Moon,* a novel of mine written more than forty years later, walks to her wedding in the neighbouring church and subsequently to a marriage unconsummated.

There is little doubt, however, that the sweet honey pears and I were consummated all right. I never knew the name of that pear and I daresay it has long since passed from the lineage of peardom. But its nature in bearing was so prolific that not only did we spend days gathering it for filling skips, baskets, boxes and trays, but it also positively rained in full ripeness from heaven, covering the long uncut grass beneath, the rotting pears themselves being covered in turn by buzzing flotillas of wasps, at which my grandfather swung an infuriated cap in the hot August sun.

Some distance away, across the square, in a short stone side street, we bought from time to time the fruit of other trees, but here in the old back garden of the coach-builder's yard, it is not the trees I remember. No solitary tree of pears, like a honeyed spire, grew there to let imagination feed on its memory until the nettle of tragedy at last grew out of it. It is the coach-builder and his art that I most vividly recall. The essence of it all is as remote from our jet-driven world as the chariot-making yards of Rome or Baalbeck, where the underground stables are huge and expansive enough to contain a fleet of a thousand buses.

But here, in this quiet, sycamore-shaded yard and street, there were neither chariots nor buses, but only everyday vehicles of both great beauty and utility, all built lightly but for strength, spokes and shafts and rails all varnished and fined down until they looked not unlike the moulded and twisted sticks of rock — spit-rock, we always called it from the habit of its makers of spitting on their hands as they pulled at the malleable ropes of sugar — we bought at feasts and fairs. Traps, buggies, milk-floats, brakes, butchers' carts, bakers' carts, wagons, wagonettes, landaus, cabs, flies, carriages of ultra elegance: all were there, finished, half-finished, shining with paint and varnish, drying in the sun. No other craft, I suppose, ever contributed so much elegance and colour to the streets of this century as that of the coach-builder. Red, blue, yellow, green, gold, black and even white: the dashing vehicles, still chariot-like, still had the streets as their own. The careering traps, drawn by high-steppers, the comforting beer-barrel buggies drawn by Shetlands, the vast brewers' drays, the double-horse delivery trucks, the charging milk-floats glistening with churns of brass and silver finish and those gracious landaus and wagonettes in which, according to class and income, you rode out to relish the summer air.

The first serious accident I ever saw in a street was between one of these vehicles, a two-horsed wholesale fruiterer's truck, and an early motor car: an event at once shattering and prophetic. The fruiterer and his truck still regarded the streets as the horse's own and unviolated racetrack. Like milk-floats, traps and of course fire engines, they drove everywhere at a pace fearful and swaggering, often in swanky, cocky rivalry. For the fruiterer to meet head-on, at a crossroads, a totally unexpected horseless carriage stinking of oil and petrol must have been a shock even greater than that of being offered a glass of milk at the Green Dragon in place of a pint of porter. But the struggling, bleeding, screaming horses of that Edwardian morning were not merely victims. They were omens; their day of elegance and street chariot-racing, like that of the coach-builder, were about to become part of a vanished world.

The tall conical pear tree, like a sweet shadow of the adjoining church steeple itself, together with the coach-builder's yard and its gay vehicles and apple trees, were only part, and that an irregular one, of my grandfather's small summer adventures in the world of fruit. Apart from these minor affairs we had a far larger and more permanent piece of business to conduct in that direction. Every summer, I imagine about the first or second week of July, when honeysuckle, hedge roses, meadowsweet and that particular variety of willowherb known as codlins-and-cream filled every dyke and hedgerow with the full flower-vintage of high summer, we harnessed the horse-and-trap – I had already mastered the business of putting on bridle, collar, belly-band and all the rest – and set off on a journey that for me was like a pilgrimage to Mecca.

If the day were very hot – and in recollection every day was hot – I cut a branch of ash leaves to stick in the horse's bridle in order to keep the flies away. Everywhere fields of wheat, early oats and barley were beginning to show that magical midsummer transformation of colour from pure green and blue green to a vaporous touch of gold. A little late hay would perhaps still lie in the meadows waiting to be carried: the air in consequence full of the scent of it, mixed with the fragrance of honeysuckle and meadow-sweet and an occasional pungent pong as the horse broke wind. I must confess that I loved the horse to break wind, especially when trotting. Both high and low notes punctuated one another until, not knowing what was next coming forth in this natural horsy symphony, my grandfather and I rocked about in a state of equally boyish hilarity in the seats behind.

Our destination was the village of Stanwick, the church spire of which was one of the nine we could see from our little farm-holding on a clear bright day. Beside the church the road wound upward on a short hill and then straightened out again. About half a mile along this road stood a four-square house of no particularly great age or architectural style, built of that warmest pleasant limestone that runs diagonally right across England from Wansford (the Wansford-in-England as the legend has it) to the Mendips in the west. The house, its windows often curtained or blinded against the July sun, had an air both unadventurous and respectable. It was a sort of curate's house, in which you could imagine a young, respectable and rather seedy prelate either writing dry, desultory notes for a sermon or making ginger-and-rhubarb jam.

The trap having been brought to a standstill, the horse nodding its crown of ash leaves against the flies, my grandfather would hand me the reins and tell me to hold hard for a jiffy until he went to see if 'the old tit' was about.

In the front garden, every bit as respectable as the imaginary curate himself, grew a green-flowered rose. I have never seen a green rose elsewhere and it remains for me, to this day, a kind of hallmark. It was, it seemed, the only green rose ever raised or grown anywhere and in addition to being a hallmark it also implanted itself in my mind as something of a miracle. It had, it appeared, been the hybridising crown of the deceased husband of the old tit, whose presence in the house my grandfather presently came back to announce as confirmed.

We then drove the trap through the front gates, up a short gravel drive and so to the back door of the house. Immediately an astonishing pandemonium broke out. The earth suddenly opened up, like an underground kennel, and let forth a bewildering army of dogs, some small, some large, some puppyish, some almost drunkenly fat-teated, all barking and yapping in what seemed to be quarrelsome savagery at once. The possible effect of all this on the horse being unpredictable – we once had one who would stand vertically on its hind legs, like a fighting stallion out of a picture by Stubbs, at the mere distant sound of the band of the Royal Welch Fusiliers – that my grandfather instantly seized the bridle, leaving me still in the trap, in a state of near paralysis, fear and wonder, not daring to alight in case my legs were chewed to the bone.

'Oh! the dear things won't hurt you. They won't hurt you a bit. They're *pleased* to see you. They're really *ever so* pleased.'

With these words, or some others of intentionally equal comfort, the old tit doddered forth. Her tiny frame quaked like totter-grass from head to foot. I see her as a kind of brownish, diminutive nun, untouched and unprotected, except for her countless dogs, from the sterner, predatory world outside. Woe indeed, wet or fine, was her recital of lamentation.

Its most consistent text was that of 'scrumping'. The garden, as I was to discover, was wandering and extensive. Its surrounding stone wall, blessed with fan-trained trees of peaches, plums and even apricots, was not in fact a protection at all but, as walls have so often proved to be in the course of history, a medium of defence merely offering challenge to an invading enemy.

'The boys have been over the wall again, Mr Lucas. There isn't a thing left. Not a cherry nor a gooseberry. I think the currants have all gone too. It's too terrible, Mr Lucas, it's too terrible, Mr Lucas, to think of –'

By now the dogs had quietened. They merely snuffed around the trap wheels. I was able to alight. My grandfather, by nature imperturbable, had little to say by way of comfort and merely puffed at his pipe instead; and since one of his favourite stories was of a day in his extreme youth when he had scrumped a considerable quantity of apples and had hidden them in the furrow of an adjacent ploughed field in the twilight and had then considerable difficulty in finding them next morning, I had every excuse to be quiet too.

The old tit now led us forth, more than ever tottering, to the doomed areas of destruction, the scorched earth left by scrumping boys. The snuffing dogs followed. A path bordered by bush-trained apples and pears, under which grew wild sowings of seeding honesty and golden marigold, together with marrows already as fat as sucking pigs, led away into the distance that seemed to be an even denser forest of plums, apples and pear-trees of positive grandeur. The June drop had passed; on all sides the trees were loaded with already fattening fruit. Here and there vast umbrellas of rhubarb leaf, waving beds of asparagus, silvery forests of seakale and mauve lakes of potato-flower proclaimed that the garden was as richly productive at earth level as in the balmy sky above.

We paused, nevertheless, for constant, twittering complaint. What the boys hadn't robbed the birds had. Fat golden and red jewels of ripening gooseberries, scarlet pearls of redcurrants, positive rosaries of blackcurrants, shining as dark grapes, grew in healthy splendour, the bushes shrouded in old lace curtains, discarded antimacassars and even shreds of female underclothing, everywhere. My mouth watered at the sight of this luscious harvest as frequently as the old tit doddered and twittered in

misery. Even today, fifty years later, the squash of a ripe red gooseberry and its seeds against my tongue are enough to recall the contradictory scene of riches and destruction.

Presently and inevitably we were escorted to the front line, the wall, the tragic breach in the defences.

'This is where the boys come over, Mr Lucas. You see where they've broken it down. You can see where they've broken the stones away. Look at the apricots – All broken down –'

My grandfather sucked at his pipe. Like me, he looked in sympathy, but in vain, for a hole in the wall, a displaced stone or two. As for apricots, my young quick eyes could see them hiding, young too as yet, unblemished behind the leaves, snug against the wall.

'It's awful, Mr Lucas. Every year it gets more awful. I'll have to have barbed wire put all along –'

Hereupon my grandfather would shout that all was well. There was nothing to worry about. Boys would be boys.

Deafness not only defeated him. It merely served to heighten the wail of lamentations. The sudden increase in twittering and tottering always seemed to me that the old tit was about to fall apart.

At some point just beyond this – later in the summer I was forbidden on pain of death ever to go within visual distance of the apricots, the crown jewels of the September scene – the wall took an abrupt turn to the right. The entire garden opened up into a semi-wilderness. The grass was long and unmown, dissected only by a narrow path along which, in single file, the dogs, in pup or not, waddled like an advance party of brown troopers. Abruptly, to the left, there was a sudden drop of twenty or thirty feet into what had once been what my grandfather would have called, and indeed did call 'a stun pit'. From here, I gathered, had been quarried the stone for both house and garden wall. The calcareous nature of the remaining soil being admirably suited to the growing of fruit, especially stone-fruit, among which apricots demand certain exceptional conditions, the late husband of the old tit, who I gathered had made a modest fortune from the invention of some patent lamp or other, had everywhere planted fruit with great prodigality.

The result was that the old tit was now the possessor of a positive forest of fruit that she had no idea what to do with. Hence the presence of my grandfather and I to survey and assess the prospect of harvest. The scene was utterly idyllic. Time had covered the lacerated cliffs of stone with grass and thyme and wild rose and elderberry and odd bushes of hawthorn; above it all rose the many fruit trees in their full bearing and prime, in particular pears of many varieties, Blenheim Orange apples, Worcester Pearmains, Cox's Orange and an apple that my grandfather called 'a summerin' apple', on account of its earliness, softness of flesh and inability to keep. This, I fancy, was ready to pick, a pleasant pale yellow in colour, by the end of July, to be followed a little later by that queen of plums I have already mentioned, the squarish apricot-like plum of incomparable flavour always known as the Stanwick Plum (has it died too with the vanished world, I often wonder?) and then in succession the many pears, the Russets, the Williams Bon Chrétien, Conference and that great lady, Marie Louise.

But in July the prospect of garnering all these was still well ahead of us. Before that time the boys, naturally, would be over the wall again; blackbirds would have been feasting; the annual invasion of wasps would have begun; summer gales would have ripped off the little remaining fruit; there would be little or nothing left. Nevertheless some assessment of ultimate harvest, pitiful though it might be, had now to be made; a gamble, a bargain, had to be struck.

In uncertain procession, dogs and all, we returned to the house. My impression is that, except when it rained, I remained outside, torn in temptation by ripening gooseberries and currants on the one hand and the cherry trees, of which there were few, on the other. It was only on really wet days that I was invited into the house, my recollection of which does nothing to disprove my impression of the old tit as a brown, diminutive nun. There lingered about the cloistered rooms an air at once ecclesiastical, stuffy, sunbaked and deeply redolent of paraffin. A few cases of stuffed birds, a fox and a stoat or two; whatnots overladen with china; a bewildering variety of chairs, stools, *prie dieux,* sofas and footstools covered either with beads, antimacassars or both, and a great gallery of photographic enlargements of Victorian gentlemen of stern and bewhiskered demean who appeared to be about to preach at me long sermons either on the evils of childish interruption in the world of adults or the rewarding piety of silence: this was the pattern of every room, overlaid even to my childish mind with an air of unhappy solitude.

After what always seemed to me a whole era of pain, the bargain between the old tit and my grandfather was finally struck. I had never the remotest idea of what sums were involved; I only knew, even then, that my grandfather's immense and inborn honesty made him utterly alien to the prospects of sharp practice. It is more than likely that the first bargain was of a preliminary nature, still guided by the prospective disasters of predatory boys, wasps and summer thunderstorms, and that the final one was struck and sealed only when the last Blenheim Orange had been borne home in the September twilight, to be stored on the floor with a thousand others in the little back bedroom where I always slept: a room of which I shall have something of singular interest to say a little further on.

A glass of home-made wine, most probably of elderberry or rhubarb, was the final signal that all talk of importance for the day was over. I always watched it disappear down my grandfather's throat – my impression is one of abstinence on the part of the old tit – with much relief. My own rewards were infinitely less generous.

'Would the little boy like an apple or something?' the old tit always asked and in due course a handful of blackbird-bitten cherries, a pear full of wasp-craters, a bruised and fallen apple or two were, in their seasons, my rewards from the old tit's tottering but affectionate hands. It was indeed good fortune that I had taken the precaution of filling my pockets with choicer, sounder fruit long beforehand. Boys, indeed, will be boys.

In due course, when we returned at some time in early August, it always seemed to me that the depredations of boys, birds and wasps had been of little account. Memory of course tends to count the good, happy years; less often the lean, bad ones. Clearly there must have been summers of disappointment and disaster. One good raging August storm, with clouds sailing in from the west like blue-black tornadoes, would wreck the Blenheim Oranges, the Doyenne du Comice and Cox's Orange, leaving underneath the trees a desolate battlefield of fallen fruit. But time on the whole paints out such dreary landscapes, leaving canvases cleaned and ready for light always brilliant, sun always warm and even torrid and trees always laden with fruit in spite of wasps, as in a promised land.

The great mystery and inquiry in my mind was how we ever managed to find time not only for the garnering of this harvest but for that of wheat and barley too. The journey from home to orchard – there were two choices of road, top-road and bottom-road – alone took an hour, very often more if we chanced on some acquaintance, some roadside stone-breaker, a scytheman at work beyond a hedgerow, a drover wetting a rough whistle on an out-door settle at a pub. Even in conversations notable for dialogue cryptic, undecorated and dry these exchanges seemed always to go on an unconscionable time.

''Ow bin then?'

'Mid.'

'I 'eered talk as she wadn't very grand.'

'Bad a-bed and wuss up.'

'Old gal come down yit?'

'Fourteen! Last Sunday. Laid on two on 'em though.'

'Swine fever over at Long Leys, I 'eered.'

'So I 'eered.'

'Well, we'd better be gittin' on, else it'll be bull's noon. Giddup there.'

'Too right. Be the way, how's Joe?'

'Gone. Took Monday, gone Wednesday.'

'Never? If it 'ent one thing it's another.'

'Too right. Giddup there.'

The entire long day was otherwise ours alone. The only other help on which my grandfather could count, besides Smack, was from that of a rather rapscallion of a character named Sam, the farmer next door to us. Compared with our puny holding his could truly be called a farm: five or six fields, horses, cows, bullock-yards, binders, wagons. Proud as any coachman in livery I used to drive these wagons, full or empty, at harvest time, handling the big shires as I manfully chewed a straw. This system of neighbourly exchange always worked well at harvest and again at threshing time and even again at ploughing time, when we imported on to that intractable gut-lugging clay of ours two monsters in the shape of great steam engines, one stationed at one headland of a field, one at the other, the plough being drawn back and forth on a long steel coil between. You might as well ask to see a Roman chariot at Ascot or a Christian-eating lion at a base-ball field as ever to see this piece of agricultural antiquity again.

Sam, who had served as a soldier in India and on the North-west frontier, might have come straight out of Kipling. His slightly swaggering, bantering manner, his capacity for beer, his rough warmth, his ability to make every syllable of reminiscence about India and the Army sound like a raging lie made my grandfather's homely innocence seem almost the equal of mine. He and my grandfather always called each other 'shop-mate', an echo of the old shoemaking days. When wet weather drove us indoors they sat on sacks of potatoes, bales of straw or even on the chaff-strewn barn-floor and argued of this and that in terms almost revolutionary, blew vile tobacco, released frequent and un-inhibited crescendoes of wind and spat, while I, the little pig with big ears sat, looked and listened.

To this scene, inhabited otherwise only by Sam's wife, son and daughter, there came, in I suppose about 1916, a stranger, a figure of touching innocence in the shape of a piece of German cannon-fodder who had mercifully escaped the holocaust of the Western Front (a certain distinguished soldier-politician, writing of a mid-war dinner at Brigade HQ, at which the customary soup, fish, entrée, roast, sweet, cheese, savoury, Moselle, Claret and brandy had been served, subsequently made the comment in his own reminiscences: 'Not at all a bad dinner, when you think of it, only twenty-five miles behind the front line,' a remark I have always thought must have pleased Siegfried Sassoon and the author of *Goodbye to All That*): a pitifully young German prisoner of war.

Johann had no English. His only means of expression was in the form of a slow, bemused, painfully bewildered smile. Truly Nordic, fair, transparently blue-eyed, gentle, he worked dutifully in a dumb world until gradually, sitting in barns or on wagon-boards, I taught him a few rudimentary words of English. Perhaps it isn't altogether odd that I should remember Johann with such clarity and some affection, since I have over and over again been convinced that this young fair pawn, one of millions moved remorselessly hither and thither in a bloody game of chess, sowed in my mind the first of my doubts on war's futilities. We all grew very fond of Johann and he of us; and later, not long before the carnage of another game of chess was about to be repeated, I painted his portrait in a story, *The Hessian Prisoner*.

It would be late September, sometimes early October, before the last of the apples were gathered in. The leaves of the pear trees were already turning to their rosy-walnut, garnet-golden, vermilion-brown. On some darkening evening, with light balloons of mist collapsing everywhere on the wide stretch of river valley, we would drive home with the last truck-load of fruit, I as usual blessed with the old tit's parting gift of a few mouldy fallings but heavily laden pocket-wise with the choicest prizes I could find. On our way we would pass the big stone water mill where later on we would bring our wheat for milling, the flour in turn to be baked into 'mucky bread'. The sound of the millrace and the grind of truck wheels on the stones of the long hill out of the valley were almost the last sounds (except my grandmother's irate 'I'll be burned if you'll sleep in my sheets with that neck. You'll be sowing carrots in it next') before I fell asleep, dog-tired, in the little back bedroom.

All winter that small room smelled of apples, ripe and sweating and laid out on chests of drawers, tables and floor for keeping. The only window faced north-westward, over the river valley. On winter nights the great glow of iron-ore furnaces lit up the distant sky with a crimson-golden glow. On the mantelpiece of the fireplace, where no fire was ever lit, a few flower-painted trinkets and Victorian china figures stood with a brass candlestick. But as if in anticipation of a fire there stood ready in one corner of the room my grandfather's entire gear as a fireman: great brass helmet, boots, axe, belt, rope and uniform. Sometimes, safely alone, I used to try on boots and helmet, only to collapse under the sheer weight and size of them.

One winter night I awoke to the startled impression that the iron-ore furnaces were burning brighter than usual. A few moments later my grandfather rushed into the room, dragged on boots and helmet and uniform, grabbed axe and belt and rope and clattered madly downstairs. After some further minutes someone else, my grandmother or my aunt, came in and took me from my bed. I rather fancy I was five. The curtains having been drawn back, I was held at the window to watch the great fire. Less than half a mile away a boot factory was burning with brilliant ferocity. Pretty soon it was threatening a long low row of stone and thatched cottages. In one of these my grandfather had been born and from that same one, on that winter night, he was bearing away a baby in arms.

The 'Divinity that shapes our ends' appeared in fact to be at work again. The baby was eventually to become my wife.

X

If there is one description that occurs more often in the slow progress of my schooldays towards the end of the war it is the single word 'apathy'; Mr Gaul, master of Latin and Scripture, further amplified this to 'lethargic'. Perhaps I am by nature inclined to be dreamy; perhaps it was the war, with its ever increasing pattern of doom, with the long lists of killed, wounded and missing growing ever longer, the shortage of food, the interminable delays to passenger trains so that the vast ammunition chariots from the industrial Midlands and north often delayed my evening homecoming until after nine o'clock; or it may have been the growing squad of schoolmistresses passing on to us, in their man-starved world, their own lethargies and frustrations.

Of mechanics, mathematics, chemistry and so on I knew, and still know, practically nothing. Others might find the mysteries of changing colours in test tubes a sort of magic; to me it was as remote a mystery as trying to read Sanskrit. The simplest explanation of all, perhaps, is that I was merely abysmally bored. So desperate at one time did I become that I joined a voluntary squad of potato pickers, thus exchanging for a few weeks my classroom for the vast acres of the estate of the Duke of Buccleuch, of which the memory of the great yellowing avenues of elms on misty oyster-cold autumn mornings remains with me yet, more vivid than any chemical formula or any trigonometrical mumbojumbo.

There may be those who deduce from all this that I was not

merely bored, but also rebellious. With this I am inclined to agree. I have a notion that it was a sort of inborn cussedness that for example made me take so little interest in Latin, a fact that I now much regret. I have a natural and insatiable appetite for words, not necessarily those of a nature long and abstruse (I run a mile from intellectual swank words such as 'esoteric' and 'proliferate', which crawl out of their various holes from time to time) and I like taking them apart, as some people do old clocks, to see what makes them tick. The shaky nature of my foundations in Latin here puts me to much disadvantage and I now often wish that I had attended with greater application to the exploits of Caesar instead of lighting outrageous candles on the back row of the fifth form, thus leading the short-sighted Mr Gaul to the confused impression that the sun had suddenly come out with supernatural brightness.

Rebellious, perhaps; unambitious, certainly. My solitary ambition at this time was to become a painter. My father's ambition for me was, I am quite certain, that I should become either a minister of the church or a musician of sorts. It is, however, a sad thing that whereas our family and indeed my own take the very greatest and most affectionate interest in music none of us have ever yet succeeded in performing on or with any kind of instrument, except my father with his splendid bass voice and my younger son, who briefly mastered the euphonium to a point where he could play 'A Farmer's Boy' and 'Bless This House' with a competence and fervour that on occasion reduced his mother to tears of adoration at school concerts. Alas, I am sorry to say, I followed the general family pattern; crotchets and quavers and clefs and minims meant even less to me than sines and cosines.

But for art I had a genuine interest and appetite; I looked forward to art class as to no other lesson. We were taught by a Mr Gash. In the late Victorian or early Edwardian era Kettering had produced a painter named Alfred East, later Sir Alfred, a performer of conventional competence who had at one time exhibited at La Nationale des Beaux Arts in Paris and whose work, I note, is now returning to some favour, as with other painters of his period and kind. Mr Gash, I fancy, had been a pupil of his. A kindly, simple, local man, he had evidently got it into his head that he ought to talk to grammar school boys in an accent other than his own. Thus misled, he constantly beseeched us to bear in mind such rules as 'the heighth of the heye'. Others thought this funny; I didn't; and for once I was earnestly sitting at someone's feet, waiting to be taught.

Nothing, in those days, gave parents more pleasure than to be able to demonstrate that their offspring could either paint pictures or play the piano. 'My mother,' Henry Moore has said, 'had no knowledge of art. Like many parents, she thought that whatever I did was jolly good.' So with my painting; as I sketched, painted flowers and copied the various classical prints that hung about the house I found myself much praised, so much so that it was strongly hinted that I ought to take lessons (to this very day I am constantly being urged by my family that I ought to take up painting; in answer to which it is quite useless for me to point out that writing is as much a graphic art as drawing and that words themselves are a form of paint.) Time and expense, as well as diffidence, precluded any idea that I should seek tuition under Mr Gash; instead I discovered that the eldest of four sisters living opposite our house gave painting lessons and it was to her eventually that I went, with my new box of oils and brushes, to receive lessons at, I think, the princely sum of a shilling an hour. It may well have been less, since it isn't many months since I was told by a painter of distinction that attendance for instruction at Jacques Emile Blanche's studio in Paris at the end of the last century cost half a franc, plus another half a franc if M. Blanche himself gave you a personal hint or two.

The results of my all too brief lessons in painting were remarkable. They are not to be seen in the Tate, the Prado or the Metropolitan Museum of Art, but in my mother's best front bedroom. They are a most extraordinary and inimitable pair of pictures, since they are beyond all doubt the two worst pictures ever painted by man. In strict truth, perhaps, I ought to confess that their horrific badness is exceeded by one other, a landscape. When I last saw this masterpiece it was being used by an aunt of mine in the sitting-room grate as a means of keeping soot from falling down the chimney in summertime. When I asked after its origins she replied with immense pride 'It's yours! Don't you remember?' Mercifully time had obliterated everything; my career as a painter was long since dead; my final masterpiece was stopping a hole to keep the soot away.

Here, unless it should be thought that my life has been governed by a sort of celestial traffic warden whose inspired duty it has been to prevent me from taking the wrong turning at street lights or one-way streets, I must apologise for yet again drawing some attention to the movements of the 'Divinity that shapes our ends'.

Hitherto, such movements may have seemed to be of relatively small importance. The next were not. Moreover there were two of them; and they took place together.

The war ended. The grey and dismal morning of the official proclamation was as vivid, for me, though falsely, as the golden days of orchard and harvest-field. The church bells in the ancient and structurally unsafe steeple of the church at Rushden, unpealed in all probability since the relief of Mafeking, pealed gallantly out again, as if to say 'We have won. Ring out wild bells! and damn it all.' And damned indeed we were to be.

At school there was little or no evidence of any change for a term or two. Then gradually our erstwhile mistresses began to drift away. (One of them at least was well-sculptured and pretty and there used to be stories of favoured members of the upper sixth being invited to her flat to enjoy the seductive solitude of tea and buttered crumpets; but I was too young for that line of luxury.) Soon we had a staff seven-eighths of whom were men, most of them soldiers from the wars returning but one of them a Welsh International soccer player of much skill who once helped me put the ball into the opposing net eight times for the First XI, for whom I played when I was fourteen. In *The Old School* I have stated firmly that 'I believe I still thought of becoming a professional footballer . . . but I longed most of all to leave the place and never see it again.'

Then in the autumn term of 1919 the hand of the Divinity moved again and something of a miracle occurred. Our instructress for English, a gaunt, carroty Scotswoman, under whom I had suffered in steadily mute retrogession of interest in that subject, had left us at the end of the summer term. Anything of even the minutest improvement would have been welcome to us as we reassembled for that autumn but greatly to our surprise (in my case a stunned surprise) there eventually walked into the classroom a young ex-infantry officer who looked, facially, at any rate, as if he had been mercilessly battered by the shovel of a drunken navvy. He also limped; he also had some difficulty in holding the chalk as he wrote on the blackboard, a fact not surprising since he had lost three of his fingers. Nevertheless the painful distortions of the face, already showing signs of healing from a sort of disordered parchment map into something recognisably human again, couldn't conceal that here was a very English face, once good-looking and still alert, kindly and unembittered by all that war had done to it. The injuries to face and hands had been caused by a single German hand grenade and the limp in the legs by the presence of uncountable bits of shrapnel, many of whom continued to roam about the flesh for some years to come, now and then appearing on the surface in order to provide some proof of their existence beside pain.

Edmund Kirby, son of a Northamptonshire farmer, has somewhere described, I believe, the hypnotic presence in the classroom of a pair of vividly blue, enraptured young eyes, ceaselessly watching him as he taught. If his own were thus keenly observant those of the young pupil he was watching, also the possessor of a very English face, can only be likened to the 'transmogrifying magnifying glasses' whose use was urgedby the elder Weller, in Mr Pickwick's unfortunate court case,on Samivel.

If it is possible to change human vision, or at least to waken it, by the stimulus or even shock of a single experience, then this is a perfect example of it. I do not think I am putting it either too highly or fancifully to say that in that one morning in the autumn of 1919 I not only grew up; I grew up into what I was to be. Fanciful as indeed it may sound, I date my literary career from that moment. 'Write me,' the young ex-infantry officer said to us, 'an essay on Shakespeare. I mean from your own point of view. Don't tell me he was born in Stratford-upon-Avon in 1564. I already know that. Don't tell me either that he wrote *Macbeth* or *The Merchant of Venice*. I already know that too.'

In case my already expressed self-criticism as the possessor of a rebellious nature may have been misinterpreted as indicating that I was constantly in a state of war against something (though I don't deny that I often am) I ought perhaps to explain here that by rebelliousness I simply mean being told or ordered to do something by somebody in somebody else's way rather than be left alone to do it in my own. For this reason I have never discussed a word of a poem, play, story or novel with anyone before writing it, a process that D. H. Lawrence called 'the give away' and which was once excellently illustrated by Miss Rosamond Lehmann, who confessed that whenever she was asked what her next novel was to be about always replied simply 'Two women and a man.'

Thus left to my own resources, instead of being chivvied about, I succeeded in writing an essay about Shakespeare without mentioning Shakespeare. Whether this was good or bad I have now no notion of knowing. But one thing is quite certain: it was exactly as if, not having run a race in my life, I had suddenly run a hundred yards in ten seconds dead. I suddenly knew, incontestably, that I was or was going to be, a writer. This empowering fact (it belonged neither to the region of hope nor desire but simply *was*) I confided to no one, first because I had as yet no one in whom to confide, though this omission was shortly to be remedied, but also because the outrageous impossibility of such a fact would have seemed as senseless to others as if I had suddenly revealed that I had stumbled on a process of turning strawberry jam into gold.

Secrecy in ambition is a great fertiliser and in secrecy, for a time at least, my ambition flourished. It now seems to me both interesting and odd that whereas I can remember clearly the various examples of compulsory reading I had endured under the stern gaze of the carroty Scotswoman, among them *A Tale of Two Cities* and a whole year, if you please, on *Kenilworth,* I found myself in some confusion in trying to place exactly the first year's reading under

Kirby. I am inclined to think that it consisted in some kind of hyper-sensitive diving into a magical hat: a sweep and a whirl that produced Keats, Shelley, Drayton, (*Fair Stood the Wind for France*), Shirley, Herrick, Lovelace, Milton, Chaucer, Tennyson and so on, a great jewelled jumble coming teeming out of what had been, until then, thin, arid air. Of specific books I recall only one, Milton's 'a speech for the liberty of unlicensed printing in the Parliament of England': *Areopagitica*.

That book, short though it is, first brought me face to face with the greatness of the English language, so flexible and capable of constant flowering in comparison with the unflowering, grammar-ridden French or the impossible suety garrulity of German; a neatness so ordered and yet musical, so lucid and yet pictorial. As I read Milton's logical but impassioned plea (and it would do us no harm to remember it from time to time) it is not too much to say that I was not only dazzled as by a great vision but that I realised for the first but by no means the last that prose, in our malleable, delicate, incomparable English, can also be poetry:

> I cannot praise a fugitive and cloistered virtue, unexercised and unbreathed, that never sallies forth and sees her adversary, but slinks out of the race where that immortal garland is to be run for not without dust or heat. Assuredly we bring not innocence into the world, we bring impurity much rather: that which purifies us is trial, and trial is by what is contrary.

Little though such words and their singing order may mean to most of the present generation of young writers, many of whom appear never to have taken the trouble to learn anything of the use of language and who appear to care for nothing but slinging words haphazard on to the paper, apparently at their happiest when using those formerly mostly favoured by thugs and gutter-snipes, they meant a very great deal to me. I believe there was a time when I could very nearly quote the whole of *Areopagitica* off by heart and I had also reached the point where I was going around with the symphonic nobilities of The Book of Isaiah pounding away in my head, a scriptural piece of reformation which much astonished Mr Gaul, who had now confessed that he recognised my talents but deeply deplored the misuse of them. 'Ah! Bates, Bates,' he would say. 'You with your gifts, you with your gifts,' and then shake his poor patriarchal head, giving the wayward lamb of my talent up for lost.

It is curious that though I was so carried away on the bright flood-stream of English poetry and the poetic prose of Milton and the Authorised Version I had as yet given no conscious thought to the idea of writing verse myself. I have long supposed that poets write not merely with their own and often secret voice; they need a comparable voice, often secret too, to listen to them. That voice, as far as I was concerned, was still missing. The warm, encouraging voice of a schoolmaster, together with a guiding hand, was admirable but not enough. I needed, without knowing it, another voice, together with another volcanic bang of transformation.

Presently, in the late autumn of 1919, these both arrived: in the shape of a girl.

Before I put down a word about the second of these revolutionary influences I ought to say a little of a third. Somewhere about this time there one day appeared on the morning school-train a complete stranger. For some days we spoke of him merely as 'the chap in the green cap'. As a gang the dozen or so of us catching the early morning train were inclined to be both clannish and boisterous. We sang popular songs all the way to school, among the ditties being one which Anthony Powell was apparently hearing at the very same time at Eton, namely 'K-K-K-Katie, beautiful Katie', together with that moving tribute to young beauty: 'The tender blossoms on the tree cannot compare with Mary-Ee. One of our number was also ingenious and daring, preferring very often to spend the journey swinging from carriage to carriage on the outside of the train, hanging on with his nails at fifty or sixty miles an hour, instead of sitting comfortably inside.

But the boy in the green cap, a couple of years my senior, was neither clannish nor boisterous. He seemed to be coolly exclusive, serious, apart. His pale bespectacled face gave him the appearance of being swotty. He always carried an armful of books in his hand and was always reading, instead of singing, in the train. Soon he had changed his green school cap for our own and soon he and I were walking part of the way home together.

Henry James Byrom was a Lancastrian who had moved from an older and much more distinguished school than our own in the southern part of the county by reason of the fact that his father had died and he was now living with his mother and uncle, who had come to be headmaster of that very same national school where my father had played his tricks so long before and where in fact my future wife was also to spend her schooldays. One of his ancestors had been John Byrom, composer of that Christmas carol still so often sung, 'Christians awake! Salute the Happy Morn'. There seems in fact to have been a strong musical streak in the family and Henry himself was musical too.

The pale face and spectacles did indeed conceal a character that was not merely swotty; it was fantastically brainy too. It was also, as it turned out, warm, witty and affectionate. The brains were of the kind that makes off with high honours in exams as easily as most children lap up ice cream. This did not prevent him from being, like me, a tolerably good footballer and a great lover of music and the countryside and, unlike me, a good amateur actor. He was the sort of young man who inevitably plays the part of Brutus, Richard II and Macbeth in school plays while the Bates of this world hang about at the back of crowd scenes, growling like unfed dogs and now and then crying out miserably 'Hail Caesar!' or something of that sort. His scholastic background was unmistakable. In his uncle's house the regular daily newspaper was *The Times,* which Harry read with the solemnity proper to a London club-man rather than a country schoolboy, whereas ours, as befitted a good Nonconformist Liberal family, was the *Daily News,* For the rest of his time at school Harry's scholastic lustre outshone that of all the rest of us, until he finally departed for London University under 'Old Gollancz' and subsequently to a mastership at Stephen Spender's old school, U.G.S., where Spender confessed in Graham Greene's anthology that his father allowed him sixpence a week pocket money. I can only say here that Spender was lucky. I am pretty sure I am right in saying that I had fourpence, for which I was expected to clean a few shoes and chop a few sticks in return.

But Harry Byrom was, for me, a most lucky turn-up. He was, at that very moment, the very person I needed. His mind, though brainy, was not sticky. In summer we launched out into long country rambles, revelling in the blossoming of bluebell woods, the coming of hay and harvest, the darling buds of May and the beauty of old churches. In the longest days of summer we were up at six, clad in running shorts, ready for a three-mile training session. In winter we sang Handel, Schubert, 'There Was a Lady Sweet and Kind' and 'Riding Down From Bangor' at the piano and gobbled greedily at the only musical fare the town in those days had to offer, a choice finally lying between *Messiah* and Haydn's *Creation* on the one hand and *Patience* and *The Pirates of Penzance* on the other. As is the fashion of growing youth we argued with passion and what we thought was subtlety, thinking ourselves great fellows, and looked down on girls, who in those days mostly wore their hair tied in large funereal black bows at the back, as an unfortunately necessary nuisance to be tolerated distantly. It will perhaps complete the picture of Harry Byrom if I say that he read *Ovid* as other boys read Edgar Wallace and was on occasion prone to quote Latin to the summer skies or, if we found mushrooms of incomparable quality on some dewy September morning, address them with Keats' joyous cry, 'Full of the true, the blushful Hippocrene'!

If you conclude from all this that 'the narrow road to a certain demesne of secluded priggishness' was about to open to me you will conclude correctly. Brains are not all; brains, as a critic has recently pointed out with some wisdom, are not for instance necessary for the writing of novels, whereas imagination is; brains may father *The Theory of Relativity* but not Sam Weller. The world of making fiction, which at the time of which I am writing was only three or four years away from me, is not one of mathematical exactitudes or soluble equations, but one of lying and distortion. Art, as Picasso has rightly remarked, is not truth.

Fortunately I was about to be turned from the narrow path leading 'to a certain demesne of secluded priggishness' into one as totally different as it was unexpected; a circumstance brought about by a combination of accident and Shakespeare.

I have never been ardently fond of school plays. The painting of scenery, the ramifications of stage lighting, the dressing up, the learning of long speeches, the smell of dust and greasepaint have always given me a certain pain. Painful too has always been the presence on the Great Night of fond parents, ready with handkerchiefs to suppress stinging tears if a nervous offspring should fail with 'the quality of mercy', and adoring young ladies from neighbouring schools worshipping some new and newly-moustached Mark Antony. My heart still thuds for an extremely small boy given the task of entering the stage from the auditorium at the cue, in *Julius Caesar*, of 'Here comes one in haste,' only to see him fall, at the critical moment, flat on his wretched face.

Nevertheless school plays, like church and funerals, have sometimes to be compulsorily attended, at least by pupils. What play we were giving in the autumn of 1919 I have now forgotten, but a certain uneasiness in the memory suggests that it may well have been that messy last infirmity of a noble mind, *The Tempest*. Be this as it may, I went to the Saturday afternoon performance with another friend (Harry Byrom being conspicuously on the stage of course) and much reluctance, no doubt thinking of football.

After a few minutes the play bored me. Certain of my friends tell me that when I am bored either by conversation or persons, two pale blinds slowly come down over my otherwise brilliantly blue eyes, successfully shutting me away. On this occasion the exact opposite happened. In the semi-darkness of the school hall I was bored but my eyes were opened. I found them constantly drawn not to the stage and the doings of Ariel, Prospero and Caliban, but to the dark-haired handsome head of a girl sitting in the seat immediately in front of me.

It is not too much to say that I was hypnotised by this head and the smallish, dark-eyed face which now and then turned sideways. In the inevitable agony of such occasions I also found my-self tortured between the notion that this sidelong movement of the head was either merely casual or that she was covertly and flirtatiously trying to look at me. By the interval I could stand it no longer; I had to know who she was. 'She's my cousin,' my friend said and it was like the onset of a new disease.

At the end of the play we were introduced to each other; I was dumbstruck and, wordless, duly departed. All that weekend the liquefaction – I humbly borrow Herrick's perfect word from one of the most perfect of all lyrics – of those dark eyes refused to let me rest. I was, as countless generations of men have been before me, a goner, held in the bonds of calf-love. Though we had hardly met, I found myself already tortured by the repetition of such lines as 'parting is such sweet sorrow' and 'Farewell, thou art too dear for my possessing'. Monday and school seemed a million years away.

When both came I got hold of her name and address and, in trembling and trepidation, wrote to her. To my utterly con-founded astonishment there came a reply. It was in an envelope, fashionable in those days, lined with deep, rich purple tissue paper. I was addressed as 'my dear'. The ecstasy of this piece of intimacy immediately drove me into a distracted secrecy; I could speak to no one; I could hardly join in the singing on the train and there are still times when the repetition of Anthony Powell's ridiculous 'K-K-K-Katie, beautiful Katie' haunts me almost as much as Purcell's 'When I Am Laid in Earth'. Indeed if there had been no reply to my second letter I believe I would gladly have followed the example of that most melancholy of lines.

But there was a reply; we were to meet. We met, as I remember it, in the First Class waiting-room on Number Three platform at Kettering station. There is no practical reason whatever for there ever being erected a plaque on a house in London saying 'H. E. Bates lived here'; but if there were any justice whatever in the history of railways and twentieth-century novelists there should be a plaqué on the door of the First Class waiting-room on Platform Number Three at Kettering station, saying 'H. E. Bates loved here'.

Con appeared to me even more hauntingly beautiful, on that second meeting, than at the first. With her black shining hair, her liquid black-brown eyes and her strong well-developed figure, her gym slip accentuating the shape of her fine young bust, it seemed that Byron's line 'She walks in beauty like the night' was the one most fitted for her. Confronted with this vision, two years older than myself, I was shy, bumbling, stiff and troubled.

We promptly talked, astonishingly, of literature; she loved, it seemed, poets such as Mrs Hemans but also Shakespeare. Indeed she loved all poetry and had herself actually written some. Had I?

Again if there were any justice in the history of twentieth-century literature these two words would go down with the immortality of 'Et tu, Brute?' and 'Dr Livingstone I presume?' Had I?

No, I said, I hadn't. I had never even thought of it.

'Why not?'

'Well, I don't know – I don't think I could.'

'Of *course* you could.'

'What makes you think so?'

'Oh! I sort of *know* you've got it in you.'

'How do you know?'

'Oh! you've *got* to write a poem. You've *got* to write a poem for me. Or else –'

This is not, of course, a truthful transcript of the conversation that took place between us but both the sense and tension of it are all there. I say tension advisedly, for, as I was later to discover, this beautiful young girl was also dominant, insistent and a schemer, passionately set on having her own way. I use the word tension because somewhere in that conversation lay a burning threat that if I didn't write her a poem it was more than possible that she would never see me again. The thought was something I couldn't bear.

It might well have been that, in such circumstances, I should have gone flying for solace and inspiration to the Elizabethans, taking something like Suckling's 'Tell me not, sweet, I am unkind' as a model or that stricken piece from an anonymous writer of 1658 which starts:

> Oh! what a pain is love:
> How shall I bear it?

and ends:

> I cannot work or sleep
> At all in season:
> Love wounds my heart so deep
> Without all reason.

Instead, I did nothing of the kind. I have already indicated that the outbreak of war had an effect of saddening gloom on me; its end was even worse. Happily my father had neither sister nor brother, and was himself unfit for service, and my mother only one sister: so that from the point of view of wounding or bereaving us we had been spared the more grievous of war's trials. But the effect of those long, black, mortifying lists of killed, wounded and missing that filled column after column of every morning newspaper had made a searing impression on me that has never left me; nor can I ever forget the little improvised street shrines decorated, as one still often sees in little Italian cemeteries, with faded photographs of the dead and a few jam jars of fading flowers.

Thus affected, I wrote a poem on 'The Tomb of the Unknown Warrior'. I suppose it had the piety of extreme innocence about it, but in its way it was not only the first thing I had expressed in verse but probably the most serious I ever was to express in that medium. Shown not only to Con but to Edmund Kirby, it suddenly brought me much adulation.

'*There* – I told you you could do it. I *knew* you could. They're going to print it in the school magazine, aren't they?'

Yes: they were going to print it in the school magazine, that universal graveyard of so many budding poets, and they duly did.

For myself it was the first of a host of embarrassments of seeing myself in print; for Con it was a moment of triumph. She basked in reflected glory; I was her discovery.

'You see, I *told* you you could. You've got it *in* you. Now you've got to write *more* poems. Lots and lots. Promise me. Lots and lots and lots and lots.'

It was all rather like being pushed into playing in a football match without knowing anything about the game and then doing a hat trick. Suddenly, ridiculous as it may now seem, I felt myself propelled along by bounding waves of inspiration. Most of this was instigated by Con and 'the love that wounds my heart so deep without all reason', and the rest by the more reasoned sobriety of Edmund Kirby's praise. A man of few words, even to the point of being phlegmatic, sometimes even sardonic, Kirby was by no means an easy mentor to please.

For the next several months I not only wrote poems. Con and I entered into a long and passionate correspondence. Sometimes our letters went by post, at others by less orthodox means. I should explain here that the grammar school and high school at Kettering in those days were contained in one building, boys in one half, girls in the other. Though this did not mean that we were in any sense a coeducational establishment it did mean that girls and boys perforce shared certain classrooms though at different times, notably the chemistry labs, the library and the art room, so that it was by no means uncommon for the progress of the boys' upper fifth towards the chemistry lab, on the second floor, to find itself barred on the stairs by the jostling descent of the girls' lower sixth on its way to a lecture on Wordsworth in the library. As a result there was inevitably much confusion, dropping of rulers and notebooks, giggling and a great rustling of paper.

As an echo of all this I recently had a letter from a lady, now in her sixties, who wrote: 'I am married to Dickie X., who was one of your class-mates. I wonder if you remember me? I used to carry Con's love-letters to you up the leg of my knickers.' So does the romanticism of first love sometimes survive, with at least some little part of it undiminished over half a century.

But it wasn't until the following spring that there occurred the first real moment of conflagration in first love. Con, as I have said, was a schemer, a feminine characteristic not unknown even in schoolgirls ('Their need is great,' I once heard a girls' head-mistress say and the words still seem to me to have in them a truth bordering on poignancy) and one of the first of her schemes was to arrange for me to spend weekends at the house of my friend her first cousin, who lived in the same town a couple of streets away. At first the cousin and his sister, a pretty girl dying of consumption without fully knowing it at that time, used to make a wandering foursome with us to explore the surrounding fields and woods, where wild purple rhododendrons and primroses grew in great profusion. But soon the cousin and his sister were learning to exercise an anti-gooseberry diplomacy, so that Con and I were left more and more to ourselves. This seemed to me marvellous; I grasped at every opportunity of being alone with her, simply to talk of literature, flowers and my new poetry. It was all I needed; I never even remotely imagined that there could be anything more.

One warm fine spring evening we wandered along the wooded banks of a brook, probably a small tributary of the River Welland. Primroses, kingcups, white and purple violets and Shakespeare's Lady-smocks bloomed everywhere about the marshy earth. After some time I stopped to climb a stile and then, suddenly turning my head to look for Con, found myself caught up in an un-expected, swift and passionate embrace, and then kissed long, fully and ardently on the lips.

How I recovered from this totally unexpected but delicious ravaging of my boyhood innocence I find it hard to say; it sometimes seems to me not at all impossible that I might have been left speechless for the rest of my life. There was certainly, at that ecstatic moment, nothing to say; nor could I have said it if I had wanted to; instead I could only offer my lips in further sacrifice, surrendering to an ardour returned by lips ecstatic, compulsive and not wholly inexperienced. It was no longer a question of sweet, devoted friendship; the moment was more like the fusion of two white-hot wires. I was more than slightly shocked and intoxicated in consequence; it was now a case, in Herrick's words again, of:

> Thou Art my Life, my Love, my Heart,
> The Very Eyes of me;
> And hast command of every part,
> To live and die for thee.

The over-sensitive intimacies of first love demand, as I have already indicated of poetry, a particular kind of secrecy. Any other mundane, timetable-ridden, meal-ridden, family-ridden world must be shut out. First love develops in its own sacred, suspended, breathless, often wordless vacuum. It generates, and revels in, its own pain. It has no language of any known syntax or coherence that can express to others outside the vacuum what ecstasy it feels, always believing that others have either not felt it or not in the same way, never pausing to enquire after the fact, as old and inevitable as dawn, that a million million others have.

So we began to meet in secret, or what we thought was secret: under dark railway arches, in remote woods, in hayfields, under wet oak trees dripping with rain, in railway carriages and inevitably, when all else failed, in the First Class waiting-room on Platform Number Three. (We chose the First Class waiting-room because there were never any First Class passengers.) We deluded ourselves that only the most intimate of friends and confidants knew of these things; of course everybody knew. Even the porters at the station knew and occasionally came to spy gleefully on us as we were locked in blind embrace in the First Class waiting-room. The masters at school knew. Now, however, I was no longer bombarded in class with sallies of crushing reprimand such as 'I see our friend Bates is dreaming again'. The approach was more subtle, the sarcasm infinitely heavier. 'I see that our friend Bates has his head in the clouds again. No doubt with eyes on something of more pressing importance than the Treaty of Paris.' The word 'pressing', of course would draw much laughter.

I did not care if Scott knew; but I think Con was perpetually alarmed at the prospect of discovery by her Headmistress, a certain Miss White, of secret meetings in corridors and the passage of *billets doux*: hence the constant need for the clandestine up-the-knickers postal system. On my fourpence a week I couldn't afford many stamps, though Con, who already earned money as a pupil-teacher, my entry into which realm of education would have given Scott so much pleasure, could afford both elegant notepaper and gifts to me of the works of Shelley and Keats richly bound in purple or olive suede at Christmas or on my birthday. In return I once presented her with a sixpenny bar of Cadbury's milk chocolate for which I had saved up for three weeks, only to have it rejected on the grounds that I ought not to waste my money. My remorse at such intolerable spurning of my gift was so great that my entire soul was lacerated, a tragedy that didn't prevent my eating the whole chocolate bar myself on my lonely way home in the train.

All this time, egged on by Con and almost silently encouraged by Kirby, who in his wisdom would rather say nothing at all than outrightly condemn or praise, I was writing poetry. That this poetry was infinitely and execrably bad I have now no doubt; mercifully all of it is now lost. A few years later when Edward Garnett had read and approved my first novel, *The Two Sisters,* which I am happy to say is still in print after more than forty years, he asked if I had written much poetry and if so would I send him some. Eagerly I replied that I had indeed and sent off a great batch of adolescent MSS for him to read. Though he had praise for one or two pieces it was not of an exuberant kind. Garnett was rarely wrong in his judgements and I scarcely wrote another couple of dozen stanzas in my life.

All this time too my appetite for literature was well served. Not only had I access to the Carnegie Library at Rushden but also to the far larger, far better Carnegie Library at Kettering; I still had my father's books and the contents, modest though they were, of the school library. Somewhere about this time my father had suddenly persuaded himself of the virtues of bribery in relation to my scholastic progress and had instituted a bonus scheme whereby I got £1 for a first place and half that sum for a second place in any subject at the end of term. As I was almost invariably certain of firsts in anything connected with literature or art I sometimes found myself three or four pounds richer when school reports arrived, and with this money I sometimes bought books.

Among them, as I remember it, were *A Shropshire Lad* and Hardy's *Satires of Circumstance* but in case these should seem a rather superior taste for a boy of fifteen I should here add that I still loved the secret readings of *Chips* and *Comic Cuts* which my grandfather and I held as often as possible under hay-stacks or in the tool-shed on wet afternoons, I sitting on the bran barrel as I read out to him the exploits of 'Weary Willie' and 'Tired Tim' and the inhabitants of 'Casey's Court', he half asleep on a sack of chaff while westerly rain lashed at the cobwebbed windows and the blue tea can hotted up on the paraffin stove. My love of the two comic papers was all the greater because my father, in yet another example of his stringent Methodist rules, had always conceived them to be a source of mischief, if not indeed of downright evil and corruption, and had long forbidden their entry into the house. By contrast my grandfather adored them, reserving for 'Weary Willie' and 'Tired Tim' all the adulation he had once given to 'Little Tich', for whom he had made the renowned long boots, and such Victorian stars of the music hall as Dan Leno and Marie Lloyd. Pressed by me he would some-times also sing songs:

> Rollin' round the town,
> Knockin' people down,
> 'Avin' a rare old booze I bet,
> Tastin' every kind o' wet,
> Rollin' round the town –

and sometimes a song of the Irish, 'On the Boat that First Took Me Over', some lines of which went:

> They brought me fat pork
> On the end of a fork,
> And said 'Paddy, ate that.'
> I said 'I can't, it's too fat,'
> On the boat that first took me over.

Thus for all my progress towards the first standards of some sort of sophistication I still never lost track with the land, the characters on it and the ripe, rough Midland vernacular. A drover staggering home from market, with burning eyes, three parts drunk, would still stop off at the little farm to tell us a rambling tale or two; we still laid nightly snares for hares in the hedgerows; a convoy of gypsy caravans coming up bright-coloured against the skyline would sometimes stop and pass the time of day; my grandfather had nothing but friendliness for gypsies and sometimes one of them, a blind man, would alight and come to greet him.

This meeting always had in it for me a great moment of wonder. One of the more remarkable physical characteristics of my grandfather was that he had a double thumb. This thumb, though congenital, looked as if it had been roughly crushed into twice its normal shape by a heavy press. I used, as a child, to fondle its rough spoon shape with an amazed disbelief. In silence the blind gypsy from the caravan would handle it too. It was a certain sign of recognition between two old friends who hadn't, perhaps, met each other for a year.

'It's George,' the gypsy would say. 'Old George.'

Hereabouts, no doubt stimulated by the slightly older company of Harry Byrom and Con and the encouragements of Kirby, to say nothing of my father's bonus scheme, I began to work harder and with more conscious direction. 'I am become a man and put away childish things', is perhaps all too pale and tame a description of the fantastic stimulus of the injection given by puberty somewhere between the ages of twelve and fourteen, possibly the greatest single miracle wrought in man. Growing up, growing pains: these too are descriptions too pale for the sudden upsurgent skylight into adolescence.

But now, also, I had a more practical reason for work. There loomed ahead of me, some time after my sixteenth birthday, the forbidding challenge of what was then known as the Joint Oxford and Cambridge University Certificate. It was the sort of thing that Harry Byrom could, and indeed did, dispose of with less trouble than eating toast and marmalade at breakfast. Not so I; many of the defections in my earlier scholastic progress were like old sores – nothing, it seemed, would heal them now. Nor was there any kind of precedence for supposing that love, sweet though it was, would perform some alchemic miracle in the exam room. I do not waver, and have never wavered, in my belief that love is of far greater and more rewarding importance than trigonometry or calculus, but my position for proving this proposition to either my tutors or the examining magistrates at Oxford and Cambridge was not exactly a tenable one. A pass of some degree of excellence in the Certificate might well mean a passage to University. I had not, at that time, thought about University. As at a meal, I had merely concentrated on getting through the bread and butter; the cake might come afterwards.

The summer of 1921 was incredibly long and hot. No rain fell for several months. A summer virtually beginning in February lasted on until November. Great cracks, almost chasms, broke up the clay of harvest-fields. Beans shot from their grilled black stalks like bullets. There were many fires. My grandfather and his fellow firemen, already considerably frustrated by a pair of greys who, somehow sensing fire, always either reared up on their hindlegs or reverted to the disposition of donkeys at the mere sound of the alarm, were further hampered by the fact that the greys sometimes also lay down and then took a good half hour to harness, so that very often the fire was out before the scorching chariot arrived. More often than usual that summer we heard the fire-bell clanking up the road. Instantly scythe and rake and pitchfork would be dropped as we rushed to harness the horse, just in time to follow the chariot and its fuming greys, now at full pelt, as they

passed the farm gate, the firemen hanging on to the engine and shouting with the enthusiasm of small boys going to a bun-fight. Somehow I was always just in time to hang on to the back-board of the truck, eventually to arrive on a scene where the only source of water, a brook, had long since dried up in the drought, and a row of thatched cottages or a couple of haystacks smouldered like black funeral pyres in the intense heat of afternoon.

By July, the time of the exam, the heat was intolerable. Already I had got into the habit of getting up at half past five or six, both for the purpose of working on old exam papers in the cool of the morning, and of catching an earlier train in order to snatch a few precious moments with Con. There has always been in my character this strong pull of conscience on one side and a disposition to flout authority and rule on the other. The results of this, call it antagonism or cussedness or what you will, have sometimes been bad; sometimes, on the other hand, good. I think they were good when I was able to enjoy a blessed and secret hour or two with a passionate girl of nearly eighteen in a July meadow, in the shade of a sycamore tree, before the blistering heat of the day began. It helped to take my mind off the exam, and also to soften some of the tensions for an ordeal the outcome of which gave me little hope and even less, I fear, to my mentors.

I was also relieved on the first of those torrid mornings – we were actually allowed to sit in our shirtsleeves, normally an unheard-of thing in those days – to observe that one of Con's sisters, Dora, a pretty girl and already a fully-fledged schoolmistress, was the exam overseer for the day. She gave me the sweetest of smiles as the exam papers were given out and I suddenly felt confident and at home. Con was one of a large family of brothers and sisters, mostly older than herself, and one of her brothers had that not uncommon knack of improvising on the piano, which provided him with an evening job in the local fleapit, pitching in at the right moments with yearning music for lovescenes, desolations in a minor key for the dying and the Overture to *William Tell* for every runaway stage coach and every pursuing cowboy. Whenever we watched the stirring doings of Pearl White, the mad pursuits of the Keystone Cops or the genius of Chaplin and perhaps the even greater talents of Buster Keaton, Con and I sat on the far back seats, pressed in long embrace in the darkness, hushed as always in deep secrecy, she fondly believing that her brother on the piano was a great a genius, though unsung and undiscovered, as Keaton and Chaplin, so that I almost wished, then, that I had learned the piano.

As for the exam, it seemed to me that I did well with all that was connected with Literature; tolerably well with History, Geography and even Mathematics; appallingly with Latin and so blankly and with such negation with mechanics and the sciences that I actually walked out of the exam room after the shortest permitted span of endurance, on each occasion bumping straight into Scott outside the door, each of us giving the other a glare cold enough to have frozen a polar bear. It seems to me that Scott's pervading fault was contained in a stern Scots inelasticity which, poor man, he couldn't help. I am assured that in the Scottish household of today the man is still undisputed master of it; all others must obey; if the 'meister' feels the need of a tonic in the middle of the night and orders 'Wumman, get me a wee dram, I dinna feel so good', then the wife too must obey. So with Scott; he seemed to see himself as an instrument whose sole purpose was the creation of an endless line of other school teachers, bank clerks and chartered accountants. These were the ultimate ideals in life and those who obeyed the rules to achieve them were sure of his blessings, dour though it might be. But Scott in his entire career had never come across a pupil who instead wanted to be a writer and he had neither the perspicacity nor imagination to do a sensible thing about it. It was rather like running a school for computer-training, only to find that the sole object of one pupil is to write a Sonata for Clarinet and Grasshoppers.

Happily, as the exam ended, so did term; the hot, blistering summer, however, went on; and soon I was back on baked, cracked stubbles, the great dry beards on the wheat-sheaves rustling like the flare of a suddenly started fire itself, the thistles withered to wands of needles and white down long before the scythe ever touched them. Brooks, ponds and dykes were now all dry; when we went to collect water from the brook we might as well have taken a spoon to collect it in. In the orchard of the old tit there was a mighty murmurous congregation of wasps, so that it was almost impossible to pick a plum without being stung. The garden was parched and flowerless, wholly un-decorated except for the ghostly silver pennies of honesty seed, ready to join the floating flotillas of thistledown. But for me, at any rate, it was again all pure joy; blessed by massive suns, the apples, plums and pears tasted more sweetly than ever, and in the heart of such an idyll I quickly forgot school, exams, and the results of exams.

I was therefore stupendously shocked one morning to see Harry Byrom rushing up the garden path to our house, waving *The Times* and crying 'Third, old fellow, third, third!' Mystified as well as astonished, I asked what third?

'Honours,' he gasped. 'Honours. You. Look, it's here in the first column.'

Seeing my name in *The Times,* I suddenly felt as if I had been elected Member of Parliament or something.

'No exemption for matric, or anything like that I'm afraid,' he said. 'Still, you can do matric standing on your head now.'

Honours, honours, I kept saying to myself and felt like a strutting but unbelieving peacock.

It is my impression that in those days matric, or exemption from it formed the first necessary passport to university. I was therefore much surprised when, soon after the beginning of the autumn term, my father one day called me aside and said:

'They think you ought to go to Cambridge.'

Whether he meant soon or later I was too flabbergasted to ask.

'I've thought a lot about it,' he said. 'It'll take a lot of money.'

How much? I wanted to know.

'Every penny I've got,' he said. 'Every penny.'

Then, I informed him simply and with no hesitation, I wouldn't go.

I have never been sorry about that decision. I have never regretted University. My two sons, offered precisely the same terms, though without the financial stringency attached, in due course made precisely the same decision. Perhaps we are not a university-minded family; perhaps they also incline to the view that scholastic degrees, letters after one's name, the acquisition of much knowledge and a certain social cachet do not necessarily constitute education. I like to think that Renoir, Sisley, Cézanne and Toulouse-Lautrec went to neither Oxford nor Cambridge, Winchester nor Eton. I was far from embittered by the prospect of Cambridge being snatched away from me; I rather welcomed it as a relief from any further exercise in scholastic regimentation and later, not very long later either, was actually glad of it as having been an escape; for by the time I was twenty my first novel was published and only a few years later I had added two or three more books to my name and had begun to establish for myself a certain reputation. My two sons happily followed the same pattern of success; they were sensible enough to recognise that life needs a great many things that a university curriculum cannot teach: which, in the present state of much university unrest and disruption, is perhaps just as well.

But what did embitter me was to be told by my father that since I didn't wish to go to Cambridge I must therefore leave school at the end of term. That was truly the unkindest cut. I was too saddened at the time to reason that since I was still only sixteen I therefore needed at least another two years at school before entrance to Cambridge could be hoped for: all a further drain on my father's pocket, since he had my sister and brother to educate too. One of the troubles with my father was that he had no business brain; he was a pillar of unimpeachable, almost naïve honesty. During the First World War he had seen mushroom fortunes made by boot manufacturers who had no scruples whatever about taking advantage of mistakes by ill-informed government departments or by a sly wriggle or two in the tax net. His strict Methodist conscience would have no part of these things. Yet at the same time, and just as naively, he would weekly enter competition after competition mainly in the new Harmsworth publications, solving ingenious problems, composing ingenious ditties and so on, in the passionate hope that he would one day win £20,000 for himself. I think the most he ever won was a fountain pen. Similarly deluded by some bucket-shop literature about a great new venture in rayon that would make him a certain fortune overnight he had, about the time of the Cambridge project, lost all his spare capital and thereafter, for the rest of his life, kept the worthless share certificates locked in his bureau, for ever hoping that the God whose praises he sang so fervently every Sunday would take a Divine hand in the much-needed restoration of their value.

So, having accomplished a success I had never dared hope for, I left school at the age of sixteen and a half. Not only was I young; I was also extremely naïve, extremely gauche, extremely sensitive and still locked in the twin secret bonds of firstlove and poetry.

What was I to do? Which way to turn? I hadn't the remotest, vaguest idea.

For several weeks in the New Year I mooched about: waiting,

like Mr Micawber, for something to turn up. Even the mere promises of opportunity in a town governed by one staple industry are thin, however, and for some time nothing did turn up. There did come a suggestion that I should apply for a post in the foreign department of a London bank but my father wisely reminded me that such a path could only mean my spending the rest of my life with figures; and I often thanked him for that. As for the staple industry of the town he was still adamant on that score and therefore that path too was closed.

It must have been nearly March before something else turned up and this time it seemed too good to be true. It appeared that a local newspaper, and also a very old one, the *Northampton Chronicle,* was looking for a junior (very junior) assistant reporter for its newly-opened Wellingborough office. Accordingly I was requested to go for an interview one afternoon with a certain Mr Bretherton who could tell me all about it and assess my potentialities. Filled with a glowing belief that a job on a newspaper was surely the way to learn how to write, I duly went along and found myself in the presence of a smallish, fattish man of untidy appearance and slightly alcoholic air. Mr Bretherton was also effusive. He proceeded to instruct me in the wonders of the journalistic world and how greatly they would profit me. I was of course most fortunate, he kept telling me, that this was the spring of the year. The best time was coming. In Mr Bretherton's view nothing could equal the joys to be obtained on the provincial journalistic roundabout, especially in summertime; undoubtedly I should have the time of my life. Fêtes, garden parties, flower shows, tennis tournaments, regattas, Sunday school treats, cricket matches, bun-fights of all kinds: the picture was idyllic. Did I like the thought of it? If so the job was mine: at ten shillings a week.

I accepted. When earlier I recorded that in the eighties of the nineteenth century my mother worked for two shillings a week it did not at first occur to me that an increase of five times that amount in forty years could hardly be called either progress or munificent. At that time I was far from caring; ten shillings or no ten shillings, I was to be a writer by profession. It was great. It might even be, wonder of wonders, that my work would appear in newspapers. They might even print my poems.

I duly went off to the Wellingborough office, which was just off the old market place, in sight of the ancient Hind Hotel, every morning by train.

Outside the station at Wellingborough there always stood an old green horse bus, in charge of and driven by a rather unkempt, long-coated gentleman who looked for all the world like a seedy descendant of the father of Sam Weller. 'Straight up to the town! No waiting!' Passengers, if in ones or twos, might on the contrary wait twenty minutes, or even more, before the driver decided he had passengers enough to make the long uphill trip to the Market place worth while. What his charge was for both journey and waiting time I never gathered; such luxuries were not for me.

Out of my ten shillings I had of course to pay train fares and this left nothing for lunches or even a cup of tea. As a result I had to evolve a special method for actual survival. This meant leaving the newspaper office at twelve o'clock midday, running all the way to the Midland Station at Wellingborough, about a mile out of town, and catching the 12.25 to Rushden. This journey, if the fireman didn't misfire with the transfer key to the branch line at the signal box, took seven minutes. Since the return train left at 1.19 this meant that I had to run every inch of the way home, again nearly a mile, gollop the lunch my mother had waiting for me and then run all the way back to the station again, with about a minute to spare. Small wonder that I was thin as a rake and developed no little prowess as a runner.

The early morning train got me into the office about nine o'clock. An inevitable smoky air of grey dreariness hung over everything. Some of my erstwhile schoolfellows, now bank clerks, suitably dressed in bowler hats, pin stripes or smart Lovat checks, had warm and comfortable banks to which to retire for the morning's work. I had a dingy upstairs room with bare floor boards, a table, two chairs and the black basket sort of fireplace you see in Cruikshank's illustrations for Dickens. My first job of the day was to rake out the ashes, go to the cellar for coal and a few broken pieces of old boxes and get a fire on the go. It never seemed to be anything but perishingly cold in that office. While the fire slowly drew up I did my best to keep warm by sweeping the floor, tidying Bretherton's desk and actually doing the sort of exercises, flapping my arms back and forth across my chest, that you still see outdoor workers doing in the dead of winter.

By about ten o'clock it was time to make the first two calls of the day: one to the Coroner's office, the other to the police station. As the Coroner's office was only just round the corner, in the shadow of the church, in a narrow street of black brass-knockered doors that itself looked Dickensian, I almost always went there first. In the hush that pervaded the inside office you could almost hear the scratch of quill pens, again straight out of Dickens. My purpose in going there was to discover if anyone had been murdered, committed suicide or had surrendered life in any other way that called for an inquest. It was very rare that anybody had. Sometimes a man had fallen dead of heart failure in the street but mostly my answer was 'Nothing this morning,' as if I were the baker, the milkman or the butcher.

I then went to the police station. Not that it matters a great deal now, but I feel bound to record that on the whole the police of Wellingborough at that time, on duty or off-duty, were the most uncouth, most bog-headed, most foul-mouthed collection of humans I had ever met. Later I played several games of football against them. The air of the dressing-room was a cess-pool of filth calculated to make the language of Newgate gaol seem like the whisperings of a convocation of Sunday-schoolteachers. I disliked them for other reasons. One practical joke on a new, young green cub reporter is to be expected; two or three can be laughed off; after that it isn't very funny. One day, inquiring whether an unsuccessful suicide would be charged or not, I was solemnly informed by no less a person than the station sergeant 'No. They give them a second chance these days.' Another day I was sent traipsing a couple of miles to investigate a fire that never was. Two days later, once bitten, twice shy, I failed to heed the news that a big factory had been burned out the previous night. Naturally it had.

On Thursdays I collected the charge sheet drawn up for Friday's proceedings at the weekly petty sessions. Petty is here the *mot juste*. A drunk or two, a labouring man knocking his old woman about, the theft of a skin of leather from a factory, two schoolboys breaking windows, a case of assault, another of breaking and entering: the petty pattern was invariably the same. Nevertheless I always enjoyed the courts; it was always hard to say whether or not the magistrates were odder than the defendants and I daresay many of them were, in some way or other, just as guilty. It didn't take me long either to detect that the Clerk of the Court had seen to it that most things were carefully cut and dried before the court began and had already made up his mind, in spite of much pleading by learned gentlemen for one side or the other, what the result of each case should be. The taste left was unsavoury but in spite of it I scribbled madly away in the reporters' box, my little pigs' ears as sharply open as ever they had been under the wheat stooks in my grandfather's harvest-field.

Another piece of Dickensian survival that I attended was the Board of Guardians. This, if memory serves me correctly, met at the local workhouse. If it wasn't quite like *Oliver Twist* it still had about it the old grim air of Victorian charity. A wholly estimable number of middle-class ladies and gentlemen sat about a long mahogany table, armed with writing paper and notes, and discussed for entire wearisome afternoons cases of need and hardship or abuse of both, while I made desultory notes and stared out of the window, imprisoned again, looking for the sun.

Presently it turned out that Bretherton the giver of all good gifts, the barker selling the joys of the summer journalistic vaudeville and roundabouts, was a very different person from the journalist actually at work or under pretence of work at the office. Bretherton, I soon discovered, rarely turned up at the office. When he eventually did so it was in a state of alcoholic stupor bordering on rage or sheer sleepiness. The former usually spent itself on a spluttering lecture to me and my woeful deficiencies ('No bloody good sitting here all day. Got to get out. Got to meet people. Got to *ferret*, see, my boy, got to ferret. The rabbits are out

there, boy – got to ferret 'em out, got to ferret 'em out') and the
latter in a long deep sleep in front of the fire or with head sunken
across his desk. Sometimes too came Bretherton's buddy, his
father-in-law, alcoholically embalmed too, so that presently the
pair of them were asleep, lost in a happy afternoon duet of snoring
so that I, since we had only two office chairs, was perforce pitched
into the street.

That I was a very bad reporter was indisputable; I will not even
start the pretence that I did my best. I had no best to do. I was
revolted by Bretherton and the office; I was bored by visits to
confectioners to discover what size a wedding cake had been, how
many guests had attended the wedding and what they ate. I was
equally bored by brides' mothers, from whom it was my duty to
extract lists of presents. This boredom was now and then alleviated
by my attendances at the monthly meeting of the County Football
Association, at which the chairman wore a strange Churchillian
bowler hat which he never took off, and when I was sometimes

invited to pick out of another hat the teams competing in the next County Cup draw. These committees were composed of jolly, homely characters, often considerate enough to close their meetings early, so that I should not miss the last train home.

Not only, however, was I bored; I was very lonely. Indeed it would be fair to say that I have never been so lonely before or since that short spell of drab, journalistic penury. I hadn't seen Con for many months and for a good reason. All that time she had been in hospital. Flying along a school corridor at full pelt one day – she was something of a tomboy – she had put out her hand to hold back a swinging glass door and had slit her arm, and with it an artery, almost from wrist to shoulder. This accident had removed her as completely from my life as if she were dead. I didn't even know the name of the hospital.

Soon April came and with it a new daily nightmare. Early every spring there spreads through the British Isles a disease, a rampant epidemic, known as the flat-racing season. Newspapers are suddenly read as if only horses and their jockeys occupied the universe. Form, tips, runners, prices: millions think of nothing but horseflesh and all that appertains to it. It is a world in which I have not, and have never had, the remotest interest; but suddenly I found myself remorselessly caught up in it. Until that time the afternoon edition of the paper had suddenly turned up from head office by bus, in bundles, like so much waste paper. Now there began to arrive special racing editions, similarly issued by our rivals next door, the *Northampton Echo,* who had what seemed to me an army of swift-footed newsboys rushing about the streets yelling what I at first thought was 'Sporting Tissue in 'is shirt!' It took my bewildered and innocent brain some time to work out that this meant 'Sporting Tissue Edition'. It was my duty somehow to combat this onslaught on the waiting layabouts, dead-beats and out-of-works who mooched and lounged about outside the office as if awaiting news of a dying monarch. All afternoon the telephone rang incessantly. All afternoon I scribbled down the names of winners, runners up, starting prices. Frantically I set them up in type in one of those rubber stamp printing outfits that boys still delight to be given at Christmas-time, banged the resulting lettering (which I only *hoped* was correct) on a purple ink-pad and so to the stop-press columns of mountains of afternoon extras, which in turn were grabbed up by impatient newsboys waiting to join 'Sporting Tissue in 'is Shirt' on the streets outside.

If anything was guaranteed to pole-axe my fond notion that working on a newspaper would be a sure way of teaching me to write this was it. Rapidly, for some time, I had been working up a hatred of the dingy office, the weddings, the political meetings, the Coroner's office, the police station, the daily sprint home for dinner, the alcoholic snoring Bretherton and his father-in-law. It now suddenly occurs to me that I have neglected to mention a charming habit of Bretherton's: namely that of spitting into the office fire. In periods of sobriety his aim was occasionally near accurate, sometimes actually accurate. A brief sizzle on the hot coals indicated a bull's eye. In moods of insobriety the results were quite otherwise. Great gobs of phlegm missed their target by inches, sometimes feet, each outburst of firing preceded by a noise of gyrating machinery as Bretherton cleared the depths of his throat and, as he put it, 'fetched it up'. The resulting decoration of the old Dickensian fireplace was singularly charming.

But with the onset of the racing season my nausea at all these things suddenly went beyond hatred. There is a condition of impotency in anger which, being inexpressible in either deed or language, is more frightful than action itself. It was becoming a case of 'I rage, I melt, I burn'; I knew I couldn't last much longer; I knew that I was not only a bad reporter but would never be a good one. The poet in me, once as fresh and burgeoning as any spring blossom, had committed, or was about to commit, dark suicide.

Hereabouts, as if to make things worse, something else happened. A letter from Con told me that she was out of hospital and could we meet? Accordingly, I think on a Saturday afternoon, I went over to Kettering and we met where we had so often met and had so often made oblivious and passionate use of the First

Class waiting-room. As we faced each other for the first time for several months I was assailed by a chill and inexplicable doubt; I felt that we were strangers. We walked out into the country, not talking much. At first the little we had to say to each other was normal, trivial, estranged too. Soon there came over me a further, even chillier feeling: that she had greatly changed. In vain I searched for some remnant of the warmth we had shared before her accident and before my own trial by boredom on the paper. My search merely yielded a stunning and unpalatable truth. Always inclined to be dominant and demanding, it was now clear that she was also unutterably spoilt. Long weeks of doting and devotion by nurses and doctors had covered her with an enamel of impossible, selfish aloofness. Almost all of what she had to say was of herself and nothing but herself and the distance at which it was said grew unhappier and greater as the afternoon went on.

The birth and growth of first love is a great wonder; the death of it is fearful; the premonition of its demise perhaps more fearful still. As I went home that day I must have experienced something of the feeling that a sick patient, petrified by the thought of a feared diagnosis of some malignancy being confirmed, at last has it confirmed. For my own part I knew that love was not merely in danger of being extinguished; it was already shrivelled. For some days I searched the territory of my own emotions trying to rationalise the whole affair as being the result of my own miseries with police courts, 'Sporting Tissue in 'is Shirt' and the gobbing Bretherton. But in the end self-analysis had no such comforting solution to offer. It was a case of 'Since there's no help come let us kiss and part', with all the nagging regret of that poem's final lines to bruise me further. With a melancholy that deepened to an inexplicably deeper loneliness I knew that it was all over.

I was now rapidly approaching a condition well expressed by H. G. Wells in his own *Autobiography*, a condition which in his case arose from the fact that he was indentured as a draper's apprentice (for which his mother, incredibly, had put down the munificent sum of fifty pounds) for a total period of four years, of which he had served only two. I was not so indentured, but the fact is that Wells, after two years, and I, after only two months, had reached precisely the same point. Wells, though frequently urged by his poor harassed mother to pray for help 'in the right quarter' had nevertheless decided 'that the drapery business was a dismal trap and I meant to get out of it'. This he duly did and in later years he had this to say of it:

> I had reached a vital crisis of my life. I felt extraordinarily desperate and, faced with binding indentures and maternal remonstrances, I behaved very much like a hunted rabbit that turns at last and bites . . . I had discovered what were to be for me for some years the two guiding principles of my life. 'If you want something sufficiently, take it and damn the consequences . . . If life is not good enough for you, change it; never endure a way of life that is dull and dreary, because after all the worst thing that can happen to you, if you fight and go on fighting to get out, is defeat, and that is never certain until the end which is death and the end of everything.

It was rather after this fashion, if not in exactly such words, that I now felt strongly disposed to speak to Bretherton. As it turned out, it was Bretherton who spoke to me; but before that happened an incident occurred which seemed of no importance at the time, but the results of which were of singular value thirty years later.

On a dark, cold and dismal evening I had been given an assignment by Bretherton to go to Rushden Hall to interview the owners and occupants, Mr and Mrs Sartoris, on what pretext I cannot now remember. The present Hall at Rushden is of Elizabethan date; but an earlier mansion on the same site was said to have been erected by the renowned John of Gaunt, Duke of Lancaster, 'which was under a grant from the King to this famed personage'. The position of the house in modern times is extraordinarily incongruous: an oasis of trees and avenues, the chief of which is (unless a rumour of its recent demolition is correct) composed of sixty-three ancient Wych elms, surrounded on all sides by boot factories, nineteenth and twentieth century developments, with all the chapels, bakeries and fish shops I have already described, together with today's supermarkets and coffee bars. But on that dark frigid night when I went to keep my assignment it was rather like penetrating to the heart of a medieval stronghold deep in a silent wintry forest.

Two great wooden gates were the only means of entrance on the town side, within sight of the tall-spired church, whose first incumbent had been Thomas de Northampton in 1231. By the gates stood a small gate-keeper's lodge with leaded windows and after I had rung the big iron-handled bell-pull the gate-keeper let me in. It seemed, and probably was, all of a quarter of a mile to the house and there was nowhere a light to be seen. Finally a glimmer or two emerged from beyond the heavy avenue of trees and after I had rung another bell at the front door of the house a maid let me in. I have an impression that the name Sartoris is French and I have a vivid recollection that the Sartoris' were extremely courteous and charming to me. I have an equally vivid impression that the house was like a refrigerator. A huge log fire burned in an enormous open fireplace but the effect of this on the great frigidity of the atmosphere was that of a match being applied to the walls of an iceberg. The walls were of panelled oak which either time or wood smoke, or both, had turned completely black. There seemed to be a wholly unnecessary number of doors in the large room where the Sartoris' greeted me and each was draped in a curtain of heavy wine-red velvet, rather as if in the hope of keeping further cold out or the relative warmth of the room in.

It has passed completely from my mind what I had come to interview the Sartoris' about, or what they said to me. Two impressions, however, remain unfaded: first, my own incomparable nervousness which, further actuated by the cold, kept me constantly shivering; and secondly the strangest feeling that the shaping Divinity had actually sent me there for a purpose which then appeared to be totally obscure. All that I bore away with me into the freezing blackness of the winter night was, in fact, in no sense real; it was in some sense both haunting and prophetic.

In fact it was not to become real for another thirty years, when that same room became the setting for the first chapters of a novel of mine. But since one room, like one idea doesn't necessarily make a novel, it was opportune that somewhere about the same time I had had another experience, even briefer but just as singular in its importance. One morning, as I went to catch my morning train, a smart pony-drawn gig drew up at the station and out of it got a tallish, dark, proud, aloof young girl in a black cloak lined with scarlet. I had never seen her before and never saw her again. Such a vision was not, in fact, ever to be seen in that town and I surmised, rightly or wrongly, that she came from the Hall.

In the writing of novels there must necessarily be a fusion of negative and positive. In this case the cold, dismal, wintry Hall was the negative; the girl in the scarlet lined cloak, seen for two minutes, was the positive. In fusion, thirty years later, they became *Love for Lydia*.

Bretherton now took it upon himself to speak to me. One

morning he arrived at the office about eleven o'clock, in unsober, parsonic mood. It became clear that he was about to deliver a lecture, perhaps even a sermon, for my benefit. Its tone of alcoholic piety was incredible to hear. He addressed me as from some pulpit aloft.

I had now been with him for several weeks and what had been achieved? Nothing; precisely and absolutely nothing. I was lazy. I lacked initiative. I dreamed. I declined to ferret. Beyond the windows of the office lay a world teeming with incident or potential incident, not to say excitement. Had I ever investigated it? Never. It was a fundamental principle of journalism that it was no use waiting for events to come to you. You had to go after events. This I had failed, and failed dismally, to do. 'Everything comes to him who waits' was an adage of great falsity. On the contrary nothing came to him who waited. I had waited. Result, not unnaturally in Bretherton's opinion, nothing.

In parsonic alcoholic tones Bretherton urged me earnestly to take note that he was saying all these things not for the good of his own soul but for my own. My behaviour, he confessed, pained him greatly. His hopes of me had been high. It was now incumbent upon him to have to tell me that these hopes had been dashed; I was, in short, a failure. It was extremely doubtful if I should ever make a journalist. That some potential in me existed he had no doubt, but how many times, if ever, had it shown signs of becoming reality? Few, he declared dolefully, few, very, very few.

He aimed to spit into the fire and missed. A greenish glob of phlegm dripped from the surrounding fireplace. The remonstration piously went on. It contained, I remember, a section on Opportunity. Great indeed, Bretherton painfully reminded me, was my Opportunity. He himself was a journalist who had served on great newspapers. He had made his mark in London. He now gave the impression that fate or the gods or some other power had sent him into my life to offer me the Great Opportunity. In this direction he was only too ready to serve, even to sacrifice. That I had talents, far off and deeply latent though they might be, he did not doubt. But that I had made not the slightest perceptible use of them he did not doubt either. It was all sad, all very, very sad. At this point it would not have been at all surprising to have seen a welling of tears in Bretherton's eyes. Instead the sermon ended with a benediction. I was dismissed not only with Bretherton's blessing but with the earnest beseechment that I must pull myself together, try to do better and above all to seize the Great Opportunity. I accepted both blessing and beseechment in silence and Bretherton nipped over to the Hind for another whisky.

Bretherton was a fair example of the old journalistic alcoholic fraud. Shabby, even scruffy, the Great Opportunity long since lost in mists of alcohol, he was a figure at once distasteful, despicable and pathetic. In one of Shaw's plays there is a devastating portrait of a journalist who resembles, in fact, a human ferret dressed in seedy, greasy mackintosh: a kind of younger Bretherton before the rot finally sets in.

That morning I could cheerfully have swiped Bretherton: not physically, small and overweight though he was, but metaphorically and mentally. My rage at the piety of that lecture of his brought me, as I rode home in the train, to a pitch of impotency very near to tears. Of all human attributes the first and foremost I cannot stand is hypocrisy and that morning my cup of it was full.

Next morning I informed Bretherton, and then my father, that I had turned my back on the Great Opportunity. In all my life I have never been so relieved.

XI

I was now once again at the crossroads; and once again there was no visible signpost or hand to guide me.

Again I mooched about, waiting for something to turn up. The horizon was empty. Out of the generosity of his heart my father had bought me a second-hand bicycle for thirty shillings. It was never quite in tolerable working order but on it I clanked and squeaked about the spring countryside, drinking in the joys I had missed in the dingy office of the *Northampton Chronicle,* where one afternoon an incomparable young vision had turned up with her father, the proprietor, to cast an appraising eye on the impossible office and myself, as if I had been an inmate in a debtors' prison. I have often wondered what that aloof, lovely creature thought of me, the office and its dreary Dickensian fireplace choked with ashes.

In between my rides into the countryside I went to the reading room of the Carnegie Library to study advertisements both in London and local papers. The shadow of the Great Depression was by this time not far ahead and already jobs were difficult, if not impossible, to find: so impossible that it was only a year or two later that I found myself standing, in common with about three and a half million others, in a queue for the dole.

But presently I came upon an advertisement that seemed to offer something, if not a great deal. 'Clerk wanted for warehouse; good references; apply own handwriting etc.' More in desperation than hope I applied. Some mornings later I received a letter favourable in that it was at least a summons for an interview. It was from the manager of a firm of leather and grindery factors housed at an address a mere stone's throw from the gateway beyond which the genesis of *Love for Lydia* had taken place a few weeks before.

Duly presenting myself to what had once been an old paint store owned by the father of a former school-friend of mine, I met Mr Smart, the manager. Mr Smart was kindly, considerate and perceptive. He appeared to be impressed by my appearance and my Third Class Honours. Two days later I got the job: salary one pound a week, double what I had been getting from Bretherton and the Great Opportunity.

I should explain here that boots and shoes are not merely made of leather. They require an infinity of accessories. Hessian, linings, thread in all colours, cords, cottons, eyelets, rivets, nails, sprigs, insoles, heels, backstraps, glue, wax and heaven knows what: all these, together with a few skins of kid – the capacity of the old paint shop was too cramped for any heavier grades of leather – we kept in the old two-floored warehouse, which actually stood at the foot of the garden of a dear and attentive old lady, a certain Mrs Fountain.

On my first morning at the warehouse I was greeted by a short, rather abrupt man who announced himself as ' 'Emmings. I come to show you the ropes for a week or two.'

The first of the ropes Mr Hemmings proceeded to show to me was the outside lavatory, which was kept continually locked against possible night intruders. 'Got to keep this clean,' Mr Hemmings said. 'I do like a clean 'ole.'

The necessity of keeping the lavatory impeccably clean having been duly noted I accompanied Mr Hemmings on a tour of the warehouse and its mysteries. I scarcely understood a thing. Downstairs stood great piles, in sheets, of what seemed to be grey cardboard, together with bags of grindery, sprigs, nails, rivets and so on, and sacks of powdered glue. Upstairs were the various threads, cottons, hessians and linings. There was also in one corner a tiny office built of varnished match-boarding, containing a desk, a telephone, a few files, a typewriter and a petty cashbox from which I could extract an occasional few shillings for stamps and so on. All these things, Mr Hemmings explained to me, were to be my responsibility.

For the next two weeks Mr Hemmings showed me, and showed me very adequately, the ropes. Among other things he taught me the only thing that I can still do in a professional manner with my hands: namely, packing parcels. Now and then Mr Smart appeared, took an appraising glance or two about the place to observe that all was in order, did the *Daily Express* crossword puzzle and then disappeared on his commercial travels. His territory ranged from northward of the Nene Valley, where desecrated little villages such as Finedon, Ringstead, Burton Latimer and Raunds all had their typical nineteenth-century shoe factories, to as far south as Wollaston and even Olney, William Cowper's town, over into Buckinghamshire. All these were small fry in comparison with the many factories of Rushden and Higham Ferrers combined where, as I have said, huge mushroom fortunes had been made in the years of the First World War.

After Mr Hemmings' eventual departure it did not take me long to assess that I held a position of unique and exceeding advantage to myself: I was alone practically all day and every day. A few orders having been executed, a few telephone calls answered, I found that I had little to do between 8.30 in the morning and 5.30 in the evening. I at first took advantage of this to read voraciously. I devoured Conrad, Bennett, Wells, Galsworthy and Hardy; I gnawed into *Of Human Bondage;* I somehow discovered the American writers Joseph Hergesheimer, Edith Wharton, Willa Cather and James Branch Cabell; I grasped at *Madame Bovary* as at the fruit of a rare tree; I practically exhausted the contents of the shelves of the Carnegie Library, consuming in the process a mixed menu of May Sinclair, W. W. Jacobs, Tennyson Jesse, Perceval Gibbon, Stacy Aumonier, John Russell, Chesterton and a particular little gem, greatly formative in its influences on me, Hilaire Belloc's *Hills and the Sea.* I even kept a sort of diary, a record of the things I read, and soon its pages were fat to overflowing.

All this was far removed from what might have been my curriculum at Cambridge, but it must be remembered that I was still only seventeen and that in any case Cambridge at that time would still have been some distance away. The direction of my voyage of literary discovery was now, come hell or high water, to be of my own choosing. I had no one to teach me navigation. It is true that I went back one afternoon to school for the purpose of hearing a lecture by De la Mare, an exercise in the way language might be used that I have not forgotten; (De la Mare took as his text the sentence 'Won't you dine with me tonight?' and then with skill proceeded to demonstrate how, by the change of emphasis from word to word, the entire meaning of the sentence could be shifted half a dozen times) but this was all. Instead, the first of my own foragings began to yield unexpected fruit. One afternoon – it may well have been the one on which I had gone to listen to De la Mare – I was waiting for a train by the bookstall at Kettering Station when I spotted a large-paper remainder called *The Windmill*, an anthology of stories, essays and verse put out by the firm of William Heinemann, whose imprint the windmill was. I bought the book, I think for two shillings.

Much of its contents surprised and fascinated me. There were authors of whom I had never heard. Two in particular were Herbert Crackanthorpe, a name utterly unknown, I fancy, to the present generation, and Stephen Crane, who was represented by a story called *The Five White Mice*, a highly economical and vivid tale of a gambling joint which took its title from a ditty that went:

> Oh! five white mice of chance,
> Shirts of wool and corduroy pants,
> Gold and wine, women and sin
> All for you if you let me come in –
> Into the house of chance.

It was not, however, the ditty that impressed me so much. It was the way the story began:

> Freddie was mixing a cocktail. His hand with the long spoon was whirling swiftly, and the ice in the glass hummed and rattled like a cheap watch. Over by the window, a gambler, a millionaire, a railway conductor, and the agent of a vast American syndicate were playing seven-up. Freddie surveyed them with the ironical glance of a man who is mixing a cocktail.

The vastly mature tone of this pictorial piece impressed me greatly. Whose was this new voice? I had heard nothing like it before. A considerable number of years later I pointed out, in the *Modern Short Story*, that a short story can be likened to a horserace; it is the beginning and end that count most and of these two it is probable that the beginning is of the greater importance. In this respect Crane's story went almost as well as that of *The Prodigal Son* in the Authorised Version, where in six words the author of that incomparable little story, consisting as it does of a mere 130 words or so, succeeds in introducing his three main characters. In a single brief paragraph Crane introduced five. Nor was this all. Crane was also making his words work overtime, not only bringing his characters to immediate and vivid life, but succinctly setting the atmosphere in which they were ready to move.

A new light now opened up for me. I thirsted for more Crane and indefatigably set out on a hunt for him. The Carnegie Libraries offered nothing. I drew blanks at bookshops (only a little later I was to draw equal blanks when searching for Donne.) I could find nothing in catalogues. How it finally came about that I succeeded in tracking down *The Open Boat* and *The Red Badge of Courage,* that most extraordinary epic of the American Civil War which had shot Crane into stardom in the 1890s, I cannot now remember, but eventually I did, later finding also *The Third Violet* and *Bowery Tales.* Later, when I mentioned my Crane enthusiasms to A. E. Coppard he reacted with no little scorn, declaring 'Crane me no Cranes', perhaps not an altogether unexpectedly blind admission from a writer who had been unwise enough to take that most elephantine of bores, Henry James, as the chief of his models. For my part no charge of explosive could remove me from my ironclad admiration of a man who could start a story, *The Open Boat,* with the nine words 'None of them knew the colour of the sky'. When you read a story beginning in that fashion you begin to revise very sharply your preconceived notions of the way a story can be written.

It is to Crane, therefore, that I really owe my first conscious hunger to begin writing stories, which I did when I was seventeen. Crane had also begun writing when very young but, as far as I was concerned, with this pregnant difference: unlike me but like the young Maupassant he had arrived on the literary scene fully equipped. He had nothing to learn. He never really knew how good he was. Just as Maupassant had amazed and shocked his established elders with the unparalleled maturity of *Boule de Suif,* so Crane had stunned the American and English literary world with *The Red Badge of Courage,* an epic of a war in which Crane had not, and could not possibly have, taken part. Its authority alone is dazzling enough; its realism cuts like a scalpel. Yet the book, after someone had declared that it outdid Zola, Tolstoy and Kipling in one breath, suffered at first a critical fate dismal in the extreme. All manner of excuses were offered for its rejection: it had no love story; it was too grim (this of what was then the bloodiest war in history); veterans of war found it insulting, unpatriotic, damned nonsense; others felt that it betrayed the memory of the slain; as to the author himself and his then revolutionary style 'it was passionately urged that no decent youth should describe emotions in terms of colours, that his grammar was wildly mouldy.' Nevertheless, thanks in no little part to 'the blaze of English reviews', the book became stupendously successful and Crane found himself famous – fatally famous it would not be too much to say – by the time he was twenty-four.

The Red Badge of Courage is not a long book. Though packed with action, blood and the emotions of the starry-eyed young hero who goes to war in the expectation of glory and leaves it chastised by the white heat of disillusionment – emotions that certain horrified critics believed should not and could not be expressed in colour – it somehow conveys the impression of epic structure. As a comment on this it is interesting to note that *War and Peace,* Tolstoy's 'endless panorama', annoyed Crane. 'He could have done the whole business in one-third of the time and made it just as wonderful. It goes on and on like Texas.' Exactly. Not for the first time, nor the last I fear, had sheer length and size seduced readers into the mesmerised belief that they were in the sacred presence of greatness.

It was not only the painterly quality of Crane's prose that attracted me, nor the forceful insistence on describing emotions in colour, but also a sharp and dominant element of poetry. Though I can find in D. H. Lawrence's letters no mention whatever of Crane it seems to me that there is much in common with the early short stories of Lawrence and those of Crane. It is a well known fact that when a scientist unravels a problem of fearsomely intricate nature in one part of the world it is a fair bet that some other scientist, or scientists, are about to make a similar revelation in another (the discovery by William Harvey of the circulation of the blood is a celebrated example of this.). When therefore I read in Lawrence's *Odour of Chrysanthemums* the passage

> The small locomotive, number 4, came clanking, stumbling down from Selston with seven full wagons. It appeared round the corner with loud threats of speed, but the colt that it startled from among the gorse, which still flickered indistinctly in the raw afternoon, out-distanced it in a canter,

I can almost hear the echo of it in Crane's 'The battle lines writhed at times in the agony of a sea-creature on the sands. These tentacles flung and waved in the extreme excitement of pain,' and I know also that I am in the presence of two men who, though oceans apart as far as terrestrial distances are concerned, have arrived at an identical point where they have simultaneously discovered that writing is not merely done with hand and brain, but also with the eyes. Young as I was I recognised in Crane, and later in the earlier Lawrence, proof that words, as well as pigments, can also paint.

It was some months however, before I began to practice my apprentice hand at short stories. Poems I was still writing: poems that went, like unwanted strays, from editor to editor, bringing back, like faithful puppies, nothing but rejection slips between their teeth. Neither the remotest hint of an acceptance, nor an encouraging word, ever reached me.

In the autumn of my seventeenth year, however, I decided to write a novel. My system of getting the greater part of the warehouse work finished by about 9.30 every morning having proved almost consistently successful I went off one evening and bought myself the thickest quarto writing pad, in pale blue, that I could find. I bought it in fact from a shop run by two elderly maiden sisters, one half of the shop being devoted to books, stationery, inks, pens and so on, the other to rather exclusive brands of chocolate, sugared almonds, toffees, marzipan and various sweet-meats such as crystallised violets, rose petals and those silver bullet-like balls that are used to decorate wedding and birthday cakes. For some reason the two ladies, both of whom wore those high-necked collars of lace that at once give an impression of stiffness, disapprobation and aristocracy, seemed to disapprove of me. Perhaps they had not unfounded suspicions that I found the young girl behind the stationery counter particularly attractive; perhaps they were also suspicious and mystified that a youth of seventeen could possibly need so much writing paper, even for writing letters – perhaps love-letters? – at one time.

I bore home that massive chunk of writing-paper with a feeling of rare and peculiar excitement in my heart: an emotion arising from a particular sort of anticipation that has since been repeated a thousand times. Talking only the other day to a celebrated painter I discovered that she too had shared, over and over again, the same anticipatory thrill: hers from a blank area of canvas, mine from a naked quarto of paper. What, eventually, is going to illuminate the canvas, what the paper? The question is still, for me, the most exciting one of a writer's life – out of, and by means of, the simplest materials, will come what? The mere fact of not knowing is over and over again responsible for a positive, impossible excitement.

Almost every morning that autumn and winter, after lighting the big coke-burning stove, called I think 'the tortoise' and not inappropriately, I settled down to write in the warehouse. Sometimes the telephone bell, a customer, a drayman from the railway goods yard interrupted, but progress was mostly un-disturbed, peaceful and rapid. Though filling both sides of the paper I was not long in returning to the lace-collared ladies and their charming assistant for a fresh supply. As my novel grew so, it seemed, did the coolness of the ladies' disapproval. What *could* a young man possibly need with so much paper, and so often?

They did not know; and nor, in fact, did anyone else. I wrote like a hermit. This is not to say that I cut myself off completely from the world of football, Chaplin's *Easy Street* and Griffith's *Birth of a Nation* at the cinema, or, when summer came round again, from cricket, tennis and much bicycling into the country-side. That hermit-like part of my existence was merely a first demonstration of the indisputable fact that creation, in art of any kind, is of necessity secret. The fusion between writer and paper, painter and canvas cannot, or should not be, shared. Such sharing was called by D. H. Lawrence, with complete aptitude, as I have already said, 'the give away'.

It is beyond all dispute, I now have to confess, that my hermit-like industry did not prevent my novel from being an untidy, verbose and appalling shambles. In Crane's words 'like Texas it went on and on', and unhappily, I fear, to no purpose. When it was finished I sent it off, in MS, since I couldn't afford the cost of typing, to Edmund Kirby, who in reply permitted himself a few comments of such a guarded nature that I was disposed, with melancholy but justly, to submit to the verdict that I had spawned a shapeless, amateurish, useless monster. Indeed I had.

A certain buoyancy of character is something I have never lacked and with very little of any kind of protracted pain I buried the blue bundle of words away in a drawer, like a creature still-born. But the world being full of novels that are begun but never finished I had at least this singular piece of satisfaction to comfort me: bad as it might be, I had finished my novel, all 150,000 words of it; and this, since the act of writing is, like the act of love, primarily a physical affair, whatever emotions inspire it or it may engender later, was something of not inconsiderable importance. Having run one marathon, though in unspectacular time, I assured myself that I could attempt another.

The genesis of novels and stories, as Hardy once pointed out of *Tess*, often stems from the simplest, most fleeting of moments. A word, a glance, a face are, more often than not, enough; though not, of course, for the Texan-like acres of *War and Peace*. My next novel, which in fact was to be my first to be published, *The Two Sisters*, had its genesis after this simple fashion: it sprang simply from the sight of a candle, or lamp, burning in a window. I was much given to walking alone at this time, more especially at night, and it was on a stygian, moonless night, I rather fancy in January, that I found myself walking through the tiny hamlet of Farndish, in the neighbourhood of which the Romans indisputably delved for iron. Halfway down the village street I passed a biggish, square stone house in one room of which the curtains were not drawn. A light burned inside. I stopped for a moment, stared through the window into a room of a strange and shadowy emptiness and was instantly gripped first by a haunting sense of melancholy and then by the indefinable notion that I had been there, in front of that lamp-lit window, before. I went home greatly troubled in imagination. A new genesis had begun.

The word imagination is here of no little importance. The business of writing fiction is an exercise in the art of telling lies. If the writer uses his art and craftsmanship to their fullest extension he will not only succeed in making his readers believe that his lies are truth but that they are in fact truer than life itself. The writer without imagination, or the ability to invent, is not a writer of fiction at all. It is fidelity to imagination, therefore, not fidelity to observation, that is of supreme importance to the writer of fiction, whether it be in the form of the novel, the short story or the play. I have little use for so-called novels such as *Point Counter Point,* brilliant though they may be, which offer a sort of superior parlour guessing game designed to get the reader to spot the life-size originals of the characters involved; nor have I any more use for such a novel as that absurd and grossly overpraised piece of D. H. Lawrence's, *Women in Love,* which is not only the worst of all the bad novels he ever wrote but is almost beyond dispute the worst novel ever written by a writer of international reputation. The transposition from Bloomsbury of characters such as Lady Ottoline Morrell and Co to the hills and woodlands of Derbyshire, is a piece of incongruous lunacy, resulting in a novel that is like a bad patchwork quilt, part silk, part homespun, ending in nothing but a mess. Even before *Sons and Lovers* (a considerable number of the uninvented characters Lawrence used in the earlier novel *The White Peacock* are still alive in Nottinghamshire today) Lawrence had demonstrated that, brilliant in power of observation as he was and as the early short stories and poems indisputably demonstrate, he hadn't enough imagination to invent Mickey Mouse. As for inventing a new main character for each novel as it was written this was totally unnecessary; Lawrence himself was always there to oblige as the hero and did indeed oblige, over and over again and to a point of utter tedium, until the end.

It is true to say, of course, that a very great percentage of first novels are autobiographical; and perhaps inevitably. Twenty or thirty years of a writer's experiences, whether of love, family conflicts, quarrels, soul-searching, embracing or rejection of beliefs and creeds, may well forcefully cry out to be set down in that first precious essay. All, to the young writer, is of inflaming importance; all must go in. Not so with the second novel. Here arises the hard, gristly problem on which so many writers have broken their teeth. All has gone in; what now? Mere power of observation, however penetrative and brilliant, is now not enough. Unless power of imagination is there to stimulate a new and green insurgence of character, scene and conflict, a mere desert looms ahead. A process of telling lies, of distortion, of omission, of twisting, of conjuring, of deception – call it what you will – is now the one indisputable and imperative art that will make the desert blossom.

My purpose in mentioning all this is to make clear that *The Two Sisters* was a work solely of imagination: indeed it would not be untrue to say of wild imagination, the rampaging, highly-coloured, not always quite coherent imagination of youth trying to say something but not knowing quite what it wanted to say. The only solid piece of fabric in it was the lamp in the window of an otherwise dark house on a Stygian night in January. This house I proceeded to people with two sisters, wholly different in character, a slightly unbalanced father who kept them half-imprisoned there, a young man from the outside world who comes as a bearer of love and liberation, and a servant: none of whom were based on living people I had met before. In short it was not a work of observation, but one of poetry. Nor was it a novel of chronicled realism, but one of essentials: what had been left out was more important than what had been left in. It did not in any degree follow the pattern of the autobiographical essay that was elsewhere described as 'the easy plan, in which the author declaims that "I am going to tell you all about myself and my friends, the characters and their families, and their neighbours, and their surroundings, and their past and their present and everything else just as I can think of it." ' In other words the writer who seeks to tell everything succeeds, all too often, in telling nothing. How many Victorian three-deckers ever said as much in one chapter as Crane said in 'None of them knew the colour of the sky?

Every word of *The Two Sisters* was written in the warehouse. I fear that I have perhaps slightly exaggerated in saying that I got down to the business of writing every morning: solely, perhaps, because those are the only mornings that meant anything or gave me pleasure. There was, of course, other work to do, but I can only say that I did it as rapidly as possible. I had letters to write, typing with one finger; a little simple bookkeeping to do; accounts to make up and bills to pay; orders to take and pack and despatch. Large, heavy drays, drawn by large heavy horses, arrived frequently from the station goods yard, bringing merchandise from Manchester, Bradford, Birmingham, Scotland and various parts, so that I was flung into the fierce physical activity of unloading it all and stowing it away. Sometimes an urgent call from a factory made it essential for me to set off on a half-running errand with sack-barrow, a parcel or a quarter hundredweight sack of nails on my shoulder. In winter the little warehouse became an icebox, in summer a stifling oven.

Thirsty or chilled, I was constantly being cosseted by the motherly attentions of Mrs Fountain, the lady next door. Mrs Fountain had an incurable habit of 'popping in'. At eleven o'clock in the morning she would 'pop in' with bread and cheese or biscuits and tea; in the afternoon she again 'popped in' with tea, cake and buttered toast. She fussed over me; she liked a little gossip. In her garden she had apple and pear trees and on the warehouse wall a plum; in their season she brought me the fruits of these too. I have some idea that she thought I was overworked, which in one sense was true, in another not. The warehouse work, for which after one year my wage rose to the princely heights of thirty shillings a week, was a mere necessity; it was the business of writing *The Two Sisters,* in secret and mostly at breakneck speed, and then of hiding the MS away into a disused drawer at night, that provided the overworking and in due course that lean and hungry look which Mrs Fountain and her 'poppings-in' sought to do something to comfort.

I suppose I worked on *The Two Sisters* for a year; it is hard to remember. Until a short time ago I had long been under the impression that I wrote two versions of it; but then, searching among some early papers, I discovered a third, or part of a third.

These facts provide the key to something which has been stubbornly part of my character and practice as a writer ever since: I was, and still am, frigidly and restlessly self-critical. 'I have destroyed hundreds of poems,' wrote Rupert Brooke, 'for my soul's sake.' I can say with equal truth that I have destroyed scores of poems, several plays, many short stories and three novels not for my soul's sake but simply because the disciplinarian in me thought they were no damn good.

But at last there was finished a version of *The Two Sisters* with which I was evidently not altogether displeased. Furious and blind though the urgencies of its creation had been (I once wrote no less than 12,000 words of it, among the leather, linen and thread, in one day.) I evidently felt, at last, that I had produced a work that was not only coherent but at least measurable by the standards – the standards of a very youthful nineteen, it must be remembered – I had set myself. Still no one but myself knew of its existence, but now, thanks to the munificence of my salary, I could at least afford to get it typed. Thus, in the early months of 1925, it started on its first excursion to the outside world; while I, supremely confident that the hunger of one publisher would be enough to consume it in the matter of a day or two, a week at the outside, unexpectedly set out on another.

XII

It is well to be truthful and succinct about this event. Nowadays, when we are near-suffocated by tradeunionese, councilese and Americanese, the new extensions of stodge-pudding language that have joined Johnsonese, journalese and politicalese, it would no doubt be said that I became redundant. I prefer the old way: I was unexpectedly sacked.

Whether my secret predilection to give most of my time to writing had been suddenly discovered or long-suspected and tolerated meanwhile for lack of proof I shall never know. One day I was simply told that my services at the warehouse were no longer required. It was a fearful blow; in vain I protested. Quite apart from the loss of wages, which had now risen to positively royal heights at two pounds a week, there was also a crushing loss of pride. I actually felt that I had done some sort of wrong, a notion that may well have also occurred to my employers, who might reasonably have felt that the business of trading in the accessories necessary to shoemaking, though including many odd and diverse things, did not include the writing of novels. I now feel some sympathy for them on that score.

I was, anyway, suddenly out on the street. The cloud of the Great Depression was only a short distance away; already unemployment was rising everywhere; a system known as three on and three off (i.e. three days of work and three of dole) was already operating in the majority of factories; many firms were closing down; in less than ten years the huge golden balloon of the war-time boom had collapsed to the size and appearance of a pig's bladder blown up by boys (as we often used to do) who had otherwise no ball to play football with in those ash-strewn back-alleys we called 'jitties'. A new, ungay company of strolling players had already appeared on the streets, many of them short of a finger or two, a hand, an eye or even a leg, hawking wares such as boot-laces, scrubbing-brushes, soap, polishes and so on. I observed them not with pity but with anger: so much so that whenever I read of the play *Look Back in Anger* I am inclined to laugh with brittle mockery. Neither Mr Osborne nor those who unwisely over-praised his piece or failed to recognise that its real title should have been *Look Back in Self-Pity* can have had the remotest notion what the causes of anger can be. They should have seen the decent, piteous peep-show of the mid-twenties, in which I was half-spectator, half-player, an almost ferocious predecessor of Mr Osborne's angry young man by a quarter of a century and with truer, more bitter cause.

Nevertheless a certain natural buoyancy of temperament prevented my being too pessimistic about my personal affairs. It was true that I was once again at the crossroads, not knowing which way to turn and having no guidance on the subject anyway, but at least I now had the novel. I had great hopes of the novel. I think I sent it first to William Heinemann, perhaps because they were the publishers of Crane and Maugham; then to Chatto & Windus, Constable, Dent, Chapman & Hall, Allen & Unwin, Harrap and more. From all these it duly came back. (Perhaps it was just as well that I didn't know at this time of the thirteen years' wandering of Joyce's *Dubliners* before it found a publisher: as incredible a piece of readership blindness as ever tarnished the publishing world.) And from all except two it came back with no syllable of comment. The exceptions were Dent, with whom I had a not unhopeful correspondence, more on my own potentialities as a writer, I think, than on the virtues of the book itself; and Chapman & Hall, of whom at that time the head was Arthur Waugh, father of Evelyn and Alec. Some considerable correspondence ensured as a result of their interest in the book and Waugh senior is said to have remarked 'this young man has something to say'. The interest expressed in this remark led in fact to my going to London, I think twice, to climb the stairs once trodden by Meredith, that figure so greatly revered at the turn of the century who is now utterly put away in mothballs, to discuss the merits of *The Two Sisters* with a lady whose name now escapes me but who was most generous in both intelligence and kindness. It began to appear, soon, that the book might be accepted; I was buoyed up with miraculous hopes. These were finally dashed by the verdict of Alec, who decided that, after all, the book was not for Chapman & Hall.

So on its journeyings from publisher to publisher went the novel again. It is also just as well that I didn't know that at about the same time Hemingway had sent his famous and excellent story *Fifty Grand* to every editor in America before its merits were finally observed by that acutest of editors, Ellery Sedgewick, of the *Atlantic Monthly*. Sedgewick had a sharp nose for talent and it was he, on quite another plane, who one day walked into the London offices of the *British Weekly,* asked if there was anything new to read and was told that the only MS of consequence, and not much consequence at that, was a little piece called, *Goodbye, Mr Chips.* Quick as a whippet after a hare, Sedgewick spotted the story's vast potentiality for success among an American public always ready to shed an honest tear or two, and the fame of James Hilton, whose later Hawthornden Prize-winning novel *Lost Horizon* actually and incredibly begins with that clanking cliché 'cigars were burning low', was suddenly assured.

But as yet I had no such good fortune and meanwhile funds, never very high, were running very low. From the first moment of unemployment a staunch and mountainous pride had prevented me going on the dole. But soon the arguments for this, for me, most repugnant of steps became irrefutable. I had, after all, paid my insurance stamps and insurance against times of need was what such payments were for. We were not now, I was told, back in the days of Dickens; it was no longer a question of 'going on the parish'; it was something to which I was fairly and honourably entitled.

With hate in my heart, I gave in, joining the dole queue every Friday ('signing on', I think they called it) at some small disused chapel in one of those precariously steep streets of which Rushden is full, and duly drew my dole, the sum of one pound. In the company of a rambling, coughing, shambling queue I could never quite rid myself of a sense of shame and I invariably scurried away without speaking to a soul, very often slipping out for a solitary tramp into the countryside in order to clear my lungs of those sounds of hauking, spitting and coughing which were so much part of the melancholy chorus of those days before tuberculosis had been conquered. If ever there was money that was hateful to me it was that I drew on those wintry Friday mornings in the year 1925.

All this time I was reading with my usual voracious appetite, always extending its range. During the previous August I had gone off with my parents for a week, perhaps two weeks, to Bournemouth, and had discovered in particular one of several bookshops there. The man I was after now – and I cannot now remember what first inspired it – was Turgenev. It appeared, however, that he, like Crane and Donne (the great revival of interest in Donne was still a few years ahead) was undiscoverable. But after much diligent search I at last tracked him down, finding him in a bookshop where the early Constance Garnett translations, in their plain khaki covers, were securely shut away in glass-doored cases, as if long unwanted and forgotten. I think I first bought *A Sportsman's Sketches,* at two shillings a time, in the edition of 1895. They were at once, for me, a source of great delight and influence; neither the English novel nor the English short story contained anything so poetical or so exquisitely full of the breath of summer mornings or the atmosphere of Russian birch forests clearing slowly from the cover of autumnal mists to the rising warmth of sun. Hemingway, for all his alleged toughness as a writer, was also so rejoiced and influenced and if you listen carefully you can, I think, hear the voice of Turgenev in the following lines:

The breeze was coming up and we could hear it in the high branches. It was cool in the shade, but if you stirred in the sun, or as the sun shifted the shadow while you read so that any part of you was out of the shadow, the sun was heavy . . . I could smell the heat of the day coming, the drying up of the dew, the heat on the leaves, and the heaviness of the sun over the stream.

Until I later read Hudson and Edward Thomas I discovered nothing in English prose to equal the exquisite nature of those sketches of Turgenev written so long ago. My next step, not unnaturally, was Chekhov. Young as I was, it didn't take me long to assess the vast potentialities of a writer of stories who so often says more by what he leaves out than by what he leaves in. Chekhov was followed by Maupassant, Gorki, Flaubert, Bierce and a considerable company of others whose main passion was, as mine was now, the short story. Galsworthy and Bennett, also in turn supposedly influenced by Turgenev, I had by now partially exhausted. My nose, for ever sniffing after new names, even found Knut Hamsun's *Hunger,* a book which Henry Miller still confesses he finds a great one.

Driven by these innumerable new influences I was now, undaunted by the fruitless journeyings of *The Two Sisters,* writing a good many short stories. One autumn day it happened that I was playing football in Bedford. After the match the whole team repaired to a restaurant called the Silver Grill, where my guess is that, famished after the heat of the game, we drank much tea and ate fish and chips. A small harassed waitress, run off her feet by having to serve an entire football team and several spectators, scurried hither and thither with teapots, dishes of fried plaice and mounds of bread and butter, now and then pausing breathlessly at a serving hatch to snatch up a speaking tube and send her orders to the kitchen downstairs. I watched her, fascinated not because she was pretty, which she was not, but because already my imagination, like Hardy's with Tess and my own with the lamp in the window, was excitedly beginning to weave a pattern of lies about her.

The next morning I sat down and put that little waitress on paper in a very short story called *The Flame*. More than forty years later it is still a story of which I am not ashamed and which in fact was one of the stories in my first volume of stories, *Day's End*. But it too went off unsuccessfully on its wanderings: finding, like Joyce's *Dubliners,* no sponsors, a fact perhaps not surprising in that it was looking for one in a world where stories still had to have plots or to conform to rigid house-rules designed to satisfy the specific appetites of specific readers. My little harassed waitress in *The Flame* didn't need a plot; nor had I, then or later, any need for either plots or patterns imposed by others. But, happily, changes were coming.

XIII

It would be wrong to suppose that the world of the nineteen-twenties was entirely one of bitterness. On the contrary much of it was gay: strenuously, defiantly, noisily, swaggeringly, falsely gay. The young of all classes were in protest and revolt against their elders, but their protestations took on a form very different from those of the young of the present day. Where the young now march about cities with battle cries of violence and angry waving of banners, staging sit-ins, love-ins and so on, drinking much and trading much, apparently, in drugs, the young of the twenties merely rode, if they could afford it, in fast sports cars, made a great whoopee on Boat Race nights and wore clothes thought to be just as outrageous and revolutionary as the Carnaby Street patterns, often flowered and tattered, of today.

In a working-class town, however, the form of protest was a far milder form and the cause of it invariably the same: money or the lack of it. A few of the progeny of boot manufacturers made rapidly rich during the war could afford fast smart sports cars, but most of the rest of us were lucky to have push-bikes. There were still few buses and a lot of people still walked a great deal. If you went on holiday to the seaside in August, as most people did (still for the one precious statutory week), you did so in trains crowded to the point of suffocation and subsequently lived in digs for a couple of pounds or less a week. Of social life (I speak of the world of cocktail parties and so on) artistic and musical life, there was practically none. When H. G. Wells wrote 'in this world of gramophones, pianolas and the radio, it is worth noting that at the age of thirteen I had heard no music at all except an occasional brass band, the not very good music of hymn singing and organ voluntaries in Bromley church' he might well have been talking of my own world of the twenties, a world so remote from discotheques, television and millionaire singing groups as to make the earlier world of tennis, tea on the lawn, fairs and boxing booths, shop-outings in charabancs, chapel social evenings and parades of Friendly Societies with *their* banners proudly borne aloft at Sunday School Treats, seem both ridiculous and naïve. Indeed in all probability it was; but there were compensations.

For example we danced. We danced, indeed, a great deal. Moreover dancing was cheap. If my memory serves me correctly the price of admission to most dances was one-and-six (refreshments excluded) though on occasion we permitted ourselves the luxury of some dashing affair at three-and-six. Of really special affairs at half-a-guinea (so priced in order to keep out the riff-raff) and at which the girls wore long dresses and the men, of forced necessity, dinner-jackets, we knew, and could know, nothing. Our own affairs were confined to the Parish Hall, a local Institute of some kind, the Co-op Hall or, occasionally, to some village hall ten or a dozen miles out in the country, for which we had perforce either to hire some ancient and shaky private bus or, as is described in *Love for Lydia,* some equally ancient limousine taxi.

Most of us drank little or hardly at all; few of us could afford to do so. When the time came for refreshments we dashed with gallantry to fetch tea or coffee, jellies, cakes, sandwiches and sausage rolls for the ladies of our choice. How any of them managed to be of our choice is a problem that constantly defeats me. Rarely can women's dresses have been more hideous than they were in the twenties, never less seductive. The girl of the day was presented to you as a sort of line-prop, straight, bosomless, with a skirt so short and tight that she invariably also appeared knock-kneed. To this ever-fascinating gear was added a cloche hat, which resembled more than anything else a chamberpot without a handle, and a long row of beads or pearls. Where a girl was more generously gifted in the region of the bust she wore stays that gave the impression of being made of iron and since her hair was almost always Eton-cropped you got the further disturbing impression that Nature, caught halfway in the dilemma of whether to create a male or a female, had finally come up with a creature composite of both.

But line-props, chamberpot hats, Eton-crops or what you will, we nevertheless fell for these young creatures as if they were sculptured like the Venus de Milo or the milky mountain peaks of flesh now displayed as a matter of course in such magazines as *Playboy*. I suppose that the world of straight short dresses (today's miniskirt is in a class wholly different), cloche hats and long ropes of pearls now appears as ludicrous to the women of today (at the present moment I observe that the latest Parisian fashion designers are about to compel or persuade women to go about as near as possible in a condition known, I believe, as 'starkers') as the hour-glass figures of the years of my extreme childhood. But we, the men, didn't think so. We saw, we chased and, if we didn't always conquer, we fell. Our own great moments came in summertime, with an affair that I suppose must now be considered to be as ridiculous as the cloche hat: namely the Flannel Dance. Arrayed like young peacocks, we strutted forth in coats of many colours. My own blazer was striped in black-and-scarlet; others out-flashed it in purple-white-and-green; some were white edged with blue and emblazoned with escutcheons of school or club. Thus arrayed, we clomped around, prodigiously sweating to fox-trots, quicksteps and subsequently to the gymnastic gyrations of the Charleston and the Black Bottom, joyous to the music of saxophones, 'Valencia' and 'Ain't She Sweet?'

Envious as women always are, girls who could not perform these newest of movements sat out, huddled together like sour, drab butterflies. At dances such as these there was no such nonsense as the elegant little appointment card with its pencil attached by a silken cord in which a girl booked her engagements for the evening. We, on the contrary, rode in like young gladiators in competition for whatever creature had excited our fancy. Our rewards were twofold: long seasons of chilliness from those with whom we had neglected to dance and the precious reward of seeing home the girl with whom the better part of the evening had been fused. 'Last Dance, Please', was a call as challenging as any ordering you to get on your marks for the 100 metres in the Olympic Games.

It is strange now to think that though so many of my evenings (except, of course, in Lent) were so spent in such abandoned and superficial gaiety, my days were almost utterly solitary. If I were not working on stories of my own, I was not only reading avidly of Conrad, Turgenev, Chekhov, Maupassant, Crane and many others, but often doing exercises in deliberate imitation of their styles, probing and dissecting them in order to discover how, in their various and masterly ways, they achieved their effects. In this single-minded pursuit I was not at all unlike a certain celebrated golfer who, day after day, travelled a practice course armed with buckets of golf balls which he proceeded hour after hour to putt and putt and putt and putt, until at last perfection and championships had been achieved.

But now, somewhere about this time, there appeared, accidentally as a result of the world of dancing, another writer, totally unexpected; and another person, totally unexpected too and a great deal more important.

On the edge of the town, to the south, stood an extremely old farmhouse. Built of stone, with a stone-walled garden, it still reminds me of many old manorial gardens, half in decay, that you see in almost every part of France. To one side of it ran a brook, over which hung lines of large horse chestnuts. At the back of the farmhouse were the usual cow-barns, stalls, stackyards, hen-runs and pigsties. Inside, the rooms were large and rambling. The kitchen had that warm, half-buttery, half-milky smell in which was also mingled the odour of cows and cow manure. There was also about the entire house an ancient and church-like smell, strong with wood smoke and dampness.

The farmer and his wife were upright, God-fearing, hard-working, pleasant, flaxen-haired, non-conformist and productive. They had a family equally divided into three sons and three daughters: all different in character, temperament and looks. No house could have been more English, more rural or more like a survival from Thomas Hardy or my own grandfather's boyhood. The father, in his extreme uprightness, was rather quiet: a good-looking man of typical yeoman aspect. In the mother I always suspected there lurked a streak of repressed gaiety accompanied by another of wisdom: a wisdom alive enough to allow her three daughters to have, from time to time, a party.

To one of these parties – I think it may well have been a birthday party – I was invited; why, I don't quite know, but I have a strong suspicion that various hands were at work behind the scenes. I knew hardly anyone else who had been invited except the daughters of the house and the pleasant little girl who served in the shop, among the silver balls and crystallised violets, where I had bought my first chunk of writing paper for my first novel. 'I wish I could set down with certainty,' says H. G. Wells, 'all the main facts of this phase of my adolescence'; and so do I. But much of my youthful development resembles a picture that needs cleaning; dust and varnish have clouded a good deal of it; a general outline remains but much detail lies hidden or half-hidden under the yellow coating of time. But this much is certain: as with artistic and musical life, so it was with literature. I had not a soul in all the town to whom I could talk. Harry Byrom had already gone to pursue his scholastic way at King's College, London, and I saw him only between terms. I had had, it is true, a brief friendship with a schoolmistress who belonged, or felt she belonged, to a slightly upper middle-class and with her I had been able to share, for an unpassionate interval, some of my new-found enthusiasm for, among other things, Donne. Her father manufactured mineral waters. Some idea of his attitude to music – we never spoke of literature – may be gathered from the fact that he was apt to declare, as he unwillingly listened to Chopin or Schubert on the radio, that all modern pianists played with one finger. Her mother was rather precious and came, I rather think she felt, from a good family, thus suspecting that if her daughter ever married me it would be rather beneath her station. Once, when the daughter was convalescing from some illness, I went and sat and read to them, the mother being the chaperone, choosing of all authors Donne and of all poems 'I wonder by my troth what thou and I did till we loved'. I might well have wondered, since love we never did.

But the picture of that winter night of the party at the farmhouse needs little cleaning. The varnish of time has certainly obscured many of the faces that were there, but I still see clearly the big farm kitchen, the huge low-ceilinged sitting-room, the girls in their typical nineteen-twenty dresses and the piles of home-made cakes, tarts, sandwiches, jellies, cheeses and sausage rolls. I can still smell the soft milkiness of the kitchen, the whiff of frigid cow-pungent winter air as the back door was opened and the wood smoke of the farmhouse fires. As the evening went on we ate, drank – not a single thimble of alcohol of any kind, naturally – danced, played games, gossiped and flirted.

We danced, I suppose, to a gramophone. The games were simple: mostly, I think, charades. But from time to time there was much running up and down the bare ancient oak stairs, phases of hide-and-seek and the usual hilarity, accompanied by shrieking, as if seductions of some sort were taking place in the upper darkness. For my own part I remember getting tired of dancing, exchanging shallow gossip and generally running around. At last, I suppose somewhere towards midnight, I found myself sitting on the half-dark stairs with a girl I had never met before: fair-haired, blue-eyed, rather petite and barely seventeen.

I have always fancied myself to be rather quickwitted but she, it turned out, was just as quick. Though she was in fact a stranger to me I got the impression that I had in fact met her before. The truth is that I somehow mixed her up with someone else. This led to a certain confusion, further leading to light banter, in the conversation.

I asked her name.

'Marjorie,' she told me. 'But most people call me Madge.'

I told her my name.

'I know,' she said.

Soon after this, since it was only a day or two beyond Valentine's Day, I teasingly hinted that she must have received a heap of Valentines. By so doing I opened up a mystery. There was a certain special Valentine she could not account for. She didn't suppose that I could? With a growing sense of mischief I hinted that it wasn't beyond the bounds of possibility. With excitement and curiosity she begged to know who had sent it, while I, with the sense of mischief growing all the time, succeeded merely in making the mystery grow darker and darker, more and more excited. Without my ever having uttered a word to confirm it, it was clear before midnight that I was the Valentine's sender. I had in fact never sent a Valentine to a girl in my life but that night it was an unsent Valentine – unsent by me, that is – that introduced me to the affections of the girl I was eventually to marry. To this day she doesn't know the sender of that Valentine, except that she still strongly suspects me, and nor do I. The entire affair remains a classic example of the fact that if you tell the truth people rarely believe you; whereas if you tell lies, or hints of lies, they nearly always do.

We kissed in the protective darkness of the stairs, kissed again on the way home and finally on the porch of her house. Thereafter we began to meet very often and go out together. The thing that struck me at once was that she seemed far older than her years: a fact not altogether surprising since she had lost her father and several other members of the family during the war and had rather been pushed, since then, from pillar to post, having to fend for herself a good deal. Her life and mine could hardly have been more different, although we lived only a street away from each other, had played the same street games and shared a number of friends. She showed an amazed disbelief in the fact that I wanted to be a writer and a still further disbelief that, having been blessed with a little higher education, I was still unemployed. She herself had attended that same national school where my father had worked out his tricks in the late nineteenth century, a building that had changed little, if at all, in the intervening years. By a painful coincidence its headmaster at the time of her attendance was none other than Harry Byrom's uncle, a rigid disciplinarian of the old school for whom she had little respect and less affection. She was not only a girl of immense popularity in the school itself but a girl, even at that early age, of great spirit: so much so that one day during the war she had seen her brother subjected to such a blatant beating in open class that she had instantly fled from the school to home, there to collect a soldier uncle, conveniently home on leave. Fresh from the blood-stained fields of France, powerful in body, artillery spurs jangling, the soldier uncle proceeded to wage with the headmaster a battle of which the issue was, I understand, never remotely in doubt.

When I say that we met and walked out together I mean walking in the same sense as I had walked, as a boy, with my father. Indefatigably we walked and walked and walked: very often for long distances on winter nights, when the blackness of remote country roads was often so intense that I am not ashamed to say that I was frightened, and when at last we saw, with great relief, rows of green-yellow lights winking out for miles across the wide river valley. We also had bikes and on these we could go farther afield: often on Saturdays to Bedford, that rather enervating town that with its pleasant promenade by the Ouse reminds me more than a little of certain towns on the river banks of central France. In Bedford, in those days so much the haven of retired Army gentlemen who had seen service in India, Singapore and so on, there was a bookshop and a good bookshop at that. With not more than a shilling or two in my pocket I spent hour after hour in that bookshop and its fusty but well-stocked second-hand department, picking up precious items for my still small but growing library. Blessed bookshop, Hockliffe's.

But we went, also, to the remoter stretches of the Ouse, to its lovely serpentine course where the names of the villages are composed of consonants so softly ethereal that you feel you must whisper them. Here we discovered long, unpeopled, overgrown stretches of water, often of backwaters, where Monet might have painted his waterlilies. Here the big white flowers were as crowded on the water as the fish, mostly roach I fancy, that lay in shoals under the big leaning willows and poplars that shaded the back-waters on hot summer afternoons. Gigantic hemlocks brooded in the shadows like the ears of green elephants. Willowherb and meadowsweet and yellow mimulus and purple loose-strife lined the river banks. Of sounds you only heard, sometimes for hours on end, the turning, a whisper too, of poplar leaves, the plop of a rising fish, the gentle dive of a water vole, a breath of wind lightly brushing the stiff tall swords of reeds.

Armed with kettle, frying pan, eggs, bacon, sausages, bread, cheese, fruit and tea, we picknicked here over and over again, I finding wood for the fire, Madge doing the cooking. Young appetites staunched, bodies replete, we then lay in the sun, locked in long ecstatic embraces, half asleep. A voice at last of some cow-man bringing his cattle back to the meadows after milking-time would eventually remind us that the afternoon had dreamed itself away. Then we made tea again, fed the appetites of youth yet once more with cakes, buttered scones and tins of fruit. Sometimes in the business of washing up Madge would take off her shoes and stockings and dabble her feet and legs – the best legs in town, as my friends often and rightly reminded me – in some more shallow patch of water among the reeds. Presently cows and cowman were silent again and we found ourselves embalmed in a final hour or so of utter peacefulness, in an abandoned world in which an occasional kingfisher broke like a blue and copper firework from shadow to sunlight and a pair of swans with a family of following cygnets steered a course of matchless grace through the waterlilies and the long combed green hair of underwater weeds.

Nearer home, within walking distance, I had discovered a small wood where dark purple violets grew so thick on the floor that you almost felt you had to take off your shoes and stockings before you picked your way among them. They were followed later, in midsummer, by crowds of butterfly orchids: strange, cream-green stalks of a Chinese-like delicacy, a sort of floating ghostliness in

the petals and a fragrance so exquisite and strong that when we took them home indoors, the heavy exotic breath of them was more overpowering than that of lilies. A little farther afield I discovered, one late April afternoon, another wood, this time rich with primroses and that rarity of the primula family, oxlips. It was very quiet in the warm broken sunlight and suddenly I found I was not alone. In a hollow walled by exposed old tree-roots of oak and hazel I had come upon a whole family of dancing, prancing little foxes ('give us the little foxes, that eat our vines, for our vines have tender grapes' – it would seem, I am told, that the little foxes, in France and elsewhere, still eat the tender grapes), a sight so enchanting in its mischievous grace that the following day I took

Madge back to the wood to see them. To my great delight they were there again and in absolute silence we lay, half-hidden by hazel boughs, and watched them, gambolling and fooling and chasing each other in their first exercises of growing up, so that once again we were locked in a world a million miles from the stink and noise of factories, leather and machines and Monday morning fires of leather-bits in which we had both been born. I don't think, unless memory one day completely fails us through utter senility, that we shall either of us ever forget that dancing ballet of the little foxes among the sheets of primroses and oxlips; nor do I think that either of us, from that moment, ever doubted that that world of factories, leather, chapels and factory hooters was a world we somehow had to escape from.

Some time not long after this I went home with Madge to discover, strangely enough, in her mother's modest front parlour, a writer and a book both quite new to me. How Henry Lawson's *While the Billy Boils* ever found its way into that room I have not the remotest idea; but as soon as I opened the book and started casting an eye over its fifty and more stories and sketches of Australian life in the latter part of the nineteenth century I was acutely aware that here was a voice to which I had to listen. I suppose that the fact of my having been brought up in a working-class family, in a working-class town, in a working-class school and with no other friends than those among working-class people might well have given me a sense of resentment against democracy and the vernacular, at least as far as literature was concerned. On the contrary: it was the strong and vivid appeal of the vernacular in such stories as *Maggie* and *George's Mother* that had done much to attract me to Crane and which now in turn attracted me to Lawson.

Lawson's territory was mostly the Australian 'road, the bush, the track, the shearer, the "selector", the pub, the wharf, the river and the street': a world as remote from that of Henry James as the conversation pieces of the eighteenth century are from the prostitutes of Lautrec. Lawson had written most of his pieces for the famed *Sydney Bulletin*, but others had appeared in the *Sydney Worker*, *Sydney Truth*, the *Brisbane Boomerang*, and various New Zealand periodicals. He had also written poetry, but a poetry of such badness, 'of rattling humour and sentimentality', that it has been likened to 'a voice speaking to you through a bad telephone'. Lawson was not a 'literary' writer; his matter is of more importance than his manner, which is much inclined to be rough, crude and tough. He is less of a literary man than a reporter and it is worth noting that Crane had been warned, in his turn, not to mix reporting with his writing. Perhaps Lawson may best be described as a 'realist-humorist', and it is certain that *Stiffner and Jim (Thirdly Bill)* is worthy to stand among the most hilariously funny stories ever written. But note, too, the rapid sketch-like quality of the style, colloquial, pictorial, snappy, as vivid in its effect as a Phil May drawing:

> We were tramping down in Canterbury, Maoriland, at the time, swagging it – me and Bill – looking for work on the new railway line. Well, one afternoon, after a long hot tramp, we comes to Stiffner's Hotel – between Christchurch and that other place – I forget the name of it – with throats on us like sunstruck bones, and not the price of a stick of tobacco.

No poet? How often it is – take good note here of 'sunstruck bones' – that the poet finds his expression in prose. But Lawson, besides being colloquially funny ('You know one or two of these mugs. Bite one of their ears'), could also be sad. *The Union Buries its Dead* is almost offhand in its sadness but is saved from cynicism by a singular perfection of realism and truth, as in the description of the burial – 'the fall of lumps of clay on a stranger's coffin doesn't sound any different from the fall of the same things on an ordinary wooden box.' Let the shabby modern purveyors of four-letter words, many of them women, try their hands at doing better than that; if ever a sentence had a melancholy, dying fall it is that simple one of Lawson's. Yet of even greater sadness is *The Drover's Wife,* a mere sketch, not a story, of a drover's wife living a life of lacerating loneliness, 'in a landscape of the everlasting, maddening sameness of the stunted trees', as she waits for a husband to return from the long droving spell up-country: a piece that caused at least one critic to say of its significance in two short pages that 'even Tolstoy has never done better'.

But curiously enough, much though I admired and still admire Lawson, he did not influence me as Crane, Bierce and even O. Henry had done. I rate style as high as matter; and at this particular period of my life I rated style, if anything, the higher of the two. If I had not very much to say of great profundity at the age of twenty I was determined that when at last my literary voice, so to speak, was properly broken, I should at least be in some command of the manner of saying what I had to say. I wanted words to be my servants, not my masters.

XIV

I think if you had asked my grandfather what he most wanted me to be he would have said 'a Member of Parliament'. If you had put the same question to my father he would most probably have replied 'a minister of the Church'. Both, happily, were doomed to disappointment; and of the two my father's was undoubtedly the greater.

My father's position may be likened to that of a diligent and dedicated farmer who had tilled his earth industriously and sown his corn with care, only to observe coming up, in due course, a crop of tares. I was the tares.

The good sound corn that had been sown Sunday after Sunday on my dutiful trottings off to Chapel, Sunday school, Prayer Meeting and Bible class had at last brought forth exactly the opposite of the crop intended. It could not even be argued that some seed had fallen on stony ground, since the ground too had been prepared and nurtured to a condition exactly right for receiving it. In brief I suddenly and dynamically revolted. In vain my father pointed out that several of my school-friends were 'to enter the Ministry'. He may also have taken the problem of my violent recalcitrance, as H. G. Wells' mother did, to the 'Heavenly Father, who remained, as ever, speechlessly enigmatical'. I do not know; but it is to his eternal credit that he offered no show of violent or even mild remonstrance on my unforeseen backsliding; we had neither argument nor quarrel on the matter. Suddenly I no longer went to Chapel and that was that; suddenly I saw all organised religion as a bony bore, a monstrous fraud, a body of hypocrisy with no drop of living blood in its veins, no purpose in all its works. For some time there had been crystallising in my mind the proposition that prelates, politicians and actors all come out of the same eggshell of vanity and that of the three of them the prelates, steeped in humbug, are the worst. As if sent to prove for me the truth of this theory there appeared on the religious front, in the usual three-year circuit which is common practice in Methodism, a reverend gentleman of unparalleled vanity, ill-manners and such a capacity for feeble sermonising that in adolescent outrage I quarrelled with him in a revolt the violence of which I have never regretted.

I will not go so far as to say that I never went to Chapel again. I went at least once, simply in order to appease Madge, who had been brought up as a Baptist, but so far had my contempt for organised religion advanced by that time that I spent the whole duration of the sermon reading a volume of Chekhov's stories thinly disguised between the covers of a hymn-book. The sowing of that particular handful of corn did, however, bear fruit. The next morning I sat down and wrote a story called, not inappropriately, *The Idiot,* the genesis of which had started in the middle of a hymn whose every word, like those of many more, I knew and still know by heart. I had now, in fact, reached the stage my grandfather had reached so long before me. He had long been sick of 'popery, humbug and singing in nightshirts' and now I, on a parallel plane, but in a different faith, was sick too.

Some time before this my grandmother, a long and cruelly tortured sufferer from asthma, had died. My fondness for her and fear of her recurrent spasms of illness had led me to read Culpepper, whose herbal had long been treasured in the household. In the course of so doing I discovered that asthma, in company with some twenty other ailments ranging from ague to stone in the kidneys, would yield to a concoction largely compounded of the roots of elm trees, boiled. I duly boiled some. They were very little roots, having been torn up with my bare hands from suckers springing up from trees large and mature and

I boiled them for hours, to my mother's continued vexation, on the gas stove in the kitchen. The resultant fluid, when strained, was a kind of litmus pink and thickish, like bad tomato ketchup. I longed desperately to create with it, like some youthful witch-doctor, a miracle of a cure for the sufferings of my grandmother, but its efficacy as a medicine was never tested. Both in consistency and colour it grew thicker and thicker until finally, unpleasantly pungent, it was thrown away, leaving my faith in Culpepper much shaken too.

After the death of my grandmother it seemed to me that my grandfather was already a breaking, if not broken, man. We are accustomed to think of the Victorians as stuffy, tedious, strait-laced, cocooned in piety. It is my own conviction that they were by no means to be despised; they were hard-working, dedicated, inventive, even courageous. It required a brave man, I have always thought, to start out in mid-life, as my grandfather had done, to conquer with nothing but wheelbarrow, spade, fork and hoe a piece of English earth that would, in the course of time, go far towards killing him. In these days, when men not infrequently draw money for not working and when trade-unionese is the language used in talks arranged, in industrial disputes, to begin talks, it seems lunatic to a point of near-fantasy to think of a single-handed farmer toiling twenty summer hours a day with a half-broken down pony to extract a bare living from the soil and at the same time to retain a dignity, a purpose and a pride in the land.

In due course, in the late twenties, the land grew too much for him. *Thou thy worldly task has done, home art gone and taken thy wages* – the task was certainly done, the wages, in the form of a pension, were pretty meagre. Now, however, instead of struggling with plough and harrow over the intractable valley clay, while I harnessed the pony, mixed the pigswill or dropped seed-potatoes into newly opened furrows, we were able to go about on more leisurely business, gathering watercress, fishing, blackberrying, gathering herbs, such as hounds-tongue, for some ointment in which he still had undiminished faith, sometimes even making toffee. I found time to walk with him a good deal and one of my

favourite walks was down an ancient cow-trodden lane bearing the regal name of King's Meadow Lane and which led eventually to the Nene. There seems little doubt that the Romans trod this lane and perhaps grew, in a field beside it still called Vine Hills, their grapes. Tall bushes of misty-purple sloes (slons in the particular dialect of that part of the Midlands) almost met overhead; there was a great richness, in due season, of dog-roses and hawthorn, meadowsweet, kingcup and willowherb.

When we finally paused at the bridge over the river it was to look out on a valley unenriched except at hay time, when the thick deposits of silt left by winter floodwaters made every meadow a cornucopia and sometimes even led to the miracle of hay-harvest all over again in September. The Nene Valley at this point has none of the idyllic lusciousness of the Ouse but it was still not too late to see an occasional horse-drawn coal barge being drawn slowly downstream past the ruined Wharf Inn, where on the Victorian Sundays of my grandfather's youth men got roaring drunk, fought, argued and even drowned themselves. The ruin today goes further. Gravel pits of vast size scar the valley's entire width and a procession of trucks lumbers away day after day, some of them bearing some prized mystic and newly-discovered element found in the gravel, richer than all the hayfields of Edwardian days put together.

Long before this the hiring fairs, the distribution of largesse and breakfast beer and the annual invasion of the Irish had disappeared, but one great event still remained: the feast. What wakes are to the English north, so feasts are to the east English Midlands. No other day of the year, except Christmas Day, had the same rich inducements and excitements to offer as feast Sunday. On the first Sunday of July there were celebrated – and I hope still are – no less than fifty of these feasts, so that the day was called Big Feast Sunday. The dates of these feasts, rigidly fixed, are closely tied to the Church and they remind me, in several ways, of the *Pardons* of Brittany. With the celebratory day fixed by the Church there grew up, over the centuries, the usual secular accompaniments: the coconut shies, the shooting galleries, hoop-las, helter-skelters, gingerbread, darts, roundabouts and spit-rock. In Brittany, at the many *Pardons,* they sell *pommes frites,* candy floss, knick-knackery of all kinds, hideously embellished models of the Crucifixion in plastic, religious relics, balloons and all the rest of it. 'The people o' Dublin,' says Captain Boyle in O'Casey's *Juno and the Paycock,* 'think more o' Charley Chaplin and Tommy Mix than they do of S.S. Peter and Paul.' And in the same fashion it is my guess that the people of Higham Ferrers, on the second Sunday in August, cared more for the beer in the Green Dragon, the Griffin and the Chequers than they ever did for the blessed Virgin to whom their Church is dedicated.

We awaited that day – and not only children but all grownups too – with a positive fever. The affair was a rite. It was truly a business of feasting. It was an occasion for dressing-up, beer-swilling, parading the streets, family reunions, torchlight processions. I had often heard my grandfather speak of the public tumult that greeted the relief of Mafeking and I always fancied that Feast Sunday was the next best thing. We began, first of all, with an enormous midday dinner: roast fowls and stuffing, roast beef and Yorkshire pudding, plum pies, a plum pudding left over from Christmas. Not to have been present at this rite would have been the equivalent, in a Roman Catholic, to rejecting the Sacrament. The house always seemed full of strange relatives, even stranger visitors from remote villages, seen only once a year. A great succulence of roasting meat filled the air and we eventually fell to our plates like a flock of Sunday-dressed vultures, my grandfather choking over the ferocious hotness of his home-made horseradish sauce, my grandmother tucking furtive silver threepenny bits into dark wedges of Christmas pudding. Shame, I think, would have descended on any house that ever failed to provide a comparable feast. 'Have some more, Albert,' would be my grandfather's continual cry, 'Go on, man, have some more,' but my father, replete, would retreat in polite refusal. Not so a distant relative samed Sip. Fat as a sow in pig, slow of mastication, benign of countenance, hungry of eye, Sip had come to the Feast to eat his fill and, though ordinarily looking as if about to burst, did so with bland, solemn and determined justice.

The ritual of that day continued after a tea almost as large as dinner itself – masses of bread and butter, the bread brown, white and currant, scones, sponges, apricots, pineapple, jams of blackberry and plum, celery, cheese with both celery and cake – with a slow family procession to the market place. Everyone was dressed up: the women in long sweeping skirts and huge hats feathered or flowered and blouses with mutton-legged sleeves, the men in best suits and straw-hats and often with buttonholes of carnations and even of big, purple shaggy asters: so that memory tells me that it all looked, by the time we reached the thronged area of the Green Dragon and the little, chestnut-shaded market square, like something medieval, a pageant, one of those pictures one sees of Merrie England. It was here, in 1793, that the cele-brated diarist and traveller, the Hon. John Byng, later Viscount Torrington, stayed at the Green Dragon en route for the north (Breakfast 9d, Dinner 1/6, Wine 2/6, Brandy 3d) and after Sunday breakfast powdered his hair and repaired to church, where the reigning parson 'drawled the prayers and delivered a sermon . . . about the Philistines and preached to us about the Pharisees. Some poor weak singing . . . most people slept at the sermon;

I was often on the brink,' after which he crossed the Nene to Artleborough (still so called in my boyhood), and not as now, Irthlingborough, and so on to Kettering and 'cold Venison pastie; upon which and cold lamb, I supped with much relish.'

Torrington's description of the Green Dragon, at which my grandmother before her marriage had been 'in service', the superb west door of the church, 'one of the most beautiful sculptur'd porches that can be seen', the Bede House and the delicate grammar school built by Chichele, prove that in appearance the small and ancient borough had changed little since the days of the French Revolution. A vanished world? – change and decay? 'At the town's end they have, even with this week, demolish'd several upper windows, arches etc., of the old College.' With melancholy Torrington went on to complain that 'our grandfathers cared for nothing of this sort! My grandsons will have nothing to see.'

Happily Torrington's pessimism was unjustified – it was still all there for me to see much as he had himself seen it on that hot Sunday in 1793. He could not of course have seen the fair as I saw it, with the great steam traction engines of brassy power (now so assiduously collected by enthusiasts of at least that part of a vanished world) and the switch-backs crazy with gay models of the new horseless carriages. But the sight of stalls selling spit-rock (so called, as I say, because the rock-maker spat on his hands before twisting and moulding the great bronze-cream ropes of sugar), brandy snaps, gingerbread and whelks, might just as easily have come from that world of his when brandy was a mere threepence a glass and parsons droned on and on much as they do today. He might have seen too the giggling boy-and-girl exchanges of confetti, the swingboats, the fortune tellers, the wild man from Borneo, the bearded lady and the tricksters selling this and that bargain to the gaping country crowds. What he certainly couldn't have seen was the new biograph in its dark sweaty tent, the new miracle of motion pictures, and above it all the splendour of the great church spire, like an enormous inverted ice-cream cone, gleaming silver-gold in the reflection of electric light, gas flares and paraffin lamps against the blue-black August sky.

In due course we played a sort of return match at Rushden on the first Sunday after 19 September, when our feast too was celebrated, but the medieval air that still belonged to Higham Ferrers was never there. The town had no central market square; everything was more circumspect, more material, more scattered; the fair was held a mile from the church. Torrington would never have recognised the world of shoe factories and chapels, with not one parson but a dozen droning away at rival denominations

Rushden.

Sunday after Sunday. It is true that we ate as well as at my grandfather's; the ladies' hats were still as large, the buttonholes of asters and carnations still as flamboyant and ostentatious, but it was never, never quite the same. Among the pear leaves turning purest copper and gold in the garden there was also always an air of sadness. Summer was ending; and there was an old saying 'The Feast is over. Now you can shut the back door and claim (I suppose truthfully acclaim) winter.'

Winter having been claimed, there was nothing much more of excitement in Higham Ferrers, in those early days, until

Christmas, except harvest-home suppers, the inauguration of a new Mayor and the pot-cart. It says much for the character of these Edwardian autumns and winters that news of the arrival on the Market Square of a man selling from a horse-drawn wagon a load of cheap tea-services, dinner plates, washbasins and ewers and chamberpots should have spread about the town like news of the Battle of Waterloo. Even Rushden had its pot-cart, just as it now had its first semi-vaudeville, semi-cinema picture house at which Chaplin appeared both in person and on the screen. The days of the travelling penny gaff, presenting *Maria Martin* and so on, all the winter entertainment my grandfather ever knew except a rare night excursion or two to London to see Irving in Shakespeare, were long since over.

Now on winter evenings I often walked over the hill that separates the two towns and took my grandfather an ounce or two of tobacco or a few peppermints, generally known as 'stripes', and played dominoes with him in front of the fire, under the black bars of which and above the gleaming steel fender a few potatoes were generally roasting for supper. With the gaslight glowing above the red chenille tablecloth and its pattern of black and white dominoes the scene must have looked very like one of those warm bourgeois family pieces so beloved and well recorded by Vuillard and Bonnard. By the time the old American clock on the wall, with its garish picture of the town of Philadelphia, had struck nine it was time for my grandfather to light a candle and go to bed.

To this scene I was determined to introduce Madge, reasoning that if my grandfather approved and liked her all would be well. To my great delight he liked her instantly. The fact that she was, as he said, 'Higham Ferrers born-and-bred' was another point immensely in her favour; people who had been born otherwise were slightly beyond the pale. His pride and interest in the old town was in fact immense and as he learned that she too had been born a native of it he immediately wanted to know where?

'In one of those little thatched cottages under the walnut tree,' she said – a walnut tree of immense size and age, sometimes alleged to have been planted in the reign of Henry VIII, stood at the bottom of the street, close by the farm where my grandfather had regularly failed to drink his pint of breakfast beer in his boyhood – 'the second one from the top.'

'Dall it, that's the house I was born in too,' he said, greatly marvelling, and it was as if they were both, and always had been, of the same family.

I was now twenty. As 1925 came to an end I was still unemployed, still on the dole. I had now written not only novels, short stories and poems but also plays, mostly one-act plays, into one of which, *The Last Bread*, I had caustically poured some of my bitterness about the post-war twenties, not having read Knut Hamsun's *Hunger* for nothing. Of all these efforts not one had attracted a whisper of success. *The Two Sisters* was now with a tenth publisher. Not only did it seem that I had failed in my burning intentions to be a writer – a certain impatience in my character clearly led me to expect too much and too soon – but in the world of factories and chapels I still knew scarcely a soul with whom I could exchange a word on writing and literature.

Nevertheless there were certain compensations. I hadn't been to Cambridge; instead I had been to a University of my own, both as taught and teacher, undergraduate and tutor. I have been told that I learned to write much as Renoir learned to paint – *au musée*. However that may be it has always seemed to me that, left to my own resources, I discovered much about writing that no orthodox seat of learning could have taught me. Unguided, I had done a long, hard stint as undergraduate, alone. Now I was about to graduate.

A few days before Christmas, 1925, there arrived for me a letter from a firm of publishers, Jonathan Cape, lately of No. 11 Gower Street, now the home of *The Spectator*, but recently moved to more elegant premises at No. 30 Bedford Square.

In their letter they expressed their great interest in *The Two Sisters*. They liked it and wished to publish it. They also wished to meet me and wanted me, in turn, 'to meet our reader', whose name was not disclosed. They were prepared to offer me a contract for the book and the sum, in advance of royalties, of £25.

It was a fortune. I was so excited that I took little notice of the fact that I had been addressed in the letter as 'Dear Miss Bates': an enigma which needs, and will get, a solution later. All that seemed to matter, in that utterly unexpected event, was well expressed in Lawrence's words – 'Look! We have come through.'

THE BLOSSOMING
WORLD

I

On a damp, grey morning in the first week of January 1926 I boarded the 8.40 train from Wellingborough, bound for London's St Pancras. I was five months short of my 21st birthday. I had already written two novels, several one-act plays, a number of short stories, a batch of verse, almost all of it very bad, and a radio play. The occasion of that damp New Year journey imprints itself firmly on memory as one both momentous and exciting but touched, at the same time, with a certain apprehension. I was in fact on my way to meet my first publisher, Jonathan Cape, his partner and their reader, whose name I did not know, in the semi-hallowed precincts of Bloomsbury.

The great drab glass dome of London's St Pancras station, that towering château of Victorian Gothic, has often seemed to me to be very like the massive wingspread of a giant eagle brooding with smoke-blackened wings over the restless nest of platforms, trains and travellers below. It has also sometimes seemed to be, as eagles often are, both a symbol and a monument: symbol of a departed and lamented era of railway steam and a monument to an area, also departed, but utterly unlamented, of what were once some of London's most squalid and putrefying slums. The entire area of what now consists of one of London's three great railway termini serving the Midlands and the north was formerly a sink of rotting slums, thieves' kitchens, gin-houses and prostitution whose squalor and contagion were evidently a combination of the London of Fielding and Dickens at its worst. There are some who

St. Pancras Station

see in the half-ecclesiastical mass of St Pancras, with the faded splendour of its once great staircases, grill-rooms and dining-rooms, a certain nobility. But for me it has long had that monumental broodiness, an air of steamy, smoky shadow.

It was by no means my first visit to London and St Pancras. On the way southward for summer holidays I had often stopped for refreshment of some sort with my parents at the huge, smoky, steamy station. To enter the grill room in those days was like going into a palace. There was everywhere an air of opulence and grandeur, of palms and brass, of marble and mahogany. A huge black-hooded grill, its charcoal glowing scarlet, was presided over by men in white tunics and chefs' white hats. Chops, steaks, cutlets, sausages were all laid out in readiness for your selection, to be grilled to your taste. Sirloins of beef, legs of lamb, saddles of mutton reposed under the gleaming silver domes of trolleys, to be produced for the delectation of customers by conjuring carvers armed with steels and knives. The head waiters wore frock coats. The napkins and tablecloths were almost brittle with starchiness. The carpets had a deep plushiness almost royal. The feeling about everything was one of splendid amplitude. I have a haunting memory of delicious apricot tarts; another of my father casually tipping porters; still another of my father holding easy discourse with waiters not as if he had sprung from the painful poverty of a little Midland boot-and-shoe town, as in fact he had, but as if he had been moving in the elevated circles of St Pancras station restaurant and its counterparts all his life. Splendidly, almost embarrassingly at ease in this world, he guided us through lunch before at last escorting us to the fresh grandeur of a taxi that would take us across town to another station, so that we could embark on the third lap of our journey to the seaside.

And this, it must be remembered, was a railway restaurant; the great Midland Railway, in its proud maroon livery, had a similar restaurant in every station of any importance from London to Edinburgh. The traveller of those days was not to be treated like cattle. Today it is an undisputed fact that if in Switzerland you are in doubt as to where to eat, the wise course is at once to seek out the railway station, the Bahnhof Buffet; it is incontestable that you can hardly eat better than at the large Swiss station restaurants, a state of affairs just as true of France, for which the celebrated *Guide Michelin* issues a special guide for *Restaurants à la Gare*.

But on that morning in early January 1926 I had no time to linger in what were still St Pancras' opulent rooms; nor had I any money for taxis. I set off, in fact, to walk through Bloomsbury's Squares to Charing Cross Road and its bookshops. Opposite St Pancras there still stood the old grimy King's Theatre, at which, only a year or so later, you could get into a season of Shaw plays for as little, if memory serves me correctly, as a shilling a time. There were still trams in the streets and still open-top buses. London still had its wintry cloak of mist and soot through the gloom of which the naked, spotted trunks of plane-trees in the Squares stood like elephantine creatures, brooding and waiting. I stopped somewhere, I think at an ABC, and got myself a cup of coffee. The morning was raw; and it was not only the plane-trees that were brooding. There was also a greater, darker brooding, its roots social and political, in the air. The year was to be eventful, in fact, not for the publication of a certain young novelist's *The Two Sisters*, but for the General Strike, a circumstance hardly opportune for the publishing world or any other. Half the nation looked ill-dressed, lost, underfed, if not emaciated. But happily the path of youth, in my case at any rate, was single-minded; and though I had already expressed my bitterness at the cankering poverty and dole queues of the twenties in a searing one-act play, *The Last Bread*, I had really no time, that morning, to do my own brooding on social injustice and social inequality. I had to meet for the first time my publishers, Jonathan Cape, and their reader, in order to discuss a contract which was to offer me a fortune of £25 and further to discuss some few points of criticism in my MS that 'our reader' had raised.

I had a couple of hours to fill before my luncheon appointment in Bedford Square. Memory isn't always sharp over a distance of more than forty years but there is little doubt, I think, that I spent most of that morning in Charing Cross Road, with its double lane of bookshops. I was book-mad; I suffered from the chronic and ever increasing disease of reading. I could scarcely have read more at a university than I did on my own account; moreover my particular syllabus was my own. That morning therefore I was again searching for my own chosen idols, Turgenev, Chekhov, Maupassant, Crane, Donne and various others, and with an almost total lack of success that by now had become a commonplace. Charing Cross Road, dingy, seedy, depressed both architecturally and in atmosphere, has always seemed to me to be the oddest place to have become, whether by accident or design, the Mecca of bookshops. It also wears a slight air of shame: accounted for perhaps by the fact that it stands on the very door-step of the notorious Seven Dials, through which even as late as the years immediately before the First World War it was hardly safe for the respectably dressed citizen to walk with

Jonathan Cape
30 Bedford
Square

impunity, and further by the fact that, in 1926 at any rate, almost every other shop was an emporium for contraceptives, together with pills and potions for the promotion of male vigour, other restoratives, probably of the same concoction, for the restitution and rejuvenation of lost potency and immoral books of dubious authorship calculated similarly to stimulate or restore the sexual appetite by means of words. It was also notorious for that particular sort of shop which is always 'Closing Down Stock Must be Cleared Regardless of Cost. Great Sacrifice': the sacrifice always being made, of course, by the meek lamb who, licking the steam off the window, falls at last for the 22-carat gold, 50-jewelled watch at twenty-five shillings that is displayed before his very eyes in the window. It is a trap I myself know only too well, having fallen into it headlong, not on that January morning, but on a summer afternoon that same year, when I at last decided to plunge for a window-bargain 22-carat gold, 50-jewelled wrist-watch at twenty-two shillings and ended up in the clutches of two Jewish gentlemen whose gripping attentions reminded me of the words of the hymnal 'Oh! Love that will not let me go', except that they eventually did let me go, short of a fiver and the possessor of a gun-metal watch that had probably been stolen anyway.

Such was the innocence of the young man who finally found his way to that most beautiful of London's Squares, part of the vast inheritance of the Bedfordshire dukedom: the elegant, plane-tree shrouded, Adam-built Bedford Square. At No. 30 I was greeted by a young receptionist who appeared to be scarcely less than a goddess – a singularly distinguishing feature of the Cape regime of the twenties and thirties was the remarkable propensity on the part of Jonathan Cape himself for filling his offices with marvellously attractive young ladies, some of whom I adored and all of whom had to be remarkably quick-footed in the presence of the master – who seemed to be more than slightly taken aback by the arrival of an author looking not much more than a schoolboy.

I was duly taken, by the young goddess, up the magnificent Adam staircase to Cape's own equally splendid Adam room on the first floor. I fancy Jonathan was also no little surprised at my own extreme youthfulness. As I have already indicated in Vol. 1 of this work my sex, as the author of *The Two Sisters*, a novel of young female love, had been the subject of some argument and discussion among Cape, his partner Wren Howard, who presently joined us, and 'our reader', whom I was yet to meet. The ultimate majority opinion among them had been that I was a girl: a decision resulting in my being addressed, by letter, as 'Miss Bates'. This trifling mistake I had put right by confessing to being a 'mere male', which still didn't prevent both Cape and Wren Howard from peering at me rather as if I *ought* to have been a girl, firmly masculine though I was.

Cape was tallish and dark, Wren Howard spruce, military-like and fair. Cape had laid the ground-work of his publishing career as a traveller in, I think, the firm of Duckworth. Wren Howard was a specialist, and a very good one, indeed in some ways revolutionary, in typography. Both were shrewd. I will not give offence to their memory by saying that they were also mean; let it merely be said that they were not notable for a glowing generosity. That they seemed almost royally generous to me on that drab January morning does not alter the point. When you first rapturously kiss a beautiful girl you do not pause to wonder if she has holes in her stockings or has forgotten to change her knickers overnight. Similarly I was not disposed to be concerned, that morning, with the parsimonious nature, or otherwise, of publishers. That they were publishers, and were about to be my publishers, was enough. I should add here to the credit side of both men that they had succeeded, in the space of a mere five or six years, in producing the best-looking books in the entire London publishing world, an achievement for which undoubtedly the flair and taste of Wren Howard were in large degree responsible. Their books were a delight to the eye and a joy to handle. What was more, the distinguished wrappers held behind them a collection of authors, many of them American, of parallel distinction: Louis Bromfield, Sherwood Anderson, Dorothy Canfield, Hemingway, Eugene O'Neill, Sinclair Lewis, Manuel Komroff, Kay Boyle and Sarah Orne Jewett on the American

L'Etoile
Charlotte Street

side; A. E. Coppard, Liam O'Flaherty, Pauline Smith, Martin Armstrong, Laurence Housman, Doughty and others of much distinction on the English. It was a matter of extreme and intense pride to me to join such a company, representing as it did a scintillating segment of the golden age of the twenties and thirties, an age beside which all too many of the productions of the fifties and sixties look like the cast-offs of a flea-bitten ragbag.

After we had been joined by a young man from the editorial department, Gilchrist Thompson, we all went off to lunch in order to meet 'our reader', as to whose identity I had still no clue. On the way to Charlotte Street, a mere five minutes or so away, I walked with Cape, who among other things asked if I had read Eugene O'Neill and when I replied that I hadn't at once promised to send me copies of the American's plays, a promise duly kept, thus introducing me to an author whom another American once called 'our greatest playwright – unfortunately'.

In Charlotte Street we reached the Etoile, a restaurant long celebrated not only for its cuisine but as a meeting place for literary men, and happily carrying on in the same tradition today. My few excursions into the station restaurant at St Pancras constituted almost my entire experience of the world of eating in London and I was in consequence no little overwhelmed by the Etoile's continental menu and atmosphere. I felt nervous and out of my depth. I was confused by the offerings on the menu and eventually got out of the problem of what to order by ordering what everyone else did, namely minestrone and escalope de veau and spaghetti. Even then I was so utterly uncertain of myself and everything else that when the offering of parmesan cheese was finally made I had no idea whatever as to what it was for and had to be shown, like a child, by Gilchrist Thompson.

It was somewhere about the time of my innocent struggle with the parmesan that there walked into the restaurant an arresting and extraordinary figure. I have already described this moment and this figure in terms* on which I do not think I can possibly improve and I now therefore quote myself:

Edward Garnett: a Memoir by H. E. Bates (Parrish 1950) out of print.

There came into the restaurant a semi-patriarchal, semi-diabolical figure in a floppy cloak-like overcoat, a grey scarf wound round his neck like a python, and a preposterously small felt hat. He had grey hair, grey jowl-like cheeks that quivered ponderously like the gills of an ancient turkey, and he appeared to have lost himself completely. He appeared also to be an extraordinarily clumsy person; he was something over six feet tall and big-boned in proportion, but he was in fact extraordinarily agile (as I shall show later) for so large a man. His thick-lensed glasses gave him an appearance that was in that moment, and remained for me for a long time afterwards, quite frightening. He staggered about for some moments like a great bear unable to recall the steps of a dance he had just begun, and then hung up his coat, hat, scarf and walking stick on the hat stand. He then smoothed his hair with his hands, gave several painful snorts of breath through his mouth as if the whole procedure had winded him completely, and advanced towards us.

I stood up, hypnotised and terrified by this enormous and grizzly figure, and as I shook hands there was in the air a faint smell of herbal cigarettes and a weird glint of myopic eyes.

'Mr Edward Garnett,' someone said and I could have fainted.

Just as it is characteristic of youth that youth's immaturities are rarely self-evident, so youth is inclined to see as old, or even ancient, anyone over fifty. If Edward Garnett were alive today he would be exactly one hundred. When I met him on that first devastating occasion in Charlotte Street he would therefore have been only fifty-eight, or five years younger than I am as I write these words. Yet such was the gap between fifty-eight and twenty that the words 'patriarchal', 'grizzly' and 'ancient turkey' seem, even in far retrospect, to be accurate and just descriptions. They are not of course exactly so, but this was the eye of youth observing, and this is the man youth saw: a man apparently so absent and unworldly and clumsy that as he sat down at the restaurant he immediately performed the sort of act so characteristic of him. Stretching out his hand for the parmesan cheese he let the sleeve of his jacket fall into the minestrone: without, of course, having the faintest notion that he had done so. Rather in the same way he brought his gaze to bear on Cape, Wren Howard, Gilchrist Thompson and myself as if slightly bewildered by the fact that we were there at all.

If Garnett had been dressed in city morning coat, pinstripe trousers, bowler hat, grey necktie and pearl tiepin his effect on me that January day would have been no less impressive than it was. If Cape had previously informed me that I was going to meet as 'our reader' John Galsworthy, Desmond MacCarthy, Gerald Gould, A. E. Housman or Hilaire Belloc I should have been suitably impressed but by no means awed, still less bowled over. I had read them all; some I viewed with respect, some with admiration. But my meeting with Edward Garnett may well be likened to that of a cub-reporter of an earlier generation finding himself in the presence, for the first time, of Dickens or Hardy.

Garnett had already been, though he did not know it, one of many formative influences on me. I had read and eagerly digested his prefaces to his wife's, Constance Garnett's, translations of Turgenev; and together the prefaces and translations had made on me an immense and guiding impression. Today, as I turn back to them and similarly to Garnett's critical assessments of Chekhov, D. H. Lawrence, Stephen Crane, Sarah Orne Jewett, Henry Lawson, Sherwood Anderson, Robert Frost and many others I find no reason for doubting either their rightness or perspicacity. Garnett, if I had been asked to make a literary choice, would have been the man I most wanted to meet in a generation when literary figures were by no means small.

Of the general pattern of conversation at lunch that January day I now remember little. It is the impressions of conversation after lunch, when Cape and his partners had returned to Bedford Square and I was left alone with Garnett, the coffee and the herbal cigarettes, that remain indelible to this day. This conversation consisted mostly of catechisms on Garnett's part and answers, some eager, some diffident, on my own. How had *The Two Sisters* come to be written? Was it autobiographical? Or a work totally of imagination? Had I written anything else? If so, what else? Stories, poems, plays? What, above all, did I read?

I believe it was Garnett's turn to be astonished when I let out a list of my gods: Chekhov, Turgenev, Tolstoy, Ibsen, Maupassant, Crane, Conrad, Gorki, Bierce, Flaubert. Conrad alone, perhaps, produced no astonishment in him, since he had already rightly detected his influence on *The Two Sisters'* every page. But his astonishment at the rest was enough to cause him to inquire what university I had been to? Since, like me, he had been to no university himself but had, again like me, provided and pursued his own literary syllabus, my reply of 'None' delighted him as much as the list of my gods. Now and then, as I gave my answers to his many catechisms, the oyster-like myopic eyes rolled, the herbal cigarette ash dropped all over the waistcoated bosom, and the red, loose, pouting lips let forth a juicy and approving 'Yes, yes.' He had also much approval, with some reservations, for *The*

Two Sisters. It was remarkably perceptive, most poetic; an achievement, for a young man, of no mean kind. The influence of Conrad was, of course, clearly discernible, though not necessarily obtrusive, as he afterwards confessed. But would *they* understand it? That was the point. There was the rub. Would *they* recognise the quality of so youthful yet perceptive a work? He was clearly highly dubious of their wit to do so and was generously insistent, throughout the rest of the meal, that he write a preface to it in order to guide them from the dark errors of their ways.

They were the critics; the philistines. It is hard to say whether Garnett had a lower opinion of the average literary critic of his day or of the general public; but on balance I would settle for the critics. 'They don't *know*, you see, Bates, they don't *know*.' Indeed they didn't know; nor, of the greater part of them, can it be said that they know today. The tendency to behave like a wasp, irately stinging everyone in sight; the propensity to bumble useless as a bee; the illusion that speculation is criticism; the pretension to self-glorification; the manifest use of clichés and jargon while condemning them in others; the sheer love of wounding for wounding's sake, so evident in literature ever since its Edinburgh inception inspired Byron to the wrath of *English Bards and Scots Reviewers*: all these are as much part of the contemporary literary snob-pit as they were of Garnett's day. 'They don't *know*, you see, Bates, they don't *know*,' was Garnett's often repeated, scornful, mournful truth, to which he might well have added that of Ibsen, who perhaps of all nineteenth century writers suffered more than any other from the obtuse 'slings and arrows of out-rageous fortune' and sheer purblind bigotry: 'there has never yet been a memorial to a critic'. Indeed there never has.

So we talked that day until nearly four o'clock; until we were the only persons, except for the last few tired waiters, left in the restaurant; until at last Garnett, hitherto oblivious of the fact that our presence was becoming something of an embarrassment, became aware of the situation and decided we must go. Outside, in Charlotte Street, I have described my progress with him as being rather like that of 'a spaniel puppy without a collar trotting by a shaggy and lumbering sheepdog whose wind was not very good and whose eyes were not what they had been'; and I see no reason to alter the description today. As we came to say goodbye, somewhere near Bedford Square, he shook my hand affectionately and made me reiterate my promise to send him every manuscript I had written, stories, plays or poems, as soon as possible, and this I declared I would do. One of his gods that I hadn't mentioned, and who had so far escaped me, was W. H. Hudson. He promised in turn to send me Hudson's little masterpiece of a story *El Ombú*, adding his fervent praise of the new offering. It was characteristic of him that he left it in a restaurant the following day.

My response to Garnett's request for MSS must have been extraordinarily prompt and his own reaction to them hardly less so. It was in fact only 4 January when in the characteristically generous and unselfish way that marked his entire approach to creative as opposed to destructive criticism he was already writing his first letter to me, praising some of the stories I had sent him, lightly rejecting others. It was also characteristic of him that he could be practical too:

> I am sending *Once* to Mr Middleton Murry and hope that he will take it for *The Adelphi*. It is beautifully rendered, the woman's absorption in the baby and the man's absorption in both, and the Bank Holiday travel – all is beautifully felt.
>
> *Encore* is almost as good . . . If you could cut the sketch down to say 12 pages and send it to me again, I think we might try *The Criterion* or some other magazine.
>
> The poem 'Clamour' I am sending to *The Nation* and I only hope that this editor will think as highly of it as I do. But people are often insensitive to the genuine thing.
>
> *The Flame* shows that you have mastered this form of the short sketch. It is beautifully felt and written. You must do others in this style – terse, with not a word thrown away. I will send it somewhere.
>
> *The Unbelievers* is a very good idea and has some excellent

passages . . . but it is 'romantic' or romanticised. Later on you can rewrite it, but not now.

Possession is also unreal . . . *Defeat* is very well written but here again the atmosphere and accessories are too romantic . . . *The Lady Poverty* has charm but there is a 'stock' element in it . . . It's not up to your level.

And so on, characteristically: criticism both creative and constructive, sound advice, practical advice; already a pursuit, on behalf of myself and my stories, of celebrated editors.

The response of some of these was also prompt. Within a few days Leonard Woolf had accepted *The Flame* for *The Nation*; presently he was sending me books to review. Small wonder that I was carried away by elation: an elation rather tempered by the fact that I had neglected to tell Garnett that I had already entered *The Flame* for a short story competition run by Robert Lynd for the *Daily News*, never really dreaming that it would gain a prize. It didn't in fact gain a prize but was accepted for publication almost on the very day that Leonard Woolf gave it his blessing; a state of affairs that had to be rapidly adjusted in favour of *The Nation*.

It is scarcely surprising that after the momentous experience of meeting Garnett in London I returned to my native Northamptonshire, its boot factories, its rigid nonconformity and its harsh, barren red brick, in a mood of rarefied elation which the news from Leonard Woolf and Middleton Murry rarefied still further; nor was it surprising, since I was still so very young, that this elation should also have been tinged with a certain pride which, though some considerable distance from actual conceit, may well have been misconstrued as aloofness. Indeed I was, and felt, aloof.

It might well be truer to say that I felt very alone, though not lonely. I had no one, with the exception of an old school-friend, Harry Byrom, now at King's College London and whom I rarely saw except during vacations, and my old English master, Edmund

Kirby, with whom to share my newfound exultations. I did not speak of my writing much, if at all, to my parents. Even Madge, whom I was eventually to marry, seemed to cast some doubt on the truth of the fact that I was about to publish a book; but then she too was very young and could at that time claim no acquaintance with the world of authors and authorship, a defect that the ensuing years were to do much to remedy.

My life, in fact, divided itself into two parts: the one in which I played football, went with Madge to dances and cinemas, was mildly social and so on; the other in which I retired for hours at a time like a brooding young hermit to the little boxroom my parents had now given me as a study and from which I escaped for occasional relaxation for long solitary walks into the countryside, there to brood also, hardly seeing a soul with whom to pass the time of day, almost my only company the stark black elms so characteristic of that scarcely inspiring Midland winter landscape. That I was not lonely in doing all this and that I can still endure hours of being alone without any hint of being beset or oppressed by loneliness may well be due to the fact that, in the summer of 1911, in that glorious year that has been called the *Annus Mirabilis*, when I was six, I fell victim to a stroke of physical ill-fortune.

On a beautiful hot Saturday afternoon in July that year I was taken to a garden party. Again I am sure that it was, pictorially at any rate, a cross somewhere between a painting by Renoir and some pages out of *A la Recherche du Temps Perdu*: gay sunshades, mutton-leg sleeves, sweeping skirts, straw boaters, bright blazers, the ribboned hair of little girls; scarlet geraniums, blue lobelia and yellow calceolarias, that most hideous of Edwardian horticultural clashes, in the flower beds; gloxinias of purple and wine-red trumpeting behind the glass of conservatories; and then madeira cake and doughnuts and raspberries and cream for tea. On the raspberries and cream I gorged so piggishly that I was warned over and over again that I should pay for it. And pay for it I did.

Next morning, Sunday, I woke to find myself generously covered with bright raspberry-red spots. I also felt singularly unwell. This, I was told, was the clear result of my unheeding

Saturday sins; the raspberries were leaving their mark on me. The joke, however, was short-lived. Presently my head was aching; then it was no longer a head but the piston of a steam engine, wildly bumping; soon I was in a half-trance, partly light-headed, only vaguely aware of mundane events, the victim of a strange feeling of groping intoxication, a fearful impression of floating helplessly away.

The doctor arrived to diagnose scarlet fever: not surprisingly, since the town was being swept by an epidemic and a girl in the next street had already died. I do not recall any anxiety of any kind about my dying also, but only of being put to bed in an enormous brass four-poster, from which I eventually emerged to a sentence, (unheard of in these present days) of eight weeks' solitary imprisonment. It is wholly for this reason that the summer of 1911, the *Annus Mirabilis*, remains so indelibly imprinted on my memory. I saw its great beauty only from the windows of my bedroom. Not that I was utterly solitary. School-friends came to play street games with me under the window; I blew bubbles from a clay pipe and watched the diaphanous balloons float away over the roofs of the boot factories in the crystalline summer air; and in the evenings my father came and sat with me and puffed, for the one and only time in his life, at cigarettes of a particularly nasty brand in the fond belief that the resulting smoke wouldkill germs, a belief fully in accordance with another notion prevalent about the turn of the century, namely that smells and odours obnoxious would inevitably result in complaints that were 'catching'.

Scarlet fever is not among the most aesthetic of diseases; nor, any longer, is it a killing one in the way that it was fifty years, and even less, ago. But I duly went through the unpicturesque process of 'peeling' and survived. And it was during all this that I learned, I think, to be alone and above all not to mind being alone. This, perhaps, is one of the compensations of illness: that the enforced detachment of it acts as a sort of balm. Another is that illness tends to magnify trivialities, so that little things, a soap-bubble floating over roofs in the sunshine, voices in the street, the finger tendrils of a Virginia creeper grasping the raw red brick of a wall, become things of fascination and importance. I used to watch, all that summer, the way the Virginia creeper grew: up and along the walls and out of sight along the next door houses and the walls of the boot factory and slowly, like tiny fingers drawing an invisible body up from drowning somewhere at the foot of the wall, over the windowsill. In that way I am perfectly sure I first learned, and even liked, to be alone. It is perhaps also from this cause that some part of my temperament was shaped, so that my present doctor tells me that I am the most philosophical patient he has ever known.

Thus was I able easily to adjust myself to the solitude of the little boxroom that I converted into a study, furnishing it with an old Victorian armchair, a table, a bureau and presently a few bookshelves. Like a contemplative snail I retired, sometimes from eight o'clock in the morning to eight at night, into my self-constructed shell. In a town built round a single industry the day's hard timetable is inexorably fixed. At half past seven every morning the factory hooters and whistles wailed, preceded for some minutes before by the sound of workers' running feet and then followed by the clatter of odd stragglers through the sudden silence that meant they had 'missed a quarter'. At precisely the same hour you heard the factory engines start up, bang, chuff-pause-chuff, pause, bang, chuff-chuff-chuff and so into steady rhythm. Thereafter a great silence spread over the town's grey slate roofs and with it a curious sense of guilt: a feeling that *you* too ought to have been working, a prisoner until half past twelve behind factory bars. At that hour the factory hooters and whistles wailed again; wild streams of workers, many still struggling into jackets, disgorged from factory doors like released prisoners, running and cycling in all directions as if at the start of a mad marathon. At half past one the hooters and whistles wailed again; the silence and the accompanying sense of guilt spread and brooded once more over the town, not to be broken until a quarter past five.

I should add to this 'if all went well'. But in the mid-twenties all was not well. The slump lay on the country, and most severely on one-trade towns such as Rushden, like a dark disease. Dole queues were long; three-on three-off was almost a blessing when compared with long weeks of shutdown, sometimes bankruptcy. The quick wartime fortunes were everywhere dissipating; under the demoralising blight of short time, vain hope and utter idleness, war veterans wandered lamely from house to house pushing or carrying baskets of shoelaces, polishes, brushes, cheap underwear, buttons, dusters, safety pins. An occasional gypsy knocked on the door, clothes' basket full of pegs, household bits and pieces crudely made, sometimes with some cure-all mysteriously concocted ('It'll put you right, dearie, it will in no time. Any old rags to spare, dearie? Something you don't want, dearie, eh? It'll put you right, dearie, I'll tell you. You're lucky, dearie. You're lucky. You've got a lucky face, dearie. I can see that. God bless you. A lucky face.') My mother, like my grandfather, never refused gypsies. Whether they got to know her as a soft touch I never knew but they used to come back, year in, year out, with the old moaning, droning, pleading back-door whine, the sure cure-all for everything, the well-acted eternal promise, the eternal 'God-bless-you-dearie,' for eternal good luck.

But it needed more than gypsy-wished good luck to see a worker through the barren ways of the mid-twenties and perhaps for this reason I counted my own good luck, precariously secluded though I was in my self-made snailshell, as godsent, yet another example of the hand of the 'Divinity that shapes our ends'. I could surely be forgiven if I felt that I was lucky. An advance of twenty-five pounds on my first novel, five guineas for a story, three guineas for another, two guineas for a review: riches, luck indeed. In addition to all this the BBC had accepted for broadcasting a one-act play *Loyalties*, for which I got the staggering sum of ten guineas. I had also sent my angry-young-man broadside, *The Last Bread*, to the Labour Publishing Company, run by E. N. and Monica Ewer, and that too had been accepted, though without advance, and was presently to be published at a shilling, thus becoming my first published book, preceding *The Two Sisters* by a month or two.

Presently, also at the instigation of Edward Garnett, I was

sending stories to the *Manchester Guardian*, whose perceptive literary editor Allan Monkhouse ran a back-page short story of about 1000 words every day of the week in that then great newspaper; and to the *New Statesman* and the *Bermondsey Book*, the latter one part of a project, the *Bermondsey Centre*, designed to give some sort of hope to a particularly blighted corner of a blighted world. Whether it was the godsend to the poor of Bermondsey that it was intended to be I never quite knew, but the *Manchester Guardian* was a godsend, and in more ways than one, to me. To write a short story of 1000 words may appear to be as easy, on the face of it, as one of those tricks with three or four matches that are sometimes presented to you, but that, in practice, turn out to be vastly more demanding. The task of pruning down a story to Monkhouse's desired length was an exercise both admirable and exhausting. It took me, lesson by lesson, through the exacting art of making one word do the work of two, and even sometimes of three or four. So great was my devotion to that particular lesson in fact that I was presently able, in one instance at any rate, to become master instead of pupil.

Among the few writing friends I had at that time were a group of local newspaper reporters who used to meet, mid-mornings, at an old Temperance Hotel-cum-café for coffee: a decaying, fusty, shabby haunt complete with bubbling hot water geysers, marble-topped tables, aspidistras, a general odour of stale tea and cabbage and an air of half-sanctified lassitude not so very far removed from my childhood Sunday schools. Here I sometimes used to join the reporters for a morning half an hour or so. I was induced to see in one of them, a rather podgy, groping fellow, a picture of myself as I might have been if I hadn't mercifully sacked myself at a tender age from the squalid local office of the *Northampton Chronicle*: not so much a man as a cypher, not so much a writer as a shabby collector of shabby facts for a shabby weekly, a scribbler for ever in pursuit of shattering events at bazaars, garden parties, fêtes, council meetings, funerals, weddings, police courts. While I continued to thank God I had so early made an escape from that kind of life sentence I felt an increasing pity for my older, podgy, slaving friend. He too was striving to write short stories, but with a total, dismal, stultifying lack of success. When it began to appear that I had contributed, so young, to *The Nation,* the *New Statesman, The Adelphi* and the *Manchester Guardian* he was moved, one morning, to ask if I would read what he diffidently called 'one of his efforts'.

It was a sprawling, fleshy, verbose thing, stuffed with clichés, of some 1700 words. I read through it, over coffee, on the marble-topped table. The eye already guided by Garnett and made keener by the demands of Monkhouse then proceeded to take its podgy author through it, word by word, performing surgery on sentence after sentence as with a scalpel. I think, as he saw his many precious words mercilessly cut like diseased tissue and thrown out, he was near to despair; I even suspected he might well have thought I was merely showing off. But when the operation was at last over he seemed to revive a little under my assurance that the whole piece now had both air and shape and might be printable. 'Send it to Monkhouse,' I advised, 'at the *Manchester Guardian,*' which he duly did: to enter, a week later, for the first time, the joyous realms of acceptance.

If this incident and the various successful experiences that led up to it prompt the conclusion that my life was now all roses and honey let me at once dispel it. The elation of first success is not for ever. But of one thing I was positively, stubbornly, un-remittingly certain: I was never going to be, ever, come hell or high water, anything but a writer. I would never, God being my helper, take another job. But youth, as George Moore has pointed out, 'goes forth singing', and no doubt I was, as he has also said, 'lapped in the evanescent haze of the edge of the wood, the enchantment of a May morning'. As to how deep the wood would be or that the May morning would surely lose its first innocence and evanescence I did not bother to think. I did not pause to examine the questions that I was about to take up a profession that offered no certainty of employment or reward; no steady office hours, no fixed salary, no promotion, no holidays with pay; that can promise no pension, no superannuation scheme or redundancy pay, as they are now fancifully called; that provides no trade union for the protection or promotion of those employed; that accepts criticism, though often libellous, mischievous and capable of injuring the livelihood of the criticised, as 'fair' and 'in the public interest'; a curious world in which a writer's reputation, however great or profitable, cannot be sold as 'a going concern', with 'goodwill', in the open market, as a business manufacturing soap powders or soda water can be; where authors' copyrights pass into the public domain 'at 10% thirty years after an author's death and wholly, for free, after fifty years'; where one copy of an author's books can be read a hundred, two hundred, five hundred times at a so-called 'free' public library, while the author himself draws the royalty, somewhere perhaps between a shilling and half-a-crown, for the sale of only one copy; a profession mostly if not wholly unorganised, with no 'pressure groups' to pursue its interests in high places; and where, well within living memory, it was the practice for publishers to give 'a baker's dozen' for all copies sold, thus depriving the author of his due royalties on one dozen of every gross of his sales.

No; I never once thought of these things. Blindly and happily youthful, I simply went forth singing.

II

The subsequent publication of *The Two Sisters* (which after forty-five years is still in print) inspired in me no sense of elation. My guess is that for the most part artists, whether writers, painters, sculptors or musicians, feel only a sense of cold detachment from their work once it has, so to speak, passed from the privacy of their possession into the public domain. This may express itself further in sheer embarrassment, even revulsion; in the most self-critical it may well emerge as hatred. I myself, though not expressly hating *The Two Sisters*, was simply aware to a highly painful degree of its many faults; I could scarcely bring myself to open its pages, beautifully printed as they were in the celebrated Cape image, still less to read it. I do not now recall that I even bought another copy to add to the traditional half dozen free ones that an author receives; perhaps I did; I recall only a sort of guilty embarrassment compulsive enough to make me want to forget my first curious and not altogether coherent exercise in fiction.

As if to confirm my own doubts and guilt the first review was a bad one. Several subsequent ones were no better. A few others were of such abysmal stupidity that they even had the effect of goading me, paradoxically, to a wrathful defence of something I well knew not to be very good. What is one to say of a critic who amazingly compared the book to *The Young Visitors*? What to the conjecture that the novel was strongly influenced by Henry James, a writer I had never even read and whom to this very day I cannot read? Not one single critic, in fact, made an even remotely accurate estimate of who and what were the sources of the book's inspiration; none was perceptive enough to recognise what Garnett had spotted as simply as a swallow spots a fly on the wing: namely that the main and indeed only influence was Conrad, at whose feet, along with those of Chekhov, Tolstoy, Turgenev, Maupassant and Crane, I had long been religiously worshipping. So strong and obvious was the influence of Conrad that I had in fact, at Garnett's insistent suggestion, toned it down, even then still leaving evidence enough to show even the blindest fool that I had drunk deeply at the well of the author of *Lord Jim*.

What Garnett had also spotted was something that has been supremely well expressed by Alan Hodge in an excellent note to a translation of Maupassant's *A Woman's Life*: 'Often there is a fine bloom about a first novel which its writer never quite achieves again, however more expert he becomes in technique, or more nearly universal in his sympathies.' Not only was this patently true to Garnett, who had intuitively perceived the talent that lay behind the book's many imperfections. He also warned, in his preface to the novel, of the difficulties, struggles and even disasters that for the young author, still only twenty, might well lie ahead. 'The path of art, endlessly difficult,' he warningly wrote and the words so imprinted and seared themselves into my young brain that I have not only never forgotten them; I have never lost sight of the chilling profundity of their truth. Nor, after nearly fifty years of writing, has the path become even minutely less difficult than Garnett's prediction warned it would be. Art knows no easy passage; its course is for ever through troubled, uncharted and all too often perilous waters.

During that troubled spring and early summer of 1926 I saw Garnett many times: sometimes at his favourite restaurant, The Commercio, in Frith Street, where a few years earlier it had been his weekly custom to forgather with other writers, among them W. H. Hudson, greatest of our nature writers but still, at that time, a figure I hadn't really discovered; occasionally at Bedford Square; sometimes at the old 51 Restaurant in St Martin's Lane, heart of the theatre-land I longed, but longed in vain, to conquer;

but most often at No. 19 Pond Place, Garnett's flat, at which he puffed, coughed over his herbal cigarettes, spilt ash over his un-done fly-buttons as he half-lay, half-sat on a *chaise longue*, like some mischievous, irate, slightly forbidding potentate of letters, verbally bashing the heads of critics and public alike, his constant text being 'They don't *know*, Bates, you see, they don't *know*.' Once, I remember, he took me to a Russian restaurant, where we ate *borscht*; once to meet Desmond MacCarthy, who didn't turn up; once or twice to the theatre. Always he was alternately for-bidding or charming; serious or diabolically jocular; soothing or critically keen as a fresh-sharpened sword. Always his god was literature, his temple art, his altar that of good taste.

I met him also at the Cearne, the stone cottage which a disciple of William Morris had built for the Garnetts, in medieval style, on a beautiful pine-clothed slope of the North Downs. My first visit there was on a warm late May afternoon when the air was richly aromatic with the scent of pines and when the entire Weald of Kent, where my own home was eventually to be, lay spread out below the hills to a seemingly infinite distance, like some miraculous landscape by Constable. That so superlative a day should have been, for me, one of apprehension is explained by the fact that, having already met in Edward a puffy, forbidding, asthmatical bear, I greatly feared that I might be about to meet a comparable she-bear in Constance, on whose many translations of Chekhov, Tolstoy, Turgenev and Gogol I had already fed with great avidity and much fervent admiration. I felt not at all unlike a penniless youth trying to screw up courage enough to ask a fearsome father for the hand of a rich, distinguished and clever girl in marriage.

I needn't have worried. Constance Garnett was certainly not rich, except in brains and charm. Anyone less like a she-bear it was impossible to imagine. When I first saw her, frail, white-haired, short-sighted, she was feeding chickens on the edge of the pine-wood, in a little orchard, that lay behind the Garnett house. Instantly she reminded me of my great-grandmother, whose sister, physically, she might well have been. It also struck me that she might well have spent all her life in busy pursuit of homely, country tasks such as that of feeding chickens, gathering eggs, weeding flower-beds, sowing carrots and things of that sort. She looked totally unlike the brilliant woman who, after a girlhood spent in a household darkened by an atmosphere almost Brontë-esque, had won for herself a three-year scholarship at Newnham College, Cambridge, and this at a time when universities, like clubs, were virtually male preserves and when the conventions of female behaviour in public were of such strictness that her father warned her on the day of her departure for college never to be seen in a hansom cab, an act which would instantly have condemned her as being disgracefully fast, if not plain wicked.

At Cambridge she at once showed a brilliant aptitude for languages, in particular Greek. (It was from her, indeed, that I learned much of the correct pronunciation of classical plant names, so that to this day I constantly shudder when I hear gardeners pronounce them in a way that would have filled her own classical brain with horror.) Painfully shy, awkward and becoming progressively more and more short-sighted, she nevertheless won for herself the great distinction of eventually being bracketed top in the Classical Tripos, equivalent in those days to a first class honours degree. This enabled her immediately to earn her own living and presently led to her meeting the young Edward, whose chief virtue at that time appears to have been hanging about bookshops and bookstalls, a pursuit that he may well have thought might do something to compensate for the fact that though his father, Richard Garnett, was Keeper of Printed Books at the British Museum, Edward had had, unlike Constance, little of what could be called conventional education.

Edward was in fact virulently anti-convention, anti-academic, anti-government. His son David has explained this 'repudiation of the respectable academic approach' as being in part a reaction to the atmosphere and ways of the British Museum and it may well be that this same dislike of the conventions had some part in attracting him to the brilliant young girl from Cambridge, who, though she may not have ridden in hansom cabs, had by now become unconventional enough herself to belong to the Fabian Society, attend Socialist meetings and make friendships with Russian revolutionary exiles and such firebrands as Bernard Shaw. Not only did Shaw, in fact, ask her to marry him but it was a favourite story of Constance's that more than once, as she walked home with him after some Fabian gathering, she would forcibly and eloquently propound Socialist theories of her own, only to see them, a few days later, appear as an original article in some weekly periodical, the author of course being Shaw.

Happily the marriage never came off, Shaw explaining in typical fashion that he couldn't afford it and that a marriage of improvidence would have ruined his career as a writer: a remark of such typically Shavian charm that many a woman less nice than Constance would have promptly punched him on the nose. Instead she married the improvident and unconventional Edward, who was by now working as reader for the publishing firm of Fisher Unwin, where his uncanny perception in search of new talent was already earning him both reputation and success. The marriage in due course produced an only son, David, who has recounted how his mother, 'in the enforced idleness of pregnancy' brought her brilliant brain to the study of Russian, which she learnt with such singular speed that she almost immediately began to translate Turgenev, the first of whose novels she published in 1896, four years later. As if this were not feat enough Constance then further proceeded to demonstrate her own disregard of the conventions by announcing her intention of visiting Russia, alone. The fact that her child was only two years old must have seemed, to the conventional eye, to make a crazy proposition crazier still. It must further have been labelled even more lunatic by the fact that she proposed to carry with her, in ten-pound notes, a largish sum of money which had been collected in England for famine relief in Russia, where that year the grain harvest had failed. A further and yet more dangerous hazard in this extraordinary trip by this frail young mother was that she was not only carrying with her a large sum of money in cash but also letters and proposals for the arrangement of channels of communication between Russians exiled in England and secret revolutionary organisations in Russia.

Not only did I know nothing of all this as I had my first meeting with the little woman feeding her chickens on that soft, warm May afternoon; I would never have believed it at that moment if anyone had told me. It would have been rather like being told that Little Lord Fauntleroy had habitually killed lions in the Colosseum in Rome. There was no hint in the frail and gentle woman of sixty-five as she presently led me into her garden gay with scarlet poppies, columbines, pinks, lupins, pansies and aubrietia, of any immense physical courage, revolutionary or otherwise. I had been prepared for a she-bear and in a totally unexpected way I had been, in a sense, confronted with one, though I didn't know it then and the she-bear looked infinitely more like a shepherdess of sheep. That all this was a youthful misconception on my part scarcely matters now; what does matter is that all my fears and apprehensions as to that first weekend were instantly blown away like dandelion seed on a warm May wind. Though there was a difference of no less than forty-four years in our ages I immediately felt that I had known Constance Garnett all my life and that she was, warm, gentle and a passionate lover of flowers and the countryside, my sort of person. A great bond of affection between us was wrought that afternoon and for my part it has never broken.

The two main strands in that bond were flowers and the Russian classics. I had inherited my passion for flowers from both my father and my maternal grandfather and the sudden emergence of my green fingers at the Cearne prompted in Constance much delight and the eventual remark that at last a successor to D. H. Lawrence had arrived, an author with real feeling and love for flowers. Constance had made her garden on a difficult hillside, on intractable sandstone, by sheer hard labour, lugging rocks into place for flower beds and wheeling down from the woodlands above huge quantities of leaf mould. She was never, or scarcely ever, to be seen standing up as she gardened. So wretchedly poor was her eyesight that she was always kneeling, spectacles a mere inch or two from the ground as her hands groped to distinguish gentians from weeds or seedlings from cuttings and so on. My enduring impression of her is one in which she is always in that prayerful position, brown bloomers exposed, thick spectacle lenses glinting, her frail hands fingering the soil half blindly, as if trying, not very successfully, to piece together some extraordinarily complex jigsaw puzzle.

I suppose I went to the Cearne some scores of times after that first visit, almost always taking with me seeds or seedlings or cuttings from my father's garden and always plunging with youthful energy and enthusiasm into helping Constance in her garden tasks, weeding, digging potatoes, gathering peas and raspberries, slaughtering the dying rubbish of autumn flower beds. The abiding impression of all those days is one of constant joy and light. The days when Conrad, Hudson, Stephen Crane, W. H. Davies, Galsworthy and all manner of other celebrities of the turn of the century had been constant visitors there had long passed, and of Edward's new discoveries, Sean O'Faolain, H. A. Manhood, Geraint Goodwin, Liam O'Flaherty, Malachi Whitaker and many others, none ever came as visitors to the Cearne while I was there. But young visitors of some kind there always were and it may well have been a deliberate scheme on

Constance's part to invite them, since all of them in recollection seem to have been girls, purely for my companionship. I recall a pleasant niece of Edward's and a Swedish girl of great glamour, a veritable goddess, with whom I confessed to falling in love, though doing nothing more positive about it than worship her from the other side of long rows of raspberry canes.

If the constant impression of those days at the Cearne is one of continual joy and light it must be said that this had little or nothing to do with creature comforts. It was a characteristic of the Garnetts, as David Garnett himself has justly pointed out, that they viewed worldly comfort with much suspicion and worldly success with something approaching scorn. The latter, in my experience, seems to be an almost exclusively English trait, more especially where art and literature are concerned. It really isn't quite nice, in certain English eyes, to make money out of writing and painting; it really isn't done; the right thing is to wait patiently for Parnassus; you really can't have your rewards up there and enjoy them down here on earth too. So it was that Edward, after the initial elation of some new discovery of his had worn off and the discovered one himself had found success – a success that all too often Edward had predicted with the fiercest pessimism the obtuse British public would never have the perception to allow – frequently abandoned the protégés he had so brilliantly spotted and had so unselfishly and tirelessly fought to see established. Of these Galsworthy was, I suppose, the clearest and most notable example. The prodigious success of *The Forsyte Saga* (I speak now of its literary success and not of its still vaster success on television) caused Edward's back to be turned on what was probably the most eminent of his discoveries and drew from him the remark that Galsworthy would 'always see life from the windows of a club'.

So if the atmosphere at the Cearne was not precisely spartan it was certainly not luxurious. There was no electric light; all cooking and lighting was done by oil; the privy was in the yard. (I am supported in this recollection of a certain spartan air at the Cearne by an occurrence that took place some few years later, when Edward paid his first visit to my wife and me after our marriage and, on going to bed, immediately ripped off the sheets and, much to my wife's annoyance, proceeded to sleep in the blankets.) At meals we ate simply but not frugally. If Edward was present for the weekend we invariably had wine, though he could never afford the best. If it was Edward who, in his typical fashion, frequently teased dear Constance about what he called 'her Scots caution' it was he who mixed water with the sherry (making, in fact, a very pleasant drink) and often retired with a hunk of plain bread to eat with a final glass of wine as he read in bed and far into the night.

If Constance and I shared a passionate interest in gardens we shared an equally ardent one in literature. Her range in that direction was vast, her taste never less than impeccable: so that if Constance was sometimes moved to praise a story of mine I was not merely greatly flattered; I always, unhesitatingly, took it as gospel. And though her eyesight, always poor, had pitifully deteriorated, her mind had most certainly not, evidence of which was always there in the long, fertile and perpetually rewarding and amusing discussions we had on books and in the literary parlour games we often played in the lamplight after supper. In one of these Edward would read out various passages from various authors, leaving us to guess who had written what; and in this, since I had long since made a deliberate study of style for, so to speak, style's sake, I was often fairly good; but when it came to making as many words as possible out of, for example, the word 'conscientiousness' it became, as far as Constance and the rest of us were concerned, a case of a thoroughbred running against a gang of donkeys. In the space of minutes Constance's prodigiously quick brain, so long trained in languages, would produce shoals of words, sometimes well over a hundred, while the dunces about her were struggling with mere dozens.

We also shared views on other matters, notably on what we both deemed to be the decline in poetry. Fervent lover of the Elizabethans as I was and still am, it seemed to me that much modern poetry could be likened to turnip wine; and in this view

I had in Constance, a woman nearly fifty years my senior, an ardent supporter. She, in fact, confessed to having given up reading it altogether, in despair, while I, in turn, also in despair, had given up all thought of ever writing verse again. This disillusionment of hers as to the use, or misuse, of language seemed to me to have a parallel with another: that of a certain disenchantment with the socialism she had once so bravely championed and for which she had, for all her frailty, risked so much. I may be wrong in this; but she had, of course, been brought up with, and had made friends with, some of the foremost intellects of her day. Though beautifully human and sweet, she had nevertheless been almost fearsomely well educated, so that she could hold her own in any company and could, as she had demonstrated, take even a man like Shaw for a ride. It was perhaps not surprising therefore that when, in the late twenties, the voice of socialism started to express itself through men like Bevin and J. H. Thomas, she found herself listening to it with some of that same despair with which she listened to the abrasive rattle of modern verse. In this theory of mine – and something in me seems to testify that it isn't wholly a theory – I am supported in a recollection of sitting with her one evening at the Cearne, by the radio, listening to a speech by a leading Socialist. The voice was what I can only call a cloth-cap voice, but to her, who had been brought up politically with the élite and had 'heard great argument' it must have seemed like the voice of some bumbling ignoramus who could neither use nor respect our English tongue. Her few words of total disgust were surpassed only by the pitying scorn that suddenly lightened up her failing eyes.

III

It is scarcely surprising that these new and exciting contacts, through the Garnetts and others, should presently have induced in me a stronger and stronger dissatisfaction with my redbrick, chapel-ridden, factory-ridden, provincial scene. I became increasingly aware, that summer, of a great restlessness.

Back in my Northamptonshire valley there were not, as I have explained, more than half a dozen people with whom I could talk of writers and writing, music and literature. Whenever I came back from the Cearne or from London I was aware of entering some totally negative wasteland. The people of my native Rushden, warm-hearted though so many of them are, will not perhaps thank me for this; and perhaps if I, like Robert Herrick the Elizabethan poet, had visited the town in the early seventeenth century as a guest of Sir Lewis Pemberton, squire of the Hall in which I later set *Love for Lydia*, I might have been able to express myself differently. But this was 1926, not 1626; and this is how a young man on the exciting but bewildering threshold of a career that was presently to give him rather more pain than joy felt in that otherwise not very golden year: the year that was presently to lead to that other long dark shabby wasteland, the Great Depression.

Of the half dozen people to whom I could talk of literature and companion things two were younger than I; one twenty years older. All came from working class families. Sam Smith, the older man, unlike Constance Garnett, was virtually self-educated, though later, as a shoehand in his forties, he was offered a scholarship to Cambridge, an opportunity he declined. A small, virile, athletic man, not entirely uninterested in the arts of boxing and ladies, as well as pubs and literature, he had been a soldier in the First World War: rifleman, stretcher-bearer, foot-slogging it out in a very different wasteland. We too found common ground in books, countryside, flowers and even boxing. H. N. Ginns and A. G. R. Britten were two other good examples of the truth that not all the best brains come from the richest families. Harry Ginns' father was a blacksmith whose forge stood opposite the church, where in fact it had probably stood since Herrick had turned into Sir Lewis Pemberton's parkland domain only fifty yards away. A brilliant boy, he rose in time to be Deputy Chief Engineer at the Ministry of Transport. Arthur Britten did equally well by becoming headmaster of one of the largest comprehensive schools in the south of England.

These were my closest companions, though hardly ever by day. By day I frequently stuffed a sandwich and a book of poems into my pocket and did my own foot-slogging far out into the countryside, pausing to stare at pike lying in the shadow of river bridges, lying in woods and gazing in solitude at the broken blue of sky above the branches of oak and hazel, gathering mushrooms, dozing on grassy banks in the sun, sometimes scarcely seeing another soul, just occasionally passing in some remote lane a girl on a horse, she aloof, I too shy even to bid her good-day. On these excursions I grappled with wild thoughts for stories, built for myself great towering steeples of ambition, wrestled with my growing restlessness and was lonely.

I was prompted at last to seek help from Edward Garnett, begging him to do something or other to help me escape from a solitude now made worse by the fact that Madge, for a reason never coherently explained, had suddenly decided that she wanted no more of the impetuous, impatient and sometimes imperious young author who had courted her so passionately along the rich banks and woodlands of the lovely Bedford Ouse. Deeply hurt, even lacerated, I snatched at the chance Edward found for me with his typical kindness and promptitude: that of a job with Bumpus, the Oxford Street booksellers then housed in the old Marylebone Court House and presided over by that king of booksellers, John Wilson, who had already shown his own kindness and help by pushing *The Two Sisters* whenever and wherever he could. Nobody could sell books as John Wilson did and quite what he thought of me, dreamy, unpunctual, impractical, indolent and more or less useless in his busy territory I never really knew at the time. Perhaps it wasn't wholly bad, since we were afterwards good friends for many years.

Presently I found digs at thirty shillings a week with two old ladies somewhere off the Bayswater Road and John Wilson put me into the Children's Department of the celebrated bookshop in Oxford Street. The old ladies fussed over me with drinks of hot lemon at night as cures for the colds that continually assailed me that autumn and in the bookshop I slightly assuaged my conscience by writing for John Wilson a little children's book, *The Seekers*, which he promptly published and which is today something of a collector's rarity. But my loneliness persisted and in an effort to assuage that too I sought out the prettiest girl in the shop, a beautiful, well-built goddess, and asked her out to dinner. To my infinite chagrin she refused and I think we never spoke again. But many years later, such are the inexplicable ways of woman, she wrote and asked me if I remembered the incident, amazingly adding, as if to rub salt into an old wound long forgotten, that she had never read a single book of mine, leaving me to ponder, also amazingly, as to why on earth she had written in the first place.

Before long, however, I made three friends, two young men whose names I have now forgotten and a shyly nervous, sensitive, bespectacled girl some few years older than myself. These three

cajoled me into going to Promenade Concerts while I in turn shocked them by expressing a savage hatred of the brassy vulgarities of the Wagner they loved. We forgot our musical differences in a mutual love of Keats and Shelley and the girl gave me Keats' letters to read. We ate cheap lunches at tiny tea shops and I was hardly ever free of indigestion.

Soon the girl was presenting me with other books and more and more and more we were going out together. Margaret was the daughter of an architect who lived in one of the many pleasant squares of Bloomsbury and sometimes she took me home to dinner. The impermanence of our friendship was solely and entirely my fault and I regret the wounds it caused; but Margaret is nevertheless important in my life for the reason that it was she who held the key to another door beyond her own and which in turn gave access to yet another and in turn to that blossoming world of which I am now writing.

That this friendship was on my part purely and utterly platonic there can be no shadow of doubt whatever; that it was something totally different on her side, though I did not in my selfish stupidity grasp it for some long time, is equally certain. I believe that she loved me deeply and suffered, as a consequence, much and in silence. But I in turn had no love either to declare or to offer and it would have been then, as now, an hypocrisy to pretend that it was otherwise. When a man is friendly with a girl who never makes his heart beat the very minutest fraction faster there can be no question of his having love to give, however great the love may be on the other side. Margaret, shy and sensitive, was too proud, perhaps too genteel, to declare her love and not subtle enough, or gifted enough with what are sometimes called feminine wiles, to express it in other ways. Her continual gifts to me of beautiful and expensive books, typical as they were of her nature, were simply not enough; nor was her deeply enthusiastic praise of my writing. When she did at last bring her femininity to bear on the problem, I suspect in desperation, it was to invite me out into the country for a Sunday picnic. Its effect on my emotions may be likened to applying a match to an iceberg; all afternoon I never once experienced the very remotest desire to kiss her. I would even go further and say, cruel though it may sound, that if she had suddenly stripped off every shred of clothing and offered me her pale naked body I should not only have refused. I believe I should have walked away in silence and embarrassment.

On my part, therefore, I was merely content that we should be, as is often said, just good friends; and this, for me, is how it was. But Margaret's importance to my life lies in the fact that without her brief intervention it might well have taken a totally different and perhaps less fruitful course. One day I received a warm and glowing letter of praise for *The Two Sisters* from a lady whose name then meant nothing to me but was soon to mean a very great deal. Violet Dean, sister-in-law of Basil Dean, the celebrated theatrical producer, was herself a writer and came from the family of Longman, the publishers. She was also Margaret's cousin.

It was from this new friendship that the full pattern of *The Blossoming World* will presently be seen to emerge. Violet Dean was a remarkable woman who was never happier than when solving, or trying to solve, the unhappy problems of others. If a man should have been confronted with the painful problem that his wife was about to commit certain suicide he had only to find Vie, who would undoubtedly have sorted out the whole matter in no time. She was not only ever willing to unravel the problems and tragedies of others; she unselfishly revelled in doing so. Paradoxically, as so often happens with people of her kind, she had problems of her own that she found insoluble. Sometimes, indeed, I shrewdly suspect that she may not have wanted to solve them: that she was in fact one of those people for whom trouble is, if not an actual source of satisfaction, certainly one of excitement. These are the people who, having no trouble on hand, speedily set out to make some. If they fail in making some they swiftly seek to find it in others.

Thus Margaret was the key to Violet Dean, who in turn was the key to another new friend: one of the most beautiful women I have ever met.

She too, with her ravishing beauty and great talent, caused my world to open its petals in a remarkable way.

IV

Violet Dean not only moved much in the world of literature and the theatre but in that of music too; she was a woman of no little influence in spheres still far removed from mine. She, like Margaret, had read and praised *The Two Sisters*. Now she began, in her typical fashion, to impart her enthusiasm to others.

The result of this was that presently I received, on deep grey notepaper and in a handwriting both exciting and excitable, another ecstatic song of praise for a book in which, on its publication, I had virtually lost all faith and affection. The writer in this case wrote that 'your book is, for me, like a dark red rose'. This lovely sentence was flattering enough in itself but when I read on and found that the writer had read the novel at the instigation of Violet Dean I knew that the fates had been once more working hard for me.

I suppose that when she wrote that first letter to me – the first of very many as it turned out – Harriet Cohen was almost at the height of her fame as a pianist. She was certainly at the height of her dark, distinguished, Russian-like beauty. After I had replied to her letter, imparting in it my own delight that so celebrated a musician had found my book to be a thing of beauty, she wrote back immediately, inviting me to lunch. That lunch, like her letter, was the first of many.

When I duly turned up at her flat in Bryanston Square I found her to be a woman of ravishing loveliness. Like many Jewish women she radiated a strong sexual warmth, so that merely to be in her presence was to feel under the influence of someone disturbingly sensual. But the fact that she also had brains together with a great single-minded dedication to her art made her attractive on two planes. I will not go so far as to say that I instantly fell in love with her; it was more truthfully an affair, on my part, of utter adoration. Nor, for all the passion with which she returned my subsequent kisses, was there any question of her being in love with me. It is true to say that she was irresistibly and compulsively attractive, full of a strong sexual feeling that nevertheless always stopped just short of that complete and blind abandonment which must come of true love. The best expression I can find for her is that she was a seductive tease. Even this is in no sense a full description of her. She recurs constantly in memory as rather like the dark red rose to which she had likened my novel. The deep sensual perfume attracted you with the ravishment to the heart of the flower; then, as you prepared to drink of it to the full, the petals either dropped or were snatched away.

It was never possible to resist this strong physical attraction. Indeed from the very first she encouraged it. On only my second visit to lunch she met me at the door of her flat, walked side by side with me upstairs, paused half way up to kiss me and then with slow deliberation took one of my hands and drew it to her exquisite breasts. This appeared surely to be an invitation to love but in fact was not, either then or afterwards. Not that I worshipped from afar – and worship it most certainly was; on the contrary we were constantly in the embrace of rapturous intimacy without ever reaching the ultimate moment of making love. That this was an experience both lovely and enduring is proved by the fact that we remained deeply fond of each other for another forty years, until that very last moment when I stood in the crypt of St Paul's Cathedral, where so many great figures from the arts have been given their last requiem, heard the choir sing with great beauty some of the Bach she loved and found myself unable to suppress the tears of thankfulness that welled up in my heart in sorrowful gratitude for the part of her life she had given me when I was very young.

That part of her life was, in my twenty-first year, another great key in mine. My acquaintance with music and the world of music was really ludicrously slight. She, on the other hand, besides being world-famous, knew almost all the great composers, conductors and artists of the day, and soon she was seeing to it that I met many of them too. She took me to the old Queen's Hall so that I could meet Vaughan Williams, Arnold Bax and Frank Bridge. She took me to Broadcasting House and let me sit by her piano while she did a broadcast, the only other person there being her equally charming sister, who turned the pages of her music for her. Always eager in musical experiment, she played for me, and sometimes gave me records of, composers of whom I had never heard. Thus I first heard de Falla and Sibelius. With rapidity, thanks almost entirely to Harriet (always Tanya to her friends, since she did indeed look strongly and beautifully Russian) my musical horizon widened. In due course it was embracing Mahler, Bruckner, Poulenc, Ravel, Debussy and a host of others, so much so that to this day, though I cannot read a note of music, I still sit down frequently and briefly at the piano and improvise for myself ten minutes or so of some *eine kleine Nachtmusik* after the manner – and very much after the manner I must confess – of one of those composers she first championed and introduced to me.

She was also vastly interested in literature – indeed she was an intelligent writer herself – so that my horizon also widened in that direction. She too, like Constance Garnett, knew Shaw; she knew Arnold Bennett and Somerset Maugham; her mind was keen and it helped to sharpen mine. Some of her many friends were rich and it was one of these who, one afternoon at tea, heard that my Nonesuch Press Bible, one of the many expensive presents Margaret had given me, lacked the volume containing the Apocrypha, and promptly sent me a copy the very next day. To these friends, rich or otherwise, musical or literary, she also imparted her enthusiasm for my work, especially my short stories, so that the little reputation I had already acquired began to be enlarged too. With Violet Dean also industriously singing my praises (it was somewhere about this time that Margaret's mother worriedly inquired of Vie whether or not I was trifling with her daughter's affections?) I began to be better known and more talked about in circles which, only a few months before, I had never remotely dreamed of entering.

If all this creates the impression that I had now become a literary personality, a social figure, lionised and feted and sophisticated, let me at once dispel it. I had by now returned to Rushden, to my self-made shell, and was working on the long novel which Edward, much as he too admired the sketches and short stories I was constantly producing, had been for some time strongly urging me to write. 'The outlook,' he had already reminded me, 'is pretty bad for literature and literary men. It's a luxury trade and the printers' strike is going to mess things up for the publishers badly, not to speak of the fact that the public isn't going to buy books in unsettled times.' The production of a long ambitious novel was therefore, he also pointed out, of very great importance to me; and I now prepared myself for the long hard slog on a 150,000 word affair that was to be called *The Voyagers*, a task that was to occupy me for almost a year.

All through that long and exhausting task I still roamed the countryside, much of it half-decaying under the growing shadow of depression, alone; played football and cricket in their seasons; danced a lot; flirted a great deal; had many more lunches with Harriet, revelling always in their passionate and sometimes enchantingly musical aftermaths; and often went to see my grandfather, to help with the threshing on cold gusty autumn days or to play dominoes with him by the fireside on dark winter nights to the sound of the old American clock ticking away on the wall and the fragrance of potatoes baking on the hearth.

The times were indeed far from propitious for literature and literary men and the immediate struggle ahead wasn't merely to be hard; it became a sort of literary penal servitude. I scarcely ever had more than ten pounds in my bank account and once I was so flat broke that I had to borrow exactly that sum from Edward, a debt I repaid in less than a couple of weeks, greatly I think to his astonishment. How indeed I got through that year financially I shall never know. I was too proud to borrow from my parents and still too dedicated to my iron resolution never to be anything but a writer and therefore never to take a job. To these financial hardships there was, however, added something far worse. As the portentous pages of the novel grew and grew (and sometimes I worked eight or ten hours a day on it, ending in utter exhaustion) there also grew in my heart the souring, torturing suspicion that the book was bad. It was in fact to turn out to be something infinitely worse: an utter, absolute disaster.

It is now to this disaster, since it was probably the most precious but important turning point in my entire career, that I must turn; but before I do so it is necessary to say something of another Garnett – namely David, whose place in my writing life was to become as influential, and as much touched with affection, as that of his father and mother.

I had so far been more than fortunate in the friends who had influenced me in literature, the last four of them women, the last three of them leading, as if by some mysterious design, from one to the other. I was now to be further blessed.

I am often told, and I think it correct, that I have a singularly good memory; but every memory has its blanks and lapses and I am not now sure quite when David Garnett first wrote to me from his home, Hilton Hall, in the neighbouring county of Huntingdonshire. Here I must also confess to another lapse, though not one of memory. For some inexplicable reason I had never then heard of David Garnett, though I had been reading his mother's translations and his father's criticism for some considerable time. For all my excursions in literature I had somehow missed David's famed *Lady into Fox*, which had collected both the Hawthornden Prize and the James Tait Black Memorial Prize.

This is now, however, a minor point compared with the gigantic effect on me of the simple word Hall. In Northampton-shire especially, but also in other counties, the word Hall really means something. One instantly thinks of huge houses such as that splendid half-ruin Kirby Hall, or Haddon Hall and great houses of that style and standard. When therefore I was invited to go to spend a weekend at Hilton Hall I was at once put into what is nowadays called no end of a tizz. Two subsequent visits to Windsor Castle failed to scare me half as much.

Many questions vexed me. First what kind of wardrobe should I take? Would my two very ordinary suits be good enough? Should I go out and buy or hire a dinner jacket? I had chilling visions of grand tables adorned with silver; of valets, even butlers. When Edward had first invited me to the Cearne he had been good enough to allay any such fears by pointing out that he and Constance lived very simply and that 'we are quite without fuss'. This David unfortunately neglected to do, thus leaving in my head the discomforting notion that the word Hall couldn't be anything but synonymous with grandeur.

This highly uneasy illusion grew larger and larger as the day of the visit drew nearer and nearer the following Spring. Though I didn't buy myself a dinner jacket for the simple reason that I couldn't afford one I nevertheless spent two days pressing my suits until the trousers were knife-edged and about the same amount of time on my shoes, until they shone like new-fallen chestnuts. The only new thing I did buy was a suitcase, comforting myself in doing so that at least its outward appearance would satisfy Mr Garnett's butler and valet, even if the contents didn't.

When my mother's front doorbell finally rang on a warm May afternoon I had been waiting in readiness for Mr Garnett of Hilton Hall for more than an hour, growing more and more nervous, even half-hoping he wouldn't come. Finally, in deep trepidation, I went to the door to meet him and there had one of the great shocks of my young life.

On the threshold stood a man of large stature, immensely untidy if not even shabby, shod in great heavy shoes and dressed in clothes that might have been handed down from some mid-Victorian navvy or farm labourer. There can be little doubt that David will be much amused if and when he reads these words but I beg to assure him that the occasion, for me, was very far from being funny. For a few wild moments I even thought that Mr Garnett, unable for some reason to come himself, had sent one of his many gardeners to fetch me. But somehow I managed to murmur 'Mr Garnett?' and when he answered 'Yes' asked if he wouldn't come in and perhaps stay for a cup of tea? He declined, murmuring that he had to pick up his wife, who was shopping in the town. I duly went to fetch my brand new shining suitcase, which now looked disconcertingly grand, and we then got into Mr Garnett's very small car, which in its own shabbiness made the suitcase look more ludicrously and painfully aristocratic still.

There then began one of the most extraordinary journeys of my life. After we had picked up Mrs Garnett, a small, shy, dark-haired woman, we started the thirty-five mile drive from Rushden to Hilton, not far from St Ives. In my beloved Higham Ferrers I pointed out the beauty of the little square, with its charming little town hall that is also a court house and which looks today almost exactly as it did then; I also pointed out the magnificent twelfth century church; I think I may also have mentioned that the town was at one time to have been a university town, its associate body being All Souls, Oxford; and I added one or two other passing notes on the little borough of which I was devotedly proud and where my grandfather and mother had been born and where I myself had spent some of the happiest, sovereign days of my childhood. I think I most probably also have mentioned that the town, and more especially the church, formed the setting of *The Two Sisters*.

To all this I got no word of reply, no single syllable of comment. At first I put this down to the fact that the car was an open one and that I was sitting in the dicky, which made the passage of conversation a little difficult anyway. But as mile after mile went past with scarcely a word falling from the lips of the Garnetts I grew more and more profoundly wretched. What had I done? Why, if they wouldn't speak to me, had I been invited in the first place? Was I not of their elevated Hilton Hall standard? Not grand enough? Miserably puzzled, I thought of Constance, charming, full of animated and amusing conversation and laughter, and then of Edward, to whom I could and so often did talk, with ease and profit, for hours. I fell to pondering on what among my deficiencies could be the one that had forged this iron forbidding barrier of silence. Perhaps I was after all a pitifully bad writer, not up to the standard of the author of *Lady into Fox*? Perhaps I had merely been invited in a gesture of duty, out of deference, as it were, to Constance and Edward? To all of these questions I got no reply except one from deep inside myself: a ghastly, growing sense of homesickness. I wished profoundly that I had never heard of Mr Garnett and that I were back home, playing cricket or roaming the fields among the darling buds of May.

The explanation of this strange, almost wholly silent journey through the charming little town of Kimbolton, then St Neots and then on into the almost soporific pastoral countryside of Huntingdonshire, where surely grow the most splendid, most royal cowslips in all England, rich and golden as the sun of heaven itself, lay in fact in Mrs Garnett, Ray. This small – and as I discovered later, charming, talented and intelligent woman, was the victim of a shyness so vast and stultifying that it amounted almost – and I think this is by no means an exaggeration – to a disease. And it was eventually Constance, who herself had to suffer the same long, painful disconcerting penalties of silence as I, who at last explained it all to me. It would appear that Ray's father, if not actually tyrannical, had belonged to that race of parents whose household gospel is based on the ruthless text that children should be seen and not heard. Unless my supposedly good memory now serves me very badly Constance even went so far as to say that in that particular household it was actually forbidden the children even to speak, or indeed to make any kind of noise, in the presence of the father. Thus Ray had been cursed, from childhood onwards, with that cruel affliction of enforced dumbness, the terrible, wickedly engendered shyness that so be-wildered, mystified and pained me on that May afternoon more than forty years ago.

As a result of all this, since people who marry and live together tend very often to become more and more like each other, David seemed to have contracted the disease of silence and shyness too. Scarcely credible as it may now seem I too presently fell victim to the same infection. I too began to feel that to speak at all was something wrong. This in turn induced in me a gnawing, unnatural shyness that engendered in turn miseries of uneasiness and still further homesickness. I longed for Monday to come, so that I could go back home.

There was, however, one comforting feature of the visit that awaited me. Hilton Hall was not grand. It did not, in fact, measure up at all to the standard that the word Hall denotes in my native Northamptonshire. Instead it turned out to be a pleasant red brick house, a sort of Lord of the Manor farmhouse, perhaps of a date slightly earlier than Queen Anne, standing in a garden both pleasant and unpretentious. It was rambling, untidyish and friendly. David, who had for some time been in partnership with Francis Birrell as a bookseller, had acquired for himself in consequence an excellent and handsome library which he housed in a biggish room, its elm floor bare and uneven, upstairs. And it was that room, friendly with its many books, that first started to dispel the discomforting disease of shyness I had so suddenly and unexpectedly contracted. Soon I was torn between liking Hilton Hall and its garden, and then wanting to flee from it. It would be foolish to pretend that I was ever at ease or quite myself that weekend but my miseries slowly dispersed as May suddenly gave all the best of its incomparable self: so that from all the bewilderments and discomforts there still stand out a few indelible lyrical moments, among them the cowslips, then my planting a lime tree in the garden, and then the three of us, Ray, David and myself, standing by a hedge of hawthorn and listening to a band of nightingales singing their hearts out at the height of noon. That at least was a moment when human speech, for once, was unnecessary.

One of the consequences of pain very often comes in elation. And it is perhaps the strangest thing of that strange weekend that I went home elated. The conviction that the Garnetts after all didn't dislike me (David and I have remained firm and affectionate friends ever since) was coupled with a new mood in me that was both uplifting and creative.

It is not too much to say that I felt a new bloom to have spread over my life. Alas, in my stupefying folly, I was to proceed to destroy it.

The long, grinding stint of *The Voyagers* ended in early August or perhaps late July, 1927. Utterly exhausted, I snatched at the chance of a short holiday in Germany, my first trip abroad, like a fainting man snatching at a brandy.

That holiday had really come about as a result of a supper, some time before, at Edward's flat in Pond Place. The only other guest was the Irish writer Liam O'Flaherty, author of the celebrated *The Informer*, and whose wonderful short stories of Irish life both Edward and I so greatly admired. Supper being over, Edward suddenly produced his last Will and Testament and begged that O'Flaherty and I should witness it, as we duly did. Rising at last to go, I was checked by O'Flaherty, who asked if I had come across a bookseller named Law, who kept a bookshop somewhere in the region of Red Lion Square. I replied that I hadn't. 'Remarkable feller,' said O'Flaherty in his rich, winning Irish accent. 'A rare boyo of a character. German. You must drop in on him. I'll write you his address. Tell him I sent you.'

When at last I got time to go along to the bookshop in Red Lion Street I found it to be little more than a cubicle, about 12 feet by 8, its walls lined with books, paintings and drawings from ceiling to floor. Its owner, whom I had thought to be Law, turned out to be Lahr, a German who had run away from his native village near the pleasant little Rhineland spa of Kreuznach, where some of the most expensive hocks in all Germany are produced, before the First World War. Charley Lahr, with his slightly eccentric habits, one of which is going about practically bare-footed at all seasons, has been a familiar figure in London's book world for more than fifty years. Of slightly more than average height he was, when I first met him, possessed of a singular, almost maniacal energy which enabled him to cycle, run or walk about London in a passionate and tireless search for books. His devotion to literature and writers, and indeed to painters, was phenomenal; and his shop, never capable seemingly of holding more than six people, always seemed to be populated by a couple of dozen, with more chatting and lounging away in the passage outside.

They were men and women from all walks of life: poets, novelists, artists, solicitors, schoolmasters, business men, book collectors in search of first editions or autographed copies, journalists and editors. It would take far too long to name even a fraction of the persons of small or considerable eminence who forgathered there; but among artists there was Pearl Binder, now Lady Jones, wife of a recent Attorney-General, and William Roberts; and among writers Rhys Davies, O'Flaherty, T. F. Powys, Nancy Cunard, Rupert Croft Cooke, Malachi Whitaker and a host of others. Together with an uncanny gift for nosing out first editions and rarities in the Farringdon Road, on market stalls and back alleys, Charley always seemed to have on hand, in some garret or other, a tame old printer ever ready to earn a few pounds by printing pamphlets, tracts, odd poems, small magazines and smaller books, including those limited editions which were then the craze of the book world. In pursuit of this sideline he would cajole young and scarcely known writers such as myself to produce stories for slim volumes or magazines, poems for Christmas cards or somebody's wedding and all manner of bits and pieces, often of a rude or revolutionary nature, for pamphlets. For a time he co-operated with an editor in the production of a magazine called *New Coterie*, for which Roberts and others provided pictures and a not at all undistinguished band of writers provided prose and verse. Copies of *New Coterie*, besides being pretty rare today, provide an illuminating guide to what was going on among up-and-coming writers in the late twenties. For such books as I and others did for him Charley offered no contracts; all was haphazard, if not indeed plain mad; and when we were paid, as we always were, it was in cash, in unexpected dribs and drabs, to which Charley would often add some handsome book or two as a bonus. I cannot speak for others; but for myself those dribs and drabs were welcome manna indeed.

Not that I was ever far from being nearly flat broke; and it was solely for this reason that when Charley first suggested I join him and some others to go on holiday in Germany in August 1927 that I had to refuse; I simply hadn't the cash. Charley instantly countered this by saying that he would pay the fares if I could somehow conjure up enough for food and hotels, adding further that if I couldn't do even that I could borrow from him and pay at some unspecified date later. It was all madly and delightfully vague but nevertheless an opportunity too good to miss. The rest of our companions were to be Rhys Davies, William Roberts, his brother and a book collector, a lawyer as I now recall it, whose name I have forgotten. Quite where our final destination was to be God only knew.

Accordingly we set off one warm August night to catch the night ferry from Gravesend to Rotterdam, arriving in Holland early next morning. The subsequent breakfast and a breakneck tour of the city set the pattern of all that was to follow later. I felt as if caught up in some half-real, crazy maelstrom. From Rotterdam we rushed like a gang of dotty refugees fleeing from some unnamed wrath to Amsterdam. There I had a mere hour or so in which to decide that I liked the city very much before we were again on the train, belting it into Germany. Cologne, Mannheim, Mainz, Coblenz, Bingen, the Rhine and the Lorelei passed in a lunatic flash. I had just time to decide that I liked the Spa of Kreuznach very much too when we were off again, this time walking as I remember it, lugging suitcases and rucksacks, across hot and dusty roads lined with pear and apple trees and sometimes winding through valleys along which could be seen the tents of companies of the British Army of Occupation. Always Charley was fifty yards ahead of the wearisome rest of us and always he concealed from us, with careless laughter, all clues as to where the hell we were heading.

Those roads, weary though they made me, nevertheless remain with me to this day as something marvellously idyllic. Wild yellow snapdragons, scarlet poppies, blue chicory, white yarrow, meadowsweet, reddening apples: it was all like some early glowing pastoral piece by Renoir or Monet. So idyllic did it seem then, as now, that I later wrote a novella about it all, calling it *A German Idyll*, its setting being not only the flower-blessed roads but the tiny remote village of Steinbockenheim, Charley's birthplace, now revealed as our destination.

The return of the prodigal son to the bosom of a large farming family living in a large and ancient farmhouse was as mad as the wearying business of getting there had been. We were instantly regaled with vast quantities of hock, the excellence of which I was too inexperienced to appreciate, and then equally vast quantities

of scrambled eggs, potatoes, bread, fruit and cheese. There was also, as I vividly recall, redcurrant wine, which for my uneducated taste seemed far nicer than the hock. For ever I shall remember the great beauty of its colour, a distilled crystalline crimson-scarlet. It too symbolises, across forty years, all that was lovely in a Germany which, though outwardly so beautiful to the eye, was in fact at the bottom of the darkest pit. Those were the days of a mad despair that made our own crazy journeys by train and foot seem of not more account than a child's street game: the days when a German farmer or peasant could take a cart-load of potatoes to market in the morning and come back with a load of Deutschmarks in the afternoon, only to find them totally worthless next day. Never have I seen such quantities of money, so many millions of marks, as I saw in chests and chests of drawers in that tiny village, all of it paper, all of it worthless, all of it being hoarded by farmers and peasants in the pitiful, touching belief that one day God would produce in the financial world of a Germany bludgeoned and bled to death a miracle that would at last raise them all to the standard of millionaires. Small wonder that in one farmhouse the farmer had installed for himself a tap connected by pipe to the cellar below, so that if and when despair or thirst moved him in the middle of the night he could refresh and perhaps restore his faith with a draught or two of wine.

There is in one of Chekhov's letters, written about 1896, a passage in which he describes his being at a Russian wedding and in consequence being drunk for four days. I won't go so far as to say that my five companions and I were, for our four days in Steinbockenheim, quite in that same parlous state; let me simply say that there were times, drowned as we were by the hospitality of those simple and generous Germans, it sometimes seemed like that. For all the singing and rejoicing and dancing I finally reached a point where I never wanted to see, let alone drink, a glass of hock again.

At last, having paid such few bills as we had been allowed to incur (we lived for about three shillings a day) we set off for another crazy railway journey through pine forests illuminated all along the boundaries by wild yellow evening primroses, to Leipzig and then Berlin. Suddenly, in Berlin, my heart sank, covered in the pale cast of homesickness. The reason for this was all too painfully simple. Some time before this Madge had decided that, after all, she wanted to see more of the impossible young writer she had lately rejected, so that we were once again together, more in love than before. The fact that I found Berlin a city of depressing coldness may have had something to do with my sudden longing to go back to her and England. But back I knew that I had to go and presently Charley put me on the Warsaw-Ostend express, and I was back home the next afternoon.

A few days later I heard what Edward Garnett had to say about my novel. It was a moment I had long dreaded.

Nor was my dread misplaced. On the morning of 5 September 1927, Edward put on a sort of Jack Dempsey literary punching act, using me as the punchbag. He wrote not merely that my novel was terrible, impossibly terrible, but that it simply could not be published. It was written in a 'facile, flowing, over expressive, half-faked style'; it was cursed with 'generalities, vague cynicism, washy repetitions'; it was 'Hardy and water. Hardy at his worst romantic side'; it was 'hollow-sounding, repetitive, semi-poetic, semi-journalistic'; it was 'unreal, long-winded, romantic and cynical'; and so on and so on and so on, each sentence of criticism more ferocious than the last. In fact Edward, that morning, hit me with everything he'd got.

Two things are worth noting, I think, about this long and blistering letter. The first is that there was in it a brief sentence which said simply: 'Don't despair. You have a facile demon in you, who gets hold of the reins, as well as the real artist in you who retreats into the background.' I interpreted this as meaning, quite correctly, that Edward hadn't lost faith in me. This in turn was responsible for the second thing of note: my astonishing and quick recovery from that morning of disaster. I hadn't, in other words, lost faith in myself; and this is how, in *Edward Garnett, a Memoir* (now out of print) I expressed my feelings:

It is something to my credit, I think, that I recovered from that letter in a day. It blasted me; it skinned my soul; it seemed momentarily to sever every hope I had. But the very fierceness of its chastisement, which I knew to be just, was purifying in its complete chastening. It induced in me a great sense of isolation and above that a great stubbornness of determination not to be diverted from the things I wanted to do. It touched, deep down, the fibres of that part of me that slept, ate, dreamed and thought of nothing but writing all day and every day without lessening of tensity or rest. In fact, in the finest sense, it woke me.

It has often been said that behind every successful man there is a woman, whether she be wife or mother. I think it may also be true to say that behind every good novel there is a bad one. *The Voyagers* was my bad one, though not by any means the last of mine to be written and rejected. But with a natural buoyancy of character and an infinite determination not to be deviated from my set course I put it behind me like a bad dream. And it is now only just to say that, for all the severity of his judgements, there was in Edward a singular streak of sweetness and generosity. In only a few days after that catastrophic mauling I had received at his hands he was sending me comments on two stories, thus: 'I am delighted to know that you returned home relieved and soothed in spirit. Both *The Dove* and *The Voyage* I think are admirable. Both are spiritually true and delicately expressed. I don't see anything to criticize in either.' So was I finally restored.

It may well be, as George Moore has said, that 'youth goes forth singing'. It is equally true that it goes forth making a damn fool of itself. And now, as if I hadn't made enough of a damn fool of myself by wasting an entire year spawning 150,000 spurious, stupid words, I was about to make a damn fool of myself again.

But this time in quite another direction.

V

I have already explained, in *The Vanished World*, how strictly I was brought up at the Methodist altar. I have also described how the good corn my father so diligently sowed Sunday after Sunday finally came up, to his intense disappointment, as tares. In these matters of church and chapel there was much in me of my paternal grandfather, who scorned in no uncertain terms 'popery and humbug and sciencing about in nightshirts'. His true God, like mine, was really Nature.

My own scorn for all organised religion took the form of angry revulsion somewhere about the age of seventeen. It was not merely piety I suddenly found myself despising and rejecting; more truly it was those who dispensed it. I conceived for the Methodist clergy, most of them ill-paid, it is true, some of them fools, a few humbugs and certain of them spongers, a very icy

contempt. Not long later I turned my back on the polished pine pews, the phoney stained glass windows, the pained preachings and the all too often baleful singing for ever.

As a result of all this, when my mother's front doorbell rang one summer afternoon and I went to answer it only to find a parson standing there, I was ready with my sword of scorn, spitefully sharpened and dipped in acid. My moment of asinine truth was about to be unveiled. The man I saw there was tall, fair, bespectacled, pleasant-looking, indeed handsome. Politely he introduced himself as the new incumbent, at which I declared with a smart, rude lack of tact and manners that I didn't care a damn for him, his church, his cloth or his faith and that if he wanted to know why there were no doubt plenty of his flock who would be ready, even eager, to tell him.

He took all this very mildly, raised his hat with courtesy, said he was sorry about it all and bade me 'Good afternoon'. That this grossly stupid display of rudeness on my part might have made me an enemy for life is all too patently true; instead it turned out to be a remarkable example of the Christian turning the other cheek and unexpectedly made for me a wise, amusing, witty and generous friend for many years.

Bernard Harris in no way fitted into the Methodist parsonic mould as I then knew it; in fact I had chosen entirely the wrong man as victim of my scorn. Bernard was broad-minded, unfond of ostentation and show, whether of church or otherwise, gifted with a great sense of humour and an even greater love of literature. He was also fortunate enough to have a wife who, besides being charming and broad-minded too, was very well blessed, in her own right, financially. There was therefore never any thought or necessity for Bernard Harris to go through the nauseating act, as so many ministers did, of sucking up to rich boot manufacturers who paid handsome premiums for their back pews, paid pitifully low wages in their harsh red brick factories, believed on Sundays that the Lord was their shepherd and spent the rest of the week worshipping the theory that business is, after all, business. Intelligent, educated, unbiased of mind and eye, Bernard saw through them with a clarity of mind that matched my own.

His quick discovery that I had written and published books with the highly reputable firm of Cape immediately caused him to invite me to the Manse to tea, all as if he had utterly forgotten every moment of my asinine sword-attack. We instantly got on well. His wife was gracious and intelligent too; his two children, Dennis and Catharine, were delightful. Dennis was later to be killed in action in the Second World War, a young officer worshipped by all his men, and Catharine, by then a brilliant linguist, was to write a deeply touching memoir of him that proved that she had a splendid mastery of her own language as well as of others.

Bernard also had a brother, Frank. Not a strong man, he had given up ministerial practice in order to collect and sell first editions, manuscripts and rare books, a business in which he proved to have a judgement both rare and shrewd. On his not infrequent visits to Rushden we invariably met and Frank would often bring with him some new and uncommon discovery to show me or tell stories of others he had found. Among these was an early pamphlet by Norman Douglas on, I think, the exploitation of children in the Lipari island quarries, that had been published by the Stationery Office: price, one ha'penny. Having discovered the great rarity of this early item Frank shrewdly wrote to the Stationery Office and inquired had they any left? They had. He promptly bought up the whole stock, some fifty or sixty, I think, at a ha'penny a time, and made himself a modest fortune.

Another book he brought to show me was some voluminous work by his notorious namesake, Frank Harris, who had presented the copy to Joseph Conrad. Conrad's reply, in letter form, declining the book, was pinned to the title page and constituted one of the most blistering items in literary history ever written. It has always reminded me of Conrad's long and devastating criticism of Edward Garnett's play *The Breaking Point*, which it must have required formidable courage to write and even more formidable courage to read. That Edward was courageous there is no doubt; that he had also little experience of things theatrical is proved by David's description of the play's first night, when all that Conrad had feared and predicted came horribly true, with the result that 'the agony was prolonged and the effect was nightmarish'. In turn Conrad tore into Harris as an infuriated tiger might tear into a bloated rat, the result being that the book, as a collector's item, was of much historical literary interest.

Another result of Bernard's brother's excursion into the book-collecting world was that Bernard and his wife, most likely at Frank's instigation, were now kind enough to begin buying MSS of some of my short stories. The few modest guineas they paid were like manna added to my frugal and uncertain income and soon, happily, they were followed by others. Hugh Walpole, at Rupert Hart-Davis' instigation, bought the MS of a novel. A lady in Suffolk, another collector in California, Charley Lahr and some of his customers in London: all from time to time now bought MSS, thus adding a little more to the Bates' till. The most important of these collectors was without doubt Sir Louis Sterling, the wealthy head of the Gramophone Company. Louis Sterling is the classic example in reverse of the poor Jewish boy going west to get rich; instead he came east to London, from New York, to make his fortune. With only a few dollars in his pocket he came across the Atlantic in 1903, on a cargo boat, bringing a few modest books in his baggage, and got work as a commercial traveller. Soon he was collecting books and then manuscripts both old and modern, finally acquiring a library embracing almost all that is notable in our literature, the whole of it now being housed in the library of London University.

Louis Sterling was a friend of both Harriet Cohen and Charley Lahr and once again, in these friendships, I cannot help seeing the hand of the 'Divinity that shapes our ends', since it may well have been at the instigation of Harriet, as it certainly was of Lahr, that Sir Louis now bought an early MS draft of *The Two Sisters*, 218 sheets long, to which I added the note 'This is the earliest draft, much shorter than the final but contains almost all the story, if not all the scenes, from that from which the work was set up. The pages are numbered awkwardly and the style is awkward too, but was a product of only a month or two before the other.' For this first MS Sterling paid me £150, a sum so vast that I suddenly felt like the millionaire he himself was. Soon he also bought *Catherine Foster*, 357 sheets, *Alexander*, 97 sheets, *Charlotte's Row*, 380 sheets, *The House with the Apricot*, 70 sheets, together with other shorter items, all of them proving by the copious and complicated nature of their deletions and corrections that I was at this time taking Edward's preachings and injunctions greatly to heart and was working like a diligent beaver to rid myself of silly and extraneous influences and take firmer step after step towards becoming a wholly conscious writer.

It may seem slightly fantastic to say now that if I had only trusted to the instinctive artist in me instead of looking so much to others for influence, Edward's lambastings of me might not have been necessary. As early as 1925 I had written *The Flame*, an economical little sketch of a tired waitress of whose technique and feeling even Edward could find no adverse word to say; a little later I was beginning a story, *Fear*, with the words 'on the horizon three thunderstorms talked darkly to each other', thus getting more atmosphere into ten words than Hardy ('one of George Eliot's many miscarriages', as George Moore has well said) and his kind could often get into a page. Not that I was out of the wood by a long way yet. Much evidence exists, in fact, to show that I was still stupid, recalcitrant and slow to learn.

Among other stupidities I did a blindly silly plagiarisation of Tolstoy which Edward rightly pointed out had neither sense nor virtue and who was then very angry, also rightly, when I accused him of 'throwing mud at me'. To this Edward retaliated with words so wise that it amazes me how I could possibly have missed the penetrative point of them. 'Don't you understand that both my being upset and the necessity (after reading your cool and airy letter) of making you realize the position – is the very best proof of my interest in you . . . You don't imagine, I suppose, that it is a pleasure for me to strike you with a hammer to reach the sensitive spot in your perceptions.'

It is not in order to draw continual attention to my short-comings and dunce-headedness that I reiterate these things – I could go on to the point of utter tedium in that direction. It is rather to draw attention to the extraordinary nature of Garnett's devotion to literature, and of his rare combination of critical insight, profound sympathy and infinite enthusiasm, all so great that it is perhaps not surprising that few of his kind, if any, exist to succeed him today. He was no mere ordinary publishers' 'reader'. I am truly convinced that he believed his sole mission in life to be literature; his vocation was to bring the bud to flower. How many reputations he discovered, made and nurtured it is quite impossible to say, but it is David's firm contention that in all his life Edward never missed a single talent, and I believe it to be true. He saw reputations soar with dazzling brilliance and rapidity only to expire, after a book or two, like damp fireworks; he saw writers ruined by success; he saw the temporary extinction of writers such as Conrad in the inevitable period of reaction immediately after death; he must have seen scores of cases where legend overshadowed talent; he saw the furore cast up by that silliest of books, *Lady Chatterley's Lover* and passed on it the final, blistering, crushing verdict – 'it's the last pressing of the grapes, Bates, it's the last pressing of the grapes'. Indeed it was.

So I went from crisis to crisis, now producing something good, now something bad. In those moments of dark misgiving and depression which beset every artist, leaving him with the lacerating conviction that either he will never paint or write again or if he does so that it will be either atrociously or without success, I took my problems out for long, solitary walks, incapable always of sharing the often insoluble equations with another person. Nature, sometimes in the form of primrose woods, hayfields and harvest, skating or merely gathering mushrooms, and often and often in visits to the gardens at the Cearne, was always my healer.

That I was all too frequently in need of a healer there is no doubt. The hard continuous slog to master my craft presently began to affect my health. For weeks on end I would suffer acute abdominal pains which in turn induced bouts of depression accompanied by tensions both mental and nervous. This condition I had increasingly to endure for another twenty years until at last an operation removed it. I suspect that the Garnetts sometimes discussed this harrowed condition of mine and there was an occasion when a chance remark of Constance's, only slightly veiling her concern, seemed to indicate that she thought I was suffering from the disease which finally killed D. H.

Lawrence. Happily this was not so. I shall tell later, I hope in not unamusing terms, how what was wrong with me was at last diagnosed and in an extremely unusual manner.

H.E.

Perhaps I can best explain my feelings about my condition, back in the 1920s, by saying that I continually felt that I was looking at the world not through the rose-coloured spectacles of youth but with the slate-coloured ones of a premature middle age. There is a portrait of me done by William Roberts, when I was perhaps twenty-two or twenty-three, which shows a young man gazing out at the world with a clenched, harrowed intensity. It is not only a remarkable likeness of the person I then was; it brilliantly reveals the inner struggle and even torture that was going on behind what have been called my vivid and hauntingly blue eyes. It may give some further indication of my state in those days when I say that, as I write these words more than forty years later, I feel not forty years older but a good forty younger. Furthermore, without at all wishing to lay all the blame on ill-health, I will confess that I was more than a little difficult to live with, so much so that I wasn't merely an angry young man; I sometimes acted with an almost savage intensity and impossible selfishness against those who either didn't agree with me, wouldn't or couldn't understand me or who drove me to anger or irritation by what I thought were their own stupidities. One result at least of this was that my American publisher lamented to Edward Garnett that 'Bates behaves like a prima donna'.

No man, in fact, ever felt less like one. Finally, early in 1929, driven almost to despair by the gnawing ache of ill-health, I fled from Rushden, where the winters always seemed to be of an equally gnawing, chilling bitterness, and took a brief holiday in Bournemouth, where there were a few good bookshops and a resident orchestra, and which also had, reputedly, a soft winter climate. It was early February; on the day I arrived the first crocuses were brilliant and wide open in the warming sun. The next day there began, with a huge blizzard, a winter of such prolonged intensity that there was scarcely a sign of leaf on any tree until the end of April. The sea froze. From the cliffs hung vast icicles, like glassy inverted church steeples. The wind was wicked, solid ice. Your eyes, hair and bones froze as you walked the sea front. My blissful dreams of softer climates than that of Northamptonshire were utterly shattered.

There followed a miraculous summer: very hot, very dry, with long months of drought. In its scintillating brilliance I retraced with great happiness some of the steps of childhood, some of them leading to a little earthly paradise consisting merely of three narrow meadows flanked by a stream where often and often as a boy I had gathered watercress with my grandfather. I suppose they were perhaps really very ordinary, those meadows and that stream, but to me they were then, and still remain today, like the distilled essence of paradise. Here and there the stream ran shallow over white and sepia stones; in a few places it deepened into black holes shadowed by ancient bushes of sloe. In spring silver and yellow sallows positively seemed to dance with bees. Little fish darted, silver and gold too, in and out of shadow and sunlight. In August forests of pink willowherb, of the sort known as codlins-and-cream, softly filled long stretches of the banks, together with purple loosestrife and tall cane-like reeds, feathery brown at the tips. On hot days cows sought shade under vast old hawthorns, rubbing their backs against them until the trunks shone like polished mahogany. The air, bereft of bird song, whirred with that concentrated chorus of grasshoppers that seems in the strangest way to deepen silence, so that the air was hotly and hauntingly hushed. Even the yellowhammers, on those intensely hot days of late summer, were silent, as if thirstily asleep, and on many an afternoon I lay, sweating in some pool of dark parched tree-shadow, and slept too. And thus I would find myself healed again.

Perhaps some day someone will write a treatise on imagination, both of what it is and of how it can affect, through periods of concentrated use, the centres of nerves and emotions. It is a subject of which, I feel, we know very little. Is imagination, either in part or whole, a sort of sixth sense? The theory fascinates, and in the holding of it I am supported by certain strange things that have, from time to time, happened to me as a writer. On not one but many occasions I have written stories, inventing their characters purely and wholly from imagination, only to meet the same characters, in almost precisely the same situations, in real life, some months later. In a novella of mine called *Summer in Salandar*, where every incident and character is drawn exclusively by the power of imagination, a woman both rich and selfish sets out, having left her own husband, to destroy, rather after the manner of a spider with a fly, a young man she meets while on holiday on an island. Her name being Vane, I fitted her out, in the story, with an expensive set of matching luggage, each piece stamped with a V. Two years later, travelling by ship to the same island on which the story is set, I saw the set of matching luggage, each piece with its V, going aboard ahead of me and then watched, for the next three or four days, the woman of whom I had written, rich and selfish, proceed to her spider act of destruction. Is this an example of the workings of a sixth sense? or what? Oscar Wilde tells us that life imitates Art. Is it perhaps not also possible that imagination creates life, as it were by some process of magical foresight, before life itself does? The temptation to say that all human life exists as a pre-ordained pattern is one which has, for many people, a strong appeal. Are some of my stories, in some strange way, preordained? I wish I knew.

Some time before this a curious event seemed to have occurred in my fortunes. One evening Liam O'Flaherty had rushed into the office of Jonathan Cape in Bedford Square, excitedly urging 'Get *The Two Sisters* reprinted. Bates has won the Hawthornden Prize.'

Bates had not in fact won the Hawthornden Prize, but that there may have been some slight substance behind the rumour is shown by the fact that for a good many years afterwards it was not at all uncommon for me to meet people who, on hearing who I was, would instantly declare 'Oh! yes, you're the man who won the Hawthornden Prize.' The prize was worth £100, a pretty fair sum in my youth, and it is not impossible that if I had won it Madge and I might well have made our decision to get married earlier than we did.

When we did in fact make it at last we were both sure of two things: that we would, if possible, go to live far away from our native Rushden, in the south country of W. H. Hudson and Edward Thomas if possible, and that we would ask my former schoolmate, Harry Byrom, to be best man. On visits to London I saw Harry pretty frequently, one of our joint pursuits at that time being the theatre, in which he had recently made an exciting discovery, as he wrote to me, of a brilliant new young actor. We accordingly began to follow this young man all over London, whenever he appeared in some new production. Charles Laughton was not then famous as the ebullient King Henry VIII throwing chicken bones over his shoulder; he was merely a small part actor of much intelligence, content to be playing small parts for the sake of experience. One of these parts was that of a slouching, slippered layabout in Molnar's *Liliom*, with its repeated refrain of 'Wake up, wake up, you vagabonds, the damn police are after you!' a part that Laughton played with such comic realism that we were convinced, and correctly, that here was one of the great actors of our time. Many years later I dined with Laughton, then world famous but sick of the theatre, as in fact I myself was too, and found him to be a man of charm and an intelligence far above the average of the acting profession. I told him how much and how often he had enriched my youth and he was, I think, touched to feel that he had done so.

At all events many other affairs and persons – Violet Dean, Harriet, Louis Sterling, Charley Lahr, Bernard Harris, the selling of more MSS and stories and the increasing if relatively slight success of the novels I was now managing to write – were all adding up to the same course: marriage. The event itself was still some time ahead but meanwhile I had prudently introduced Madge to the Garnetts and on a number of occasions we went to the Cearne together, often making it a centre from which to look for the cottage we eventually wanted. Though we met with no success it was good to know that Constance, and indeed also Edward, of whom Madge was at first terrified, approved of the girl I had chosen, a girl whom they had rather feared, I fancy, might turn out to be a flashy and useless piece of goods, though for the life of me I could never think why. These visits also had the effect of endearing Madge to the south country, so that presently there was no atom of doubt in our hearts as to where eventually we would make our home.

With all this in mind my wanderings about the Northampton-shire countryside now had a new purpose. I cycled from one country house sale to another, picking up for a few shillings odd chairs, corner cupboards, chests, china, glass and bits and pieces of all kinds. Together we searched antique shops and junk shops and pretty soon I developed a fair nose for a bargain, though there were many (a set of six genuine Georgian mahogany dining chairs was beyond our financial range at £6!) which we had to forgo. I had also been given an excellent tip, which I still think holds good, by Margaret's architect father: namely that one should always ask oneself if one could get a piece of antique furniture made today for the price being asked for it. If the answer is no then you have a bargain.

This is now the moment, I feel, in which to reintroduce Margaret into my life, though I fear rather painfully. There had evidently been some growing crisis behind the scenes and certainly there had been some talk of 'that young man trifling with my daughter's affections', as Violet Dean was later to tell me. The resulting tensions were soon to become unbearable, so that presently I was to receive a letter from Margaret in which she bared her heart, and indeed her soul, as far at least as feminine pride would allow, and asked what, if anything, was I going to do about her and the great affection, if not indeed love, that she felt for me? I was stunned. Since there had been neither inconstancy nor duplicity on my part I found it hard to bring myself to believe that she could think I had misled, deceived or cheated her. But this, though she didn't say it in terms quite so explicit, was clearly what she did think and it was all too desperately clear also that she was on the verge of being broken-hearted. Sad as I was about this, it seemed to me that there was no point in being otherwise than honest about it, telling her that I did not and indeed never had loved her and that if in my purblind stupidity I had wounded her I was deeply sorry. With as much tenderness and understanding as I could summon I told her about Madge and where indeed my real love lay.

Precisely what all this did to her it is impossible to know. The ecstasies of first love, even when returned, engender a pain peculiarly their own; when they are rejected God only knows what torture and torment follow. I deeply blame myself for all this, and long ago though it now all is I can only wish that I had had the wit and perception to see that it would surely happen. Alas, I was too obtuse to have done so and the heart of a charming, generous, intelligent girl was surely broken. It says much for her character that I think she forgave me and, bitterly painful though it must have been to say so, that she understood.

It is now a good moment also to bring Violet Dean back to the scene. Our search for a cottage having been unsuccessful (it was now 1930 and the nearest we had come to buying a cottage was in my grandmother's little Bedfordshire village, Souldrop, a sketch of which may be seen in *The Vanished World*, the cottage in left foreground, the little church steeple behind) I now sought the aid of Vie, the tireless helper in time of trouble. Indefatigable and willing as ever, she responded by inviting us down to Kent, to her manor house at Little Chart: a lovely but strange house, with dark episodes of history, standing on the edge of a large rolling park from which the Great Depression had just evicted its owners, leaving behind a trail of shattered tree tops where formerly had stood a noble splendour of ancient oaks, elms, sweet chestnuts and beeches. There was an air of sadness about that littered wreckage, a lovely pastoral piece of England shattered as if by war, that lives with me still.

It was February, 1931, when we took the train to Kent. Spring seemed to be coming; the air was damp and fresh and you could almost smell the not too distant sea in it; thrushes were singing and along the dykes a few varnished celandines were waking and here and there even a primrose or two. Rain fell all through Saturday night and on into Sunday morning, cheerlessly.

The village of Little Chart, though very small, is divided, like Gaul, into three parts. The centre contains a few dozen houses, a church, a pub, a shop and two small lakes on the edge of which stands a paper mill where, three quarters of a century ago, was made a good deal of paper, by hand, on which books of the Kelmscott, Ashendene and Doves Press were printed. Alas, hand-made paper is now also part of a vanished world. Another piece of the village, containing what is reputedly the oldest hop-garden in

England, stands a mile or more away, and here too was once a church, unique in that it contained a Roman Catholic chapel under its Protestant roof, and now blasted to a ruin by a Hitler doodlebug. The third part lies another mile from the centre in another direction and consists of a village green of great charm, called the Forstal, surrounded by a dozen houses of stone, half-timber and that soft bronzy red brick seen at its loveliest in villages such as Goudhurst, away towards Sussex, westwards.

The Forstal
Little Chart

It was on this elm-fringed green, the Forstal, that Vie, after her miraculous fashion, had discovered a cottage that she thought might suit us. The rain stopped at lunch-time and after lunch we walked out to see the house. It was a horror. Much depressed, we were about to walk back when its owner declared that he might have one further possibility to offer. This was a building for conversion, a granary. We walked across the sodden grass, then only a rough area of pasture with a shaggy brown horse grazing on it, today mown smooth as a bowling green for cricket, to look at it. It stood in a half-flooded farmyard: an oblong building of stone, weatherboard and tile, open to the winds on the ground floor, still littered with straw and grain upstairs.

We looked, poked about a little, went upstairs and pondered. We went outside, looked and pondered again. We stood for a few minutes by the thick, yellow-lichened old stone walls and suddenly the sun came out. Its rays were the very faintest degree warm and we saw now that we were facing due southwards. Madge looked at me and I at her. We said nothing; but in that moment of sunlight we suddenly knew that this was it.

Once again the mysterious Divinity, this time in the person of the unfailing Vie, had shaped our ends and performed its miracle.

VI

Within hours we had decided to buy the Granary. Within a couple of weeks the plans for its conversion were ready.

For the stupendous sum of £600 we were to get a large living-room, four bedrooms, a study, a bathroom, a kitchen and nearly an acre of land. Between us we had something over £400, some of it due to much hard work by Madge, the larger part of it thanks to Louis Sterling, and I decided to borrow the rest of the £600 on mortgage. We had almost enough furniture to make a tolerable start and the chief of the things we needed were curtains, cups and carpets.

There were instantly several immediate reactions to this decision of ours. Constance Garnett was profoundly alarmed, even horrified. She, who had as a young mother travelled alone or in the company of strange Russian gentlemen by sleigh and *droshky* across a Russia that was largely without railways at that time, indicated even if she didn't actually say so, that we were committing some kind of sin in going to the extravagance of buying a country cottage *with a bathroom*. I think perhaps it may be putting it too strongly to suggest that there was a streak of masochism in the Garnetts, but it is nevertheless true that David has said of his parents that they viewed with severe suspicion the world of creature comforts. That Madge and I were to commit the even greater folly of installing electric light and an indoor lavatory were only further reasons for Constance wondering whatever sort of sins against the Holy Ghost of prudence the impecunious young were coming to. She did not suggest that we

The Granary.

were actually mad; her Scots caution merely indicated that we had gone far beyond mere imprudence into the regions of the unwise.

It soon became clear, however, that both our families and our circle of friends and acquaintances also thought we were stark, raving barmy. Of course you never knew with these writer fellows – they clearly hadn't got their heads screwed on the right way. They were not as other men. But whatever was *Madge* thinking of? – a sensible, hard-working girl from a respectable working-class home – going to live in a *barn*? The very thought was outrageous. The scheme was a lunatic one that could only have been invented by a young man slightly if not utterly deranged. A *barn*? It conjured instant visions of straw and hay, bare brick floors, bare earth and even perhaps of Madge and me sleeping, like the good infant Lord himself, in a manger.

Most amazed and disbelieving of all our friends was, I think, Bernard Harris. Bernard had only the very vaguest idea of what in fact the countryside consisted of. For him, I think, it was a kind of uncharted wilderness in which unidentifiable trees and plants existed to form a general pattern of greenery in spring and summer and a forbidding, naked nothingness in winter. He marvelled at my knowledge and passion for it, confessing that he himself (perhaps a little with his tongue in his cheek) didn't know a cabbage from a potato in growth, and confessing still further that in his botanical ignorance he was quite unable to identify an ash from an oak. He too found himself quite unable to swallow the idea of our living in a barn. It was clearly one of an astonishing craziness. Many years later, when he came to stay at the Granary, when we had *two* bathrooms, I truly believe he thought we had in fact committed a further sin of actually telling a lie about the barn in the first place. He really couldn't quite grasp that the cow-barn of his first conception had turned out to be, after all, a very comfortable, elegant house.

£600 down the drain too: further madness. It must of course be remembered here that in the early depressed 1930s the idea of converting this, that and any other kind of building into houses was utterly unthinkable. Today we live in a world where people thirst for, and even pay heavily for the privilege of, being able to convert pigsties, cow byres, old windmills, malting houses, oast houses, henhouses, warehouses, old railway stations, old signal boxes, disused forts, ancient barges and almost anything else into places in which to live: these are the new, the modern status symbols. But in 1931, when you could have bought such places for a song we were, among the people we knew, the only people to dream of such a thing – the one exception being H. A. Manhood, also a short story writer and a protégé of Edward's, who lived in a converted railway carriage which he had bought, I think, for £25.

That summer was wet and cool. On some evenings, even in July, you needed to wear an overcoat. The previous summer had been better and in the August of it I had persuaded Madge to come away with me and share some of the joys of foreign travel that I had known in Germany and that are of such enduring enchantment still. We accordingly went to Brittany. We travelled to St Malo by night boat, slept on deck and were very sick. From St Malo we went on to the old and beautiful town of Morlaix and thence to the little coastal village of St Jean de Doight, once the home of the late-impressionist painter Gustave L'Oiseau. It was all very like going back into the world of Maupassant or of Gauguin and his friends who had painted at Pont Aven, living there, as we now did, for a few modest francs a day. The country restaurants full of peasants and farmers all eating at one big central table, the insular suspicions of the Bretons towards strangers, the flowing native cider, the fishing boats with their pink and blue seine nets that later Christopher Wood depicted so well, the street markets where live ducks and hens sat with their legs tied to wheelbarrows or cartwheels, the little train that ran from the main street in Morlaix across the pink-purple moors of heather to the coast where the tide ran out for miles, leaving great black castles of rock exposed on deserts of pure white sand, the strange angelic white headgear of ancient Breton peasant women sitting asleep in the sun: I remember it all as an idyll, perfect in every degree, as if it were yesterday.

From St Jean de Doight we went south to Rouen, where the Seine, the waterfront and the old city too were Maupassant-like and we once paid the staggering sum of fifty francs, less than ten

MORLAIX

shillings, for a dinner, instead of our customary ten francs, an event that caused me to come out in a long hot-cold sweat. From Rouen we went on to Paris, where we met Margaret, who was staying with American friends. One of the characteristics that least endeared me to Margaret was that she was an impossible chatterbox and I seem to hear her still, prattling away like some light pianola as we toured about a tiring, torrid Paris in an open taxi. Paris has never, except on one or two occasions, seemed so lovely since. Nor will it ever be so cheap again.

It was also during that summer, if memory serves me correctly, that I paid another visit to David Garnett at Hilton, a visit that is worth recording for several reasons. I recall that David and I bashed a cricket ball about the lawn with his two young sons, Richard and William, David showing that colossal physical strength which had so staggered D. H. Lawrence and which made him such a powerful swimmer. Shortly afterwards there arrived a young Welsh writer, a strange, taut-looking girl, fair and blue-eyed, dressed in a black velvet cloak. Dorothy Edwards was an ardent socialist who wrote only two books, *Rhapsody*, a volume of short stories, and *Winter Sonata*, a novel. In *Rhapsody* there is a short story, *The Country House*, which I deem to be one of the best in the language. The strange thing about this strange girl and her writing is that I find it impossible to trace what influences, if indeed there were any, lay behind her work. Its perfect simplicity reminds me only of the work of that greatly gifted painter Gwen John, sister of Augustus. It is the work of a quiet but evidently deeply troubled mind.

Soon there arrived another visitor, heralded by the gigantic roar of a huge motorbike. The sight of this great Brough Superior machine and then of the slight, blue-eyed figure of its rider, dressed in the uniform of an RAF. aircraftman, was enough to tell me immediately who he was: none other than Colonel T. E. Lawrence, alias Shaw, alias Ross, the author of *The Seven Pillars of Wisdom* and that also deeply troubled book, *The Mint*. He was intro-duced to us as Mr Shaw. The fact that he had breakfasted with Mrs Thomas Hardy far away in Dorset and had roared his way across half England in a matter of a couple of hours or so had no sort of effect on Dorothy Edwards, who merely remained utterly ignorant as to who he was.

We finally went into the house for sherry and lunch, during which Lawrence began a discussion on Greek poetry, a subject on which he was no small authority. This sudden excursion into the realms of classical verse had the immediate effect of putting Dorothy Edwards' back up. Her instant conclusion was that this aircraftman, this Erk in his ill-fitting blue uniform, was showing off; could there be any other explanation for a mere serviceman holding forth on Greek poetry? The air grew tense. By this time it had also dawned on both David and his wife, as well as on myself, that the ardent Welsh writer-socialist hadn't the slightest notion that she was talking to a man who had become so much a legend in his life-time that he had sought to flee from it into the monastic anonymity of the RAF. The air grew tenser still, the argument more aggressive, not to say belligerent.

To David, Ray and me all this had about it a certain air of comedy. Not so to Dorothy Edwards, for whom the situation merely worsened. It may be that Lawrence, sensing that his identity hadn't been disclosed to her, worsened it deliberately and that he too was secretly enjoying the fun. The entire situation had about it something not a little Thurberesque or perhaps rather in the vein of those shorter farcical plays of Chekhov.

But, as so often in Chekhov, the epilogue to the story is not comic, but tragic. Not long after that meeting both T. E. Lawrence and Dorothy Edwards killed themselves: he accidentally, on his motorbike, she deliberately, by throwing herself under a train.

Soon, with the prospect of the Granary lying before us, Madge began to undergo a slight period of madness of her own. There was good reason for this. From that sunlit moment in February when we had stood by the lichened walls in Kent to the moment when she walked into the house on her wedding day in July she never once set eyes on the place where, in our supposed craziness, we were going to live. From time to time I really believe she wondered if it actually existed. It is true that I myself made one or two visits to it, once I believe from the Cearne, and went through such mundane essential business as measuring the windows for curtains and discussing paint and drains.

It was in fact the curtains that were the cause of Madge's temporary aberration. For economy's sake she had decided to make them herself, a reasonably simple enough task except for the fact that she could never be sure that I, never very good at practical matters anyway, had got the measurements of the windows exactly right. This worried her to such an extent, even to preying on her mind, that the poor girl actually began walking in her sleep, hanging the curtains in the middle of the night at her mother's bedroom windows. It finally turned out that I had miraculously got the measurements right and all was well after all.

I have the impression that I wrote little or nothing at all that summer. The chief task that now occupied me was to raise vast numbers of plants, both from seed and cuttings, for the garden I was determined to create in Kent. Inspired by the Cearne, I raised primroses, polyanthus, pansies, poppies, alpines and heaven knows what else; I begged from other gardens, including the Cearne itself, from which numbers of things still survive in a garden that is now nearly forty years mature.

The story of how this garden was created out of the wilderness of an old farmyard is not unfascinating; but before I tell it I ought to speak of another friend whose importance to me has been considerable. Somewhere about this time there had come to Jonathan Cape a new editorial assistant: Rupert Hart-Davis, now Sir Rupert. Handsome, tall, friendly, a great bibliophile, Rupert eventually became perhaps the best publisher's editor in London, as his masterly editing of Oscar Wilde's letters goes to show. We at once got on supremely well together. Rupert was very much my sort of person and of my generation, which the two partners of Jonathan Cape were not. Rupert therefore became a liaison officer between the heads of the firm and myself, so that I found myself able to take to him problems, financial and otherwise, which I found it difficult to take to them.

Rupert had also been to Oxford at a particularly fruitful period and numbered among his fellow students Peter Fleming, Osbert

Lancaster, John Betjeman, Louis MacNeice, Quintin Hogg, Harman Grisewood, Alan Pryce-Jones and John Sparrow as well as others of talent and influence. One of these was the then literary editor of *The Spectator*, Derek Verschoyle, who at Rupert's instigation now began to give me books to review and to ask for other articles. *The Spectator*'s list of writers in the early thirties makes rich reading: Graham Greene, Peter Fleming, Alastair Cooke, Dilys Powell, Stephen Spender, C. E. M. Joad, Kate O'Brien, L. A. G. Strong, William Plomer, Rupert himself and many other talents of brilliance. A year or two later Rupert was responsible for further kindness, so that I was given *The Spectator*'s weekly 'Country Life' column to do, an opportunity that gave me the very first regular income, a magnificent 6 guineas a week, that I had had since first beginning to write; but of this I shall say more later.

What chiefly strikes me now about the dawn of the 1930s is the great richness, literary-wise, of the times, not merely on our side of the Atlantic, but on both; we have nothing comparable, on either side, today. The consequence of this was that the period was one of the most stimulating and exciting for a writer, especially a young writer, to be living and working in. As in a great period of painting – i.e. Impressionism – or music, the sudden birth and fusion of great numbers of talents at the same time has an immensely dramatic influence on the rise in the general artistic temperature. This in itself creates a climate which is not only right but perhaps, above all, infectious. Men and women of true artistic talent find themselves frustrated by a climate that is either sour or sterile, as happened in the 1950s, or that of the 1960s, which have seen literature descend, as that excellent actor Richard Hearne recently pointed out, to the depths of the snob-pit. It would be tempting to pursue this theme but perhaps it is better simply to say that when art sinks so low it is its own destroyer.

In the 1930s there was nothing of this. There actually existed, amazingly, a large body of writers, not merely young but drawn in fact from three generations, who actually cared, and cared greatly, as Milton and Donne and Shakespeare and Dickens and

Tennyson and hundreds of others had done before them, what English should look like on the printed page. The word charm had not become derisory; there were still writers who fashioned their words lovingly, not regarding them as lumps of offal to be cast down for dogs to eat. Of the generation before the First World War, a very considerable number of big figures were still highly active; though Conrad was dead, Hardy, Galsworthy, Shaw, Wells, Maugham, E. M. Forster, Belloc, Masefield, Bennett, Housman, D. H. Lawrence, Huxley, W. H. Hudson, W. H. Davies were still very much on the stage; of the writers who had survived that war Sassoon, Graves, Linklater, Compton Mackenzie, Richard Church, A. E. Coppard are only a small part of a lineage that was also rich; finally when we come to the generation that had been too young to bear arms in the war we are confronted with a truly astonishing array of talent: Evelyn Waugh, Graham Greene, Peter Fleming, V. S. Pritchett, William Plomer, John Moore, W. H. Auden, Stephen Spender, C. Day Lewis, Sean O'Faolain, Frank O'Connor, James Stern, William Sansom are only a few of the host of talents making up that exciting company. Nor was this all. Across the Atlantic another army of writers, headed by figures such as Hemingway, Faulkner, Erskine Caldwell, Katherine Anne Porter and Sherwood Anderson were helping to lead yet another generation of younger talents away from the sterile folly of merely imitating second-rate English talents and to discover for themselves the rich indigenous veins that were awaiting exploration over there, so that an entirely new, fresh, living flow of ore was about to be tapped.

It could not have been otherwise than, immensely exciting to be part of this new generation, a generation which, in my view, has remained unmatched ever since. It was surely closely comparable with being a young painter at the time when Pissarro, Sisley, Signac, Seurat, Bonnard, Van Gogh, Picasso and Matisse and many others were so enriching French painting towards the end of the nineteenth century. Like Sisley and Pissarro I was poor, but cash or the lack of it was of all things at that early period of literary flight of the least importance. The path of art, endlessly difficult', I had been told and had not only found it so but was still so to find it, for many years, time and time again. To this eternal truth I was now conscious of adding another. I was now more than ever dedicated to a situation 'where the artist's power of compelling imaginative persuasion transforms them (i.e. his stories or novels) into a living truth'.

The apparent folly of marrying on nothing, and in a converted barn at that, did not therefore seem to me to be folly at all. It was rather a compulsive challenge; and it is of this long and severe challenge and how I met it but often didn't conquer it that I must now proceed to tell.

VII

In August 1930 Madge and I had tramped over a good part of Kent, rucksacks on our backs, looking for possible houses in which to live. One day we walked little short of twenty miles from Canterbury to the village of Pluckley, which stands on the very edge of that ridge that lies, like a long step, between the North Downs that the Pilgrims to Canterbury once trod and the vast Weald that stretches away in its wide magnificence to the South Downs of Sussex. At Pluckley there is a small forest, perhaps a surviving part of the great ancient forest of Anderida that once covered so huge a part of southern England. As we toiled up the last mile or two to reach the ridge we passed a small church standing on a grassy hillock above a stream. Sheep were grazing under the old stone walls and Madge paused to take a photograph. We didn't know until later that that church, with its safely grazing sheep, was to become a closer part of our lives.

This then was Little Chart; and to it we finally came, newly married, unable to afford a honeymoon, on a July afternoon in 1931. It must now be recorded that there was a certain slight element of irony about our wedding day. I, the parson-hater, the rebellious chapel-goer, rejector of the Methodist faith in which my father had so strictly brought me up, had at last been married in the realms of strict nonconformity, in chapel, and furthermore not by one parson but by two, Bernard Harris, jocular and kind as ever, being one, Harry Byrom, my erstwhile school-mate (the *only* member of the upper sixth at Kettering Grammar School) being an admirable best man. The affair was a simple one; and what I think perhaps lingers sharpest in my memory of the after ceremonies, simple as they too were, is the face of my grandfather, reflectively sad that we were leaving our native heath and were going to live, as I think it must have seemed to him, a thousand miles away. For him, I think, it was really a farewell. Exaggerated though it may be to say that our going broke his heart, it is true to say that I saw him only once or twice again and then in decline. Just after the publication of *The Vanished World* there occurred, in Higham Ferrers, in the little ancient square we both loved, one of those episodes that from time to time occur unexpectedly in life, forming a sort of late epitaph to someone or something long lost. On a beautiful October morning I met there a man who introduced himself as the person who had taken over the little farm my grandfather had once worked, where horse after horse of his had dropped down dead, where I had bird's-nested, tried in vain to lift the great sheaves of bearded wheat and had looked for skylarks' nests among the yellow coltsfoot flowers in the spring ploughed land.

We talked briefly of his, and my, vanished world: of the days of labour on land intractable and unyielding, long ago. Suddenly he asked me if I knew what that field of my grandfather's, back at the beginning of the century, when horse and man were almost the only means of traction on a farm and where he had tried with all his strength to wrench a living from soil almost as unyielding as rock, had always been called. I confessed that I didn't know.

'The Sorrowful Field,' he said and on that soft October morning, warm with sunlight, there were sudden tears in my eyes.

But in Kent, on that afternoon in mid-July, when the air was smothering with the odour of sweet chestnut bloom, the field was not sorrowful. It suddenly seemed miraculous, happy and fertile, full of promise and of an infinite beauty. Not that there really was a field, as such; our Granary stood in what seemed to be a wasteland of giant dock and thistle and old grass grown yellow with summer. Nowhere was there to be seen the remotest sign of the garden I dreamed of. All this, and much else, had still to be created and fought for.

In what was to be the garden stood a decaying haystack. Beside it stood a decaying willow and beside that another. There was still another, huge and old. Piles of rock and rubble lay strewn about in this forest of dock, grass and thistles. Beyond a raw, new, ugly snake-fence lay a meadow and this at least had features of splendour, surrounded as it was by a rectangle of great Turkey oaks, perhaps two hundred and fifty, perhaps three hundred years old, cylindrical, majestic and almost black in full summer leaf.

Ludicrous though it may now seem there is an incident both small and trivial that marks the start of the garden that I now see from my window, the giant golden Turkey oaks backing it on a rainy autumn morning in the field beyond. It is the sowing of a packet of radish seeds. Is it sometimes the very smallness of things that makes them linger so long in the memory? Not a packet of gentians, of rare campanulas, of fabulous lilies, of Himalayan blue poppies, of alpines; but radishes. This tiny ridiculous piece of creation was the first I ever achieved on my own piece of English earth. Since then I have sown thousands of seeds and planted thousands of plants, bulbs and shrubs, but still those radishes remain in the memory like a string of white and scarlet pearls.

Every penny we had, with the exception of some twenty pounds, had been sunk into the house, and the problem now was how to survive while Madge attacked the house and its domestic affairs and I the garden. The result was that we lived on two pounds a week. Fortunately food was very cheap but at the same time there was nothing to eat as yet from the garden. Once or twice a week a travelling greengrocer called in on us, his produce in an old-fashioned covered cart, not unlike a small replica of those prairie wagons you see in Western films. After nearly forty years I have utterly forgotten what the man himself looked like. It is the face of the young daughter who was always with him that haunts me still as it also haunted me all that long time ago. It seemed to me a face moulded out of yellow clay: a face born to tragedy. I believe it is true that Hardy saw his Tess only once and also in a cart, in a country lane, and from that fleeting experience, haunted also by a face, created his celebrated novel. Soon I was to create mine shaping it into a story called *The Mill*, a story that was not only far and away the best thing I had written up to that time but the story that firmly and beyond doubt established my reputation as a writer of stories and revealed me at long last as a fully conscious writer, wholly aware of what I was doing, a master of the craft I had worked at so relentlessly and intensely. It is said that Chekhov, like me a great lover of flowers, wanted to turn the whole world into a garden. So too did I: but with the difference that I wanted to do it, if possible, overnight. As a young man I cannot flatter myself that I was exactly patient, but the fact that I have still not finished the garden after forty years of toil and thought on it perhaps goes some way to proving that the impatience of youth has been replaced by something less volatile in middle age. At all events I began the grand attack on my piece of earth: uprooting vast quantities of gigantic docks, mowing down nettles and thistles, seeing to the removal of the haystack and the burning of the more useless of the willows. I worked like a slave, from early morning to night, writing nothing and therefore earning nothing, my bank balance dwindling with frightening rapidity. Too proud to borrow in case it should prove to the disbelieving that after all we *were* mad to have got married on nothing and madder still to have chosen a barn in which to live, I was saved from utter penury by the arrival of a few late wedding presents in the form of cheques, each of them a godsend.

Sometimes, however, it was necessary, if only for sanity's sake, to escape; and so sometimes we did, occasionally to the sea, most often to the great beechwoods which lie so majestically along the North Downs, three or four miles from the house. Seen from a distance these woods look like thick, gigantic bearskins; when you enter them they become like vast cathedrals, pillared by thousands of immense beeches whose elephantine trunks show up like bleached grey bone against the black frames of numbers of scattered yews. In spring these cathedrals are strewn all over the upper edges with millions of bluebells, a festival and miracle of purple. In autumn, shining in the sunlight of October and November, they look like golden temples. We visited them over and over again, always in a state of perennial wonder. From the primroses and bluebells of spring to the wild strawberries and golden yellow rock roses and even wild columbines of high summer we felt, I think, that this was the shrine at which we had come so far to worship. Beside it our native Northamptonshire seemed bare and cold and desolate. From these hills you can see, on very clear days, the sea. A black whip of smoke, in the days before oil replaced coal, marked the passage of ships up and down the channel; and there were days of crystal sea-whitened light and running breeze where you felt that below you lay half the world, pasture separating woodland in the same repeated pastoral pattern for miles and miles. This, you told yourself, was ageless, an affair of eternal greenness, sea-washed light and snow-pure cloud. This, you told yourself also, must have been what the climbing pilgrims saw; and perhaps Caesar and his legions too.

It wasn't long before we were faced with a new problem. To the labour of the garden was suddenly added the prospect of another kind of labour. Madge had begun to feel distinctly ill in the mornings. It was to Violet Dean that we at once turned and she, in her typical fashion, ever eager to help in time of crisis, took Madge off to her doctor, who confirmed what we really knew already. Our first child was on the way.

Whether we were part fearful, part excited it is now difficult to say. I only know now that I believe every act of creation to be re-creative. I am strongly of the opinion that the way to negation, even unhappiness, even disaster, lies in fighting against the current of the creative stream. In other words I knew, now, that I had to work like hell.

And work like hell I did. Often, again like Chekhov, I wrote a story between breakfast and lunch; an article between lunch and tea; a review between tea and supper. I wrote until my hands trembled and I could scarcely see straight; until I was appetiteless, half-sick and cursed again with a greyness of vision and the gnawing ache of abdominal pains.

Any artist who works after this fashion, at such blind pressure, will tell you that sometimes there comes a moment when he is not quite of this world. I do not mean by this that he becomes wholly or partly insane; he simply ceases for a time to know what day it is. Such an experience overtook me one day when, after a long penal spell of especially hard work I went to London to meet and have lunch with Violet Dean, who was ever good to us. After wandering round the bookshops of Charing Cross Road during the morning I suddenly found myself standing on an island in the middle of the street, my mind black and blank, unaware of who or where I was, why I had come to London, who I was going to see or what time it was. I suppose the experience lasted for less than a minute, but when I presently came to myself and looked at the nearest street clock it was to discover that I was already an hour late for my lunch with Vie, who was waiting for me somewhere far down in the City, beyond St Paul's.

It is not an experience I care to repeat; and I mention it now only as an answer to that all too common remark that readers often make to writers: 'aren't you lucky?' I do not rebuke them, however, for that. Perhaps it is difficult for them to understand that there are times when the gift of imagination can also be a curse.

That first autumn in Kent was long and mild. Many leaves stayed green on the oaks until Christmas. By December hazel catkins were in flower. By January primroses were blooming in the woods and I remember how, once, we gathered them by moonlight.

A letter to Edward Garnett in the mid-winter of that year tells me that I was now working on a novel, *The Fallow Land*. The successful completion of this book was of the very greatest importance to me. If it could be successfully brought off I knew that I would be able to draw an advance on it in the spring: a desperate financial necessity, since the baby was expected in May.

It would seem that the book was going well and that I hadn't committed another folly; for this is what I wrote to Edward:

I feel immensely pleased with it . . . I have done roughly 250 pages, which is roughly half way, and I can't hold myself. This is the book I have always wanted to write – the struggle against the soil, the whole exactly a woman struggling to live on the land. I have made her a shrewd, quiet, level-headed creature with a sort of fatalistic streak in her; she has a will like a mule and a head for money; her husband is exactly her opposite – spoilt and a fool about money. She saves the money and he wastes it. Her children, of whom she is passionately fond grow up and grow like their father.

It would also appear that I had taken Edward's excellently sensible advice and was getting the first chapters of the novel typed so that he could take a critical glance at them instead of leaving the entire affair until it was fully completed, thus putting myself into the painful position of *The Voyagers* all over again. That this was a most wise course is clearly indicated by another letter to him, written in the middle of January:

Your letter was like a gallon of wine – I went rollicking off to the novel drunk with delight. I can't tell you how glad I am that you like it.

Drunk with delight: that indeed is how I must have felt after all the caustic castigations of the past. At last, perhaps, my world was beginning to blossom.

The setting of *The Fallow Land* was precisely that part of the Nene Valley where I had grown up with my grandfather as a boy; and in a sense it was his story, his struggle, that I had transposed to the woman, and her struggle, in the novel. It now occurs to me that, if I only had known of it at the time, *The Sorrowful Field* would have been the apter title. However that may be, it is certain that there was a hint of the paradoxical in the fact that although the great beauty and variation of the Kent countryside had already inspired me to rhapsodic love for it, it had also succeeded in making me see with a clearer, far more objective vision the native Midland land I had left. Perhaps it was a case of standing back and letting the dog see the rabbit; but it remains a certain fact that I was to write another half dozen novels of that native Midland soil before at last war, with its many revolutions, not the least of which was in the countryside, together with other causes, decided me to leave it and turn in other directions. Novels such as *The Fallow Land, The Poacher* and *A House of Women* are not written today; nor could they be. They are, in a sense, historical novels, portions of a world that has vanished as surely as the world of my boyhood street games has vanished. War, the senseless destroyer, kills not only men; the Second World War revolutionised the countryside as nothing, not even railways, had done before, killing all hope, in the process, of a writer of my kind ever being able to write again of man or woman battling their guts out in order to tame by means of horse and hand fields that were sterile or sorrowful.

However, the completion of *The Fallow Land* was a happy and important event; and was presently to be followed by another equally so. In May, at the time of the blossoming of that 'loveliest of trees, the cherry', our first daughter was born; and I was presently able to write to Constance Garnett that the child had 'intense blue eyes, and a lusty voice with which she cries all night.' Her first name was Ann, her second Catharine – the spelling of the second being the result of a promise to Bernard Harris, who had insisted, as he had done for his own daughter, on the classical middle 'a'. Ann, in fact, was cast in the classical mould herself: the classical, blue-eyed, flaxen-haired Anglo-Saxon mould of the Midland valleys, the world that had produced her mother and grandmother and still produces some of the loveliest girls in all England. It was fitting, I always thought, that my beautiful first daughter should have been born when, in A. E. Housman's immortal words, the cherry was 'hung with bloom along the bough'.

A disturbing thought now occurs. In Chekhov's *The Cherry Orchard* it is the sound of the axe striking at the trunks of cherry trees, in pre-Soviet Russia, that symbolizes the prophecy of doom for the old régime. Today, in Kent, the home of the cherry in England, precisely the same thing is happening. Everywhere cherry trees, so black of branch and so white of blossom, are falling under the axe. A symbol of doom, the end of an era, of the further tightening of the straitjacket of the State, or what? I find the parallel of absorbing, sad, disturbing, even tragic implication.

But in the summer of 1932 neither war nor the axe that falls on cherry trees had begun to cast either their sinister shadow or echo. Madge was now a mother, I a father; the garden was growing; my world was, as it seemed, blossoming: perhaps not so splendidly as that of the cherry trees, but let us say modestly.

And perhaps this, it would seem, is a good place in which to say something of my own mother.

VIII

It may have seemed to certain people an odd fact, even a deficiency, that I had little or nothing to say, in the first volume of my autobiography, *The Vanished World*, of my mother. It may well have been thought that, for some unexposed and unexplained reason, I had largely left her out of it. This is not so.

The two great influences on my earliest years were my father and my grandfather. To the first I owe my literacy and love of music; to the second my love of Nature and the countryside; to both, perhaps, an ability that has sometimes been called the faculty of 'thinking through the pores of my skin'. My mother, excellent mother though she was, exerted no such influence on me.

Born Lucy Elizabeth Lucas, in 1878, elder daughter of my shoemaker grandfather, my mother is now in her ninety-second year, her life thus spanning almost all of what is indisputably the most revolutionary century of all time. It says much for her that she is not merely alive but lively; possessed of all her faculties both physical and mental; keenly interested in domestic and world affairs – an ability and interest she undoubtedly gets from her father; avid reader of newspapers and watcher of the television box; living alone in the largish house built by my paternal grandfather at the turn of the century; still able to stitch and sew beautifully, to do her own cooking, housework and shopping; devoted to visiting, coach outings, church-going, and what my father and grandfather would have called 'shop window fuddling'; highly critical of what she deems to be the deplorable decline of manners and language and especially of the sponging indolence rife under the contemporary umbrella of the Welfare State; forthright in opinion, reserving the higher of her scorn for political tricksters typified largely by so-called socialists.

One of the Old School: that, I suppose, is the readiest and commonest description of her and her kind. When I read of men tottering into fumbling retirement at the age of sixty, so often to moulder away through what should be the riper years of male maturity, afflicted with the grey blight of pensionitis, I like to think of my mother, thirty years their senior, entirely unpensioned because she happens to be a victim, by reason of her age group, by that iniquitous and infamous gap in the cradle-to-the-grave graph of the Welfare State, staunchly holding to her

nonagenarian independence and still extracting interest and pleasure and amusement from living. Perhaps her generation is still better exemplified by a friend of hers, even further advanced into her nineties, who when solicitously asked by my mother if there was anything she needed by way of extra comfort in life replied after singularly brief thought:

'Yes: three things. A new pair of specs, a new set of teeth and – a man.'

My mother was born, like my grandfather and my wife, in the pleasant little stone Northamptonshire shoemaking borough of Higham Ferrers, where she began work at the age of ten, thus doing a little better than her father, who had begun at six, scaring crows. Her starting wage was two shillings a week. This doesn't sound so bad when you remember that it was for half time only. My father was similarly a half-timer: school in the morning, work in the afternoons, or vice versa, I am never sure which. For this splendid sum, anyway, my mother tied knots in a shoe factory, later rising to a position, like her father the shoemaker, where she worked only on special orders demanding exceptional skill.

Northamptonshire, like its neighbouring counties, has long been a stronghold of Nonconformity and at the earliest possible age she was dedicated, as I was later to be, to the cold and un-remitting altar of Methodism, my grandfather, as I have explained in *The Vanished World*, being contemptuously of the opinion that the Church of England was composed of nothing but a psalm-chanting gang of Papists. Methodism, she was telling me only recently, claimed her at half past six every Sunday morning before breakfast; she had a good mile to walk to Sunday School. The disciples of Wesley, in those days, had no use for idle hands. Prayer and parsons and all the rest of the frigid paraphernalia of Wesleyanism kept her, as Chaucer says, 'narwe in cage', until the last session of Sunday School began at 5.30.

Not only Nonconformity but liberalism greatly helped to shape her. On each side of the fireplace in my grandfather's front parlour hung portraits of John Bright and William Ewart Gladstone: the revered twin gods of Victorian liberals. And a liberal she has remained all her life: scorning the soppy hum-bug that surrounds so much of socialism and the flabbiness of character among modern youth that, in her view, so largely stems from it. She is not one to show emotion easily, though this by no means indicates that she is incapable of feeling it. Her capacity for self-reliance has given her a quite extraordinary aptitude for sitting still; she can embalm herself for hours in an aura of peace but at the same time is ever ready to put on her best hat and gad out for a while, either on some shopping expedition or 'just for the ride'. One of her characteristics that has perhaps diminished least with age is her derision of humbug in all its forms. She scorns falsity, arrogance, fuss, self-pity, ostentation, palaver, showing off, high-falutin speech and above all snobbery, whether of rich or poor. She can detect it all from a mile off and this, I am glad to say, forms a good part of my inheritance from her.

Physically she is also cast in that pure Anglo-Saxon mould which, as I have said, has made and still makes the people of the English Midland valleys the best-looking in England, perhaps in Europe. The girls here are renowned for their good looks and my mother, in the days when girls really dressed like girls and looked like flowers, was one of them. I see all the special features of that fine Anglo-Saxon type not only in her but repeated also in my wife, my daughters and my granddaughters: the delicate bones, the fine soft skin, the blue eyes, the fair, light-textured hair. Age may wither, but time cannot alter the bone structure of a face; and at ninety my mother displays a profile beautifully clean in line, handsome and almost unwrinkled, so that she really looks some twenty years younger than she really is.

Does she carry a cross about with her because she once worked for two shillings a week or that she was once so poor, in her early married life, that she was left, one Friday morning, with only sixpence in her purse? Not, as they say nowadays, on your nelly. Today the statisticians would put her last remaining sixpence fifty fathoms deep below the poverty line. But statisticians have no code index for pride and it so happens that the word poverty is not, and never was, in her language. Perhaps she remembered that her own mother had once sat up half the night, by candlelight or even a farden rushlight, and made shirts at sixpence a time; and perhaps it comforted her.

In turn I confess it rather comforts me to be told that as I grow older I tend to become, in looks, not more like my father, whom earlier I was said so much to resemble, but much more like my mother. It would, in fact, not at all surprise me if I too didn't one day inherit her astonishing capacity for sitting still, in prolonged meditative contemplation, a capacity that is, perhaps, the secret of her great age and the smooth, almost unwrinkled shell-like quality of her face. I have an early photograph of her, probably taken about 1883, in which she is wearing an extraordinarily elaborate coat for one so young, a sort of furbelow affair, and in which she is staring at the camera not merely with uncommon gravity, but with a glare positively pugnacious: as if to say 'Life, I'm going to lick you'. It reminds me a good deal of the portrait William Roberts did of me in my early twenties. There is something pugnacious about that too.

In speaking of influences it now occurs to me that the business of contracting early influences in writing and painting may perhaps best be likened to that of contracting common infectious diseases in childhood. The victim comes out in clearly defined but rather nasty spots, all over. Thus an artist such as Christopher Wood contracted nearly all the possible influences, chiefly French, available at the time, before unhappily putting an end to himself at the very moment when he might be said to have gained a clean certificate of health. So it was with the author of *The Two Sisters*, except that gradually, painfully and certainly he shed the contagious influences of his early youth as he had also shed the peeled skin of an early attack of scarlet fever.

The near-fatal lesson of Hardy having by this time been well-learned, I now determined that any new influences on me should not by any chance lay that particular curse on me again. I now in fact fell under the spell of no less than four new masters, two English, W. H. Hudson and Edward Thomas, and two American, Hemingway and Sherwood Anderson, but this time not fatally or even dangerously, but with singular profit. I contend that these two widely separated pairs of writers have a good deal in common. That Edward Thomas was influenced by W. H. Hudson is pretty certain; that Hemingway was influenced by Sherwood Anderson is undoubted. It has also always seemed to me possible that Hudson, being a great friend of Edward Garnett, must have read Turgenev in Constance's translations, as Hemingway most certainly did. Indeed Hemingway actually called one of his shorter novels *The Torrents of Spring*, which of course is one of Turgenev's own titles. This book, intended as a parody of Anderson's *Dark Laughter*, itself a book that clearly reveals a certain lack of self-criticism in Anderson, ironically ended up as an even greater parody of Hemingway himself, with the result that the two books are equally bad. This, however, does not detract at all from the great and revolutionary influence both Hemingway and Anderson conferred on the modern short story. Anderson's own contribution on that score was to break with what he himself called 'the cold, hard stony culture of New England', where the established and cultured writers saw everything as 'a preparation for life after death'; and then to turn away to find the indigenous material of the Middle West, where he began to record, with no touch of false romance, the lives of poor whites, remote farmers, negroes and boys who hang about race tracks, obscure dreamers in the back streets of Chicago, country schoolteachers and lawyers of frustrated ambition living in the desolate dust of forgotten townships and unloved women who walked 'out of nowhere into nothing'. If I were called on to pick one story that is the very essence of Anderson it would be, I think, *The Triumph of the Egg*, an essay in the tragedies of frustration that must surely rank as Anderson's masterpiece.

Anderson, like Hemingway, showed us life not in woolly, grand or 'literary' prose, but in pictures. E. J. O'Brien put this succinctly and well by saying that 'almost for the first time an American artist attempted in his fiction to present a picture rather than to write an ephemeral play', though 'the pictorial values of Sherwood Anderson were not at first apparent because his pictures lacked colour'. Hemingway performed in much the same way, going for that same direct pictorial contact between eye and object, between object and reader. To achieve this he cut out a whole forest of unnecessary verbosity. He trimmed off explanation, discussion, even comment; he hacked off all metaphorical floweriness; he pruned off the dead, sacred clichés; until finally, through the sparse trained words, there was a view:

The road of the pass was hard and smooth and not yet dusty in the early morning. Below were the hills with oak and chestnut trees, and far away below was the sea. On the other side were snowy mountains.

So simple, so un-literary and yet so powerful in pictorial effect were such pieces of Hemingway that they had a great effect on me; and in consequence I learned much from them.

To Hudson I had come rather late, although his book of South American stories *El Ombú* (he had in fact been born in the Southern American continent, in a house called *The Twenty Five Ombú Trees*, the *ombú* being a tree of great size) had been the very first book that Edward Garnett had ever given me. But now, living as I was in that part of England, so rich in wood and downland, so splendid in its great variation of scene and wild life, I turned to him and discovered not only a new master but one with whom I instantly felt the closest kinship. It is largely to Hudson, though also to Edward Thomas, that I owe the enrichment of my ability to put the English countryside down on paper. Galsworthy, who had also been influenced by Constance's translations of Turgenev (that melancholy idyllic little scene of old Jolyon dozing away in the garden in *The Forsyte Saga* is, unless I am much mistaken, almost pure Turgenev) called Hudson 'the rarest spirit, and has the clearest gift of conveying that gift . . . Without apparent effort he takes you with him into a rare, free, natural world, and always you are refreshed, stimulated, enlarged by going there.' Conrad perhaps put it even better by declaring that 'this man writes as the grass grows', which indeed he does. It is evident too that Hemingway also knew Hudson's work, since he refers on one occasion to *The Purple Land*, one of Hudson's two South American romances, peopled as it is with the most gorgeous and seductive of dark-haired beauties, as 'a highly dangerous book to put into the hands of a middle-aged man'.

So Hudson not only enlarged my vision of the natural world, and in particular those parts of it that were now topographically so close to me, but also my ability to write of it. I think that, in the thirties, I must have read almost every word of Hudson and came away, as Galsworthy says, refreshed, stimulated, enlarged. The step from Hudson to Edward Thomas was an inevitable one and though there is unhappily far less of Thomas than of Hudson to be read, I nevertheless rate Thomas' *The South Country* as indisputably the finest piece of prose ever written about the countryside of southern England. Not only is it incomparably beautiful as prose and equally so in its pure quality of evocation, but it serves to reaffirm a truth I have long held to be indisputable: namely that you do not necessarily have to express yourself in hexameters in order to write poetry. *The South Country* is of the purest poetry and Thomas, with Hudson, our greatest nature writer.

Are these two prose-poets read by the generation of today? I cannot say; if not, more's the pity. I will only say that when the snob-pit and the sewers of the 1960s are lost in the limbo to which they are clearly doomed to be sunk, Hudson's truth, expressed in *The Purple Land* will still be valid: 'Ah, yes, we are all vainly seeking happiness in the wrong way'; just as his prose, like that of Thomas, will still be poetry:

> The blue sky, the brown soil beneath, the grass, the trees, the animals, the wind, the rain, and stars are never strange to me; for I am in, and of, and am one, with them; and my flesh and the soil are one, and the heat in my blood and in the sunshine are one, and the winds and the tempests and my passions are one.

Is it possible that in this almost Biblical passage there can be found the finger-post pointing to the happiness that so many in our subtopian, permissive, soured society are seeking but in vain? Perhaps. But there arises from it a thought I find worth pondering on. Perhaps it would do us no harm to try, for a change, living as Conrad rightly maintained Hudson wrote: 'as the grass grows'.

W. H. Hudson

IX

Soon, just as grass grows in the somnolent heat of June, my garden began to grow. The labour of hacking it out of a ruined farmyard, on virgin soil, was inevitably tough; and it soon became clear to me that my own hands, extremely small as they are (it is said of my mother that when I was born she took one look at my hands and made the instant declaration that '*he'll* never get his living by hard work') were not going to be adequate for the job. Ill though I could afford it I knew that I had necessarily to get in, as help, some good strong labour.

I was fortunate enough to find two good men. Alfred was a hefty, cheerful Romney Marsh man of eighteen, his theme song when at work being that then popular ditty *Oi'm 'appy when oi'm 'oikin'*, which he belted out lustily almost all day long. The second man was not eighteen but eighty, and not from Kent but from Cornwall. Very soft spoken, very courteous, very strong for a man of his years, Mr Haley possessed a horse and cart, or could borrow them: I cannot now quite remember which; but immensely useful they turned out to be.

I should now explain that the Granary, in its beautifully squared rag stone, was in the shape of an ▮, the shaded part only of which belonged to us; the rest was a disused stable. I knew that I could, God one day being my helper, buy the stable portion for £100. But God not being a bank and I having about as much chance of finding £100 as I had of striking a pot of gold under the willow tree, I had spoken to Edward Garnett about the possibility of borrowing the money from him, promising to pay him back in five or six instalments. Edward was very willing to help but it was I, not he, who at the last moment got cold feet, fearing that I would never be able to repay him.

It was here that the 'Divinity that shapes our ends' took yet another hand in our affairs. One of the first things that Alfred had persuaded me to do on coming to work for me was to buy a ticket in the Irish Derby Sweepstake, which I did, though rather reluctantly. Shortly afterwards the telephone rang one evening and a telegram informed me that the ticket (pseudonym 'Lucky Ann') had won £100. Since the owner of the stable (one of the often repeated maxims in his puritanical creed was 'the greatest good for the greatest number', on which I used acidly to comment 'Yes: Number One') had already issued thinly veiled threats of turning the stable into two bungalows, thus ruining The Granary, I now felt that I could either have said a thousand prayers or wept for joy. In no time the entire building was ours.

After this blessed stroke of fortune I felt freer to pursue the most important of my horticultural passions: namely the building of a rock garden. But rock being expensive to buy and deliver, this possibility began to seem almost as remote as the £100 until suddenly the hand of Violet Dean again generously stretched itself out to us. In the parkland on which stood her house there also stood a disused rock quarry, and from there, Vie was good enough to tell me, I could take all the rock I wanted.

So began a period of great and exciting toil, in which the man from Romney Marsh, the man from Cornwall, myself and the horse and cart all took strenuous part. Alfred had never heard of a rock garden being built before and now entered into the spirit and sweat of the thing with an ardour that seemed a compound of a fiendish enthusiasm and a kind of disbelieving joy. We might have been building the Pyramids. With equal but quieter strength Mr Haley joined in. Armed with picks, shovels, crowbars, spades and levers we went almost daily to quarry rock: great cheese-green lumps of it, beautifully mossed, often weighing several hundredweight. These Mr Haley, the man of eighty, used to lift bodily into the cart as if they were mere newborn babes.

My role was largely that of instructor; I was the architect. I had swotted everything up; I had soaked myself in the Gospel According to Reginald Farrer. In consequence I knew that a rock-garden should not resemble a cake with stone almonds on top or the grave of a dead elephant stuck about with naked tomb-stones. As a result we were soon moving the huge lumps of our lovely Kentish rag-stone, which somehow in its mossy-green-cream-yellow appearance reflects all the beauty of this southern countryside, into natural order and place. I was excited and happy in doing it all and Alfred sang *Oi'm 'appy when oi'm 'oikin'* with even more joyous gusto.

Alfred, in his youthful strength and ardour, was soon also engaged in another activity. He was digging my first herbaceous border. At some time in his still young life a man had taught him the technique and advantages of what is known as 'double-digging'. With almost an air of guilt Alfred informed me that this would cost me 'half-tidy bit o' money' – wages at 10*d* an hour! – but would pay 'half-tidy middlin' dividends' in the long run. 'Double-digging' in fact takes at least three or four times as long to execute as plain digging but the dividends are indeed truly rich. After thirty-eight years Alfred's border is still as fertile as when it was first made and yet has never had a spoonful of manure or sprinkle of fertiliser on it since the day it was first planted.

From the first the soil was unbelievably rich. It had the substance and appearance of dark brown sugar. The top layer of it went down for a distance of three feet and everything in consequence grew with miraculous rapidity. Roses climbed as if they were Jack's beanstalk. Great pools of the richest gold appeared where Siberian wallflowers grew to a width of a yard per plant; Canterbury bells were like great towers decorated with ballooning old-fashioned bloomers in purple, pink and white. Splendid steeples of delphinium rose. We had a row of peas which grew to a height of eight feet. That no true alpine could survive for long on this over-rich diet of brandy and Christmas pudding was not to be revealed to me until much later. All that mattered now was that my soil, my little plot of England, was heaven-blessed in its fertility. I had inherited the earth and to my joy it was neither fallow nor sorrowful.

After the hard graft of *The Fallow Land* all these excursions into physical activity were also a blessing. My health improved; I felt rampageous as a puppy set free in a forty acre field. It was all both restorative and exhilarating, deeply satisfying and exciting. It is said in fact – and it is not impossible that it is true, since Kent is virtually an island, two-thirds of its boundaries being water – that this particular piece of England, more especially this village and its environs, enjoys an air that is more than usually rich in iodine. But whether true or not you certainly feel that as you breathe it you are breathing something compound of champagne and the sea; and sometimes in those days, when smoke still blackened London and the homeward trains, you felt as you stepped back into the country that you were breathing an air that was not merely pure, but paradisaical, distilled.

The following year, in November, we were still further blessed: this time by the arrival of Ann's sister, Judith. Petite, with the most perfect of heads and lightest, thistledown hair, she too came to us in the pure Anglo-Saxon mould.

At the foot of the narrow little lane that runs by the house flows the young River Stour: shallow, softer than Thames flowing softly, its course taking it through meadows lying under the fringes of woods of hazel, sweet chestnut, alder, poplar and birch, all of them home of a million bluebells in spring, the scent a total embalmment of the air. In spring too the alders bear russet-brown-gold catkins that dip down to the surface of the stream and in summer the banks are lined with meadowsweet, purple loose-strife, willowherb and wild yellow mimulus. In summer too long emerald water weeds skein out into the currents, sinuously, and water ranunculus sprinkles the surface of the pools with white flowers. Today the stream is stocked with trout, but in those days you saw only a few shoals of roach and perch, an occasional pike lying in wait under the little stone bridge that spans the stream by the lane, and there were crayfish under the stones.

Just as I had once spent golden days with my grandfather gathering watercress on the little tributary of my native Nene, so I now began to spend days just as golden, indeed even richer, by the young Stour gently flowing. There is something of endless fascination in these smaller streams; they evoke an affection that I find all too often that larger rivers fail to inspire. You couldn't row a boat on the Stour at this point; but you could sit and watch and dream an afternoon by, see a heron poised like a predatory grey statue among the tall bottle green reeds and watch snipe and kingfisher swoop swiftly, royally past you.

In the lane itself bracken grew higher than a man, thick green in summer, gold-brown as the turkey oaks become in November, when at this moment, as I write, they are like purified gold against the thin blue of winter sky, above the first light fall of snow. And here in the brown-gold bracken, as winter began to turn to spring, I remember once how we disturbed a half-waking dormouse from his long hibernation and how he crept half-sleepily out and gently, like some soft brown miniature squirrel, crept up Ann's arm and sat there unafraid, bright little eyes just open, turning hesitantly this way and that, as if wondering how he had come to wake, after winter, in the spring-like hand of a child.

Such tiny incidents not only remain long in the memory. They grow in memory, their power of illuminating the past growing also as time itself goes past. I remember also other tiny things: white wild violets fat as snowdrop buds on spring banks, drifts of white wood sorrel in the woods themselves; the silent swim of water voles on summer afternoons and of grass snakes idly swimming too. And often and often simply the mere silence of it, especially in high summer, when the grand spring opera choruses of birds have died away. There are still times, when I come home from London or from some noisy journey by road or train or air, when that silence says more than a thousand orchestrated chords, so marvellously evocative that it too achieves a state of embalmment so deep that it often takes me a day or two to get used to it.

It is sometimes said of me that I evoke only the golden days. Indeed I once remember a female reviewer rather testily inquiring 'Where *does* Mr Bates get his weather from?' as if the Almighty had provided some special dispensation for me in that direction. But certain it is, as I note from a letter to Constance Garnett, that the year 1933 was a golden one. In the August of 1933 I was writing to her 'What a summer. What a parched desolation for

gardens . . . like you I feel inclined to throw it all up until crocus time.' About this time too I was writing to Edward that I was wrestling with the 'udders of imagination, hoping that milk will come'; and also about the same time to Constance of 'acute worry about money and stories and so on'; and then again that 'in the interest of trying to knock debts on the head I am planning a novel – to be robust, long, rich, full of country stuff, with a poacher-vagabond in it'.

So though the days in memory may be golden, just as I am certain they were golden in reality, the bank balance was not. No sooner had I begun *The Poacher*, in the winter of 1934, than I had to give it up in order, as I wrote to Edward:

'To try to get some ready cash. Things are for the moment a bit desperate and I have been wondering if you could lend me £20 until, say, the end of February? I have money owing me by various editors, but I can't get a cent of it and the *London Mercury* has failed and left me a creditor for £15. The doctor's bills for my wife have drained me a lot and I've insurance to meet this week too. I hate asking this – but if you could manage it I should be more than grateful. I can safely pay you back in a week or two. I am doing some country essays and stories until I find my feet again.'

'Finding my feet again' took, in fact, another year, that being the time it took to see *The Poacher* through to publication. Happily it got the best press of all my early novels; but by the time it was out I was under the enforced necessity of starting another novel, this time *A House of Women*, a book again set in my native Nene Valley. And so the pattern went: novel, expired bank balance, stories, reviews and articles in order to restore it, dunning editors for money, begging the Garnetts for their opinions on MSS, which they always freely and kindly gave; and always the struggle to pay bills, the struggle against gnawing abdominal pains, always the dread of making another botch-up with a novel and thus wasting half a year or even a year; and always the uncertainty, the irregularity of income, the constant nagging of insecurity, the fear of drying up, of greater debts, of failures and rejections.

But then, who was I to complain? This, surely, was the life I had chosen to lead, this the profession I had sworn to pursue, come hell or high water. If fate appeared sometimes to be a bit tough on me I had to be honest and tell myself that there had also been times when it had looked on me with good grace and no doubt would do so again.

It was no use weeping against the wall. Indeed it was just as well that I had in me that touch of pugnacity.

X

As the golden days increased, like my family, and as the garden grew in beauty and maturity, there also grew in me a comparable uneasiness about other things. I couldn't rid myself of a sense of impending doom.

By the middle thirties the hard-won fruits of the 1914–18 victory, so-called, had already been thrown away. The shadow of depression, large enough as it was in all conscience, seemed to me about to be overshadowed by an even greater one: that of a second world war. Possible though it may be that I have a sixth sense I do not pretend to have much skill in the realms of prophecy; yet by the year 1935 (a year when as it happens greater minds than mine had decided it to be imperative that we discover the miracle now known as radar, or perish) it already seemed to me that war, sooner or later, and probably sooner, was inevitable. In Germany the lunatic growth of Nazism and Hitler seemed to me like part of a ghoulish, terrifying piece of *Grand Guignol*, unfolding inexorably to a nightmare end. I used to talk to people who were either just not interested or could not believe in this. I for my part believed it so passionately, though with an embittered reluctance, that I used to have open fits of anger about it and sometimes inner fits of frenzy. Man had been insane enough in 1914; I found it a matter of excruciating and impossible difficulty to believe that he could be as wildly insane again and yet in my heart I was utterly convinced, though against my will, that soon he was going to be.

I was fortified – the word is ironical if you care to read it that way – by the dispatches then being sent to London by *The Times* Berlin correspondent, Douglas Reed, who was presently to expand these dispatches into a book called *Insanity Fair*, which Jonathan Cape published. My most awful fear having been confirmed by *Insanity Fair* I begged that Cape should send a free copy to every member of Parliament, a suggestion that Rupert Hart-Davis received with the wearily ironical sentence 'My dear boy, what's the use? They can't read anyway.'

The most terrifying thing about Reed's book was the accuracy of its prophecy. He had watched, listened and had been horrified by what he had seen and heard in Germany. On several visits to Germany Madge and I too had watched and heard the reflections and echoes, in reality, of those of which Reed had written: the confiscation of certain English newspapers in trains at the frontier, the nightly tramp of the feet of Hitler youth in school playgrounds, the swastikas, the swaggering jack-boots, the furtive voice of a doctor whispering to us on a Rhine steamer 'You say you have a daughter named Judith. That is a Jewish name. Are you Jewish?' It was of little avail or comfort to him to tell him, jocularly, that I had named my daughter Judith because Shakespeare had also had a daughter named Judith and that I had vowed to have at least one thing in common with him. He, the doctor, was a Jew. Nor was it of any comfort to us to be told by a young Nazi on the same boat: 'In the war you made us eat pigswill. Soon, now, we will make *you* eat pigswill.'

Reading *Insanity Fair* was, in fact, rather like eating pigswill. It made you sick: not bodily sick, but sick in mind, spirit and soul. Here, as in some hideous glass ball, the future was set out with terrifying accuracy for all to see: the Saar, the Sudetenland, Czechoslovakia, Dantzig, Austria, Belgium, France and lastly, of course, England. Every ghoulish prophecy, and a thousand more that we didn't yet know about were eventually to come true with uncanny, bitter, sickening accuracy. And it seemed to me that Reed set out his arguments with such power and cogency that no one of right mind could deny them. I certainly could not;

everything intelligent and civilised in me told me that we had looked into a glass darkly and had seen the black, diseased doomed face of Europe's future.

I used to go about trying to convince all kinds of people of the reason and realism of my fears about these things; few listened. Once I even got up and delivered an impassioned homily to a parish meeting (I was now, incredibly, chairman of the Parish Council); I might have been talking to an assembly of moles. Not that this greatly surprised me. One of the first things that had struck Madge and me on our first coming to live in Kent was the depth of rural insularity we found there; people existed, rather than lived, in a rural vacuum. There were cottagers who never went into the nearest market town more than once a year. The level of political consciousness, compared with that of the Nene Valley, where it is conspicuously high, was pitifully low. I do not much care for the word yokel, but this, more or less, was what we found: a withdrawn, dark, ungiving people, insular, defensive, highly suspicious of strangers, distrustful of all intruders, hard to make friends with. That they didn't want to listen to my impassioned prophecies of war therefore didn't surprise me; what I found ironical to note was that soon, if and when war came, as I was positive it would, it would be they who would be in the front line of battle.

Insular as they were, they inevitably had insular customs and traditions. In winter it was customary, every ten years or so, to cut down the sweet chestnut trees which almost always grow, very closely together, in small copses called *cants*. Men, as they still in fact do, would set up little huts among the thinning dark grey trunks and blue smoke from their fires of bark shavings drifted and hung about the air. Soon too, wherever the light came in, the very earliest primroses began to bloom, then crowds of white anemones, then bluebells, then petticoat-pink campions. The poles were invariably cut and split for snake-fencing or used whole as hop-poles. The Romans, it is said, first brought over the sweet chestnuts, since the nuts were part of the staple diet of the soldiery. In other copses, largely of hornbeam, charcoal burners still worked, since charcoal, so much used in the old bakehouses of London, is apparently best made from hornbeam.

And then while the chestnut was still being felled and split, the first actual work in the hop-gardens began: that beautifully fascinating business of stringing the poles so that the whole garden takes on the look of some gigantic white-gold spider web.

Then soon came the white of pear and apple blossom, the even whiter bloom of cherry, and then last the pinks and reds of apple. In mid-summer hay turners, still horse-drawn, rattled about the meadows and in August binders, horse-drawn too, clacked about the fields of oats and wheat and barley. By the time plums had grown purple-fat on trees and had been gathered the real festival of the year, the English *vendange*, the hop-picking, began, bringing the centuries old fusion of Cockneys from London and the people of Kent, in almost precisely the way peasants forgather for grape-harvests in autumn in European vineyards.

I always felt that this festival, for which surely every working family turned out, was not only gay, as indeed it was with all the chaff and joking old-buck backchat and teasing and beery fighting and wenching that went on in and around it, was something more than just the mere business of picking hops for brewers; it always struck me as being a sort of pagan rite. And thus, I always felt, the people of Kent perhaps also saw it, though not of course consciously; it was a rite that had to be attended, a festival that had to be worshipped at. Nobody, except toffs and squires, ever missed hop-picking. Every mother took every child with her to the hop-gardens and every child, except those still being suckled at the breast, picked hops, from the first dewy misty light of September mornings until the soft descent of dusk and its shouted evening benediction that rang out down the pale green lines of fallen or half fallen hop-skeins: 'Pull no more bine!'

They pull the bine by machine today and every year the Cockneys come in smaller and smaller numbers. There are things called quotas and you see somewhere every year the saddest of sights that can surely blight a fertile country: whole gardens of hops being burnt as they stand. Now too they pile fertilisers with desperate prodigality on to cereal land, so that the corn grows dark and rich and much of it falls flat, still green, at the first moderately heavy rain. In turn combine harvesters suck at the ripened grain rather like huge scarlet pigs rootling at the earth for food and in turn again the stubbles are burned, leaving scorched earth in black zebra stripes, depressing as if a burning, invading army had just passed through.

If the villagers in September escaped to their festival of hops, we in August escaped to the sea. We loved most, I think, to go by way of that strange, flat, wide-skied kingdom that is Romney Marsh, where grey-mauve marsh-mallows line the dykes and herons stand poised above the still waters and the sea seems to be for ever reflected with a pure salty brilliance in the air. I always felt a sense of flight as I crossed this marsh and its dykes, an uplifting as if I were a bird. Soon you came to stretches of shingle that lie between marsh and shore and breasted sand-dunes often as white as salt too. Wild yellow horned poppies grew about shore and shingle, together with big floppy trumpets of pink convolvulus. Long stretches of seakale in white flower stretched out, in places, almost to the edge of the sea, and sea-thistle rose everywhere as blue and sharp as steel.

In places strange little black huts lined the shore, like abandoned sentinel boxes, and in dazzling contrast blue and copper kingfishers flashed along the dykes. Black fishing boats drawn up on sand and shingle were exactly like pictures out of Boudin, and fishermen sat mending or drying nets beside them, gossiping and smoking, waiting for the turn of tide. Farther east we made for Folkestone, the harbour, the blue fishing boats and the little stalls selling whelks and cockles and mussels and soles and mackerel and plaice. I didn't know in those days that Manet's *Les Bateaux de Folkestone* marks the very beginning of Impressionism, though so it evidently does; but the scene cannot have looked vastly different to the young and despised Manet, back in the nineteenth century, than it did to Madge and me and the young Bates sisters on salty, fishy August afternoons thirty odd years ago. You could buy a good fat Dover sole then for 6*d*, a big plaice for 6*d*, a little one for a penny, a herring for a penny and enough sprats for a family for 6*d*.

For some curious reason – perhaps because they went to sea in ships and knew great waters – there was always something far less insular, far less defensive, about those Folkestone fishermen and their nearly always fat, jolly wives than about their dark, resentfullooking brethren farther inland. The men of Kent are sharp and shrewd; and even the sharpest, shrewdest Cockney, so they will tell you, can be gypped there. But for my part I always got a feeling of openness, a sort of sea-free carelessness, perhaps deriving from a sea-to-shore, hand-to-mouth existence, down in that rather shabby, often muddy harbour, with its fish stalls, fish auctions, wet fish being sliced and beheaded and pale gold nets hanging out to dry.

They, like our inland primrose woods, helped to prevent my brooding too long and too hard on the thunderclouds of war. But soon two other events of more importance took place in my life: one sad, one a further extension of its blossoming.

XI

Those were the days, the mid-thirties, as were those of William Morris, when select Private Presses flourished and there was in the air a certain slight madness about first editions. One result of this was that the Golden Cockerel Press had, in 1935, commissioned me to write a book for them. They had in fact already published two books of mine, *The House with the Apricot* and *A German Idyll*, the latter the long story I had conjured out of that half-crazy visit to Germany with Rhys Davies, William Roberts, Charley Lahr and other friends.

My memory, normally good, now serves me rather hazily; but unless I am greatly mistaken it was in June 1935 that Christopher Sandford and his fellow directors at the Golden Cockerel kindly arranged to give the book, *Flowers and Faces*, an afternoon party in Kensington, the party being in the afternoon so that guests could also see the King and Queen go past on their Jubilee Procession. I felt very flattered at all this and the affair was naturally, on a pleasant June afternoon, very gay.

During the course of it I was asked to meet a young publisher. Michael Joseph, dark, charming, intelligent, goodlooking, proceeded to tell me that he had just hung out his sign, the Mermaid, in Bloomsbury, thus setting up in his own right as publisher. We took to each other instantly and found we had much in common. We liked, among other things, football (Michael had once been selected to play for the British Army, having been chosen in the belief that he was an international of the same name), fishing, the countryside, books and especially fiction.

M. J. proceeded presently to ask me if I was entirely satisfied with my present publishers. I replied that I had seen no reason so far to be otherwise, at which he said:

'Then we'll forget the matter. But if ever you should change your mind will you remember that, of all our young authors, it is you that I would like to publish most?'

There and then, genuinely and not with that mere politeness that parties so often generate, I said that if ever at any time I was forced to consider a change, I would go to him. M. J., in fact, had already outlined several ideas about publishing that much appealed to me. He thought, quite rightly, that in those days far too many books were being published, a great many of them indiscriminately, with the result that each book got far too little individual attention and in consequence authors were poorly served. This struck me as sound sense. What I also liked was that his new publishing house was largely to be based on fiction, of which M. J. had considerable knowledge, and this of course was my field.

I do not believe, on the whole, in authors changing publishers. The impression created, as I see it, can be an exceedingly bad one. But when the time came for a reasoned and logical dissatisfaction with Jonathan Cape there was only one other publisher to whom I wished to go.

It was to Michael Joseph. But that event was still nearly ten years ahead and war, my damned inevitable war, was still to separate that gay afternoon in Kensington, with its celebratory party, its fluttering colours of bunting and pennants and flags and the King and Queen driving past in a world of what seemed happy peace, from the day I joined M. J. and his Mermaid in Bloomsbury Street.

It was another two years before the other event of importance occurred and when it did it was one of the deepest melancholy.

Edward Garnett, rising to dress himself one February morning in 1937, suddenly complained of a violent pain in his head and collapsed, fatally stricken by cerebral haemorrhage. In that moment I lost a friend, guide, counsellor, confidant, comforter and critic.

MICHAEL JOSEPH
26 Bloomsbury Street

I say critic: yet I think it right to say that I never really thought of Edward as a critic and that it is probably just as true to say that he probably never thought of himself as one either. He had a singular contempt for the academic critic, who 'he thought boiled the old bones of the great departed but could not recognise a living genius'. No doubt he cherished an equal contempt for many others of the species, most of whom are still with us: the literary club armchair critic, the critic egotistical, determined to show how far finer fellow he is than he who is under criticism, the smart-alec critic, the pontificator critic, the windbag critic, the critic who dresses it all up in jargon that only he himself can understand, the elephant critic, who never forgets old wounds, the pay-off-old-scores critic, the critic who deludes himself that success is inevitably synonymous with badness and that the seclusion of ivory towers is likewise synonymous with a rare and exclusive greatness.

In all these senses Edward was not a critic. He provided, instead, the light by which literature is discovered, the diagnosis which reveals what is only suspected. The critic, as Mr William Gerhardi (now Gerhardie) has pointed out in an admirably perceptive assessment of the novel in a preface to his own novel *Futility*, rarely teaches. He has little or nothing to offer that will assist the creative mind. He is tasting wine, sampling it with approval or disapproval, for the public appetite; the torturing mysteries of creation are utterly hidden from him. Garnett, on the other hand, being unfettered by academic training in literature, was left free to be able to penetrate the creative mind with the rarest insight and having penetrated it was capable of recognising, shaping, nursing, and bringing to fruition its infinite possibilities. That is true criticism: the criticism that is also creative; the criticism that brings the bud to flower.

In that field Edward Garnett had, and has had since, except perhaps in a few minor instances, no rival. His type is so rare, his combination of insight, profound sympathy and infinite enthusiasm (an enthusiasm that flowed till the end of his life) so great that it is not at all surprising that no one succeeds him today. The very term 'publishers' reader' is one of horror; it conjures up a picture of the wretchedest sort of underpaid hack poring over impossible beer-stained, tea-stained manuscripts in a dingy back office, anonymous, bronchial, long-suffering, eaten away by cynicism. Nothing could be further from the truth as far as Edward Garnett was concerned. A certain playful sort of cynicism, revealed by a diabolical glint or two of the eyes, the natural product of a temperament exposed to the treachery and disillusionment of modern society and modern literary and publishing society in particular ('We are not in it for our health, Mr Garnett, we are not in it for our health') undoubtedly revealed itself in him from time to time, but it was almost always accompanied by laughter; but as to the task to which he undoubtedly felt himself solemnly called, just as other men may feel themselves called to the church or medicine or teaching he brought no kind of cynicism at all – a truly astonishing fact when one considers that he was engaged in one of the most profitless and thankless of literary tasks for over forty years.

He was never a prey to deceptions. He never believed that because the surface of a work of art is light its heart is therefore frivolous; he had undoubtedly heard the precise opposite in Mozart, whom he adored, and must have seen it in his parallel in painting, Watteau. The sketchy vernacular surface of Henry Lawson's stories of the Australian outback didn't prevent his instant detection of the sadness, even tragedy, lying underneath. Nor was he deluded into thinking that because a subject is 'lofty' the sentiments extracted from it are automatically 'lofty' too. It is a sad mistake to assume, as Mr Gerhardie points out, that,

> a place of honour is assigned to 'serious' subjects expressing lofty, solemn and sonorous sentiments, betraying an unhealthy preoccupation with the other world to the exclusion of common everyday sense. The truth is, in fact, the reverse. The more deeply rooted in life, the more steeped in humorous tragedy . . . the more serious in the real sense will be the heavenly forces released in implication. And the more highfalutin the subject, the more grandiloquent the manner

and dead-earnest the aim, the more nebulous, windy, dogmatic, flat, inaccurate, woolly, lifeless, trivial, shallow and worthless will be the result because the writer has seen fit to use his own foolish tongue to state that which a wiser man would have left implied. No *intellectual* belief is required from the pure poet.

Exactly. The word to note here is 'implication', since it takes me directly back to Garnett's preface to *The Two Sisters*, in which he had noted that events were implied rather than chronicled, a truth that, when after long and painful struggle I had recognised it, finally provided me with the living key to all my work as a writer of stories. Nor was it the only truth towards which Garnett had directed me. In a preface to a volume of Turgenev's stories he had pointed out that the novel, far from being dead, as is often declared, 'can become anything according to the hands that use it'; and in an even more memorable passage had said: 'if you love your art, if you would exalt it, treat it absolutely seriously.' And this, whether the subject has been tragic or comic, light or apparently casual, I have ever since tried to do.

On a February day with the first touch of warmth in it Edward was cremated at Golders Green. Yellow crocuses were blooming about the grass and I thought of Constance and the garden at the Cearne. I could not help reflecting too that Edward, like me, had begun his literary career as a very young man. Almost all his first discoveries, Conrad, Galsworthy Hudson, Doughty and so on, had been men much older than himself. Now, by the nineteen-thirties, all of them were dead and he had reached a period, his rare enthusiasm diminished only by death, when all his stars were much younger than himself. So it was a following of very young men who stood that day to pay homage to him – H. A. Manhood, Geraint Goodwin, Hamish Miles, Arthur Calder-Marshall, Rupert Hart-Davis and myself.

All of us, but I think myself most of all, owed him much; and all of us had delighted in him.

Joseph Conrad

XII

By this time Madge and I were expecting a third baby and it will give some idea of the high state of my finances if I say that one day I accepted with alacrity an invitation from Graham Greene to lunch with him at a restaurant he had just discovered: 'You can eat for one-and-ninepence.' The place was in fact that splendidly Edwardian pub in the heart of London's theatre-land, all brass and red plush and mirrors and beer-engines and snug corners, the Salisbury in St Martin's Lane. Graham, as impecunious as I was, had discovered with delight that for one-and-ninepence you could get soup, a large plate of boiled or roast beef, roast lamb or pork, some sort of pudding or cheese with perfectly magnificent celery. It was all excellent.

Neither of us had enjoyed, up to that time, anything more than a *succès d'estime*, to which on my behalf Graham had contributed a generous appraisal of *Cut and Come Again*, the volume of stories containing *The Mill*. In it he had compared me fairly and squarely with Chekhov, saying that he didn't think me the lesser artist. In consequence my literary stock now stood pretty high and I there-fore felt that the time had come when I should attempt to build something of ambition and solid worth on these foundations.

One of the things that had long fascinated me about the English landscape was the Great House, of which Northampton-shire is particularly rich in beautiful examples, both in glory and in decay. What had further fascinated me was the subject of the growth of the selfmade man, often virtually uneducated, often

THE SALISBURY

rough and crude, who through sheer force of native energy and character had bulldozed his way to the top: yet another example of the fact that character not only assails bastions where education fears to tread but is capable of engendering a warmth and attraction that figures academic and over-civilised all too often lack. What was in my mind was to write a novel in which these two forces come together: on the one hand the grandeur of the Great House that seemed unassailable and unpossessable except to those privileged by right of birth and inheritance, and on the other by a character born in poverty, ignorance and even squalor, deprived equally of material care and opportunity, who in spite of it all forges his way through like some blundering ambitious ox until at last he is the possessor of the Great House from which, in the bitterest of winters, he once stole coal in order to keep his dying mother warm.

The theme seemed to me to call for bold and powerful treatment; it was no pastoral sketch. I saw in it not only a personal struggle but a piece of social history, a segment of the late Industrial Revolution that had marked my native landscape with so many soulless, hideous red-brick scars. In this landscape the remnants of the pastoral would serve to heighten the deadly nature of the new world of the machine, and vice versa. Its life would be robust but also lyrical, the progress of its main character ruthless but also sympathetic and sensual. Set in a mould of extreme ugliness, he was to have in fact a compelling and fatal attraction for women, for each of which, in his progress to the top, he was to feel a variety of passionate attachments.

I forged ahead with the Chronicle of Bruno Shadbolt with a conscious strength and confidence I had not experienced before. I felt, from the first, that the theme itself was right and that the foundation on which I was building was also right. I wasn't building on clay; underneath me I could feel, perhaps truthfully for the first time as a novelist, impermeable layers of rock. In the ill-fated *The Voyagers* all my instincts had seemed to warn me that its foundations and workmanship were jerry-built and Garnett had proved me right. Now there was no Garnett, either as boss or foreman, to guide my literary trowel and plumb line, but now all my instincts, tempered hard by another ten years of experience, told me that I was building true and straight. When on the last page of the book Bruno Shadbolt at last stands by the Great House he has battled for and won there is a moment when the reader must feel, if I have done my work correctly, that material gain and wealth do not necessarily build an altar of happiness. He is caught up in 'the sudden concentration of years of loneliness. He was a man without friends.' Alone, all ambition, all passion spent, he simply becomes 'one with the stones of the house'.

I had called the novel, which spans the years 1873–1931, *Spella Ho*. I had taken the title from a chance map-reference of the county of Northamptonshire. The reference, 'Spella Ho', clearly indicated 'Spella House', but there seemed to be something far more arresting and dramatic in the brevity of 'Spella Ho' and so it became. It also became, after a dozen years of toil in which there had been disappointments which anything but sheer youth could have considered heartbreak, my first commercial success. Not that it even remotely approached the contemporary commercial success that young writers, even with their first books, are apt to achieve today, when radio, television, films and the flares of publicity of all kinds shoot a writer to stardom almost before the ink on his paper is dry. But the book was reprinted three times in the first year of its publication: for me little short of a miracle.

That the miracle had arrived at the most opportune of moments is indisputable. In the July of the previous year our first son, Richard Lucas, named after his maternal greatgrandfather the farmer-shoemaker, had been born: a July that miraculously lives in the memory not only for the exquisite nature of the summer itself but for the masses of giant tiger-lilies that regaled the garden and which I have never since grown so well. A lusty and elegant young man, Richard was early so adept at conducting the garden bird-chorus from his pram, with hands of waving enthusiasm, that I wrote to my father to tell him that assuredly, at last, we had a solid musical exponent in the family. Alas, though music is high on the list of Richard Lucas Bates' passions, he too is yet another in the long line of Bates who, in the musical medium, cannot transmute worship into creative activity.

My memory is here a little vague as to immediate subsequent events, though by no means as to those which were to happen a little later. I have perhaps belaboured the theme of the 'Divinity that shapes our ends' but certainly it was at work again in the early part of 1938, when I fancy it must have been Rupert Hart-Davis who sent proofs of *Spella Ho* over to the Little Brown Co. of Boston USA. I may be wrong in this and it is possible that the passage of the proofs took place at the instigation of the Americans, since I well remember that Ellery Sedgewick, then editor of the *Atlantic Monthly*, had asked Sylvia Townsend Warner, on a visit to England, who were the young English writers he ought most to be looking out for and had received the reply 'H. E. Bates'. At any rate the proofs of *Spello Ho* duly arrived in Boston and one spring evening I was astonished to receive a cable from there not only offering me good terms for the book itself but a sum of no less than 5000 dollars for the serialisation of the book in the *Atlantic Monthly*.

I went about for days in a startling state of crazy disbelief. Apart from the immense prestige of appearing in the *Atlantic*, a magazine held perhaps in higher esteem at that time in America than any other, the money itself was the equivalent of the discovery of a gold mine at the bottom of the garden. I had never heard of such money. A subsequent letter from the *Atlantic* indicated that the novel as it stood was slightly long and that it would necessarily have to be cut for serialisation purposes. Would I object to the editor of the *Atlantic* cutting it according to their way of thinking? or would I care to cut it myself? With alacrity I not only declared I would cut it myself but that I was prepared to go to America to do so.

Accordingly I set off for America somewhere about the middle of May. I travelled by that old ladylike Cunarder *The Aquitania* and I suppose that in a way, compared with our contemporary flights of a few hours, it was rather like having an extremely leisurely meal in the mahogany panelled, palm-fringed restaurant at St Pancras station, where I had sometimes eaten with my father as a boy. The prodigious breakfasts, the heavy lunches and dinners, the lavish afternoon teas with a palm court orchestra playing *Tea for Two* or *Tip-toe Through the Tulips* seemed to belong not merely to an already distant Edwardian era but now, in memory, to something even further away.

I arrived in a New York hot, steamy and objectionable as only New York can be when the first heat of summer strikes it like a mounting fever. There can be few great cities in the world whose greeting to the passenger by sea is more depressing and revolting. The gates of the land of the free, in the grey purlieus of the downtown waterfront, are more like the portals of a prison than the gateway to freedom and prosperity. I was, however, not depressed on that first torrid sweating day as I set foot on America's sordid soil. I was borne forward on a great wave of exhilaration: a wave I was never to experience on any subsequent visit, when my impression that New York is a cardboard and concrete theatrical set liable to disintegrate and disappear overnight increased until I could no longer bear the overwhelming conviction that this is a city as uncivilised as Sodom and Gomorrah.

I spent a day and a half looking, rubber-necked fashion, at the sights New York's visitors are supposed to look at, and then entrained for Boston. It says much for my abysmal ignorance of America that it was firmly fixed in my mind that Boston was a small parochial town something of the size and nature of Cambridge, England. I can only suppose that the legend of the stony nature of New England's literary culture had created so false an impression. I was anyway astonished to discover that Boston was a vast port – and a highly entertaining one – and a city of some millions of people, including, it would seem, its own population of gangsters. In one thing, however, my preconceived notions of Boston were not ill-conceived. The *Atlantic Monthly Press* had kindly put me up at one of Boston's many clubs, an establishment that it seemed to me was far more English, far more exclusive, far more Victorian than the Athenaeum, Brooks's, White's or the Bengal Club in Calcutta rolled into one. An abiding memory of this masculine, mahogany museum is of my rising to go to breakfast on the first morning of my arrival and of meeting, on stairs and in corridors, a number of completely naked Bostonian gentlemen, all looking like uncooked kippers, on their way to take their morning baths. White-moustached, military, dehydrated, more English-colonel than any English officer who ever ordered a *chota-peg* in Poona, they gave the impression that they were daily awaiting orders from General Grant to pour the whisky and advance with infuriated dignity on the despicable rebels of the south. I have never forgotten those naked kippers.

In due course, that first morning, I went along to the offices of the *Atlantic Monthly* to meet various directors and other people, most of whose names I have now forgotten. Boston too was hot and sticky. Afterwards we went along to Beacon Hill to meet directors of the parent company Little Brown & Co. and then to lunch. It is the saddest of facts that of the people I met at lunch that day the greater part, though comparatively young, were to be dead within a year or two, it being Little Brown's misfortune at that time that its executives tended to fall by the wayside like stricken flies in the heat of Boston's summer.

I liked Boston, long-scorned for its stuffiness – that is by America's own brash, half-civilised standards – though it was. It is true that its famed magnolias, of which its streets are as gay in springtime as a Kentish orchard is with cherry-blossom, were already over but its park-like centre had charm and its central heart at least wore a recognisable badge of something civilised. It had also lots of restaurants, Swedish, Norwegian, German, French, Danish and so on at which it was cheap and fun to eat and at which I subsequently did. You could eat dinner, as I recall it, for less than a dollar a head (sometimes they even threw in a free dry martini for that figure) just as in London, at the same time, you could eat a marvellously good five-course lunch at the Café Royal for 3/6, or a seven-course dinner for 5/- – a dinner so exceptional in quality and quantity that the dramatic critic James Agate was once moved to write a whole article devoted to its gastronomical triumphs.

After lunch, on that first day in Boston, it had been arranged that I should be taken on a tour of the city – this to include all buildings old and historical, the town of Cambridge and naturally the Harvard University itself. The English visitor had to be suitably guided and impressed by those parts of the city whose history was not unconnected with that of his own country. Accordingly I was put into the charge of a young man, Archibald Ogden of the *Atlantic*, who had been provided with a motor car. My impression then was, and still is, that Mr Ogden did not wholly relish the task to which he had been assigned. I rather fancy that he reasoned – and even perhaps feared – that his guest would be an English stuffed-shirt, superior, insular, aloof, inclined if not actually dedicated to the proposition that all Americans are savages, uncouth and of dubious upbringing, who speak a language apparently taught them by semi-literate nasal apes. I rather think that he in turn thought I should speak in a near unintelligible Oxford drawl, my conversation interspersed with witless repetition such as 'I mean to say', 'What-ho', 'Frightfully decent' and 'Ifya know what I mean, old sport, what?'

Anyway we duly motored off, Mr Ogden taking me in the course of duty to see the older parts of Boston and thence to Cambridge and Harvard. We duly looked at Harvard. We duly looked at Harvard Yard. Then we duly looked at Harvard again; and dutifully yet again. Then Mr Ogden said:

'I guess you've seen plenty of universities before?'

I said I guessed I had.

'Oxford and Cambridge I guess?'

I said yes, both.

'You go to either?'

No, I assured him, I hadn't been to either. Nor, in fact, did I regret the omission.

This confession seemed not only to warm Mr Ogden; it seemed almost to cause him to begin to revise his uneasy conception of his young English companion, replacing it with the possible thought that I might even be human. At any rate he was now moved to inquire if I had seen enough of Harvard?

I thanked him and said yes, I thought I had.

'Well, in that case, what would you like to see now?'

My reply was one which Archibald Ogden, my friend now for more than thirty years, will never forget.

'I'd like to see the Red Sox.'

As if emotionally pole-axed Archie stood for some moments speechless outside the near-sacred portals of Harvard and then broke out into the wildest of grins. It was rather as if an American, asked as he stood at the gates of Buckingham Palace if he would like to meet the King had replied No, he'd rather go to New-market. The joy and relief on Archie's face were a miracle to behold.

'When,' he said, 'would you like to go?'

'Now.'

We went. I was entranced; and a strange thing happened. Our seats enjoined us to an old Bostonian sweat, wrinkled as a deflated pig's bladder, alcoholic of eye, oyster-like of gaze, tough and toothless of mouth. His mother's breasts had clearly been carved from base-balls. His vocabulary included no word by the minutest degree distant from the language of the game. His bible was the game's book of rules, both authorised and unauthorised. A certain arid cynicism, long born of the truth that all opponents are crooks and all umpires paid servants of the devil, hung about him like a grey shroud. This shroud had obviously covered him in his cradle and would no doubt cover him, embroidered with those cynical words 'Three Blind Mice', in his grave.

As the game progressed this shroud became slowly lifted. It began to be borne upon the old Bostonian sweat that he was sitting next to a grown man – none other than myself – to whom the very rudiments of a game he had sucked in with his mother's milk were having to be explained, as to a child, syllable by syllable, word by word. It was utterly beyond belief; it simply couldn't be; it just was not possible that there could exist on earth a man, a

grown man, who had no fundamental understanding of things as fundamental as pitcher, striker, home run and all that. As the game grew and the excitement grew the great wonder of his disbelief also grew, until the oyster alcoholic eyes had me fixed in a stare that told me that never again would he believe that Englishmen were anything but pitifully, primevally mad.

But by the end of the ball game one thing was certain, incontrovertibly and incontestably certain: Archie Ogden and I were not only friends but friends for life. Even Archie's drymartinis, of ill-fame and unrecorded strength, produced for my edification two evenings later and causing me to be carried home – on, I think, a bier – failed to destroy a friendship so happily begun. We discovered, among other things, that we shared a not dissimilar sense of humour, a total contempt for the pompous, a love of life and a passion for literature. Archie in turn has wisely discovered a love of England, where he now lives, and is, if I am not mistaken, now profoundly devoted to Dr Johnson's proposition that 'he who is tired of London is tired of life'.

Archie was only one of several young people then in the editorial service of the *Atlantic Monthly* and as I proceeded morning by morning to the excision and revision of *Spella Ho* for the magazine we made good friends with each other. The process of cutting the cloth of my novel according to the required American pattern was both odd and revealing. My impression that English was English wherever she was writ or spoke was one which was about to be rudely shattered. On those hot June mornings I came face to face, for the first time, with the pitiful, infantile nature of American insularity. In reading American novels or watching American films it is axiomatic for the Englishman to employ his native wit in order to translate, understand and absorb words and phrases hitherto foreign to him. Faced with the word 'speak-easy' he doesn't demand that it be translated as a 'place where illegal strong drink may be obtained'; he accepts with joy its vivid vernacular and the word passes into the language, thus enriching it. Given the words 'baloney' and 'phoney', only one of whose derivations he may be aware of, he accepts them too, taking only the very shortest possible space of time to acquaint himself with the fact that the one means crazy rubbish and the other a falsity. 'Stool pigeon'? – before the talkies of the gangster era not one Englishman in a million would have guessed its meaning, together with that of words like 'moll' and the many scores of apt, sharp, highly descriptive bits of American vernacular most perfectly exhibited by such writers as Damon Runyon.

By contrast the simple English of *Spella Ho*, some of it in the Midland vernacular but even so never obscure or complicated, had to be questioned on every page. 'You see, our readers would never understand what it meant': the strangest comment, it seemed to me, on the readership of what was certainly one of the most literate magazines in America. So morning by morning I had some simple, nearly always unobscure English phrase to delete or adapt for the American ear and not once did it occur to the editorship that it might have been the reader and not the writer who should gird himself towards the effort for change.

Of the then editorial board of the *Atlantic* at that time there was one man for whom I had the very greatest respect and affection and of whom I will speak in more detail presently, and another for whom I had none. Talentless, phoney, pompous, the worst kind of literary snob, an even worse kind of American snob, he had carved for himself a useless *niche* in which he posed, oblivious of his vapid deficiencies, as a suave, good-looking god of cultured countenance. Cambridge, England, had nurtured without educating him: and no man was allowed to forget it. In England he consorted with those who caught the right trout in the right streams and in Scotland with those who netted the right salmon in the right lochs; he shot the right pheasants, the right partridges, the right grouse, all in the right places; he stalked the right stags and distributed the right haunches of venison. Nature had endowed him with an enormous opinion of himself but had neglected, unfortunately, to teach him manners. Some years later, when my novels *The Purple Plain* and *The Jacaranda Tree* were enjoying the sunshine of Book Guild choices and an infinite number of translations all over the world, our American-English snob invited me to lunch in London, enjoining me to turn up early at his hotel for an apéritif, 'so that we can have a good talk before lunch-time'. When I duly arrived I was greeted with the most mannerless of stony eyes from the god of cultured countenance and coolly informed 'our lunch is off, I'm afraid. I am lunching with the French Ambassador.'

Ellery Sedgwick, the then editor of the *Atlantic Monthly*, was a person of entirely different and superior calibre. In many ways Ellery was not at all unlike an American Edward Garnett; in many others the two men could not have been more different. Both had the same undoubted flair for spotting literary talent where, very often, others failed to do so. Ellery, for example, had been the only editor in America to have detected in Hemingway's celebrated story *Fifty Grand* an entirely new voice: a voice that was to become not only famous and much imitated but in the end legendary. Yet every editor of importance in America had seen *Fifty Grand* and had rejected it. It remained for Ellery to see not only its inherent virtues but the vast talent of the man behind it.

This was merely one example of Ellery discovering genius. At the further end of the scale he proved himself just as adept at discovering the popular. Walking one day into the offices of the little-known periodical the *British Weekly* and asking if the editor had by any chance any MSS worth taking away to read Ellery was told 'Oh! there's that little thing over there. We're thinking of running it as a Christmas feature.' Ellery took away the MS of that little thing over there' and read it. It was *Goodbye, Mr Chips*, a sentimental piece about an ageing English schoolmaster which, the average judge might have thought, stood about as much chance in the rough market place of American letters as a slim volume of verse about love-in-the-mist by an old maid. Ellery's shrewd instinct told him otherwise. He recognised at once that brand of sentimentalism, just short of sheer mush, for which the American public is as ready to fall as a child for clouds of candy floss. Ellery took *Goodbye, Mr Chips* home to America, with results that all the world knows. He was in fact a great editor and under him the *Atlantic* became the kind of great periodical which today, alas, neither England nor America knows. Ellery's contrast with Edward Garnett was largely based on material things. The Garnetts, especially Edward, had a distaste for, even a contempt for, social or worldly success. They even went so far as positively to avoid it. If not the hair shirt, then the rough blanket of comfort, was theirs. Not so Ellery Sedgewick. Ellery, impelled by a need and desire to enjoy the worldly comforts and pleasures of life, had also recognised that he lacked the necessary financial and business aptitude to put his finances, modest though they may have been in his younger days, to the best lucrative use. He therefore had the wisdom to find someone who could do it for him. This trustworthy and expert aide had consequently invested shrewdly for Ellery, with the result that he had reached a point, when I first met him in Boston in 1938, of some considerable affluence.

His first act on meeting me was not only to praise with warmth and judgement *Spella Ho* and such short stories of mine that he had read in consequence of admiring the novel, but to invite me for a weekend to his house outside Boston. We drove there, I remember, in a mighty black Cadillac. The house itself had an interesting history and was yet further proof of the fact that the keenness of Ellery's eye was accustomed to see riches where others either saw dross or simply nothing at all. Travelling somewhere in the Southern States, I rather think Georgia, Ellery had spotted one of those gracious white colonial mansions, of the type one instantly associates with *Gone with the Wind*, falling into utter and sad decay. Unwanted and apparently irreparable, it was going for a song. Ellery at once bought it, had it dismantled and put on a schooner and sailed it up to Boston, probably from the port of Charleston or somewhere near.

On its selected site some miles out of Boston it now stood in all its refurbished elegance, white, gracious, spacious and a joy to behold. All about it Ellery and his wife had planted dogwoods, lilacs, syringas and big-flowered shrub roses which were, on my visit, in the prime of their pink, cream and white bloom. Into this setting, in his light shantung suiting, with greyish drooping moustache and hair, Ellery fitted to perfection, looking for all the world like some benign and benevolent gentleman cotton-planter from colonial days when slaves were a dollar a dozen. His adored garden was itself adorable and the fact that I in turn adored it too led to a friendship which, for all our difference in years, warmed and ripened even as we walked from rose to rose in the humid twilight of the May evening. Inside the house Ellery had introduced furniture of the appropriate colonial period, so that all was elegance. He had even papered some rooms with an antique blue-flowered Chinese wallpaper that, on some of his travels, and with his customary acumen, he had deemed to be of the right scale of adornment for his beautiful piece of Palladian colonial. I admired him greatly for it all and not least because for all its elegance and the expense it had clearly entailed, it was warm, friendly, civilised and a home.

Others, it would seem, did not admire Ellery. The Spanish Civil War was still in progress, a hateful piece of civil bloodletting that had aroused the bitterest of passions among the left-wing young, notably intellectuals and poets, on both sides of the Atlantic. It was unfortunate for Ellery that he had strong ties of friendship with the Spanish nobility and the result was a sneer campaign that seemed to label him, in some eyes, as black as Franco himself. I confess I could not follow the reasoning in this and proceeded to take Ellery as I found him: a rare judge of literature, a man civilised, liberal, urbane, highly intelligent, kindly, and for ever eager and willing to help the young in the world of literature. He was, in fact, of a kind which America notably lacks: a gentleman.

We did not, as I remember it, discuss the Spanish Civil War. Instead I rode my hobby horse, as I was also to ride it for the benefit of the younger members of the *Atlantic*, about the certainty of the coming war in Europe. It was immensely to his credit that Ellery listened with gravity to what to others appeared to be the mere prophetic ravings of a young fanatic who was somehow making nonsensical mountains out of the most trivial of molehills. Ellery, whose experiences had taken him further afield than Harvard Yard and games with the Red Sox, seemed to think I spoke with reason. That there was little he could do about it hardly mattered. The ear was sympathetic; and it was yet one more reason for the deepening friendship between us. We also spoke much of literature and he asked me, as he had asked Sylvia Townsend Warner, what names among the younger generation, particularly those engaged in the short story, he should watch out for. Like Edward Garnett, he was a man passionately interested in the most difficult of forms and had done much for it in the course of his editorship of the *Atlantic*. I gave him several names of my contemporaries, among them that of Pauline Smith, a South African protegee of Arnold Bennett's, who in a story called *The Pain* had written what I believed, and still believe, to be one of the most touching and beautiful things in the language. Much impressed by it too Ellery at once included it in an anthology he was in process of compiling, including in it stories by Thurber (the famous *Macbeth Murder Mystery*), Arnold Bennett, Katherine Mansfield, Erskine Caldwell, Lord Dunsany, and my own story *The Ox*, to all of which he contributed a penetrative and highly unacademic preface that would have delighted Edward himself. His famous injunction to remember that 'a story is like a horse race' is a classic not to be forgotten. 'It is the start and finish that count most' – a truth to which I was later tempted to add another of my own – 'and of the two I am not sure that the start is not the most important', a truth with which Ellery in fact agreed: 'I am not sure but it is the most difficult accomplishment in fiction'. Subsequent experience has taught me that it is.

My stay in Boston presently afforded me the opportunity of going northward for a few days into Vermont and New Hampshire. It has sometimes been said that the first settlers from Europe could hardly have chosen a worse refuge for their promised land, their new world, than the hinterland of what is now New England. Rocky, barren, inhospitable, it must have seemed to them a sad exchange for England's green and pleasant land. But perhaps they found compensations in the flowering of Vermont and New Hampshire in late spring. There really is of course no late spring in North America and as I drove up into New England, in early June, the heat of summer had already descended, sucking forth sap from grass, flowers and a million trees. The countryside of woods and small mountains very much recalled the Vosges or the Juras. There were many flowers, their names, alas, now forgotten by me, with one exception. I still see, with the wonder I saw it then, the great cherry-and-gold lady's slipper orchid growing unmolested along the roadsides, common as dandelions in an English spring.

All this prompted me to recall Sarah Orne Jewett's *The Country of the Pointed Firs*. This country of hers is, of course, not Vermont or New Hampshire, but the more northerly Maine. I already knew her book well, having been schooled to it by Edward Garnett, and it was now good to be on the fringe of her country of the pointed firs and that of her sister book *The Only Rose*.

Sarah Orne Jewett was descended from a Yorkshire emigrant who went to America in the mid seventeenth century, but she also inherited French blood on her mother's side. There would seem to be little doubt that her fastidious and perceptive sensitivity and what has been called by one critic 'the purity of her transplanted and strictly preserved culture' owed much to her knowledge and feeling for French literature, through which she was much influenced by Flaubert, who may be considered her master. She was an insistent admirer of *Madame Bovary* at a time when certain English critics were being decidedly sniffy, if not worse, about that novel and as a result her work, at its best, is faithful to Flaubert's own dictum – *écrire la vie ordinaire comme on écrit l'histoire*. She was a woman of delicate health; and no man, except her father, ever seems to have interested her. Her work therefore contains no clash of passions, no blighting disharmony; but it has everywhere in it the candour, the clarity and the truth whose expression she must have learned largely from the author of *Madame Bovary*. Her work therefore, for all its apparent modesty and surface delicacy and in spite of its faults, including occasional lapses into near sentimentality, touches chords that lie deeper than they would appear to do. It is consequently deceptive. It is not superficial and remains yet one more example of the eternal truth that violence is not necessarily synonymous with strength and that delicacy can express, in the right hands, profundities that sound and fury so often cannot.

As far back as 1904, in an extremely perceptive article in the *Atlantic Monthly*, a writer praised and explained Sarah Orne Jewett's work in these words:

I always think of her as one who, hearing New England

accused of being a bleak land without beauty, passes confidently over the snow, and by the grey rock and past the dark fir tree, to a southern bank, and there, brushing away the decaying leaves, triumphantly shows to the fault-finder a spray of the trailing arbutus. And I should like, for my part, to add this: that the fragrant, retiring exquisite flower, which I think she would say is the symbol of the New England virtue, is the symbol of her own modest and delightful art.

That is splendidly put; but in an equally perceptive and generous preface to *The Country of the Pointed Firs* Willa Gather goes even further. (I have incidentally never understood the exclusion of Willa Gather's name from the roll of Nobel prize winners). 'If I were asked to name,' Willa Gather says, 'three books which have the possibility of a long, long life, I would say at once *The Scarlet Letter, Huckleberry Finn* and *The Country of the Pointed Firs.* I can think of no others that confront time and change so serenely.' That Sarah Orne Jewett's art was modest and limited, as was Jane Austen's, does not detract, as I have already indicated, from its perfections. 'To note an artist's limitations is but to define his genius.' Sarah Orne Jewett took her material as she found it and made no attempt to adorn it. She wrote of

fisher folk and seaside villages; with juniper pastures and lonely farms, neat grey country houses and delightful, well seasoned old men and women. That, when one thinks of it in a flash, is New England . . . She learned early to love her country for what it was. She happened to have the right nature, the right temperament, to see it so – and to understand by intuition the deeper meaning of what she saw.

Small wonder that Edward Garnett had seen her in precisely this same light, recognising in her, as he had recognised in the Australian Henry Lawson, a talent that had been able to extract from apparently unpromising, even ugly, material, things of a touching beauty. Parts of Lawson are comparable with O'Henry; part has even been compared with Tolstoy. I cannot easily conjure up any figure with whom to compare Sarah Orne Jewett. But like Lawson she points to Garnett's eternal truth: that the novel, (in her case the short story) 'can be anything according to the hands which use it'. To create beauty out of ugliness, to make the rock flower and the stern New England fir tree blossom was indeed, as Willa Cather pointed out, 'a gift from the heart'.

If you would savour something of this 'gift from the heart', taste the following sample of it:

> I stopped to pick some blackberries that twinkled at me like beads among their dry vines, and two or three yellow birds that fluttered up from the leaves of a thistle, and then came back again, as if they had complacently discovered that I was only an overgrown yellow bird, in a strange disguise but perfectly harmless. They made me feel as if I were an intruder, though they did not offer to peck at me, and we parted company very soon. It was good to stand at last on the great shoulder of the hill. The wind was coming in from the sea, there was a fine fragrance from the pines, and the air grew sweeter every moment.

How wonderfully evocative, how beautifully descriptive and how full of scent and atmosphere that deceptively simple language is, so supremely typical of her art.

I returned from New England and Sarah Orne Jewett's country to a Boston growing steamier and steamier and more and more unpleasant every day. I had now finished my task of pruning and shaping *Spella Ho* nearer to the American's heart's desire, though whether it was of any remote assistance to the insular American reader I never knew. I had dollars in my pocket and the experience of taking the pruning knife to a large and substantial piece of prose had served to impress on me a truth all would-be short story writers should remember: 'there is no such thing as the sacred word.' The pruning of a story is exactly like that of pruning an apple tree: in comes light and the branches bring forth fruit in greater abundance.

I was now anxious to get home, to see my England, my garden, my family, my year old son. I think, before I departed, that I preached yet again from the gospel of Europe, warning of the wrath that was at hand, and I knew that even the young among my American friends had neither ear nor desire to listen. We went once, I remember, down to Boston's waterfront, to the great meat market there and ate a positive acreage of steak for dinner. You sat on roughish chairs and at roughish tables and ordered steaks of whatever size you thought you could defeat from the vast carcasses that hung around. The whole atmosphere was somehow a saloon cum sailing clipper affair that might have come out of Herman Melville. The waiters were wild men gifted with salty humour. You expected fights to break out, as in Wild Western saloons, and through the low windows of the restaurant you could see the spars and smoke stacks of shipping lying at anchor in Boston's harbour, beside a waterfront that didn't seem to have changed much since the legendary Tea Party. It was all as far removed from the white moustached kippers in a Boston club as a Covent Garden pub is removed from a Paris fashion salon. I loved it, remember it with pleasure and shall never forget its salty, beefy, maritime, Wild West air.

Financially secure for the first time in my life, I set sail for England in July, well knowing, in my heart, ironically, that she was standing on the edge of doom.

XIII

I was wrong; my immediate overwhelming impression was of arriving in paradise. I went about for some days in a state of semi-drugged, ethereal wonder. I simply couldn't believe that the garden I had only lately made from the wreckage of an abandoned farmyard was real and moreover that it was actually mine. It stood rich with lilies golden and white, delphiniums, salvias, petunias, geraniums, roses, verbenas and a hundred other things dear to my heart. There was a fragrance and an air about it that couldn't have been matched, as it seemed to me, by any garden of Eden.

Outside, in the meadows, hay was still being gathered in and the fragrance of it was heavy, as only the fragrance of hay can be, on the July air. Meadowsweet, I think my favourite among all England's wild midsummer flowers, clotted the dykes with cream. The hedgerows themselves were rich with wild rose and honeysuckle. The iron rocks of New England and Miss Jewett's pointed firs faded away against the picture of our dark Turkey oaks' brooding shadow over resting sheep in the meadows or the splendour of upland beechwoods on the hills above us. There might be no noble lady's slipper orchids, cherry-and-gold, on the open roadside, but purple loosestrife already illuminated the tranquil waters of the little river at the foot of the lane, the sweet chestnuts were in flower and the wheat had on it that miracle of bloom, half blue, half green, that clothes it just before ripeness. If there was any place where my heart justly belonged this was it.

The hills lured us to picnics. Armed with kettle, tea and food, as Madge and I had long before armed ourselves on excursions to the Bedford Ouse, we used to go on hot, breezy afternoons to a spot that lay wide open to westward, southward and the distant sea. Here had once been a copse, now chopped down. The destruction of its trees had left a certain desolation but had let in light, with the result that nature had responded with a new paradise of flowers born from seed that had long slept in shadow. It is to my regret that I never took a count of the myriads of wild flowers that you could find within the compass of that small destroyed piece of woodland; but in July it put on its supreme floral feast of marjoram and willow herb and rock rose and burnet and honeysuckle and camomile and a host of other things, including occasional orchids and some stray rarity such as a solitary maroon columbine. Among all this grew a vast crop of wild strawberries with, if I remember correctly, a few wild raspberries too.

We used to gather wild strawberries by the basket: brilliant little crimson-scarlet jewels with that rare sweet-sharp flavour of their own. Their own special fragrance lingers too with the fragrance of those days of high summer, when even on the hottest days the air, coming in from the sea, had in it that certain oceanic tang that saved it from sultriness. Often, tired of gathering the infinitude of strawberries and tired even of the sound and echo of children's voices, I merely found myself a spot among the fallen pine cones and lay back, sun-washed and half-asleep, drenched in a kind of herbal cloud of flower-scent, sunbaked earth and odours illimitable, little dreaming that presently, above these incomparably enriched hills, in parts hardly changed since Jane Austen stayed in one of the great houses in a great park just below, the flower of a new generation would be killing itself in the first great air battle, and perhaps the last, of all time. Without knowing it I was picnicking on the new front line. But there was a taste of wild strawberries on my lips and for a time I no longer cared what the author of *Mein Kampf* was up to.

But one cannot, as I think one of the poets of the Romantic Movement pointed out, live for ever on quince jelly. The summer began to pass into autumn; or as is the way when political evils are being hatched, August came in like an uneasy hen aware of predatory rats hiding and ready to strike in her run. All my fears about Europe began to come back, grey, dark and finally black. I had been too young to express to any really explicit extent my bitterness at the First World War; and all I had done, in a short-lasting aftermath, was to write a few acid verses, now lost, for a periodical called the *New Clarion*. But now I felt it was time for me to get up and say something more.

The Granary

I think I can best explain what was in my mind at that time by going back once more to the Garnetts, this time to quote David:

War is the worst of the epidemic diseases which afflict mankind and the great genetrix of many others. While it lasts it impairs the powers of rational judgement; millions are crippled and die and the accumulated riches of empires are destroyed by fanaticism and fear; cruelty and callousness are infectious and these toxins of the spirit make the unconscionable claim that all personal life, happiness, art and human expression must be subordinated to war, or serve it. That exorbitant demand is constantly proclaimed and has to be violently contradicted. Life, love and happiness go on under almost any conditions. Indeed they are quickened by war as the beauty of a face may be quickened by fever.

These words had not been written in the late summer of 1938, but they would, if written, have expressed almost to perfection what I felt about Europe's hopeless malaise. That it was hopeless was, it seemed to me, beyond doubt; that it might have been avoided if physicians of intelligence had been brought in soon enough, arriving at the right diagnosis, seemed to me to be also beyond dispute. Instead we had had as Prime Minister a man who looked something like a benign hop-sack with a pipe stuck in his mouth, followed by one who looked half like a Baptist church deacon and half like a provincial commercial traveller trying to sell sewing machines. While the voice of Churchill cried in the wilderness Chamberlain watched birds and prayed, I have no doubt, as H. G. Wells' mother had done, for guidance from 'the right quarter'. But when wild boars are ravaging and savaging the countryside it is of small use to chase them with Pekinese lap-dogs. The author of *Mein Kampf* had a pet rude name for Chamberlain; and though even in our so-called permissive society I will refrain from writing it down, apt though it was, I will nevertheless note that it is one with which Chaucer would have been familiar.

Munich was therefore inevitable. I will refrain from going over its lamentable timetable of missed trains and wrong connections and arrivals at wrong destinations. For me it merely represented the culmination of almost a decade of foreboding, fear and finally fright. I was at a football match when I heard its cruel, sanctimonious, funereal knell and I wasn't far away from an impulse to shoot, if not myself, at least the guardians of 'peace in our time'. I thought greatly, then, of my children: my two beautiful daughters and my young son, impeccable as always in his cream shantung jacket. My world, which had at last seemed about to blossom to the full, was instead about to be blighted, together with that of unlimited millions of others. I conceived and shared no illusion whatever about this. War's inevitability had been as predictable as an eclipse of the sun. This was the eclipse and I was mightily, bitterly angry.

I at once, perhaps mistakenly, perhaps without thought enough, determined to put this mood of embittered outrage into a novel. What was perhaps an even greater mistake was that I was going to attempt to see the sequence of events through the eyes of a woman, always an attitude fraught with extreme dangers for a man. Perhaps I reasoned that when it comes to war the female vision, driven by intuitions, sees things with sharper, clearer, more penetrative power. At all events it was not to be a happy book; nor was it to be born of the Northamptonshire backgrounds that had nurtured *The Poacher*, *The Fallow Land* and *Spella Ho*. My landscape must now, I felt, be widened. I was to chronicle the story of a woman bitterly bereaved by the loss of a brother in the First World War and her attempt to find, through a series of associations with men, some her lovers, the fraternal love of which she had been robbed. Not an easy theme. Nevertheless I felt that I now possessed the technical accomplishment with which to tackle it, as well as the force of moral outrage as to war and its futilities to provide the emotional and spiritual motor power. I was also convinced, and indeed still am, that it is a bad thing for a writer to stand still; it is a poor exercise that never takes him beyond well-charted ground; it is excellent, in my view, when a writer bites off a little more than he can chew. The comfort of merely satisfying a well-tried formula offers no adventure. If adventure in turn offers risk and in turn begets failure, then the writer must set out to learn what failure teaches.

The early conception of a novel or story greatly depends, it often seems to me, on setting it in the right key. Great geniuses in music often seem to make such choices in their art by some divine instinct. It is by no means so easy in literature, where there are no rules and no fixed set of keys, either minor or major, from which the writer can make his immediate or final choice. The composer knows more or less what something will sound like in C sharp minor or in F major. The writer has no way of knowing any such thing. He must invent his own key. If the key he selects is right then it is likely that his music and its themes will flow from it naturally. If the key he selects is wrong then he is likely to find himself in frustrations and troubles of every kind.

It is now my considered opinion that I somehow chose the wrong key for this novel. As to what key I ought to have chosen I have never since been able to determine. It was a book of almost unrelieved melancholy: of a woman searching for a kind of happiness that was not to be found and who could not break the fraternal stranglehold that everywhere frustrated her and for which she blamed the undying stupidity and waste of war. To the very end it had what is called a downbeat and it also went on and on, as Stephen Crane had complained of Tolstoy's *War and Peace*, like Texas.

Some time before this David Garnett had joined the firm of Jonathan Cape in his father's old capacity as reader. As Rupert Hart-Davis was still occupying an editorial chair at No. 30 Bedford Square I knew that I had at that address two allies greatly sympathetic to my work. I therefore had great hopes of the novel, more especially as Madge and I were expecting a fourth child by the latter part of 1939. The dollars earned by *Spella Ho* had now largely been used up during the long arduous months of writing something like 150,000 words and it was now highly essential that my novel should succeed and so raise in some slight degree the temperature of my bank balance.

To my infinite chagrin and pain my two allies turned out to be critics of the most remorseless nature. Having read my MS, they took me out to lunch and proceeded to hurl at me a critical bombardment whose plan they might well have borrowed from Edward. I had spawned another monster; I was the begetter of a two-headed, crooked Mongolian monstrosity whose body would have to be put somewhere darkly away. There is no record on paper, as there was with the letters from Edward, as to what was said on that dismal day, but the words are no less incisively ingrained on the memory for all that. It made it all the worse for me that I had the highest regard for both David's and Rupert's judgement. That they had a few soothing words to offer about a passage here and a passage there did nothing to assuage or disillusion me. Unwarily and stupidly I had fallen again into a great trap, having apparently learned nothing from having fallen into it before. The result was that I wasn't merely angry with myself; I was angry that the anger I felt for war and its stupidities hadn't produced the resounding bang for which I had hoped but merely a flabby moan. 'The path of art, endlessly difficult' indeed.

And where on earth, I could only ask myself, was the path going now? In this new and embittering disappointment, entirely of my own making, I could only ask myself if I really knew, after all, what I was doing as a writer? Was there in me some leaden vein of obtuseness that would never be taught, would never learn? With utter melancholy I could only tell myself that there must be. Moreover I found myself in such a state of depression that I saw no way of possibly putting it right. I had somewhere taken a wrong turning and had wandered off into a morass, a pitiless swamp forest of tragically fatuous entanglements from which I could see no way out.

By this time sandbags were being piled about the streets of London; gas masks were being issued; the full stretched wires that had been growing tauter and tauter and nearer and nearer to breaking point ever since Munich were at last at explosive point; and within a week or two war had at last begun.

A pretty picture: war; another novel ill-conceived, a failure; a general chaos of mistrust and uncertainty in the publishing world; a total assured income of about thirteen pounds a week; a fourth child soon expected. Above all, perhaps, a shattering, embittering loss of confidence.

I do not suppose that in the entire history of art, whether of writing, literature, painting, sculpture or even the art of inventing things scientific or mechanical, there has ever been anyone who did not, at some time or other, suffer this erosion of confidence in himself and his art: the shrivelling notion that he has been drained dry, that imagination has withered or died completely, above all that creative impulse will never be reborn. It has been well said that a writer may ask his reader to believe anything he can *make* him believe: to which one can only add that first of all the writer must himself believe in what he wishes the reader to believe. When such capacity for convincing himself of belief is missing, dormant or dead then the writer is lost in a desert, moribund, spiritless, forlorn.

I have said before, and it will perhaps do no harm to say it again, that the general public sees only what it is allowed to see: the picture successfully achieved, the book conclusively wrought, a pleasing whole, perhaps a success. It cannot and does not see the fragmentary, unfinished, blighted, abandoned bits of jigsaw that lie behind the façade, mouldering in the studio, gathering dust in the study drawer. It probably remains wholly unaware that such things ever happen to writers, still less to those who have attained a name and even a degree of success, and it probably labours under the further delusion that once reputation and acclaim have been achieved everything the writer touches automatically turns to gold. I assure them it is not so. Furthermore it is just as probable that the public never has the remotest notion that many writers dislike, or even loathe, their finished products, and never, after the final pain of proof-reading, ever read a word of them again. If this be true of the work that is finished and appears to satisfy its creator's self-critical demand, what of the ugly duckling, the two-headed Mongolian disaster, the thing that should never have left the womb?

In the early autumn of 1939 my own answer, from the pit of despair, was a simple one: I would never, never attempt another novel.

But some time before this catastrophe left its savage mark on me something far more pleasant had occurred. It seemed to me that if the lights in Europe were going out, as in fact they were, it might be a good thing to take a last look at them before Nazism and war cast their final obliterating shadow. In the early spring of that year, therefore, some six months or so before war actually broke out, Madge and I decided to try to find spring on the Dalmatian coast, taking in Venice on the way. We had little money, travelled third class, by slow train, ate our own food and slept on the compartment seats. When after a not very comfortable night we had crossed the Simplon and arrived at Domodossola, the snow was six or eight feet deep. It faded as we entrained along Lake Maggiore, curiously glassy in its winter suspense, and then in the warm afternoon sunshine across a Lombardy Plain without life, every dyke and water stretch rimmed with a crust of white ice.

I have never in my life seen a town more marvellous than Venice. It is perfectly enchanting, brilliance, joy, life. Instead of streets and roads there are canals; instead of cabs, gondolas . . . And the evenings. My God! one might almost die at the strangeness of it . . . warmth, stillness, stars. A gondola goes by, hung with lanterns. In it are a double bass, violins, a guitar, a mandolin, a cornet, two or three ladies, several men, and one hears singing and music. They sing from operas. What voices! . . . For us poor and oppressed Russians it is easy to go out of our minds here in a world of beauty, wealth and freedom. One longs to remain here for ever.

The words are not mine; it is nearly eighty years since Chekhov ecstatically wrote them on his first visit to Venice and the astonishing thing is, as I can testify, that they might have been written yesterday. I think perhaps I have been to Venice nearly a score of times since that first visit of ours in February 1939 but the ecstasy Chekhov felt and that I experienced likewise has never faded. 'Of all the places I have visited Venice has left me the loveliest memories', Chekhov went on to say and one can only echo him a thousand times. The February air may have been colder, sharper than iced champagne, but champagne it was. The streets were almost empty but that merely gave a better view of palaces, bridges, dark alleyways, dark still waters. The enchantment was made all the more complete in that the Hotel Bauer Grunwald, clearly thinking we were a honeymoon couple, did us the honour of giving us a bridal suite instead of the tiny box we had paid for.

Whether, in spite of the fact that we had three children, we looked extremely young and naïve I never knew; but the honeymoon myth was repeated on the pleasant little Italian steamer on which we presently sailed down the Adriatic. A party of Germans, gross, thick headed, dutifully marshalled and led by 'our Führer', a little courier of peremptory voice and manner who would have done credit to the author of *Mein Kampf* himself, eyed us with covert, curious and calculating glances that finally offered them only one answer: just married.

To make the picture one of even greater fascination Madge was also knitting something.

All down the Adriatic it rained in grey, gloomy torrents, but 'our Führer' was totally undismayed. Tomorrow, in Dubrovnik, all would be sunlight, a perfection of blue sky, the warmth of spring. Oranges would glow on the trees; narcissi and iris and anemones would greet us as we landed. And so it was. The morning was one of pure brilliance; oranges did indeed glow like lamps from the trees; mimosa glowed everywhere in yellow clouds; purple iris and white anemones shone in the gardens; and over it all glowed that amazing piece of ancient beauty, Dubrovnik, of purest white stone, its great walls encircling a city in which, I believe, there is no house later than the eighteenth century.

Some words in Chekhov's letter of 1891 cause me to pause and think: 'For us poor and oppressed Russians it is easy to go out of our minds'. Similarly, in 1939, the Germans would have us believe that they too were poor and oppressed: not enough living space, no colonies, a criminal craving to possess what belonged to others and what they supposed, by God's right or Hitler's, belonged to them. The sheep-like excursions of the party aboard the steamer had a tragicomic air. 'Lead us,' they seemed to say, 'no matter where, and we will follow.' It is only fair to add that once or twice they kindly invited us to follow too, so that we found ourselves driving out, in large open Fiats, in freezing Yugoslavian dawns, to visit remote places inland, pausing occasionally on the way at some primitive inn to knock back, at a penny a glass, fiery draughts of plum brandy as a means of partially thawing out throats frozen solid. High beyond us lay black mountains; on the lower slopes pitiful little fields scratched from nothing and fenced by low stone walls, were all that cultivation had to show. The market places of little villages had an air of starved weariness: a few goats and hens, mules, a bunch or two of root vegetables and once what we were told, with some pride, was donkey ham. From houses no bigger and better than pigsties pretty, laughing but unwashed peasant girls ogled and eyed us, giving the impression that for a few *dinars* nothing would be denied. The men were moustached, martial and incredibly handsome and in the streets elderly women stole furtively past, faces covered to the eyes, black-shrouded ghosts of the days of Turkish rule.

In the town, where there was still much of Turkish influence too, we discovered a restaurant that might have come out of the old Austro-Hungarian Empire. It seemed to belong to the Vienna of Strauss or old Budapest; it reminded me of an enchanting little film *Sunday Affair*, which is rather like a combination of Molnar and Chekhov: everybody having hours of time in which to sit over a newspaper, a cup of coffee and a glass of water, gossiping, arguing, doing nothing. A little scarlet-uniformed negro boy stood in the vestibule waiting to take your coat; the waiters wore the old traditional mid-European white aprons; in one corner a motley orchestra scraped away tunes from Strauss, Liszt and Dvorak. To me it was also a corner of dying Europe, a Europe whose death had been criminally advanced by having its heart, the old Austro-Hungarian Empire, forcibly gouged out, leaving a sinister crater filled by doctrinaire ferment, oppression and murder ever since.

But for us, during those all too short two weeks, the sun remained for ever brilliant, with the premature warmth of April. We wandered, one warm Sunday afternoon, into a little coastal town and heard music, from fiddles mostly, coming gaily from an open-windowed house. We stopped to listen; we even peered in at the windows. Within a second or two a joyful young man rushed out, seized my hand as if I were the returning prodigal son, and dragged us both inside, as if we were indeed the lost that had at last been found. We were at once in the centre of a wedding feast. We could speak no word of Yugoslavian, and no Yugoslav could speak a word of English. Our language for the rest of that gay afternoon consisted entirely of smiles. We ate much sweet cake and drank much champagne and were altogether the objects of so much delighted attention that we began to feel that perhaps, after all, the hotel in Venice and the Germans on the little Italian steamer had been right: that it was we, and not the bride and bridegroom, who were on honeymoon.

And perhaps, as I look back, it was a honeymoon. We had never been able to afford one anyway, but had through sheer lack of cash to go straight from church to the Granary. But if honeymoon over-romanticizes that brief sunlit visit to Dalmatia in spring it cannot and will never detract from the brilliance of the memory of that last look at Europe before its lights went out. It remains as vividly and affectionately in memory as a harvest field in childhood, the feel of wet watercress on my hands, the milk-warm touch of a thrush's egg against the mud basin of its nest in an April hedgerow.

That it was also sad there is no doubt. But just as illness magnifies and even beautifies, so sadness can itself heighten or deepen the illumination and beauty of memory. At any rate I returned to England refreshed, indeed more than refreshed. The past, even the immediate past, was a dead body that had to be buried. The erosion of confidence, that can spread like gangrene if left untreated, had to be checked. It was no time for prolonged inquests, self-recrimination, self-pity. The medicine, I well knew, was within myself.

If the lights in Europe were rapidly going out they were not yet going out, I told myself, in me. Nor were they going to be extinguished by the mere failure of yet another novel. Until the body itself is dead nothing can kill imagination. Imagination is the soul of the artist. My only way of expressing it, I told myself, was in words and there were, I felt, thank God, plenty of words left in me yet.

XIV

Readers of the poetry of the First World War will know that there runs through it a common note: the agony of the enlightened and enriched beauty of nature on the one hand and the contrast of appalling negation and the useless holocaust of blood and filth on the other. The first spring skylark singing above the craters of battlefields, the first breaking green shoot on a landscape populated by shattered ghouls that were once trees, the brief blessed salve of a few English summer days of leave, the soldier's relief from rats, lice, gas and the whole Dante-esque hell of pitiless, pointless slaughter. These excruciating, ironical contrasts are the things that give that war poetry much of its poignancy.

Though war had only just been declared in September 1939, and then not very martially, there was something of the same feeling in the air. Suddenly all of nature and its beauty, all that mattered of earth and flower and root and grass, became unbearably heightened in value. All too often, as I have said, it is in little things that memory enshrines its more precious moments; and so it is with September 1939. The weather was hot and dry. The wheat, uncut as yet in the fields, stood strong and straight, the ears untouched by rain and burned by sun until they were the colour of brandy. They seemed to me to have a great steadfastness about them, those fields of corn; and I felt that nothing could blemish them or lay them low.

In the warm sultry evenings Madge and I, she tired of being played football with by her fourth child, who wasn't to appear on the field until November, used to take brief slow walks in the falling darkness along the village green, listening to an odd plane flying somewhere, gazing at the odd white trumpet-shape of a searchlight somewhere far off, wondering if war really had begun or if, in a strange way, it was all an hallucination sent to mock us. And again it is the very smallest things that enshrine those evenings in memory to such perfection that they might have happened only yesterday. In this case it was glow-worms. I couldn't ever recall having seen glow-worms before. But there they suddenly were: tiny greenish lights in the roadside grass. Though so minute, they seemed on these taut, sultry evenings to glow like indistinguishable beacons. You felt that they were saying 'Don't despair. The lights are not out. We are small but we are unquenchable. Look at us and take heart a little.' We did indeed look, every evening, and take heart. The strange thing is that I have never seen a glow-worm since.

On a more practical level I had to do something to keep my family on the one hand and prevent myself from going mad on the other. If the times had been bad for authors at the time of the General Strike in 1926, they were little short of catastrophic now. I found it impossible to work creatively. The entire emotional and physical climate had now an air of senseless suspense about it, now a furious desperation as if you were on one of those moving staircases that are going down when you want to go up, thus trapping you into the frantic and crazy gymnastics of an escape that never happens. The so-called year of peace between Munich and September 1939 had at least seemed to be leading somewhere, even if only to the final confrontation of war. The phoney autumn of war was, instead, a trap; you were held in a vice from which you could get neither point nor escape of any kind.

The evacuation of children from London to the countryside was the first of the revolutions that were brought to us; and human nature, I fear, came out of it badly. Madge and I, she as always in the forefront of battles for good causes, proceeded to go on patient excursions about the immediate countryside, looking and begging for homes where children could stay. It was astounding how, suddenly, on these visits, the size of houses dramatically diminished. 'We only got one spare bedroom and his old mother uses that.' Ferocious old couples shut their doors in our faces. Old ladies comfortably supported by private means suddenly produced doctors' certificates for sciatica, bronchitis, bad legs, rheumatoid arthritis, stone in the kidney or any of the thousand ailments that noisy children are bad for. Nevertheless the children came, estranged in a land of trees and orchards and hops and cows; and for a time their East End parents came too, but all too briefly. The horrors of rural England ('only one bloody pub, only one bloody shop') were altogether too much for most of them, so that they fled back with speed and relief to Lambeth and the Mile End Road, glad to be back in the civilised world of sandbags, four-ale bars and street markets, leaving our Kentish cornfields to waste upon the desert air.

When winter came at last it was ferocious. Blizzards left their mark in vast carved drifts, sometimes the shape of great sea-breakers caught and frozen at their very crests, sometimes in giant pure bosoms milkily overhanging the hedgerows, sometimes in shapes like those of huge basking white whales, their flanks ridged in long streamlined fissures. The road clearing equipment and chemicals that now clear snowbound roads in an hour or two were not part of the war-time scene. Snow froze in jagged corrugations everywhere, making any passage into town a nightmare. Once it snowed for 72 hours without stopping, leaving us trapped for days in an arctic prison.

In these frustrating circumstances – the winter, as I recall it, lasted at its worst for seven to eight weeks – I felt that writing of some sort was my only salvation. Still locked completely in cold, uncreative mood, I now turned my thoughts to something that I had had at the back of my mind, awaiting birth, for some time. Rich as the 1920s and 1930s had been for the short story on both sides of the Atlantic, I had continually found myself searching in vain for a book that would put this fruitful sphere of its development into words, both critical and explorative, and perspective. There had been books, most of them not good and many of them merely dealing with the aspect of stories for purely commercial markets, on how to write short stories and how to market them successfully. This was not what I had in mind. Writing, like medicine and gardening, is not an exact science. There are no rules and I do not believe that it can be taught, even basically taught, in the way for example that painters are first taught to draw. In essence it is a process of discovery and it was as a guide to this discovery of what had been done and was being done in the realm of the short story that I now began *The Modern Short Story.* It was in no sense to be a textbook on how the short story could or was to be written; it was to be illustrative of what some of its greatest exponents, from Poe to Hemingway, had achieved.

If I began the book as much as an essay in personal distraction, at a time when all creative impulse was dead in me, I can only say that I ended up by producing a critical survey which has been in constant use in schools and universities ever since, on both sides of the Atlantic. Though I had had no intention whatsoever of dispensing any plan or plans as to how a short story might be written it was inevitable that my predilection for certain methods, including my own – I had already published more than two hundred short stories – could not be kept out. The chapters on

Chekhov and Maupassant, American writers after Poe (e.g. Herman Melville, Bret Harte, Ambrose Bierce, O. Henry, Jack London, Stephen Crane and so on) Gogol and Turgenev, Tolstoy and Katherine Mansfield, the Irish School (Moore, O'Faolain, O'Connor and Joyce) and the new American renaissance of Hemingway, Faulkner, Sherwood Anderson, Katherine Ann Porter and so on all served to indicate the many shapes and directions I felt the modern short story capable of taking. I had also some strong opposite prejudices. I berated the worst of Coppard while cordially praising the best; I said what I had to say of the tedium of Henry James by saying nothing; I lambasted Kipling, who in his loud vulgarities still seems to me the Wagner of literature, than which I can think of no worse insult; and I made the discovery of an interesting piece of near-plagiarism by no less a person than Somerset Maugham.

Compare, if you will, the following two passages. The first:

> Like other rich men at the beginning of this century he ate and drank a good deal more than was enough to keep him in health. Even his excellent constitution was not proof against a prolonged course of overfeeding and what we should now consider over-drinking. His liver would not infrequently get out of order and he would come down to breakfast looking yellow about the eyes.

And the second:

> I fancy that life is more amusing now than it was forty years ago and I have a notion that people are more amiable. They may have been worthier then, possessed of more substantial knowledge; I do not know. I know they were more can-tankerous; they ate too much, many of them drank too much and they took too little exercise. Their livers were out of order and their digestions often impaired.

Maugham or Samuel Butler? Which is which? I really don't think that a studied reading of these two passages will give any greater clue than a cursory one. Maugham's style is so much in the manner of Butler's that one might have supposed it to be the work of a young and apprenticed hand, guided by early hero-worship, instead of that of the author of *Cakes and Ale*, from which the second passage is taken, the first passage being from *The Way of All Flesh*.

The long savage winter ended. In the middle of it our younger son, Jonathan, was born: a restless young gentleman of quick brain ungifted with an ability to sit still for more than two seconds at a time but an astonishing opposite capacity for meticulous care in the work he now does, which is to put complicated soundtracks into highly expensive films.

When the long snows finally gave way to spring, which in turn was to give way to an almost faultless summer, you felt once again assailed by the old excruciating paradox, that of beauty flourishing, heightened and refined, against a background of foreboding, fear, and impending disaster. Primroses had never looked so eternally symbolic of spring, or so pure and lovely; daffodils may have touched Wordsworth's heart back in the early nineteenth century, but they never came as near to breaking ours as in that spring, bitterly momentous as it was to be, of 1940. Everything about the land, the woods and the garden was of an infinite, searching preciousness. I remember once how an American visitor to England during wartime, when things were at their blackest and lowest, telling me of how he was impressed above all not by the fortitude, resilience and sheer guts of Londoners under stress and fire but by the way they would stand in silence by some half-shuttered flower-shop window and gaze with solemn, hungry rapture at the few blossoms on sale inside. That is much as we felt that spring.

Meanwhile, over in France (where in certain RAF messes officers were known to have complained bitterly that the price of champagne had gone up from 3/6 to 3/8 a bottle) the snows too had melted and the warmth of spring had cleared and dried the roads. The stage was, in fact, set for battle; the phoney war was over. All that had been predicted in the aptly named *Insanity Fair* was now printed on the programme; it was merely unfortunate that certain readers of the programme were still either wearing the wrong spectacles or had left them somewhere in some dust-ridden pigeon-hole. The plan across the channel was well laid; its execution was dramatically, diabolically swift.

In the south country we lived all this time with a feeling of nakedness, as on stretched wires. The notion that we were also to be shot at as we lay there stretched out was not exactly a pleasant one and we never spoke of it. But it was there on the first exquisite days of May, when both hawthorn in the purity of its whiteness and oak-flower in its bountiful olive-yellow which always seem to me the great symbols of spring coming up to its great overflowing, (I wrote once of may blossom as being 'the risen cream of all the milkiness of Maytime') were of excruciating tautness. It became clearer and clearer every day that France was rotten. Like a neglected and diseased tree the central heart of whose trunk was mere fungoid pulp while its outward exterior looked sound it was about to fall at the first well-directed gust of wind. It did fall; and, strange and contradictory though it may now sound, great was the rejoicing, at least on my part. I shall for ever believe that on the day that France fell in the spring of 1940 many of the people of southern England – I do not and cannot speak for others farther north – felt that a great load had been lifted from their hearts and shoulders. They were alone at last and they were glad to be alone. Only we ourselves could now be traitors to ourselves. Nor did we need the words of Churchill, mighty in comfort and inspiration though they were, to tell us that that at least would never happen.

There followed a Gilbertian situation: serious enough at the time, terrifyingly futile and comic in memory, and now enshrined in a television show, *Dad's Army*. I belonged to it. I might have been better employed making marmalade. I was issued with a rifle. I was terrified of keeping the rifle in the house because of the children and equally terrified of taking it on Sunday morning parades in case I had accidentally left a bullet in it and it would go off and shoot somebody, probably the Major. I abhorred shooting and hunting in any case and as I crawled about on my belly on dark summer nights in woods, fields and churchyards, looking for an invisible enemy, I never once felt like a hunter but only the hunted. Sometimes in the dead of night air-raid sirens went off and I, ever eager for duty, would be up and dressed and at the ready, rifle in hand, in a matter of seconds, to report to HQ across the village green. Whenever I did so there was never another single soul in sight; I for ever got the feeling that I was defending England utterly alone. After an impossible interval a few sleep-drunk comrades would join me, accompanied eventually by an elderly lady from next door, so evidently eager to give her all in defence of her native land that she could scarcely walk for an armoury of gasmasks, tin helmets, stirrup pumps, buckets, spades, whistles, vacuum flasks of tea and cocoa, shawls, scarves, gas capes and almost everything else of a defensive and offensive nature except a pike and a suit of armour. Invariably, under the weight of her defences, she fell flat on her face, by which time the siren for the all clear had sounded.

The German soldier being noted for a high degree of well-disciplined efficiency I have grave doubts as to whether Dad's Army would have lasted very long in defence of its Kentish woods and hop-fields. Resolution is not enough; I had resolution in plenty but of military tactics I knew about as much as a rabbit being cornered by a stoat. Our official warning note that invasion was or was about to take place was the ringing of the local church bells and I well remember a morning when, buttoning up my trousers in the lavatory, I was absolutely sure that I suddenly heard the dread clang of bells from our local tower. I hastily sat down again. Happily it was a false alarm.

While this tragi-farce was going on at home something of infinitely greater seriousness was going on across the channel. There was about to be made the most momentous decision of the war. It is of course the easiest possible thing to marshal figures in order to prove points and whether the following figures are strictly accurate matters little now; the situation adds up to the same thing. At the time of the German invasion of Norway the RAF probably had, with the French, some 1400 fighter aircraft as against the Luftwaffe's 1500; but in second line fighter strength the Germans were probably stronger by 1000 than British and French fighters combined. Of bombers the Germans had a first line strength of probably some 2500, or about 3½ times the RAF strength, together with reserves of about 4500, or about 2½ times the strength of our reserves. On all counts, therefore, excluding the defection of France, we were very much outnumbered.

Worse still, our losses in the late spring of that year in France were frighteningly heavy: so heavy in men and machines in fact that there arrived a moment when it was clear that if they continued for another three weeks, or even perhaps two weeks, on that scale, there would be little if anything of Fighter Command left. At the very height of these paralysing losses the evacuation of British troops from the beaches of Belgium and Northern France had begun and many an embittered soldier, shelled and machine-gunned on the beaches of Dunkirk, inevitably looked up at the sky and asked himself where the bloody hell was the RAF? The answer was one of the most momentous importance. The RAF was back in England, having been brought back by the wise and courageous decision of Air Chief Marshal Dowding, who realised that the Battle of France had been lost and was consequently unprepared further to sacrifice his Fighter Command on the useless ashes of a burnt-out altar. He had therefore ordered Fighter Command back to England, well knowing that the Battle of Britain, the real Battle, was still to come and knowing equally that in fact there would be no Battle of Britain if there were no fighters to fight a Battle of Britain with. It was one of the great decisions of the war and there seems to me little doubt that if it hadn't been made at that moment there would have been no Battle of Britain to fight and that the war might well have ended victoriously for Germany in June or July of 1940.

By his action Dowding was able to rest, re-form and reinforce his fighter squadrons. That they were soon to be shattered not in the sky, but on the ground, on their own airfields, was the result of inexperience which laid more stress on lines of fighters looking trim and neat on their perimeters than on security and this, after some further paralysing experiences, was remedied by a system that became known as dispersal, whereby planes, intelligence staff, radio operators and so on were no longer assembled neatly in one place, like a well-ordered school, but scattered far and wide for safety and survival. That we managed somehow to survive those blistering attacks on airfields seems to me a miracle, but survive somehow we did.

The Battle that presently began in that torturingly beautiful summer will always be known as the Battle of Britain. Of its supreme importance I will say more in a moment. But geo-graphically, of course, it covered no more than a tiny fraction of Britain. The area of combat took place in a cube roughly eighty miles long, nearly forty broad and five to six miles high. The vortex of all this was the Maidstone, Canterbury, Ashford, Dover, Dungeness area, in which Spitfires largely operated, with the further rear centre of combat between Tunbridge Wells, Maidstone and London, largely commanded by Hurricanes.

Sometimes in the frontal area as many as 150 to 200 individual combats would take place in the space of half an hour.

To the civilian population below, who were able to see something of a battle for the possession of their island for the first time for centuries, the entire affair was strangely, uncannily, weirdly unreal. The housewife with her shopping basket, the farm labourer herding home his cows, the shepherd with his flock, the farmer turning his hay: all of them, going about their daily tasks, could look up and see, far, far above them, little silver moths apparently playing against the sun in a game not unlike a celestial ballet. Now and then a splutter of machinegun fire cracked the heavens open, leaving ominous silence behind. Now and then a parachute opened and fell lazily, like a white upturned convolvulus flower, through the blue midsummer sky. But for the most part it all had a remoteness so unreal that the spectator over and over again wondered if it was taking place at all. Nor was it often possible to detect if the falling convolvulus flower contained enemy or friend, and often the same was true of aircraft: so that the battle was watched in the strangest state of suspense, with little open or vocal jubilation.

It was of course, with its combatants, much glamorised by newspapers; but Richard Hillary was right when he said

> much that is untrue and misleading has been written on the pilot of this era. Within one short year he has become the nation's hero and the attempt to live up to this false conception bores him . . . The pilot is of a race of men who since time immemorial have been inarticulate; who, through their daily contact with death, have realised, often enough unconsciously, certain fundamental things. It is only in the air that the pilot can grasp that feeling, that flash of knowledge, of insight, that matures him beyond his years.

This was just as true of the far less glamorised bomber pilots, as I was later to discover.

Remote though it may have seemed to the spectator below

there can however be no shadow of doubt that the Battle of Britain was the most decisive of the war. Its closest parallel is Trafalgar. Both were the beginning and not the end of the long road to victory. A good many years were to elapse between Trafalgar and Waterloo; another five of bitter and extensive combat on air, sea and land were to elapse between mid-September 1940 and the surrender of the German armies at Luneburg Heath in 1945. This book offers no space in which to argue over the inter-allied conflicts and duplicity that went on in those years, bitter though their results may now seem to the British mind; it simply remains to say that if the Luftwaffe had knocked out the RAF in that unbearably beautiful summer of 1940 it is scarcely possible that we would have hoped to achieve another Waterloo.

Throughout it all I wrote little. It was a world in which you felt there was no tomorrow. You lived for the day; and the day, you hoped, by the grace of God, would be enfolded mercifully by a night in which men didn't kill each other. The nights, as I remember them, were of a marvellous starlit calm; the days broke limpid and soft and flowered into a perfection that mocked and pained by its beauty. Like an old hen protecting its brood I hovered protectively about my young family, holding it to be my duty, for the present, to see that they at least had a protective umbrella held above them. They, after the manner of children, grew to accept it all more readily than their parents, so that there came a day when a great blast of thunder broke out above the house and all of us dived under the kitchen table, the children weeping with fear until pacified by their parents' soothing words: 'There's nothing to worry about. It isn't thunder. Only bombs,' so that tears were silent and dried in a moment or two.

As the summer drew on, growing always in beauty, until once again the wheat was the colour of brandy in the fields, it became clearer and clearer that the climax of the battle was still to come. You felt your nerves begin to stretch to breaking point. Not only did it presently seem as if there were no tomorrows; there were no todays either.

At this moment Madge's brother paid us a weekend visit. Far

away in Northamptonshire he had been as remote from battle as a nurse in Kensington Gardens might have been from Sevastopol or Khartoum. He found it impossible to believe that war was being waged above his head. I don't think he slept well; but in the morning he came forth with a marvellously sensible suggestion. We would go fishing. I myself hadn't fished for years and neither of us had a hook or line to our name. Accordingly we went out and spent some magnificent sum, about two pounds I imagine, on the two cheapest rods we could find, hooks, lines, floats and shot. We dug vast quantities of worms and mixed great puddings of paste. We then armed ourselves with beer, cheese and sandwiches and set off finally for the two pretty little lakes that lie in the centre of the village, one of them containing an island of quince trees, with the limpid narrow young River Stour running alongside them by woods of alder and hazel and here and there under big old horse chestnuts and half drowned ancient willows.

An immense peace enshrouded us; in a garden an old man placed an even older ladder against an apple tree glowing with early red fruit as with lanterns; a kingfisher streaked, copper and blue, through the dark tunnel of alders; a flight of mallards winged away above the quince trees; moorhens dived and disappeared and pranced their delicate way among the tall thick summer reeds. It was hard to believe that this was a battlefield. The paradox of war and the ethereal exquisite nature of summer dissolved together to form a sort of opiate, a state where time and its senseless, fragmentary paroxysms of pain and fear no longer existed. We simply were; we sat beside the still waters; and there was nothing else that mattered.

The little river hadn't been fished for years and as we cast in our lines it was like taking chocolate from innocent and unprotected children. Fat perch and roach, sometimes a small pike, an occasional rudd or silver bream: all came to us as if we were hypnotists. Even in the heat of the day we went on hauling them in. Then suddenly the opiate heat of noon was shattered. A dog fight broke out above us with such unexpected suddenness that I thought at first it was the boughs of the big tall poplars catching noisy fire above our heads. Machinegun shells spattered down the full centre of the lake, rousing a thousand fish, big and small, from August slumber, so that they leapt out of the water in silver frightened shoals as if pursued by some monstrous legendary pike. We angled with a little more circumspection after that, seeking the shelter of trees; but though we heard once or twice again the rattle of machinegun fire there was really nothing that could ever destroy the suspended beauty of that day, which had calmed at least one troubled mind and given it hope for the future.

The immediate future was in fact to be one of blackness. With the coming of September the Germans were to make another full and deliberate attempt to destroy Britain. The full premeditated nature of the attack, based on Goering's personal orders from France, was clear: it was to smash London and with it, if possible, the entire morale of the people. The first attack, on 7 September, was the heaviest the country had ever had to face. Very heavy bombers, Dornier 215s, were used, escorted by powerful fighters, including the new Heinkel 113. The Luftwaffe bomber force, outnumbering the RAF many times over, was over London for hours, commanding the sky. Docks, stores, warehouses, masses of working-class houses and buildings of all kinds were smashed. By night, from fifty miles away, we could see from our Kentish fields the great red-orange light of London burning. Throughout it all the outnumbered RAF fought like tigers and though in the heat of battle it is never easy to assess casualties with any accuracy we claimed to have shot down a hundred Nazi planes. Against this over 300 Londoners were dead and another 1600 injured.

This was by no means the end. On 15 September a new great mass of bombers with their fighter escorts was again pitched against us, London again the main target. In one of these desperate moments when something has to be done to hide fear from children and distract them from a catastrophe about to blow up in their faces we had trundled off, pram, kettle, food, fishing rods and all, to picnic by the lake. The quinces were already turning gold on the trees by the water and the day was as golden as the ripening fruit. We had scarcely begun to fish when the sky, from the south-east, the direction of Dover, began to blacken. It was darkened all over by what seemed to be a monstrous gathering of giant starlings. Helplessly we watched them, at no height at all, flying above our heads, in relentless formation, on their way to London. As they passed there was suddenly, among the reeds along the lake, an explosion, followed by another. Though by no means loud, it frightened us more than the bombers, even long after we had discovered that it had been caused by two addled wild-duck eggs bursting in the summer heat.

Again a small, ludicrous event, remembered after nearly thirty years, illuminates an affair of far more sinister import. In the recollection of the exploding duck-eggs lies the thought, tenuous but satisfactory, that that day, 15 September, was virtually the end of Goering's effort to destroy us. Fat duck-egg as he himself looked, it was he, not us, who was that day exploded. We claimed – again, probably in the heat of battle, mistakenly – 185 Nazi planes destroyed. The precise number hardly mattered to a dozen one way or the other. On 18, 27 and 30 September we claimed a further 230 and after that the Luftwaffe fire was virtually expended.

Those who lived in the south-east that summer will never forget the irony of its ethereal beauty and its deathly, deathless conflict. When the weather broke at last, bringing autumn rain, it also brought an odd, repeated phenomenon. I had never seen it before and I have never seen it since.

It was a sundog: a kind of evanescent circular rainbow that, in unsettled weather, appears just a little away from the perimeter of the sun. It had about it a kind of ominous beauty. It might almost have been a sign from heaven: a portent, but of what you were too tired or shattered or relieved to wonder.

XV

Misery, said Coleridge, is not an exportable commodity, the market being everywhere glutted by it; and I will therefore not enlarge too greatly on it by going into that little known and other Battle of Britain, the night battle, which followed in the winter of 1940–41, when the Luftwaffe night bombers attacked London and all Britain's major ports, an onslaught of unparalleled power, up to that time, for the repulse of which we had only twelve so-called night-fighter squadrons, not one of which contained a night-fighter or even an aircraft of the required competence or even fitted with any night device for seeking out the enemy. Our fortune in escaping total destruction in this dark and little known confrontation, in which pilots were actually peering outside the cockpit in order to try to identify some object in the sky, is a mystery locked for ever in the bosom of God Almighty himself. He alone knows how we survived.

In the Battle of Britain, by day, the risk to civilian life had been relatively small; it was the pilots, five or six miles up, who had been killing each other. It was fear of invasion, that defences might be defeated and leave us naked and occupied by an enemy that induced the feeling that there were no tomorrows. When the day Battle had been won and the night Battle took its place the situation became entirely different. It was now the civilian population who were being exposed. Thousands were being killed and maimed and made homeless. Cities were being reduced to ruins. Tension, even in the south, was becoming intolerable.

Much has been written of the resilience of people under campaigns of continuous air bombardment and subsequent history has proved that resilience is not necessarily a British prerogative. But perhaps one small reminiscence of those days will serve to show that in certain situations humour is the British synonym for courage.

The story was told to me by Lady Reading, head of the Women's Voluntary Service during the war: the WVS who, in their neat green uniforms, drove about London and other cities dispensing help in time of trouble. That many of these ladies were from the now despised upper and upper middle classes (though many were not) is one of the points of the story. At one period the situation in London was so grave that a breakdown in Civil Defence services, through sheer weight of enemy attack, was threatened. Extra forces had to be brought in from somewhere and in this case some were called in from Newcastle, which had had little share of enemy attack. When the tough and highly independent Geordies duly arrived in London their eye fell with scorn on the green-tunicked ladies dispensing tea, cocoa, sandwiches and so on. The upper classes, with their southern accents, doing their bit, eh? Saving us from the enemy, eh? God help us, the Geordies seemed to say, if anything serious did happen. There would be a wild run for the exits.

That first night of the Geordies' visit to London all hell broke out over the city. London experienced its heaviest and bloodiest beating up to that date. In the morning the city was a burning wreck. Of this holocaust the WVS, well tried in battle, took little notice, but went about their appointed voluntary task of dispensing food and drink and helping injured and homeless all night long. The Geordies, on the other hand, never having experienced anything remotely like it, had endured a night of parlous agonies. But when the smoky dawn finally broke and the WVS, the despised ladies, were still at it, at least one Geordie had the grace to go to Lady Reading in humility. 'Aye,' he said, 'when we saw you yesterday we didn't think much o' you. But now we know you're best bloody bitches in t' world.'

This intolerable tension of living in the south at last forced us to a decision: we would evacuate the two girls to Northamptonshire. Not that this solved another of our problems: money. I had written little or nothing except *The Modern Short Story* since war began and it was certain that this would never make me rich. I cannot recall even having written any short stories though I do know that up to that time I had never been paid as much as £10 for one. I had once, it is true, been offered £10 for one and had accepted the offer, only to be let down by the editor, who welshed on me. Nor had I now many friends to whom I could turn. Derek Verschoyle, who had given me much work for *The Spectator*, had gone into the RAF; Rupert Hart-Davis had enlisted in the Coldstream Guards; David Garnett had also gone into the RAF to do special work for Coastal Command. I had consequently not only lost sight of all of them but was deprived of the kind of help they had long given me.

In desperation I went to *The Spectator*, for whom I had written much in the way of reviews and articles as well as the regular 'Country Life' feature, and asked the editor, Wilson Harris, if he would take me on to the staff. To my infinite surprise he said that he would and that I could in fact take over the job of literary editor. This seemed too wildly good to be true and I accepted gladly.

I will not go so far as to say that I actively disliked Wilson Harris. I will merely say that he appeared to me to have about as much humanity as a clothes prop. I once told him a slightly risqué joke, but this was received in the kind of frozen silence that would have greeted an incident of indecent exposure in the House of Lords and I never repeated it. Aloof, cold, ascetic, distant, Wilson Harris appeared to be the sort of man who had never consummated his marriage with life. As an editor he appeared to me to be a kind of bloodless public school headmaster of a long outdated type. I used to enter his study armed with proofs, books or articles like a small boy tremblingly ready to apologise that he had failed to finish his impositions, do his Latin prep, or unravel the diabolical mysteries of his trigonometry. In consequence I never felt anything but very, very small, very, very inferior, very, very unhappy.

Against this I must set the fact that I wasn't a very, very good literary editor. Perhaps my longseated hatred of journalism, however superior, that had had its inception in the Wellingborough office of the *Northampton Chronicle* (whose present editor, by the way, has recently been vastly amused by my account of my shortcomings there in *The Vanished World*) was responsible. Fortunately for me R. A. Scott James, a very good journalist who at least had some red blood in his veins and had been of help to me on occasions in the past, was also on the staff and acted as a sort of cushion between the clothes prop on the one hand and the harassed and volatile literary editor on the other. Life was certainly not easy. I used to come into St Pancras station every morning by ten o'clock, always to find that some new part of London had been devastated in the night and that streets and pavements were crowded with apparently cheerful Cockneys sweeping up broken glass and rubble and damning Hitler in the appropriate vernacular. Most days, as soon as I arrived at *The Spectator* office in Gower Street, air-raid sirens would begin their warning wailing and all the staff would go into underground retreat, thus disrupting half the day. In this way I learned to adapt myself to an entirely new system of writing: one whereby I could shut myself away in a cocoon and go on working, whether in tube or bus or railway carriage, as if the outer world never existed.

There inevitably came a day when the new boy, not having lived up to his promise, had to face expulsion and I confess it was rather more with relief than anything else that I said farewell to the clothes prop and *The Spectator*. It is, however, not quite true that I said farewell entirely to *The Spectator*, since I continued for some time to write the 'Country Life' notes, which didn't displease the headmaster and had certainly made me many friends among its readers. But I cannot forbear to say that I never now pass No. 99 Gower Street without a feeling that a headmasterly hand will stretch out and order me into the chill of the editorial study.

Where, then, to go from here? Not for the first time in my writing life I hadn't the faintest idea. If the times had been bad for writers in 1926, as Edward Garnett had well pointed out, they were now hell. That they were also hell for a lot of other people was of small personal comfort. It now seemed to me that it might be better to abandon, at least for the period of crisis, all idea of being a writer. The tension and frustrations attaching to it were becoming so great that it seemed to me better to do as T. E. Lawrence had done and seek an anonymous, part-monastic seclusion in one of the armed Services, there to bury my identity completely in a regimented life apart, uncomplicated by private struggle. I accordingly applied for a commission in the RAF – and was turned down.

In this suspended, negative moment there occurred another of those small interfering pokes by the hand of fate, or whatever it may be called, that was to alter the course of my life. Cecil Day Lewis, who is now Poet Laureate, was at that time doing work for the Ministry of Information. Whether he had heard in some way of my unsuccessful application for an RAF commission I have no idea or whether he had heard of an exceedingly unfortunate experience of mine with the MOI, I shall probably never know, but at all events I presently received a letter from him.

Before I tell of it I may perhaps tell of the unfortunate experience that preceded it. One day at lunch with Graham Greene I had mentioned to him my arid literary predicament (I hardly think his own was all that much better) and he had suggested that my talents surely had their correct place in the Ministry of Information, for which he himself was doing certain work. Very kindly he promised to put in a word for me in the right place, which he duly did, and in due course I went along to the headquarters of the Ministry, then housed at London University.

I was there ushered into the presence of a gentleman who informed me that he had been a school inspector: a tribe of whom, I understand, the teaching profession is not particularly enamoured; and after my experience with one I cannot say that I wonder why. We had scarcely begun to talk when he was called away to another room for a telephone call, leaving the interview to be carried on by an office boy. The following illuminating conversation then took place.

'What kind of work do you do ?'

'I am a writer.'

'You mean you actually write?'

'I actually write.'

'Oh! really? What have you written?'

'Books.'

'Oh? You mean you have actually written books?'

'Yes.'

'You mean the sort of books that are published?'

'The sort of books that are published.'

'Oh! good heavens. And *have* they actually been published?'

I rose and walked out, not waiting for the return of His Majesty the school inspector.

Graham Greene's fury at this nonsense, when I told him of it, was so great that he may well have communicated it to Cecil Day Lewis. He certainly communicated it to someone at the MOI and as Graham Greene isn't noted for using stale suet for words I do not doubt that the echoes of protest reverberated acidly.

Soon afterwards came the letter from Cecil Day Lewis. It contained the interesting suggestion that I might care to look at some portraits done by Eric Kennington, Paul Nash, Laura

Knight, Sir William Rothenstein, Graham Sutherland, Keith Henderson and others of some of the pilots who had fought in the Battle of Britain. I knew of course of Kennington's work from his vividly admirable portraits of British and Arab leaders alike in T. E. Lawrence's *Seven Pillars of Wisdom*. I had long thought highly of them and ever since that brief meeting with Lawrence himself I had been specially haunted by the simple but profound sketch Kennington had done of him. Simple, economical, sensitive, it seemed to me to have touched and revealed much of the essence of the man. Some years later I met Kennington, who lent me one of the few existing typescripts of that abrasive, self-destructive, unhappy book, *The Mint*, which he carried about with him like a pot of uneasy gold.

Meanwhile it was Cecil Day Lewis' idea that I should look at the Kennington and Nash portraits of the Battle of Britain pilots, see what I thought of them and then annotate them for a small book to be put out by the MOI When the portraits arrived I was instantly struck by several things: first the great variation in the faces of the men themselves, which varied from the glamorised types with their fancy neckerchiefs (one at least of these, stationed close enough to London, used to have his lunch specially sent down to his station every day from Pruniers) to sergeant pilots of calm and unglamorised composure and resolve and sensitive men who might have been poets, Oxford dons, picture restorers or prelates or indeed anything at all. The great variation of those faces was infinitely fascinating. I duly did my annotations and the little book was duly published. I had given it the title of *You Have Seen Their Faces*.

Little though I was aware of it at the time, the title was to a degree prophetic. The faces that had fought the Battle of Britain had been little seen or known until Kennington and other artists drew them. But behind them were many other faces of whose characteristics the greater part of the population of Britain were also entirely ignorant.

The opportunity to look at these faces too was now about to be given me, as I shall now describe.

XVI

Still in a state composed more of frustration than despair I wrote the following letter to David Garnett on 13 August 1941:

> I hear that you are again at the Air Ministry and I have been wondering if you can give me any idea of what chances I have of getting any special work to do in your own or any other RAF department. I have until October before my exemption expires; then I am booked for the RAF under special duties. Meanwhile I've been asked by Bobbs Merrill in New York if I'll do a book on the American Eagle Squadron. Unfortunately until recently the Eagles haven't been much in action, but now that they are I hope to do the book. But replies from the Air Ministry are slow, and one first contacts one person and then another. Do you know any personage of high plumage among the Eagles? I am very keen to do this book and if you can help in this or any other way it would be splendid.
>
> I have just done the introduction to the RAF war pictures by Kennington, Nash and others for the MOI and the Oxford University Press. They were pleased with it, and it seems as if this too might help to persuade the Air Ministry that I might be of some use. Will you anyway advise me as to what I might do? – if it is of any use applying to the Air Ministry and to whom and so on. I feel a bit desperate about getting my future outlined a bit.

To all this David acted with great promptitude, so that by 6 September I was writing to him that I had been to Air Ministry and had there seen a good friend of his (and a subsequent good friend of mine) John Nerney, the Air Ministry Librarian, 'a rock of integrity', who exercised a good deal of influence on the civilian side of RAF Public Relations. I do not remember much of this interview except that John Nerney was kindly and intelligent and furthermore suggested that I should come back for another interview in a few days' time.

It cannot have been many days later when I duly turned up at King Charles Street, expecting again to see Nerney alone but to be confronted instead by a trio consisting of John himself, Harald Peake, then Director of RAF Public Relations at Air Ministry and now head of Lloyds Bank, and Hilary St George Saunders, deputy librarian at the House of Commons and then also attached to Air Ministry.

I hadn't the vaguest idea of why this distinguished band had gathered to meet me and when they at last began to explain why I felt I had been led into some hall of dreams. Harald Peake, who was both intelligent and charming, was the leading spokesman. There had been conjured up, he proceeded to explain to me, the idea of an entirely new concept in RAF Public Relations. It was proposed to form a new department, to be known as PR II, and of which Hilary St George Saunders was to be the head. This department would, in essence, have as its aim something of what I had done with the portraits of Kennington, Nash and others. It would show not figures, statistics, bulletins, communiqués and so on to the public, but men, characters, faces. It would dedicate itself to the proposition that figures, if repeated *ad nauseam*, mean nothing, but that a pilot with a pint of beer in his hand and a popsie in bed can illuminate the troubled business of war in a way that will bring war and its participants vividly, excitedly, even painfully alive.

To this end Harald Peake and Hilary Saunders (my friend to the all too early end of his life) now proceeded to put forward not only a truly remarkable proposition but one utterly unprecedented in any of the armed services at any time. They proposed to commission me into the RAF simply as a short story writer.

I listened aghast. Why me? My further immediate reactions were first of being greatly honoured and then of being terrified. I couldn't be other than honoured by such a proposition, I told myself, but what of the not impossible situation if I should fail in the appointed task? I knew nothing of flying, flying men, aerial combat, bombers or fighters. With such faith implanted in me by men of high rank I could hardly be other than terrified.

Hilary, Nerney and Harald Peake proceeded to allay these fears by saying that they had equal faith in both my talents and me. Even this wasn't enough for me. I proceeded to explain that one of the things you cannot do is to make a writer write; you cannot put stripes on his sleeve and call him a Flight-Lieut. and put him at a desk and say 'Proceed, by the comma, quick march, and produce short stories.' Art, even in such limited form, acknowledges no keeper called regimentation.

Gifted with much intelligence as they all three were, Hilary, Harald Peake and Nerney cordially agreed. They were with me completely. They understood. I then put a further point to them. If I were to accept their proposal I should have to insist on utter freedom in time and movement; in other words I must be allowed to write when and where and how I liked, to go where and when and how I liked; to disregard authority when it threatened to interfere, to make my own rules (always within King's Regulations) and to be bound by no other commitment than to do what I was to be commissioned to do: namely to write short stories and nothing but short stories.

Again, to my infinite honour, astonishment and satisfaction, they agreed. These were precisely the things that they had in mind. They would treat me as an artist, see that others treated me as an artist and see that I was as free as a bird. I would be answerable to no narrow-minded station commander, no petty regulation, no inhibiting duties, but only to the men whose new, inspired idea this was. It was short stories they needed and it was I, and I alone, whom they had chosen to write them.

I left Air Ministry that September afternoon feeling rather as if I had been awarded a literary Victoria Cross. It was a very, very momentous day in my life: perhaps, as it turned out, the most momentous day of all.

I felt, at last, that my world had indeed blossomed. Of how it further matured, both in the RAF and elsewhere, I hope to tell fully in another volume, *The World in Ripeness*.

THE WORLD IN
RIPENESS

I

Burdened by an impossibly large and heavy blue cabin trunk, I set off on 17 October 1941, for the Royal Air Force Station at Uxbridge, there to engage in a three-week Officers' Training Course. The afternoon was utterly typical of an English mid-October: the air limpid, soft and warm as new milk, the distances touched with that same tender haze that must surely have inspired Keats' 'Season of mists and mellow fruitfulness'.

I only wish I could say the same for my own spirits; but I fear that for all my natural buoyancy, it was not so. Honoured though I was to have been singled out by Air Ministry to be the first writer ever to be commissioned in the Armed Forces solely as a writer of short stories I must nevertheless confess to having been slightly heavy of heart. I was leaving behind me a young wife, who had somehow to manage, on God only knew how little money, to feed and clothe and comfort four children under the age of eight, in a part of England where, even though the immediate threat of German invasion had receded, constant day and night raids by enemy bombers and fighters were still very much part of the day's unamusing routine.

I could, I think, have dodged this particular column, largely on the grounds that Officers' Training Courses do not have, as part of their curriculum, any special instructional periods for the guidance of short story writers; but I was determined in this, as in other matters, to seek no special favours, and I have ever since been specially glad that I did not do so.

The scene at Uxbridge was in part comic, in part sad. It rather resembled one of those appalling Old Boys' Reunions at which some men remember others only too well whereas others, either by design or the sheer passage of years, have forgotten. ('By God, it's old Jonesy. Remember? Upper Fifth. 1922. Gosh, you were a devil. Remember how you set fire to your Latin crib one day? Just got the damn thing burning merrily when the Old Man himself popped in. God! – talk about laugh! Remember?') Some, as I say, remembered; some, on the contrary, did not. An air of uneasy embarrassment hung over everything as the extraordinary motley company of players attempted to sort out their baggage, find their billets and beds and somehow accustom themselves to the thought of a sort of semi-monastic three-weeks' imprisonment.

Shopkeepers, schoolmasters, small business men, hoteliers, solicitors, commercial travellers, engineers, clerks, accountants: motley, indeed, the assembly was. Most were family men in their early or mid thirties. One was a Rugby International; another, rather fat and podgy, appeared to have been honoured with some special dispensation, since he wore on his sleeve not the miserable thin blue line that is the mark of the lowly entrant pilot officer, but the huge broad ring that denotes none other than the lofty air commodore. All of us treated this particular gentleman not only with awe and respect but a certain suspicion that he had been placed among us as a sort of guardian-cum-spy. It was not until next day that we discovered he had, unfortunately, suffered from the misguidance of an over-zealous tailor.

That night fifty or so of us were herded together as in a school dormitory. The atmosphere was in keeping; there was much farting; I slept badly. In the morning, by now turned alarmingly chilly, we paraded at an ungodly hour for the customary injection against smallpox, tetanus and so on. One of my companion officers had turned out to be an old schoolfellow, also a Rugby player, a hefty young man of some fifteen or sixteen stone. He was behind me in the queue for jabs. Suddenly I was stunned by a sound as of falling masonry and turned to see my erstwhile schoolmate flat on his back, cold and glassy-eyed.

Soon we were being addressed, in terms alternately avuncular, soothing and stern, by the commanding officer, who solemnly assured us that, as if we were about to enter Holy Orders, the RAF Officers' Training Course, Uxbridge, could bring nothing but physical, mental, moral and indeed spiritual elevation to our wretched and all too recently civilian souls. We listened in silence, as yet unconverted.

Presently we were led, with a sort of casual subtlety, into the curriculum itself. This consisted of a couple of hours' square-bashing after breakfast, followed by a short break, then followed by a lecture and then, after lunch, by a further lecture and more square-bashing. I didn't really mind the square-bashing; at least, on the suddenly freezing October days, it kept the blood in circulation. Of the lectures it is hard to say if they were worse than the lecturers; but on balance I should, in memory, vote slightly in the lectures' favour, little though that may mean.

One of the lecturers was a kind of stage silly ass type commonly seen in those appalling musical comedies of the 1920s; dapper and la-di-da of voice, he conceived it stupendously clever to enliven his sessions with *risqué* stories having neither point nor humour (A Waaf had an accident; she fell out of bed. She was swerving to avoid a child), at the same time offering us not a single improving word. Another was an ex-public school master of infinite and lofty snobbery whose constant injunction to us was 'always to remember our *Alma Mater*'. A third was a semi-illiterate whose favourite word was *personnel*, pronounced roughly to rhyme with *Rommel*. I used to listen to him, I fear, half-shrouded in sleep.

It must have been on the second or third day of the course that I fell in with an ex-hotelier from Cornwall who had earned his commission the hard way, having come up from the ranks. As a result there was nothing, absolutely nothing, that he didn't know about dodging duties, responsibilities and parades, bending or breaking the rules, always quite legitimately, and generally avoiding the harsher moments of service life. My first experience of these long-acquired ingenuities occurred on a frigid afternoon when thin flakes of snow were dismally floating through the darkening air, making the thought of an afternoon parade, without overcoats, more than a slightly forbidding one. Duty bound, spruced and ready, I was nevertheless about to leave the dormitory when to my infinite astonishment I saw my friend the hotelier lying indolently on his bed, still in his shirt sleeves. The following conversation then took place.

'It's two o'clock already. Hadn't you better get ready for parade?'

'Not coming.'

'*Not coming*?'

'No.'

'Good God, why ever not?'

'Going out.'

'*Going out*? Where on earth to?'

'Dental.'

This single cryptic word was drenched with all the distillation of long experience. Dental? Was there, I enquired, something wrong with my friend's teeth? Had he toothache?

'No.'

'Then if there's nothing wrong with your teeth why are you going to dental?'

'Well of course there might be something wrong that I don't know about and of course I shan't know, shall I, until I get the dentist to have a look? I'll be back for tea.'

The next afternoon, again snatched prematurely from winter, the word 'dental' was replaced by 'medical'. When I inquired if my friend was feeling ill he airily replied that, on the contrary, he felt as fit as a fiddle. But that didn't mean, did it, that there might not be something wrong and until you got the doctor to have a look you couldn't know, could you?

The following evening he proceeded to announce a still more audacious piece of adventure. He was going to town for the night. He had, it seemed, a pleasant little bird up there.

'But Good God, man, you can't be out of camp all night.'

'Oh! yes, I can.'

'But have you a special pass or something?'

'Don't need one. As long as you're on parade at eight-thirty next morning you can do what the hell you like with your nights.'

'But I thought we were supposed to stay in and swot up King's Regulations and all that, ready for the passing-out exam.'

'All baloney. What's the point of swotting up when you're allowed to take all your notes into the exam? What's the point of reading King's Regulations when you've got all the answers anyway?'

'I never thought of that.'

'Well, you must, old boy, you must. Listen to me. Never be too bloody diligent and all that. If you are they'll spot it like a hawk and have you posted to some hell-hole like Aden or somewhere. That's where they send the nice, good, obedient types. Not my sort. They know we can't be trusted.'

'You amaze me.'

'Glad to hear it, old boy. And let me tell you something else. *Never be on time anywhere.* Whenever you're posted always turn up a couple of days late. Why? A thousand to one the signal about you will never have got through and even if it has the bloody Adjutant or some WAAF or other will have lost it. No, never be on time, old boy, never be on time.'

With such splendid subterfuges my friend was able constantly and easily to dodge all the more arduous or boring or irksome of duties. One of these consisted of an incredible afternoon when, herded into the camp cinema for an hour and a half, we were given a stunningly thrilling lecture on the social duties incumbent upon officers, in particular 'The Art of the Social Afternoon Call on the Wives of Other Officers and the Leaving of Cards Therewith.'

When the three-week course was finally over I got the posting I expected: that of Flight-Lieutenant to Public Relations, Air Ministry. On the way out of camp my heavy cabin trunk was carelessly dropped from a truck, one of the sides bashed in. Instantly, properly inspired by the wisdom of my hotelier friend, I made it an excuse to snatch two days' leave at home. Nobody, as my friend had truly predicted, turned a hair.

II

When I eventually reported back to Air Ministry it was to find that the newly formed department of Public Relations, PR11, consisted of only four men, I now being the fifth: Hilary St George Saunders himself, an assistant Flight-Lieut., John Pudney and F. A. Walbank, who had produced one or two anthologies but, unlike John Pudney and myself, was not commissioned. In the various other departments of PR there were considerable numbers of other writers of much experience and distinction. Leonard Dodds and Dudley Barker were both later to become my chiefs and very excellent and understanding ones at that; many of the rest I never met at all and others not until some long time later. Among those I did meet, and indeed made good friends with, were Geoffrey Harmsworth, of the famous newspaper family, R. F. Delderfield, still a struggling playwright, with his phenomenally successful *Worm's Eye View* still to come, Eric Partridge, who had in fact published at his Scholartis Press a book of mine, *Seven Tales and Alexander*, Vernon Noble, Stanley Bishop, renowned as a crime reporter, John Macadam, sports writer, and Fletcher Allen, an editor. Also somewhere in the building were Alan Melville, John Strachey and Philip Guedalla, as well as artists and photographers of much distinction too.

John Pudney and I at once got on well together (indeed I can truthfully say that, with one single exception, I encountered nothing but friendliness in my entire RAF service). In sharp contrast to this was the behaviour of Hilary St George Saunders and his assistant Flight-Lieut. who daily and indeed almost all day engaged in prolonged and abusive slanging matches, carried out with a sort of rude verbal affection, love-hate, pitilessly, no holds barred. These encounters were a joy and wonder to behold and listen to. Hilary indeed was a master of fearless invective, a gift he used on not a few occasions in order to make easier the path of his newest pupil, to whom he now presently announced:

> We think we should send you first to a Bomber Station, where you can stay for two or three days in order to sense the atmosphere. The one we have in mind is at Oakington, just outside Cambridge. But first we'd like you to go to HQ Bomber Command at High Wycombe, where their head man will take you under his wing and see you on your way.

There was little I could do but acquiesce in all this, though I did so with an increasing nervousness and apprehension. Once again I was assailed with the chilling fear that I might fail in my mission. Of bombers and bomber crews I knew nothing; the vocabulary and territory of that world, celestial or otherwise, were utterly foreign to me. Suppose it should happen that I boob, put up a black? Thankfully the understanding wisdom of John Nerney, that 'rock of integrity' as David Garnett has called him, was there to sustain me as I went to say goodbye to him before leaving for this, my first assignment. Somehow he managed to imply, without actually saying it, that all would be well, and my faith in myself was re-implanted.

Next day I was on my way to High Wycombe, in my car. I had

scarcely cleared the suburbs of London before I was flagged down by a Cockney gentleman seeking a lift. In true Cockney fashion he had the new, green pilot officer weighed up in about three minutes flat: the easy, dead easy touch. His trouble, he proceeded smoothly to explain, was that he'd been supposed to meet his brother that morning, in Ealing, but for some reason the brother hadn't turned up. They were in fact going to High Wycombe to pick up a set of car tyres and the brother, see, was the one who had the money. My Cockney passenger was now, of course, as he proceeded glibly to explain, in 'somefink of a spot'. He had three quid on him all right but he needed another five so as he could get the tyres. Did I know what? – if I could lend him the fiver he would later leave it at the Poste Restante at High Wycombe Post Office and I could call for it on my way back from wherever I was going to. See?

I fell. This, among the oldest of confidence tricks, was too much for, and completely mesmerised, my innocent good nature. I duly handed over the fiver and duly turned up, some days later, at High Wycombe Post Office, to emerge empty-handed. There is, however, a true and good saying, especially applicable, I think, to writers of fiction. It is to the effect that 'nothing is ever lost'. The incident of my Cockney friend and his confidence trick never left my mind, and more than twenty years later I turned it into a story, *Mr Featherstone Takes a Ride*, for which an editor paid me 250 guineas, thus showing a fair profit on a morning in which I too had been taken for one.

On arrival at HQ Bomber Command, High Wycombe, I was assailed by the illusion that I had, by some misguidance, strayed into the portals of the Ritz. All, it seemed to me, was grandeur. I had grown used to, in my three weeks' Officers' Training Course at Uxbridge, a certain prison-like shabbiness, even if sherry was only ninepence a glass. Here at High Wycombe the Mess Bar Steward was as impeccable as a first-class Head Waiter, dressed in a jacket as white as that of an umpire at Lord's. 'And what, sir, would you care to drink? We have everything. A little sherry perhaps? Bristol Milk? Bristol Cream? Thank you, sir. The Bristol Cream.'

After a lunch of an excellence only comparable with that of the Bristol Cream I drove on to Cambridge, guided and accompanied by 'the head man'. It was, as I remember it, a grey, damp and dismal November afternoon which grew only greyer, damper and more dismal the farther north we got. By the time we reached Cambridge it was almost dark; at Oakington it was completely so, a circumstance that only served to increase my already wavering fears and apprehensions. Nor were these uplifted by the fact that at the RAF station, in the Mess ante-room, a radio was belting out a popular tune that has for ever remained in my mind as one of haunting melancholy: *Daddy, let me stay up late*, which to this day enshrines so much of the ephemeral nature of the lives of the young bomber pilots and crews I was about to meet and write about. It is not too much to say that I can never recall that song, still less hear it, without being very near to tears.

But before I ever got to the Mess still another experience deepened my gloom. It was my first sight of the giant Stirling Bombers, lined up like so many black broody birds, apparently either ready to roost for the night or to lay equally black and destructive eggs, all round the perimeter of the airfield. Huge, unwieldy, twenty-five feet or more high from ground to nose, not easy to fly, desperately difficult to handle in a cross wind, those monsters stood there in dark, sinister, ugly assembly. My one comforting thought, as I looked at them in the dimmed light of that November evening, was that I had been expressly forbidden, on Air Ministry instructions, thank God, to take any sort of part in Flying Operations. It was no small expression of Air Ministry's Public Relations wisdom that my job was to write stories and not, by the Grace of God, to get myself unnecessarily killed.

When at last I found myself in the Mess ante-room it was to be further assailed by the impression that I had somehow strayed into a gathering of Sixth Form schoolboys grown prematurely old. I think it true to say that of all the officers assembled there that evening scarcely more than a dozen were over twenty-five. One of these was the station commander, Group-Captain Adams, an extraordinarily likeable and able man who looked rather more like a sea captain from Drake's time than an RAF officer; another was an American from Texas, known naturally as Tex, a rear-gunner of small stature but extremely powerful hands who had got himself into the RAF in order to wage a purely personal war against Hitler; another was a Kentish man, Norman Winch, who had done some journalism but was really hoping to be a farmer and who, I am happy to say, is now a farmer and has been my good friend, together with his pretty wife, ever since; another was myself, so ancient at thirty-six that it would not have at all surprised me if the young pilots had called me Pop.

It was the eyes of these young but prematurely aged officers that made a first powerful and everlasting impact on me. They were not 'sicklied o'er with the pale cast of thought' or even that of fear. It was something much more elusive, profound, disturbing and hard to define. Perhaps I can best illustrate it by telling of a young Australian pilot of whom, eventually, I was to write two or three stories. He had come from a family of sheep-farmers, up country, in Victoria: lean, indeed gaunt of face, tight of lip, eyes glassy and seemingly sightless, almost, from long night fatigue. I grew very attached to him before he was finally shot down and killed over Germany.

When his parents and his sister at last read the stories that I wrote of him they had one paramount desire: to come to meet the man who had written of the son and brother they had lost. The war eventually being over, they came to see me: simple, honest, proud, rural people steeped in pride for a young man who had given his life 12,000 miles from home. With such pride as parents naturally have on these occasions they showed me a photograph of him taken when he had first joined the Royal Australian Air Force: a mere boy, starry-eyed, proud too, the new entrant on his way to the big school.

I weep as I write these words: I did not recognise him. Nor, as I handed them my own photograph of him, the gaunt-faced, glassy-eyed, weary veteran of heaven knew what hell had been his lot over Germany, did they recognise him either. In silence, they far more shocked than I, we realised that we were speaking of two different men.

Such was my initiation into the world of Bomber Command; and that night, as I went to bed, I knew that Air Ministry's suggested 'two or three days' would have at least to be two or three weeks, perhaps even two or three months. The immediate problem was to get these men to talk; but how? That was the question. I knew of course of that great unwritten RAF law: the one that forbids the shooting of lines. But somehow lines had to be shot or extracted: whether in secret, by trickery, subterfuge or even some form of cheating I didn't yet know.

Next morning I met the wing commander of No. 7 Squadron, a tough young man who viewed with a certain suspicion, if not indeed resentment, the writer from Air Ministry. Nevertheless we talked; and as we talked I solved the first of my problems: I would play the game of eavesdropping. Accordingly, that morning, I got my first story, unwittingly given to me by the unsuspecting wing commander who, in an unguarded moment, let fall some re- mark to the effect that the worst of his own problems was that of writing to relatives of men killed or even of seeing them in his office as they turned up, pitifully hoping, perhaps, that by some sort of miracle he would conjure their beloved ones back from the dead. 'It's hell,' he said, 'but then that's just the way it is.'

This, in fact, was what I called the story, *It's Just the Way It Is*, and this is how it began: 'November rain falls harshly on the clean tarmac, and the wind, turning suddenly, lifts sprays of yellow elm leaves over the black hangars.'

This clear, pictorial simplicity was, I felt, the right and only way that this story, and indeed any others, should be written. I wrote it the following day, in a couple of hours, and posted it straight off to Hilary Saunders, half-dreading what he might have to say about it. In no time there came back from Whitehall a stream of delighted cries and I was able to breathe again.

My next task was to make friends; and this I did, drinking with pilots and navigators, playing cribbage with them, exchanging purposely idle gossip, hardly ever mentioning ops, bombers or writing. Soon a certain air of tension that my arrival had built up began to be dissipated. In a week my presence was accepted, warmly, often with much humour, and without suspicion.

Almost the first thing I had noted about these bomber crews, and which never afterwards failed to fascinate me, was their international democracy. Canadians, Scots, Australians, Rhodesians, Tex the American, Englishmen, Irishmen, Welshmen, New Zealanders: the mixture of nationalities was great. Perhaps an even more striking thing was that of rank. It not infrequently happened that one of those great Stirlings would be piloted and captained by a sergeant, who might have under his command men of the rank of pilot-officer or flight-lieutenant. Rank in fact became meaningless as crews set out for the blackness over Germany. Many of these sergeants, in fact, neither wanted nor sought commissions. They preferred the *camaraderie* of the sergeants' Mess, well knowing that a sergeant, as pilot and captain, could expect and receive utter obedience and respect from men superior, however superior, to him in rank. And this, it seemed to me, was a wonderful thing.

Beer was the main drink of these flying men and off duty they swilled at it pretty heavily. It is not a drink I greatly care for but I confess to having drunk more of it in my three months at Oakington (for three months was it to become) than either before or since. Fortunately there were more refined sources of refreshment and one of these was the Arts Theatre Restaurant in Cambridge, where the excellent cellar had been built up by wines given from various college cellars. And it was here that I presently began to take a pilot, perhaps two, to dinner so that we could talk, over a bottle of wine, far out of range of Mess ears. Again I played the game of eavesdropping, never pumping my guests for stories, content always to pick up the creative crumbs as they fell.

They fell pretty frequently and I, like an artist catching a quick glimpse of a face, a scene, a horse, a bird on the wing, made from them my quick-sketched stories, using always the simple, clear graphic approach. Almost always, I think, these flying companions utterly failed to realise that it was the casual, unsuspecting, apparently irrelevant word that I was waiting for as my inspiration. I will give two instances. One evening a pilot, an extraordinarily good and tough one, let fall the casual statement that sometimes, not returning from ops over Germany until dawn was breaking, he would see the sun rise twice, once from several thousand feet up and a second time after he had landed. I could scarcely wait to get this illuminating symbolic episode down on paper and when I did so I called it *The Sun Rises Twice*.

The second incident fell from the lips of the young Australian of whom I have already spoken, Geoff Heard, and it almost drove me wild with excitement. There had been, it seemed, on a remote sheep-farm in Victoria, a couple with an only son. So precious and useful were his hands in the running of the sheep-farm that when war broke out the parents instantly resorted to every kind of trick and subterfuge in order to keep the news from him. Newspapers were cancelled, letters were opened, hidden or burnt, the radio was put out of action. All this, combined with the extreme remoteness of the station, enabled them to keep the stark fact of war from him for an entire year. Then, inevitably, there came a day when he drove a hundred miles to the nearest good-sized town for a few days' holiday, went into a barber's saloon for a haircut, picked up a newspaper and was stunned by the greatest shock of his young life. He enlisted the very next day and I called his story *The Young Man from Kalgoorlie*.

Cambridge, besides the sheer everlasting beauty of its colleges, had other civilised pleasures to offer. Two or three times a week there were afternoon orchestral concerts and to these I often went with some fellow officers not on duty, to listen to Mozart, Bach, Schubert and others. One of these officers was a small, shy, soft-spoken young Irishman who behaved and looked more like a gentle poet than a fighting man. I admired and liked him so much that I truly believe that if he had asked me to go on ops with him I would have flouted Air Ministry rules and have gone with him. Fortunately he made no such suggestion; and after lunch one day I stood on the perimeter of the airfield and watched his big Stirling take off for Brest, there to attack the two German battle-ships *Scharnhorst* and *Gneisenau* popularly known as Salmon and Gluckstein. The plane had scarcely risen to five hundred feet or so when it suddenly seemed to blossom into a great orange and crimson flower. It fell in fields, wreathed in a vast black pall of smoke, a mile or two away.

It was Canadians, mostly, who provided a physical toughness far removed from the poetic gentleness of my young Irish friend. One of these, a hefty navigator named Mac, was for ever, in true Canadian fashion, spoiling for a fight. We not infrequently went out together, often with another Canadian, Ed Baker, and Norman Winch, and sometimes with an extremely pretty blonde WAAF officer named Christine to whom we were all rather attached. One evening as we sat over drinks in a hotel bar I was amazed to see the two Canadians suddenly rise swiftly to their feet, simply seize a man on the other side of the room, frog-march him through the door and hurl him with unceremonial violence into the street. The reason?

'The guy was undressing Christine with his eyes.'

But even this brief episode of violence was as nothing compared with another memorable encounter that, a few nights later, Mac enjoyed in London, where he had gone on leave. When he finally returned to Oakington his appearance was like that of a man who had been in a fifteen round contest with Jack Dempsey, Joe Louis and Rocky Marciano all at the same time. His face was a red-and-purple mass of bruises and lacerations; his eyes were mere swollen red bags; his tunic was torn and stiff with dark, dried blood.

When I inquired as to the reason for this disturbing sight Mac informed me with calmness that it was nothing. Just nothing. Nothing. Just a fight.

'Some fight.'

'No. Just an ordinary fight.'

Mac, it seemed, had gone into the men's room at the Regent Palace Hotel, there to find three big men picking on a little one. Such an excuse for a scrap was on no account to be missed and Mac merrily mowed in.

'And how did it finally turn out?' I wanted to know.

'Oh! they took 'em away in ambulances.'

Looking at the lacerated face of my Canadian friend I could only marvel and wonder, trying to guess the state of his defeated adversaries. Ordinary fight indeed.

Not very long later Mac was on ops over Italy, where he was shot down, wounded and taken prisoner-of-war. In typical fashion, after a few days in hospital, he mesmerised a young Italian nurse into letting him have slightly more than the regulation amount of freedom and thus instantly escaped and, having escaped, promptly proceeded to walk to Rome, where he knocked on the door of the Vatican.

There he was given a suit of civilian clothes, a seat on a plane and a day later was back in England.

At lunch one day, trying to force down my throat a dreary plateful of bully beef and potatoes (the food at Oakington was on the whole sadly uninspired) I was called to the telephone. At the other end of the line was Hilary Saunders, informing me that I had been summoned to the immediate presence of no less a person than the Secretary of State for Air.

When I finally reached Whitehall, filled with a certain apprehension at my summons there, and was shown into the ministerial presence, it was to find Sir Archibald Sinclair, a man of highly distinguished appearance, indeed aristocratic of presence without being aloof, and of great personal charm and impeccable politeness. His American mother and Winston Churchill's American mother were cousins. I consequently felt no little honoured that he had not only greatly admired my stories but had sent for me personally in order to offer his congratulations. It gave me satisfaction to feel that, in spite of all my doubts and forebodings, I had gone some way towards justifying the faith that Hilary Saunders, Harald Peake and John Nerney (and also David Garnett, the original moving spirit behind it all) had had in me. At the same time I was told that the stories were soon to be published and that Hilary had been inspired to invent for me the pseudonym 'Flying Officer X'.

The stories duly appeared in the *News Chronicle* under that *nom de plume*, which in fact hid my identity for just about a single day. My imprint, it seemed, was on every word. When I got back to Oakington the first of the *News Chronicle* stories had already been widely read and I felt a sense of inexplicable unease. There was much leg-pulling; and the wing commander, I was told, was gunning for me. The station commander was fortunately far more tolerant but even so I took the first opportunity of making some excuse to go back to Air Ministry, with the avowed intention of begging Hilary to give me a few days' leave, which in his typically generous fashion he did. Later it was of no little satisfaction to me to know that the men of Bomber Command themselves approved of the stories; it seemed that the right, authentic, unheroic note had been struck; the stories were also much read, I understand, in prisoner-of-war camps and today, I am assured, still offer much interest to a generation unacquainted with either Bomber Command or the war.

When I again got back to Oakington the air was calmer, my unease had disappeared and I even found myself being congratulated by the WAAF telephone operator who had all unwittingly provided me, sometimes, with material for stories too, often in circumstances painful to her, when she had to inform me that she was afraid 'Flight-Lieut. so-and-so had bought it, over Bremen last night'. She was a girl of much quiet charm and I fear there were often tears in her eyes.

But now a momentous event occurred. The chief station intelligence officer, an agreeable man who had done much to make my early passage smooth, one day suggested that I go and have a talk with him. He had, he felt, something to tell me that might be of considerable interest. We duly talked, I being sworn to secrecy. It appeared that the captain of a Wellington Bomber shot down over France had escaped by devious routes and was now back with his squadron, which though not specifically stationed at Oakington, nevertheless shared our Mess; and it seemed that he had a remarkable story to tell.

The point about secrecy arose from the fact that in those comparatively early days any mention in public of pilots escaping after being shot down over the Continent was strictly taboo. But, the Intelligence officer informed me, I could if I wished talk to the pilot, though only on the absolute condition that I neither breathed nor wrote a word of what he had to tell. Next day I met and talked with the pilot and the seed of *Fair Stood the Wind for France* was sown.

Partly because of the immediate excitement of this, partly because so many of the men I had first known in No. 7 Squadron had now either been killed or taken prisoner (there were some deeply dark days on that often fog-shrouded fenland that winter) I felt it a propitious moment in which to leave Oakington and seek new stories elsewhere. I also felt that, regardless of all rules and swearing to secrecy, the Wellington Bomber pilot's story must, somehow, be got down on paper. I therefore resolved to tell Hilary that I needed a change of scene and a break before we could decide on the exploration of 'fresh woods and pastures new'. Hilary, ever understanding and in any case pleased that he had put his money, by some good chance, on a horse that wasn't quite an also-ran, duly gave me leave and I went home, my brain and imagination positively bursting like a ripe seed-pod under the heat and fervour of the story I wanted to tell.

I wrote as in a fever, the words nevertheless cool, simple, graphic, restrained. The seed given me by the Wellington pilot was seed only; it now had to be sown and nurtured in the soil of imagination, as of course all fiction has to be. I had first to invent the bomber crew; then their disastrous moment of being shot down; then their being hidden and aided by a French family, among whom the young daughter was of supreme, proud and electric importance. Indeed I saw the entire story as one epitomising the youth of two countries, on the one hand England almost alone in battle, on the other France alone in humiliation and defeat. I wanted to extract from this, if possible, the beauty, the pride, the courage and, if the word is not now too suspect, the patriotism of the young of two civilised countries determined that they would in no circumstances be slaves to an oppressor. If there was also an air of fatalism about it all so it had to be; it was just the way it was.

Dates and times are now a little difficult to recall with accuracy, but I think I had a fortnight's leave, in which I wrote, I can only suppose, very nearly half the novel. One more thing I had to invent was that particular part of the French countryside in which the events, especially the escape of the pilot, had to be set. The northern part of France I already knew; but south of Paris I had never been. Nor, of course, had I ever been to the city of Marseilles, where the final scenes of the novel were to be enacted. All this too had to be conjured from imagination, but at the same time with topographical accuracy and, in the case of Marseilles, with some sort of urban accuracy. I duly read my maps, my guides to France and my Baedekers. I like to think, now, that I got most of these things right, though eventually Hilary, who knew France far better than I did, informed me that I had caused sugar-beet to be grown in a part of France where, in fact, it never was.

So, at weekends, in odd moments, in a few days of leave, I wrote *Fair Stood the Wind for France*, taking the title from the immortal words of Michael Drayton, Shakespeare's contemporary who, in fact, wrote at least one sonnet comparable in quality with those of the great man himself: *Since there's no help, come let us kiss and part.* He also wrote, in the poem beginning 'Fair stood the wind for France', the perfect plan for the prevention of the D-Day

invasion of France by Allied Troops, a plan fortunately ignored by
the stupid Hitler and his advisers and generals:

> But putting to the main
> At Caux, the mouth of Seine,
> With all his martial train
> Landed King Harry.

So indeed we did land; it was by no means the first time that
Englishmen had landed at that particular point in France or, in
fact, defeated their enemies there.

In this way I left Oakington and the grey, fog-bound and so
often dismal fenlands. The countryside, except for the colleges of
Cambridge and the superb cathedral at Ely, had not inspired me;
the men of No. 7 Squadron and their ugly, difficult bombers had.

It was now decided that I should go to No. 1 Fighter Command
Station at Tangmere, just outside Chichester, midway between
the luscious Sussex Downs above Cowdray Park and the sea. The
weather was bitterly cold and the atmosphere in the Mess, alas,
hardly less so. I wandered about for days in a state of lonely
misery, scarcely speaking to a soul. There was, it seemed to me, in
contrast to the warmth of Oakington, a certain chill snobbery
in the air. I once tried an approach to an Australian, who merely
turned on me a cool deaf ear. I tried chatting to New Zealanders

and felt myself to be in the presence of aloof, petty provincials. My one and only contact with a South African merely revealed the presence of a Boer who was a boor. I was uneasy in the company of the station commander, who viewed my invasion of his hitherto jealously guarded kingdom with a certain high suspicion. Nowhere could I detect a keyhole, still less a key, that would grant me entrance into a world containing stories. I felt near to despair. In addition to all this there was no bed for me in the base and I was put into an otherwise empty house some distance away and there slept and brooded alone.

I developed a strong suspicion that this lack of co-operation stemmed from the station commander himself. I accordingly went back to Air Ministry, there to speak with Hilary about it. Hilary was vexed and firm. 'You are beholden to no one but Air Ministry and if your precious station commander fails to co-operate we shall deal with him appropriately.' After that I went back to Tangmere with spirits slightly lifted and then, by a piece of good fortune, things improved.

One day in the Mess I noticed a young squadron-leader, standing well over six feet, whom I hadn't seen before. He had no left hand. In its place he had been fitted with a metal gadget which looked rather like a complicated egg-whisk. Perhaps the shattering experience of losing his hand combined with a fanatical determination to go on flying, in spite of it, had given him more humanity than some of his fellows. At all events we talked; his name was McLauchlan; and presently he was inviting me to meet some of the pilots of the renowned No. 1 Squadron, of which he was leader. No. 1 Squadron was by now a night fighter squadron and perhaps it was the experience of flying by night that gave its pilots some of the warmth and kinship that I had so much liked and admired at Oakington. At last, I felt, I had my keyhole and my key.

One of these pilots was a Czech named Kuttelwacher. He too had had a shattering experience: namely that of escaping from his native country by the most devious and adventurous of routes through southern Europe, Turkey, the Mediterranean and heaven knew where. He was a man of much humour and gaiety and McLauchlan had dreamed up the idea of shooting up trains and airfields in France at night, operations the two of them carried out with joyous rivalry and glee. I too felt joyous, seizing on these events like a hungry dog long deprived of bones; and this is how, at the time, I described it all:

It was one of those periods in a station when the unity and life of a good squadron becomes too strong to remain a local thing, compressed within itself, meaning something to only a few people. It breaks out, and spreading, warm and energetic and fluid, becomes a large thing, meaning something to many people.

It was one of those periods when everything was good. The weather was good and calm and sunny, the sea-light lofty and pure over the sea by day. The nights were good and starry, with no ground mist and just the right cover of cloud. The squadron was good and proud and knew itself. The things it did were good and the news of its doings was in the papers. Whenever you came into the Mess or the billiard-room or the dining-room and heard laughter boiling over too richly you knew it was that squadron laughing. You knew by their laughter that they wanted nothing else than to be kept as they were, flying by night together, shooting up trains on the flat lands of northern France, shooting down careless Dorniers over their own aerodrome. They had found each other. The positive and exuberant feeling of their discovery spread over the Station, from Erks to Waafs and from Waafs to officers, until all of us felt it there.

By this time, too, winter had broken, letting in spring at last to the luscious Sussex hills, to which I used to repair with another kind of hunger, famished for the sight of bluebells and primroses, may blossom and oaks in green-gold flower. To roam those hills was an experience of heart-breaking beauty, infinitely precious. Our bodily hunger was also well taken care of at Tangmere. The Mess Fund was rich, carrying an enormous surplus by means of which the Mess Secretary was able to fill us with out-of-season delights. On my arrival he had even apologised for the fact that dinner in the evening had unfortunately to be cut down from seven courses to a mere five, a difference that after Oakington's sparse fare did not in the least depress me.

Unhappily there came a day when, going back to Air Ministry, I found Hilary Saunders no longer there. He had been transferred to Combined Operations. Worse still, PR11 had been disbanded and I found myself in a new department, PR3, among new faces. In Hilary's place, however, was an extremely agreeable officer, Leonard Dodds, with Fletcher Allen as a sort of second-in-command. On my very first afternoon at PR3 I gave Fletcher, affectionately known as Fletch, a not inconsiderable shock.

At half past three I was preparing to leave the office when Fletch stopped me.

'And where, Bates, may I ask, do you think you are going?'

'Home.'

'*You are going where?*'

'Home.'

'Good God. May I inform you that no one leaves this office until seven o'clock?'

'You may inform me but I am nevertheless still going home.'

'Good God, are you out of your mind? Are you due for leave or something?'

'No.'

'Then what the hell are you going home for?'

'I am going home to write.'

'Very interesting. *Most* interesting. Is it too much to ask, perhaps, that you write here? Couldn't you, perhaps, do that?'

'No. Not the sort of writing I want to do.'

'And what, may I ask, is the sort of writing you want to do?'

'A story.'

'And how long, if it is not too much to ask, will you be away?'

'A week. Very probably two. You see, it's a very long story. And I think a very important one.'

Thereafter Fletch was speechless but, being also human, he relented and let me go. A couple of weeks later I came back with the longest Flying Officer X story I had yet written, *How Sleep the Brave*, and Fletch, having read it at one gulp, went into raptures of excitement. So PR3 accepted me on the terms Hilary had long since promised. I was a free agent, moving and writing where, how and when I liked.

Some time before Hilary had left Air Ministry he had put his own enthusiasm for the Flying Officer X stories into the practical proposition that they should be published in book form. I felt much honoured by this but rather less pleased when he told me that he thought the firm of Macmillan should be the publishers. I said that, on the contrary, since Jonathan Cape had been my publishers for sixteen years, they should be offered the book instead. Hilary at once agreed and immediately picked up the telephone to talk to Cape. I then remembered that Jonathan Cape himself was ill and said that Hilary should talk instead to Wren Howard, his partner.

'Right,' he said. 'And why not listen on the extension?'

Hilary and Wren Howard duly talked and I listened. The attitude of Wren Howard, at first, could only be likened to a hard frost. There were long periods of silence, clearly denoting a strong air of suspicion touched with an equally strong lack of enthusiasm. Then Hilary played, quite casually, a trump card.

'You would, of course, be given all the paper you need. Unlimited paper.'

Paper being, at that period of the war, as precious as platinum, the change of atmosphere at the other end of the telephone was instant and miraculous.

'What we have in mind,' Hilary then said, 'is that our edition should be a sort of Penguin, selling at sixpence, but that you may do your own hardback edition at, perhaps, half-a-crown.'

The temperature at the other end of the telephone rose as in a heatwave.

The ultimate results of this conversation I shall describe in more detail later.

Meanwhile there came a day when Group-Captain Dodds, affectionately known to us all as Doddie, as indeed he still is today, sent for me one morning and said:

'Old boy, they are going to publish your Flying Officer X stories any moment now. And guess what?'

I had nothing I could possibly guess.

'First printing will be 100,000.'

Never having heard of a book, except the Bible and *Gone with the Wind*, selling such figures, I nearly fainted.

III

In periods of leave, at weekends or whenever I could snatch a spare day I now worked on *Fair Stood the Wind for France*, writing in a frenzy that fitted the mood of the times yet always striving to keep the style of the novel, as in the stories of Flying Officer X, clear and vivid in its pictorial simplicity. What exactly would happen to the book if and when it was finished I was as yet unable to tell. It might have been that if I had shown it to Authority I could well have incurred much displeasure since I had flouted regulations on security about escapes, which were still very strict. It might also have been that even if I incurred no such displeasure or reprimand the appropriate department in charge of security might not have been given the necessary clearance for publication. A third possibility was that Air Ministry might well have said that, since the book had been written in service time and from material provided by another serving officer, they would claim the book as theirs, leaving me without a penny profit; and Heaven knew that I needed every penny I could get.

Fortunately there now began to be slight signs that security regulations relating to escapes were relaxing; and soon, as they still further relaxed, I decided to show the now finished novel to Fletcher Allen. Ever since I had written *How Sleep the Brave* Fletch had shown an increasing tendency to regard me as his own protégé, covering me with an increasingly protective wing. I therefore thought I could rely on his discretion.

When Fletch had finished the novel he instantly jumped into a new ecstasy of admiration and excitement. Not only was the book marvellously good, he declared, but come hell or high water it was going to remain my own. The business of clearance ought not, he thought, to be difficult, after which he declared with every ounce of conviction that the book would be a bestseller. The pleasure at hearing this was presently slightly tempered by a mild reprimand. To Fletch's infinite astonishment he discovered that I had not, and never had had, an agent to handle my affairs. Such folly was unthinkable and had at once to be rectified. 'I will arrange at once that you meet my friend Laurence Pollinger.'

So, for the first time, I met the man who has handled my increasingly complicated affairs ever since. We instantly got on extremely well together and it can truthfully be said that that first meeting, like that with Edward Garnett, was dramatically to change the course of my life. Among other things it also led to my changing, after some seventeen years, my publisher.

Laurence Pollinger has ever been a tireless and watchful champion in the battle for the protection of authors' rights and the rectification of the injustices that are often done to them. He had, of course, heard of the wide success happily attained by the Flying Officer X stories and he now inquired how well, financially, I had done with them. When I replied that I had of course received not a penny other than my officer's pay he was both astounded and angry. But what, he inquired, about Cape? Had Cape not slipped a guinea or two into my hand? A box of chocolates into my wife's? They had not, I declared, nor had they slipped a drink, a lunch, a case of wine; indeed they had made no material gesture of thanks whatever, though they had sold countless thousands of copies of *The Greatest People in the World* and *How Sleep the Brave*.

This further fanned the flames of Laurence's anger. 'Do you then propose,' he asked, 'to let them publish *Fair Stood the Wind for France*?' I replied that I had firmly and irrevocably decided not to. This pleased him. And to whom, he asked, did I think of taking the book? He had only to show it to any one of twenty publishers and he was sure they would, like Fletcher Allen, jump for joy. Without hesitation my mind went back to my first meeting, nearly ten years before, with Michael Joseph. M.J., I declared, was to be my man.

Instantly there was set up, at No. 30 Bedford Square, the house of Cape, a strong resistance movement. Was I not aware that my last contract, in its final clause, gave them the option on my next two books? I said that I was well aware, but it so happens that such a clause has no validity in law. It is what is termed 'a contract to make a contract' and is not, I fear, worth the paper it is written on. So came my parting with Cape and not, I think, without good cause.

Michael Joseph, at this time, wasn't enjoying the best of health (my own, at the same time, was deteriorating rapidly, the old abdominal pains getting more and more severe, leaving me all too often grey of spirit, sleepless at night and haggard with exhaustion) and the man in charge at No. 26 Bloomsbury Street was Robert, now Sir Robert, Lusty. Bob treated me with sense and generosity, giving me a fat, unbelievably fat, advance on the book. As Laurence Pollinger was also able to sell the serial rights of it to both England and America and negotiate yet another excellent advance from the *Atlantic Monthly* I found myself, almost for the first time in my life, free of financial anxiety.

After twenty years of writing, with its several disasters and constant struggles, *Fair Stood the Wind for France* was my first wide success. The book was translated into many languages, and indeed is still being further translated, and at least one perceptive reviewer saw it, as I had intended it to be, a story epitomising the youth of two countries at a period of great conflict and agony. Part of the story concerns the amputation, in great and dangerous secrecy, by a French doctor, of an English RAF pilot's arm, and I hope I shall not appear guilty of self-praise if I say that, many and many a time, not only in England but abroad, I met admirers of the book who took one look of astonishment at me and marvelled that I still possessed *both* of my arms. This is, or should be, a verification of Thackeray's dictum that 'the work of fiction contains more truth in solution than the work which purports to be all true.' It is indeed true to say that there were times when I was writing the description of that amputation I really felt that it was, in fact, my own arm that was being cut off.

By this time the war had reached a strange, tense, darkening phase. In some ways it was rather like being trapped in a powerless train in a long, black suffocating tunnel. One felt gripped by a ghastly inertia, a ghoulish nightmare in which the end of the tunnel could not only not be seen but seemed as if it would never, never be there. There appeared to be neither daylight nor hope. Destruction of shipping by U-Boats piled up to a scale excruciating, savage, vastly perilous. There used to be a pair of lady comics, Gert and Daisy, who sang songs of cheer on the radio, interspersing them with remarks such as 'We go to bed hopeful and wake up thankful'. To this day I wonder how, at times, we had the heart to continue with either hope or thanks.

Yet, all this time, more and more people were returning to the capital. The vortex of the whole grim unease was there, in London's heart, and one felt that one had to be part of its agony. Now and then I returned to Tangmere or to other Stations, hoping, as a man mushrooming or birds' nesting on a summer's day, to find a scrap of treasure that would translate itself into a story. It rarely happened. A sortie or two over the French coast, an enemy fighter shot down, one of our own pilots lost: of great drama, as in the Battle of Britain, there was little or none. On occasions pilots went out over the Channel to have a 'look-see' and either saw little or, as in the case of the station commander of Tangmere one fine summer afternoon, got themselves killed. An era of apparent pointlessness, of pacific or half-pacific pause, seemed to have arrived. Where were we going, if anywhere? I used to ask myself. Why the hell, indeed, were we doing it at all?

Somewhere about this time, to my great dismay, Group-Captain Leonard Dodds was posted to India. He had been a wholly understanding chief, urbane of humour, understanding in matters such as giving complete freedom of movement to a writer of imagination, never once confusing a uniform with a strait-jacket. We had got on supremely well together and I knew that I should miss him greatly. My fear was, I think, that some narrow-gutted tyrant, a petty king, might take his place.

Happily it was not so. Doddie was presently succeeded by Group-Captain Dudley Barker, an experienced and very able journalist who also, very fortunately, understood that writers of imaginative ability cannot be regimented even if and when you put them into uniform. Dudley and I also got on, I am glad to say, supremely well together and it was to him, some time later, that I was to owe a great debt. He, like Edward Garnett and others before him, was to accomplish yet another revolution in my life: of which I shall have much more to say later.

One day I received a summons to Dudley Barker's desk, there to be told that no less a person than Air-Chief Marshal Portal (later Lord Portal) wished to see me: in fact not only to see me but to take me out to lunch. I had instant visions of having committed some appalling misdemeanour, which in turn would involve demotion (by now I was a squadron-leader), severe reprimand or a dismissal to some arid diabolical post, such as Aden, far from my beloved England. Happily, again, it was not so.

The meeting with Portal proved not only to be pleasant; it confirmed once again, in my experience at any rate, that the higher one got in the realms of Service Rank, the more impressive were, with very few exceptions, its members. I had already been much impressed by Sir Archibald Sinclair; I had been equally impressed by Lord Willoughby de Broke, who had always shown me, even in my modest rank of pilot officer, all courtesy, understanding and friendliness. ('Hullo, Bates. Sit down. Take a pew, old boy. What now? Splendid stories of yours, dear fellow. What can I do to help?') It was only when one met people of the middle orders – what in Northamptonshire language we should call piss-quicks – that there was aroused in one a disquieting sense of inferiority. The aristocracy did not, I found, wave their flags of superiority.

The middle and lower orders, I fear, very often did. For this reason their few members shall be nameless.

I do not now recall where Portal took me to lunch but it was most probably, I think, his club. If I had any lingering disturbances of thought as we met they were soon dispersed. I found myself in the presence of a man of intelligence, charm, good conversation and width of vision. I think I am right in saying that we had reached the stage of the coffee before he disclosed exactly the reason why he had singled me out from the company of my fellow Public Relations officers for some specialised purpose; and when it came I was slightly surprised. It was his idea, he proceeded to explain, that someone should write the story of the Night Battle of Britain, a perilous affair whose near-catastrophic events had already been allowed to slip back into a darkness as Stygian as that in which it had in fact been fought in the winter of 1941. Whereas the Battle of Britain had been blown up by infinite publicity into a sort of *Boy's Own Paper* adventure serial (and I am not attempting by one iota to detract from its formidable and high significance as a battle, comparable as it is with Trafalgar, with which it alone shares a day specifically named after it in the British calendar) the Night Battle had somehow slid away into the limbo of nightmares apparently best forgotten.

It was Portal's idea that this state of affairs should be put right. He proceeded to elaborate by comparing the two battles: the day battle an affair largely waged by one force, one section of the populace so small that its members had already been honoured as the Few; the night battle waged by comparison with scores of varied units drawn from all sections of the community, both service and civilian, as I have already described in *The Blossoming World*.

How we survived these deficiencies and their attendant and bloody ordeal, as I have also remarked in *The Blossoming World*, it is impossible to tell. Small wonder that Coventry was soon a blackened heap of masonry, its Cathedral a burnt-out skeleton, that London burned like tinder, its underground stations packed with thousands of refugees hoping and hoping for a bloodless morning, or that the ancient and beautiful cities of Canterbury, Exeter and Bristol had the flower of their long heritage destroyed.

The great and eternal wonder is that it wasn't a thousand times worse. But, as the subsequent history of aerial warfare in various parts of the world has proved, the dropping of vast quantities of wickedly explosive material on civilian populations, of whatever colour, class or creed, may kill but does not necessarily and finally destroy. In precisely the same way as Jewry has resisted and even flourished under centuries of persecution (in Britain it is at present in decline precisely because it is *not* persecuted) so a populace scourged and persecuted by bombs may emerge from the ordeal fewer in numbers but greater in resistance and strength, determined in spite of all odds not to be crushed. Whether you call this a triumph of mind over matter, of dignity over savagery, of civilisation over the jungle, it is exactly what happened to Britain in the Night Battle of Britain in 1941. We emerged bloody but unbowed.

The pamphlet was duly finished but, though approved in high places, was never published. Today it is safely filed away in the Public Records Office, from which it will doubtless never emerge. After I had finished it the war entered, as far as I was concerned, a new phase of inertia. Nor was this alleviated by my health, which continued to deteriorate, so much so that I endured almost constant abdominal pain, was unable to sleep at night and eventually was driven to beg Leonard Dodds, before his departure for India, to give me leave to go home and see my own doctor. This cry of despair followed innumerable visits to RAF doctors who, after all the usual routine checks, one by one pronounced me A1, Grade 1. Never was a verdict on man's health a greater travesty.

In due course I found myself in hospital, attended by an embarrassing number of nurses and swallowing a revolting concoction known as a Barium meal, in preparation for an X-ray. This having been done I requested to be given the plate in order to report back to Group-Captain Dodds with proof that I had in fact been under hospital scrutiny. Not the least part of Doddie's endearing qualities is a certain wry sense of humour and when I duly reported back to him with the X-ray plate of my stomach, which incidentally revealed something known as a *duodenal diverticulum* he immediately sent it to the photographic department of PR, which then spent the better part of an afternoon trying to elucidate from it which part of Berlin had been bombed the previous night. My own doctor's verdict sounded a rather more ominous note: 'One day we shall have to take a little peep inside you.'

All this, combined with the fact that I now had few if any stories to write, made me feel that the war had come to a premature dead end. It hadn't of course; but the plain fact was that the writing of pamphlets and articles was dull stuff compared with the stimulating, gay and often tragic days at Oakington, when I had been at the vortex of a whirl of action and comradeship the impact of which I knew would never fade. I longed for some opportunity, such as another *Fair Stood the Wind for France*, to use my imagination, but none was to come for another year or two. Meanwhile I did my best with bread-and-butter jobs and once even wrote a parliamentary speech for Sir Archibald Sinclair which he duly praised and delivered in the Commons.

This is not to say that our galleried room at PR was dull; very far from it. My friend and colleague R. F. Delderfield has well described it as a sort of Writers' Club, where rank counted for nothing and an atmosphere of great friendliness prevailed. Nevertheless I felt considerably frustrated, a situation in which I was certainly not alone. For what we were all waiting for at that time, I suppose, was the invasion of Hitler's Europe and there were times when the prospect of that event seemed a thousand years away.

Eventually, however, it began to build up to its inevitable climax. The air began to be full of rumours; the woods of the south country were filled with camouflaged guns and tanks. Soon, together with the rest of my colleagues at PR, I was being given my assignment for D-Day. To my great joy I was to go back to Tangmere, there to cover, in a series of despatches designed specifically for American eyes, the first fighter assaults across the Channel. The actual date of the invasion still being a closely guarded secret, I again went through a period of much frustration, idly kicking my heels between Air Ministry and home, until eventually the tension of waiting grew unbearable and I at last took the road to Tangmere.

When I arrived there on a warm June afternoon I found every inch of space occupied by fighter squadrons, many of whom were aggressive, seething Canadians, raring for battle. There was not a bed to be had. Accordingly, after receiving the inevitable hypodermic jabs for this, that and the other, I drove into Chichester and got myself a room at the Dolphin Hotel, then suddenly started to feel uncommonly ill and repaired immediately to bed. There, remembering my friend the hotelier's consistent injunction never to be on time anywhere, I resolved to sleep late the following day. It was in fact a mere half past nine when I woke, feeling much better, and went placidly downstairs to what I hoped would be a leisurely breakfast. Sitting waiting for it I was, however, horrified to hear two ladies at the next table loudly discussing the fact that invasion had begun. I instantly swallowed a cup of tea, dashed out of the hotel to my car and drove at breakneck speed to Tangmere, cursing myself all the way for being fool enough to chance my luck once too often and considerably scared of the wrath of Air Ministry to come for my having failed in my assignment.

I needn't have worried; if invasion had indeed begun there was little sign of it at Tangmere. It is true that several squadrons had taken to the air but none were yet back from the scene of the battle they had so long thirsted for. It must have been eleven o'clock before the first of them began to appear from over the sea, their gay red-and-white candy striped wings brilliant against a deceptively hot blue sky that was to be darkened, before the day was out, by a storm that came perilously near to wrecking the entire enterprise.

As soon as possible I sought out crews and pilots for interview, only to find everywhere nothing but angry, frustrated men.

Not one of them had a story to tell for the simple reason that there was no story to tell. Not a single German fighter had left the ground that morning in answer to our attack. The difficulty of defending a perimeter as vast as that which Hitler held from the Atlantic coast of France up to the Baltic is that in addition to not knowing where exactly the invader will assault you it is virtually impossible to decide, in the early stages of attack, whether the first strike is a feint or the real thing. To commit yourself too soon in these circumstances could be tragic folly. Goering had therefore not committed either himself or his fighters: hence my furious, frustrated Canadians, denied the blood and battle they had waited so long to taste.

Nevertheless a despatch had to be written and sent off by plane to Air Ministry by mid-afternoon. At first I conceived the task of writing a despatch about nothing to be utterly hopeless; then I woke to the fact that the very nothingness of it was of high significance. Accordingly I dashed off the piece, took it to catch the special Air Ministry plane at four o'clock and then crossed my fingers. Less than a couple of hours later a delighted Dudley Barker was on the phone to me, warm in his praise of a piece I had considered hopeless.

For a week or more I wrote a despatch every day. As invasion progressed there was more and more action to cover and my confidence in my ability to cover it grew in parallel. Every piece was well received in London and I have rarely enjoyed an assignment more. If its beginnings had been clouded by apprehension its end had given me some of the satisfaction of 'something attempted, something done, has earned a night's repose'.

Our foothold on Europe having been secured it was reasonable now to begin to think in terms of the war's end. In fact a whole year was to go by, a great deal of it bloody and bitter, before it did end and for my own part there lay ahead of me an adventure totally unlike anything I had experienced before and which was to make the year 1945 the most significant of my life, in some ways, since that damp January day when I had walked into Bedford Square to meet Edward Garnett.

Before I tell of this particular and exciting adventure, however, I must deal with another which, though briefer and less significant in its effects, nevertheless had its own measure of excitement.

IV

Some time before D-Day at last occurred I had been home in Kent on leave for two or three days when I woke in the middle of the night to a great and hideous noise and the sight of what was clearly a burning aircraft flying low over the roof of the house. I had never before seen a burning aircraft flying so low at night but within minutes it was followed by another and then another and yet another. All were flying in the same direction, that is north-westwards, towards London, at the same height and with the same hideous racket. I was greatly mystified and, with four young children in the house, not a little frightened.

Morning solved the mystery; these were the first of Hitler's malevolent flying bombs, aptly named doodlebugs, launched in formidable numbers, without respite, and with the object of causing infinite disaster to London and infinite damage to the morale of the civilian population. The flying bomb has been called an instrument of despair on the part of Hitler, who undoubtedly cherished the notion that what the blitz of 1940–41 had failed to achieve the impersonal evil machine of 1944 would. Undoubtedly he saw it as a softening-up device preceding the inevitable Allied invasion of the Continent. Equally undoubtedly we were unprepared for it (by 'we' I mean the civilian population; authority may have had its own information) and were taken greatly by surprise. It was not long, however, before we learned to listen for the sinister cut-out of the bug's power, the dreaded after-silence and the final inevitable bang: moments which were not funny but which had about them a dark and chilling air of doom.

At first our defences against these evils were badly deployed. For a few days London bore the blistering brunt of the attack and then defence chiefs moved quickly. It was swiftly realised that doodlebugs must be intercepted either before they reached England's southern coastline or in the immediate hinterland between the coast and the neighbourhood of the North Downs. Fighter squadrons were accordingly redeployed and pilots suddenly found themselves engaged in a riotous and unreal sort of circus in which they were fighting an enemy as impersonal and ghoulish as any robot. The doodlebug in fact proved easy meat and many were the devices said to have been used by pilots for knocking them down, one being the use of a fighter's wing-tip to flip the bug off balance and send it reeling on its earthward way.

This is not to say that the bugs did not do untold damage; nor to deny that the populace were very frightened, wearied and highly tense from nervous strain, irritation and lack of sleep. Nor was London alone in this; the Kentish countryside had the unenviable experience of being the graveyard of thousands of bugs shot down before they reached the capital. A shot-down bug was not, of course, a dead bug; as it hit the earth, whether in cornfield, village street, meadow or churchyard, it exploded just the same, all too often with fatal results. On my own piece of pastoral England more than 3,000 of these intercepted bugs fell in a few weeks, so that a map showing each fallen bug looks like a settlement of black flies on a dead carcass. Perhaps the most remarkable of these was one which on a beautiful July evening floated over my house, cut out half a mile away and fell after the usual sinister silence with an almighty bang, having ended its flight on the top of the church tower under which, so many years before, Madge and I had paused to watch a flock of sheep safely graze. The moment was a doubly sad one, since Little Chart Church was, unless I am gravely misinformed, the only Protestant church in England that contained within its walls a Roman

Little Chart
Church

Catholic chapel. Today the ruined and empty tower stands as a stark grey monument to one of war's more senseless stupidities.

From all this racket and tension I was immensely relieved, in August, to be given a couple of weeks' leave. We accordingly went to Scotland, where Edinburgh's calm and beauty formed a haven of bliss after the dreary dread and gloom of the south. The Trossachs seemed as lovely as the very Elysian fields and Edinburgh itself seemed hardly to know that a war was on, let alone that London and the south were living out a nightmare. For me, however, the respite was short-lived. After a few days there arrived from Dudley Barker a telegram ordering me immediately back to London. As I received it I instantly remembered my friend the hotelier's injunction about never arriving anywhere on time and I decided that 'immediately' meant at least another twelve hours. This was eminently sensible, since to have caught a morning train would merely have meant arriving in the capital at night, when all but air-raid wardens and their various brethren would have gone to bed. Far more sensible to catch the night train and arrive for breakfast, which I accordingly did, only to be woken in the dead of night by a guard calling 'Squadron-Leader Bates, Squadron-Leader Bates!' and ultimately to be handed a second telegram, couched in terms considerably more severe than the first.

I confess to fearing some extremely stern reprimand when I turned up, sleepy-eyed and not at all well-shaven, at Air Ministry that morning; but Dudley Barker, most amenable of men, had no word of reproach to offer and merely informed me that he wished me to fly to France on a mission the sole object of which was to seek out, and report on, doodlebug launching sites in the area of Picardy and the Pas de Calais. I was to take all the time I wanted, go where I wanted and, if I thought fit, as Dudley obligingly put it, have a look at Paris while I was there.

I departed from Northolt the following afternoon in the usual tin-can Dakota. My wretched stomach, never any good at the best of times, revolted violently on the flight and I was miserably sick for most of the journey, which finally ended at Amiens, where groups of the French Resistance Movement were still rounding up sorry-looking bands of Nazi prisoners from the surrounding woodlands. Presently I was piling into a truck with various other officers and men, to be driven out of Amiens to an encampment on the town's outskirts. All was infinitely dreary; the camouflaged tents might have been prisons; the food, if food it could be called, was ghastly.

Happily I fell in with an Australian Air Force officer, who turned out to be as depressed as I was. 'I can't bear this bloody place,' he said. '*I want to smell France. The real France.*' These were thoughts so much after my own heart that I suggested we beg, borrow or steal some kind of transport and go and spend the night in Amiens. This we accordingly did, finding ourselves a room in a crumbling little hotel which I strongly suspect was also a brothel. However, we slept well and, as my Australian friend had so devoutly wished, smelled the real smell of France again: and very good to smell it was.

Early next day I set out to seek transport for the purpose of executing my doodlebug mission. There was no transport. I then discovered a young RAF driver who informed me, with a confidence and assurance that would have done credit to my old friend the hotelier, that of course there was transport. He could lay his hands on a jeep in no time; you just had to know. Within a quarter of an hour he was back with the promised jeep and I was, as I thought, on my way to the early execution of my mission. I was, as it turned out, almost on my way to another kind of execution, since we had scarcely driven half a mile when we were abruptly halted by two service policemen who irately demanded to know what the hell we were doing with the Group-Captain's jeep? I duly sought out the Group-Captain and proceeded to eat, before him, the largest piece of humble pie I have ever had to consume.

All this, however, did little or nothing to deter my young driver, who in no time at all was back with another jeep, at the same time full of assurances that this time it had not been filched from higher authority. So we set off, not knowing quite what we were looking for or where to look for it. My French, far less adequate even than it is now, helped a little but not much as we stopped a peasant here and a peasant there in order to make our needs known. Finally we tracked down the first of our flying-bomb launching sites.

It was of almost frighteningly simple construction, consisting as it did of two lengths of railway line poised in the air at an angle of 450. Up this track the doodlebug was launched, to float away, if all went well, in the direction of England. Often, in fact, all did not go well. Not infrequently the doodlebug stalled, spun backwards and fell back on its unfortunate launchers, blowing them to exceedingly small pieces. On other occasions a bug would execute a much larger loop, falling on the equally unfortunate citizens of Amiens, with similarly ghastly results.

These launching pads were all of identical construction. The only difference was in the sites they occupied. Some were well hidden in woods; others in orchards; a few in back gardens; and one at least occupied a village street. I suppose, that morning, I saw and inspected perhaps twenty of them, arriving at last at the conclusion, fortified by complete boredom, that having seen one I had seen them all. It must have been about two o'clock when I finally decided that the sight of one more doodlebug site would drive me scatty and I remembered the words of Dudley Barker.

'Ever been to Paris?' I asked my young driver.

'No, sir. Never.'

'Well, you're going now.'

We drove southward. If I thought that the road to Paris was to be an easy one I was shortly to be much disillusioned. I knew, but had failed fully to appreciate the fact, that every bridge in France had been blown up in order to frustrate the Nazi retreat; but it was not until we reached our first river that I came to a moment of an awful realisation that it was one thing to decide to go to Paris but quite another to get there. On either side of the river there appeared to be utter chaos: groups of service-men, French citizens carrying bundles, bags of all kinds of motley belongings wrapped in newspaper and so on. There appeared to be no hope whatever of getting across that river.

Then to my infinite surprise I saw a pontoon consisting of several insecure-looking planks lashed to empty petrol drums slowly being punted on its way across stream from the opposite bank. This was a welcome enough sight in itself; but what was even more welcome and astonishing was the sight of a beautiful woman standing on the pontoon, beside a black Citroën car, waving a bottle of brandy. Clearly she was very excited.

'Hullo there, England!' she shouted, in English. 'Lovely to see you! Have a brandy.'

As the pontoon touched the shore she leapt to the bank, excitedly waving the brandy bottle, and at once proceeded to embrace me with rapturous fervour. Her charm and vivacity and her unmistakable Englishness were matched only by her husband's charm and courtesy and his equally unmistakable Frenchness.

'First time we've been able to leave Paris since the occupation.' She first introduced herself as a Countess and then inquired where I was bound for. When I said Paris her excitement mounted. Where was I going to stay? When I said that I hadn't the remotest idea she at once said: 'Then you must stay at our apartment. The concierge and his wife will look after you and will be thrilled to have you. I'll write down the address. It's in the Place des Etats Unis, just off the Avenue Kléber, not far from the Etoile.'

We drank more brandy; she wrote down her address; and then I asked where she and her Count were going.

'To our Château. Not far from Amiens. Haven't seen it since 1940. Will you be coming back that way?' I said that I supposed we would. 'Then you must call and stay with us there. I insist. No formalities. Just drop in. God, it's great to speak to an Englishman again.'

We parted, brandy-filled, as rapturously as we had met, she warmly insistent that we used her apartment in Paris and equally urgent that we call on her at her northern Château. I promised fervently to do both and then we drove on our respective ways.

As we approached Paris, however, I began to have misgivings. Had the Countess been talking or was it the brandy? On cooler reflection I decided it was the brandy and in consequence told my young driver to take me to the Hotel Scribe. This, as I understood it, was being used as a centre for radio and newspaper correspondents and innocently I trusted I should find some kind of succour there. Instead I found a madhouse. Nobody knew anything about anything. Nobody had time either to speak or listen. All was bedlam and chaos.

Then by pure chance I ran into Richard Dimbleby. Though I didn't know him personally but only by reputation I knew that he knew my agent, Laurence Pollinger, very well. I accordingly introduced myself, explaining at the same time that I could get no change out of anybody and that I had nowhere to sleep.

'You must bang the bloody table!' said Richard. 'It's the only way to get anything done in this damn place.'

By this time I was more than a little weary and in no mood for table-banging. There was nothing for it, therefore, but to navigate to the Place des Etats Unis.

Place des Etats Unis

This square, I should explain for the benefit of those who do not know it, is one of the most exclusive in Paris, and much of my apprehension returned as we drew up to the Countess' grand establishment. I need not, however, have worried. The joy on the faces of the concierge and his little wife was comparable only with that of the Biblical shepherd rejoicing over his one lost sheep that had at last been found. Fortunately I was armed with a plentiful supply of 'K' rations and a pound or two of real coffee. This in itself was pure gold and soon, in return for it, the wife of the concierge was cooking us an omelette as only the French know how to.

But before this she showed us up to our rooms. I have rarely seen anything in such palatial, perfect taste. Rare Persian rugs, fine old masters, exquisite china and glass, sumptuous period furniture: I felt myself to be in a miniature Renaissance palace.

One thing, however, disturbed me. To my considerable consternation Madame now and then referred to a 'Monsieur Barker'. Did she, in some way, know about Dudley; or did Dudley know about me and my tendency to truancy? I failed to decide. Then by chance the word 'Granville' was dropped to join 'Barker' and the mystery was solved. The sumptuous apartment really belonged to the celebrated Granville Barker, man of the theatre.

Next day the wife of the concierge was insistent that I meet the wife of another concierge. Madame Martin, who lived on the far side of the Place des Etats Unis, was, it seemed, English, though her husband was a Frenchman. Great would be her joy at meeting an officer of the Royal Air Force.

That afternoon I accordingly went to call on Madame Martin and found a tiny red-haired woman whose diminutive stature perfectly matched the tiny concierge rabbit hutch in which she and her husband, like thousands of others of their kind in Paris, somehow existed on the ground floor. The pathetic nature of this tiny box contrasted painfully with a house where grandeur was even more palatial than that of the house of Monsieur Barker. But of Madame Martin's joy there was no shadow of doubt. Her red letter day, long prayed and hoped for, had at last arrived. With touching, tearful insistence she begged that I would take tea with her; and take tea I did, the tea being made from a few pathetic ounces jealously hoarded ever since the Nazi legions had triumphantly tramped into Paris.

As we took tea Madame Martin referred on several occasions to *la Duchesse*. It was the greatest pity that *la Duchesse* was away in the country. *La Duchesse* would have been greatly honoured and delighted to have met an English officer. In her excitement Madame Martin frequently forgot her English, the opportunity to speak which had been denied her for nearly five years, and lapsed into a mongrel language composed of three parts French to one of almost broken English, so that sometimes I had difficulty in understanding her.

Many years later I saw her again. The occasion was one at which my French publishers were giving a cocktail party in honour of a new book of mine. The rendezvous was in the Place des Etats Unis and great was Madame Martin's astonishment when I walked into her tiny rabbit hutch and handed my hat and coat to her. But greater still was my surprise to find that my hostess was *la Duchesse* herself. I will refrain from giving her name but will be content merely to record that it was that of one of France's most renowned and aristocratic families. Not that it is she I remember. The figure that still haunts my mind is that of the tiny Madame Martin, with her red hair and precious ounces of tea, by no means happily married to her French husband, living a life of virtual imprisonment under conditions that many an animal lover would have found intolerable for a dog, her life sweetened at last by liberation and the sharing of a cup of tea with an English officer. Somehow she personifies France's wartime agony more deeply than any Frenchwoman could have done, just as *la Comtesse*, so rabidly English, personifies her joy.

I cannot now recall with any accuracy how long we stayed in Paris. My acutest and most abiding memory is of wandering, in a hazy daydream, by the Seine, stopping to browse over bookstalls or to chat with an occasional fisherman and then of wandering up and down the Rue de Rivoli, the windows of whose shops were astonishingly filled with goods that had long since disappeared from England.

Finally, with fond farewells, we left for the north. As we drove out of Paris we saw, at every street corner, hordes of hungry faces – hungry not for food but for a lift to somewhere out of Paris. As the jeep would hold only one extra passenger I decided that the fairest thing to do was to give a lift to no one, a resolution in which I was frustrated by a young woman who athletically leapt into the vehicle while it was moving, shouting, 'Lille, Lille, Lille!'

In vain I told her that I was not going to Lille and that I had certainly no intention whatever of doing so. She implored me, in typical Gallic fashion, to change my mind. I was quite adamant. She then offered me money. I declined more firmly than ever. Then, as we again reached the river where *la Comtesse* had jubilantly waved her brandy bottle at me, she begged me to walk along the river bank with her while we waited for the pontoon to cross. We walked as far as a stretch of woodland and here, as she paused, I realised that if only I would take her to Lille another kind of bribe could be mine for the taking. This too I very firmly declined and we finally left her in a state of tearful and angry frustration on the riverside.

Some few miles farther north we then came upon a sad sight. A young man and woman, bearing a long stout pole from one pair of shoulders to another, were wearily plodding along a road as long and straight and barren as only certain French roads can be, the pole bearing two large and clearly very weighty suitcases. The pair looked fit to drop. The good Samaritan in me that had with apparent callousness rejected the girl from Lille, rose up at once, greatly touched. We stopped the jeep and the exhausted couple fell into the back.

'*Où allez-vous?*' I said in my primitive French.

'*Amiens.*'

'*Moi aussi.*'

The noises from the back of the jeep were a strange chorus of tears and laughter.

As we drove on they explained that they had left Paris riding a single ancient bicycle – a machine which, under the prodigious combined weight of two grown people and two vast suitcases, had promptly and inevitably broken clean in half.

So we took them to Amiens, where they too, like Madame Martin, had hoarded a few precious ounces of tea, which we now gratefully shared with them, at the same time declining an offer of an evening meal and a bed for the night.

'No,' I said to my young driver, 'we have to get on.'

'Where to now, sir?'

'We are,' I said, 'going to call on the Countess.'

We duly found the Château of the Countess, a typically grey turreted house of the kind to be seen all over France, only to discover that there was, alas, no Countess. From below the low hillside on which the Château stood there were, however, sounds of village revelry, and it was here, the servants of the Château informed us, that we should find the Countess, dancing.

The astonished Countess, vastly enjoying herself at a village hop, was even more jubilant and excited at seeing us than when she had first waved the brandy at me from the pontoon. She at once insisted on leaving the dance and repairing to the Château, there to kill, if not the fatted calf, at least a bottle or two of precious wine. This we did and very soon the four of us were sitting down to an extremely good dinner, we full of our gratitude for all the hospitality at the Place des Etats Unis, she eager to hear how we had found the people and the city. I had in fact been greatly excited by the city; so much so that many subsequent visits to Paris have never quite matched my simmering fervour on that first post-war, or almost post-war, return. The evening continued and ended gaily.

Memory again serves me poorly here, since I find myself quite unable to remember if we spent one, two or three nights at the Château. I recall only that it was all infinitely pleasant, that I promised I would telephone the Countess's father when I got back to England and that finally, when we did leave, I went away burdened with gifts that seemed comparable with those borne by the three Wise Men, among them a superlative handbag for my wife. There was further a parting injunction that we shouldn't fail, on any account, to visit an Anglophile friend of the Count and Countess, some fifteen miles away. She too was a Countess and her arms, we were assured, would be open to infinite widths to receive us.

Having enjoyed the company of one countess so much, we had no hesitation in seeking out the second. This we quickly did, to discover that her house was not a Château, in the grey, turreted, almost prison-like French tradition, but a big foursquare stone manor house, a true French farm *manoir* built round a huge central stone-flagged courtyard. Here, when we arrived, a number of women servants were sitting in the evening sunlight on hard kitchen chairs, very much in the French summer fashion, knitting, sewing and gossiping. After I had introduced myself my primitive French once again elucidated the fact that, alas, *la*

Comtesse was not at home. However, I was assured, she soon would be and would we be pleased to wait?

I spent the waiting time wandering in the huge, square, typically stone-walled garden. Here, on the walls, glowed ripe crimson peaches of luscious magnificence; I fancy there were also deep purple figs; and in glass frames there shone, like green-gold suns, cantaloupe melons of such opulence that you felt they must surely burst and, like over-full cornucopia, spill out their golden juicy riches. Seeing it all I began to have certain doubts as to whether in fact the French had starved under the German yoke or if some, if not all of them, had lived in little insulated rural paradises, lushly as medieval nobles: a suspicion that, as I shall presently explain, was well supported next day.

In due course Countess No. 2 arrived: a rather older woman than the first but equally attractive, equally excited, equally delighted to have the honour of entertaining an English officer. It was she who graciously took us into the house which, inside, was even more a true French *manoir* than it appeared from the courtyard. Vast rooms, vast beams, vast doors, a vast oak refectory table laid for supper: it might all have come straight out of some story by Maupassant. One felt in it the very breath of a France feudal, burdened with a centuries-old rural tradition, self-contained and self-supporting, cut off not only from any urban, outside world but from that more sinister one of Nazi occupation.

These first impressions of mine grew stronger and stronger as we collected round the great refectory table for supper. What further astonished me was the extraordinary number of people who had now gathered for the evening meal. It was not merely that we were suddenly *en famille*, with *grandmère*, *tante* this and *tante* that, the Count and Countess and a sister or two, but there was also the farm bailiff and several other retainers whose exact *rôles* were not clear to me. Again the scene might have been one out of a story by Maupassant; again, as in the garden, there was no hint of things impecunious or impoverished; you felt indeed that war and all its attendant trials and atrocities had passed this lovely *manoir* and its opulent oasis completely by.

In the morning, at breakfast, my suspicions about the fullness or emptiness of at least some French bellies under Nazi occupation were finally and fully confirmed. In the centre of the big breakfast table I found myself gazing on a large square yellow object weighing perhaps two or three pounds. After gazing at it for some minutes in wonder and disbelief I was at last moved to inquire what it was. '*C'est du beurre, naturellement.*'

Butter! A block of not much less than three pounds of it. Fresh farmhouse butter. I couldn't recall ever having seen so much butter before except long ago when, as a boy, I used to go for my mother to the local dairy, there to watch with fascination the white-coated attendant slicing lumps of butter from a great block and smacking it into shapes with wooden pats on cold marble counters. But in wartime – the thing was a mocking miracle. The piece of butter on the breakfast table seemed soon to assume the size of a yellow tombstone and I could only wonder how large an English family, pitifully eking out its meagre rations, it would have fed and for how long.

I was then further moved to tell the Countess that I had never, or at least for a very long time, seen so large a quantity of butter: an admission which seemed to amuse her much. I was then emboldened to ask if I couldn't, perhaps, buy a pound or two of it in the village to take back to England with me.

'Today it is doubtful. Today is not a butter-making day. But tomorrow will be. So if you will stay with us another night – and we do hope that you will – we will round up a decent quantity for you. I hope you will stay for another reason – I know that some of the French Resistance boys would be greatly honoured to meet you.'

I duly met some half dozen of the French Resistance boys – and they were really not much more than boys – who promptly invited me to lunch with them in Amiens the following day.

We were to meet at midday in the central square. I was very happy to accept but breakfast the next morning made me happier still: for there, waiting for me, was my miracle of butter, about four pounds of it, together with a great box of luscious peaches, several melons and a number of pairs of pure silk stockings for my wife. I don't think I wept at the sight of these riches, but I am not ashamed to confess that as I said farewell to the Countess, her opulent garden and her Maupassant-like *manoir* I was very near to tears.

At midday, having met the French Resistance boys, I was taken off by them to a modest and typically plebeian restaurant called *Restaurant des Cultivateurs et Voyageurs*. And here, once again, I found my suspicions about French bellies well confirmed. Having eaten a large and excellent dish of *tomates provençal*, I was just preparing to relax, fully replete, when I was astonished, if not indeed dismayed, to discover that this was merely what is sometimes called a starter. To follow *les tomates* there arrived an equally large and equally excellent dish of *blanquette de veau*, with which I confess my poor war-shrunken stomach found it hard to cope.

That afternoon, laden with riches and feeling almost as if returning homeward from some fabulous Samarkand instead of from a France stricken and divided, I hitched a lift on the beer-plane to England. I name it the beer-plane because that is precisely what it was: a small hedge-hopping machine, probably a D. H. Rapide, which jumped from one airfield to another, depositing crates of beer and taking empties away.

My trip had been one of much reward and excitement. If I hadn't learned much of great importance about doodlebug launching sites I had learned, or had more truly confirmed for myself, much else. The descriptions of rural France in *Fair Stood the Wind for France* had had necessarily to be done, almost all of them, from imagination. Now my visit had proved, not for the first or last time, that imagination can take a writer nearer to the heart of truth than any amount of observation, and that instinct, rather than sheer reasoning, will often guide him just as surely. Once again indeed Thackeray's celebrated dictum had been justified: 'the work of fiction contains more truth in solution than the work which purports to be all true.'

I had now ahead of me another adventure, larger and of far wider import than the mere interlude in France; and of this I must now proceed to tell.

V

As the winter of 1944–45 came on my health grew infinitely worse. The abdominal pains I had had to endure with increasing misery since my schooldays had now become a scourge. Pain not only tortured me by day, but kept me agonisingly awake at night. I wrote little of any consequence and derived little or no pleasure from what I did. It was clear that one day surgeons would have 'to take a little peep' inside me but no such operation would be possible until a more critical stage in my physical condition had been reached. I simply had to grin and bear it.

When therefore Dudley Barker summoned me to his desk at Air Ministry one day in mid-January 1945 it was to greet me with something like these words:

'We all know what a miserable time you've been having with your health and if you want to say "No" to the proposition I'm going to put to you we shall all understand. It's entirely up to you. If you feel you must decline please decline. Nothing more will be said.'

'What is the proposition?'

'We'd like you to go to Burma. You would actually be based in India, at Calcutta, where Doddie will look after you.'

'How long for?'

'Entirely up to you. The object of the exercise is to write half a dozen pieces – even some short stories – specifically for the American market. It's felt that the Americans should be made aware that there is in fact a war going on in Burma, and a pretty desperate one at that. But, as I say, you don't *have* to go. It's neither a posting nor an order.'

'May I think it over?'

'That's exactly what we want you to do. In fact buzz off now, talk it over with your wife and tell us later what you feel. But remember – there's no compulsion.'

Oddly enough, I felt excited. My feelings were very much akin to those I had experienced when Hilary Saunders, Harald Peake and John Nerney had first proposed that I should be commissioned into the RAF solely to write short stories. Here, now, was a new field to explore, a new theatre from which I might extract stories and drama. Once again I felt excited, honoured and no little apprehensive.

For a day or two I talked it over with Madge and she, like me, felt it was clearly my duty to accept the proposition. She knew that, with four very young children, my absence would be hard for her; and I knew it too. But neither of us ever really felt otherwise than that I should go to India and Burma, and within another day or so I went back to Dudley Barker to tell him so.

Dudley, though pleased at my decision, nevertheless warned me: 'We probably won't be able to get you away before early February, so if in the meantime you decide to change your mind you are perfectly free to do so.'

I replied that I didn't think I would change my mind and I may even have said – I certainly thought it – that health wise the trip might even do me good. The only further comment I had from Dudley was the simple one that 'India is a mess'. Little did I know.

So on a day in early February Madge came with me to BOAC's air terminal in London, where we said a fond but rather dejected farewell. Scarcely had she waved her hand for the last time and disappeared into the street than a loudspeaker announcement told that my flight had been cancelled. I was home ten minutes after Madge and we were able to have one more evening together.

Next day I entrained for Swindon and thence to Lyneham. There a positive horde of servicemen and women had been waiting for an entire week for February's fogs to clear and they were full of mocking laughter at the new buoyant contingent just arriving. Nevertheless, that night, the fog did clear; morning broke white with hoar-frost and by half past eight we were airborne. An hour or two later I could see the far distant line of the Alps, looking like a crowd of pink sugar mice nestling together in the low, brilliant morning sun.

Malta

Eventually, on the dark blue sea below, a rock appeared: of such apparent and unexpected smallness that I simply couldn't believe that this was our first stop, Malta. But Malta it was and soon half a dozen of us were wandering among Valletta's white and sparkling ruins. Malta indeed was a sad sight; there was little to do or buy; and we ended the day by taking a moth-eaten gharry and driving to some remote black market restaurant and there eating what I strongly suspect was some species of dog heavily flavoured with garlic and herbs. If however I give the impression that Malta was a scene of utter desolation I must at once correct it. Its ruins apart, it was a little paradise of flowers; arum lilies, narcissi, irises, stocks, sweetpeas, marigolds and trees of fruit blossom. I marvelled and revelled greatly in that premature touch of spring.

Next morning we flew on to Cairo, arriving in time for a lunch which my tiresome stomach rejected, so that I spent most of the time slowly sucking at an orange and gazing dreamily at a vase of sweetpeas. After lunch, since our flight wasn't due to continue until the small hours of the morning, six of us, including I think two army brigadiers, thumbed a lift in a truck and made for Cairo. One had the immediate impression that that city had been shipped straight from Paradise. I recall a shop window full of sponges, a sight which so awed and transfixed us that we spent an unconscionable amount of time simply staring at it in total disbelief, not like a group of grown men but like schoolboys outside a tuckshop long out of bounds. Then there was the famed *confiserie* of Mr Groppi, sparkling with riches long denied us: chocolates, cakes, tarts, sweetmeats of every kind. Here we didn't merely gaze; the latent schoolboys in us leapt to life, positively falling over each other with mouthwatering greed. Finally we discovered – the city now as brilliantly lit as a fair – a restaurant in which two dozen chickens revolved on a spit over a glowing charcoal fire. Small wonder that we drove back to base more than a little heady on Palestinian wine.

Cairo

We flew off in early morning darkness. I invariably find it impossible to sleep in an aircraft and I sat awake for several hours, merely staring at the blackness ahead. Suddenly the blackness sparkled with jewels: diamonds, rubies, emeralds. This was our airfield; we were about to come down in Persia.

Dawn was breaking as we touched down; then we washed, shaved and breakfasted briefly. Sheiba airfield looked like any other airfield in the middle of a desert: sandy, windswept, desolate. This in fact was my one and only glimpse of Persia, yet many years later I had the strangest dream: I dreamed that I was a magistrate-cum-tax collector in a small remote Persian town and that I was to preside over the magistrates' court. The year was 200 BC (this perhaps was the oddest part of the dream, since one couldn't know, in 200 BC that in fact it was BC). Another vivid fact was the blinding, blistering heat of the day: a fact that made me decide to start holding the court immediately after dawn. Still more vivid was the sight of the shadows in the narrow Persian streets shrinking and shrinking until, at midday, under the perpendicular sun, they existed no longer.

The first strange thing about this dream is that, unlike so many dreams, it has never faded; it still has the same indelible brilliance as on the night when I first experienced it. The second strange thing is that I had not, beforehand, been reading or talking of Persia or seeing anything of the country on the television screen. My entire acquaintance with Persia consisted solely of one hour, in wartime, on an RAF airfield. How to explain it all? My friend Ann Todd, the actress, a woman of much intelligence, entertains no shadow of doubt about it. I *was* once a Persian magistrate and am now reincarnated.

After Persia we flew on to Karachi. My first experience of India (this was before the birth of Pakistan) was to drink the vilest cup of tea that has ever passed my lips and as I threw it away my heart for some reason, sank to my boots. I suddenly felt bitterly, depressingly homesick, a sensation that wasn't in any way lessened by the fact that when the aircraft took off again I found myself to be the one remaining passenger. The fact of that isolation, as we flew over India's vast desert interior, filled me with a dark and desolate gloom.

We came in to land, stickily, in a crosswind at Dum-Dum airfield. Perhaps it was merciful that Dudley's comment 'India is a mess' had remained cryptic and unexpanded. I knew, in fact, nothing of India; its history had largely passed me by; I hated Kipling; of the subcontinent's many languages and dialects I had heard only of Hindi, of its rivers only the Ganges. Ignorance may indeed, at times, be bliss, but as I stepped out into the afternoon's torrid heat on Dum-Dum's tarmac there was to be no bliss for me.

Nor was I suffering merely from ignorance. I cherished several fond if not idiotic illusions. One was that Doddie, if unable to meet me himself, would surely have sent someone, with the necessary transport, in his place. I soon realised that there was in fact no Doddie and no transport. Desperate inquiry at several offices purporting to be sections of the RAF merely brought, from young Indian servicemen, that curious sideways tilt of the head that seems to indicate something half way between yes and no but which experience finally teaches simply means damn-all. I then realised that I hadn't the faintest idea where Doddie's Head-quarters were; nor had I fully grasped the fact that the day was Saturday, nor the still more discomforting fact that in Calcutta the war stopped, every Saturday, at noon. All I knew, or thought

I knew, was that Doddie was somewhere in Calcutta, then a city of 4½ million people and some twenty-five miles in diameter. This in fact was another fond illusion, since Group-Captain Dodds was, in fact, not in Calcutta but in Hastings, twenty miles northward up the River Hooghli. Nor did I then know that the reason why neither Doddie nor anyone else had come to meet me was that authority – and this at a time when it was almost as difficult to get out of England as out of Wormwood Scrubs – had neglected to include me on the manifest of any aircraft leaving England during the three previous days. Officially I was lost.

By this time I also felt personally lost. Eventually I hitched a lift in a truck going into Calcutta, the centre of which, another fact I didn't know, was twenty miles away. In a recent article a celebrated journalist has called Calcutta the most degraded and disgusting great city in the world, a description the full taste of which I was to savour as I now drove through twenty miles of what are indisputably some of the most revolting, most stinking, most rat-ridden, most sickening and most depraved slums in the world. A dead cow rotting on the roadside in the grilling heat of afternoon, giving off the stench of putrefaction and the charnel house; a mad rush of gharries, cars and rickshaws; an old woman, a mere shrunken bag of bones, dying in the gutter without a soul bothering to spare her a second glance; a great mass of rotting filth choking every pavement, gully and alleyway; the evil stench of poverty, of hordes of unwashed bodies, of burning dung: these are merely a few of the more obvious, more odious, more sickening features of that seemingly endless journey through Calcutta's slums on that torrid afternoon.

Eventually the truckdriver dumped me, bed-roll, bags and all, on the pavement outside the Great Eastern Hotel, in the very centre of Calcutta. The hotel, used as a sort of transit camp, teemed with servicemen, a complete madhouse. Lost in utter bewilderment, I suddenly spotted an air commodore and asked him if he possibly knew where I might find Group-Captain Dodds? He stared at me as if I had asked for Jesus Christ himself. I repeated the experience with several other people, always with the same result, until I suddenly knew, exhausted and drowned in sweat as I was, that I was going rapidly and irrevocably mad.

Presently, in this utterly desperate state, I spotted an RAF sergeant in a jeep. I went over to him and begged, yet again, if he might possibly tell me where I could find Group-Captain Dodds.

'Dodds? Never 'eard of 'im. What mob's he in?'

'Public Relations.'

'Gor blimey, why didn't you say so the first time? 'Op in.'

I threw my kit into the back of the jeep and hopped in. We then drove crazily round several back streets, crushing watermelon rinds as we skidded round corners, honking at the usual press of dhoti-clad Indians, all looking like lazy brown-and-white moths. It was by now five o'clock and to my horror the sergeant suddenly muttered something about we'd be 'bleeding lucky if the office wasn't shut by now'. Eventually, however, we drew up in a narrow alley and the sergeant said:

'This is it. On the first floor. I'll keep an eye on your kit while you go up.'

Near to utter exhaustion, I crawled upstairs. At the head of them a thin squadron-leader, accompanied by a woman companion, was in the very act of locking an office door.

I introduced myself and he almost fainted.

'Good God, Laddie,' he said in strong Scots accent, 'we've been searching high and low for you all day. Where've you been? Do you not know you're not on the manifest of any aircraft that's left Great Britain for the past three days?'

No, I said, I didn't know; nor did I care.

At this point the squadron-leader introduced himself as Nickie, then his companion as Mrs Henderson. 'Mrs Henderson and her husband Tom are old friends of mine. Aye, they're Scots like me.'

I shook hands with Mrs Henderson, a small bright-eyed, cheerful woman who eyed me up and down keenly – purely because, as she afterwards explained, she simply couldn't believe that I could possibly be as weary as I looked.

'Talking of manifests,' I said, 'it's manifest that I get a room somewhere. Is there a hotel you can recommend?'

The squadron-leader laughed uproariously.

'Listen, Laddie. Calcutta's a city of four and a half million people and it has three hotels. One is a sort of transit camp, one is a brothel that when it isn't a brothel is closed because of dead dogs, cats or rats in the water supply. The other has so many bugs they eat you alive. Hotels? – you must be joking, Laddie. Joking.'

Then where the devil, I wanted to know, could I stay?

Mrs Henderson gave me another long, searching, pitying look. 'Ye dinna need worry your head about that tonight. My husband and I'll see ye have a bed for tonight.'

I thanked her warmly and a few minutes later I was piling my kit into the squadron-leader's car and the three of us were re-tracing the sordid miles of Calcutta's slums that had so sickened and revolted me an hour or so before. The second sight of them seemed only to reveal a greater squalor than the first; the dead cow putrefying by the roadside had entered an even more evil, sickening state of putrefaction; on trees and fences about it vultures were already gathering, evil-looking themselves, in readiness for tomorrow's scavenging gorge; everywhere in bazaars and streets and alleyways there seemed to be greater crowds than ever; rickshaws, both man-powered and bicycle-powered, dashed precariously among huge open taxis, all driven by dark turbanned

Sikhs; trotting, sweating coolies bearing loads on the ends of long poles, so that they looked like pairs of human scales; women with great bundles on their heads; all seemed noisier, more chaotic, more miserable to look upon.

After a long period of all this we came to a more or less open road bordered on each side by dusty bullock tracks along which both bullocks and water buffaloes were lugging heavy wooden carts, lumbering like Biblical beasts through deep rainless dust. Above them great tall palms threw long shadows, their high motionless fronds looking as if cut out of black steel against a sky almost colourless in the last half hour of daylight preceding India's swift short twilight.

Presently we came to another squalid settlement with the everlasting crowds, among which barbers sat in gutters cutting their clients' hair, and the everlasting squalor. Then suddenly we halted at a pair of enormous wooden gates, which were duly flung open in obedience to irate honkings on the car horn. A pair of obsequious Indians salaamed as we passed through into a biggish courtyard, on three sides of which stood a prison-like factory. 'Jute,' said Mrs Henderson and I then remembered that jute was the main artery of Calcutta's life-blood.

On the other side of the factory flowed the wide stewy Hooghli, its far bank already glittering with a thin scattering of lights. On the near bank, taking advantage of the last daylight, a gang of kneeling Indian women and girls were planting grass on a newly prepared stretch of red-brown earth, dibbing in each green tuft swiftly, as rice is planted. Behind them it was possible to pick out the patchwork of previous days' plantings, the nearest pale and wilting, the farthest already a brilliant emerald green.

The Hendersons' flat was on the first floor of a block overlooking the river. We climbed up an outside iron staircase, an Indian bearer, a boy of perhaps thirteen, lugging my kit up behind us. The flat was far from large and out of it appeared Tom Henderson, shortish, of typical Scots countenance, looking slightly but patiently aggrieved that his wife, as I discovered was her habit, had brought home yet another weary RAF waif-and-stray who could not find himself a bed. Tom Henderson had in fact lost an RAF son by an earlier marriage at some earlier stage of the war and in consequence, like his wife, was ever-ready to play the good Samaritan.

'Will ye no be takking a wee chota peg, mon?' Mr Henderson said.

My weary brain failed signally to translate this sentence of thick Scots, with its peppering of Hindustani, into any kind of sense and in answer I could only stare stupidly.

'Tom means would you like a drink?' Mrs Henderson said and I came suddenly to my senses, causing laughter.

For the next half an hour I drank much gin and tonic, well iced, and nothing had ever tasted so good. As we drank, Nickie announced that I was a writer, a piece of information that caused great surprise to spring into Mrs Henderson's face, as if she were unable to believe that such a species not only existed but had actually appeared in her home. But being also a practical soul, she almost at once suggested that I would surely like a bath, to which I responded with something like:

'God, that would be heaven.'

It was indeed heaven and thus refreshed I went early to bed, at last to slumber like a child under my mosquito net.

I woke early next morning, shaved, bathed again and then went out on to the terrace of the Hendersons' flat. The scene laid before my eyes in that exquisite first hour or so after sunrise was the perfect example of the fact that 'distance lends enchantment to the view'. The far bank of the Hooghli lay bathed in a soft, delicious, opalescent light, as from a 'faery land forlorn' its temples and towers and houses rising from an assortment of trees and palms in infinitely tender shades of pink and cream and green and yellow and even lavender. That there lay under this sublimely beautiful, ethereally unreal curtain a dark sink of putrefying squalor seemed totally fantastic. I could only wonder which had cheated me most, the evening of the previous day or the sweet opal loveliness of my first Indian sunrise.

India, ruthless as ever towards human life, soon mocked me with an answer. Just below me, in the river, beyond the new-planted grass, a pale object floated past, twisting in slow curves on the downstream current. It was the swollen body of a man, the first but by no means the last I was to see of the wide Hooghli's victims.

It wasn't long, however, before the first fond illusion of India's fairy dawn was to be burnt in the cauldron of rising day. In an hour or two the sun was scalding; by noon the flat was an oppressive oven in which I sweated and wolfed at iced gin and tonic like an exhausted animal at a stream. 'Och! this is nothing,' the Hendersons said. 'This is only February. We've no begun to warm up yet. This is really the winter.'

Afternoon wrapped me in a long siesta, from which I emerged to the blessed refreshment of tea flavoured with fresh green limes. Soon afterwards Nickie appeared, announcing his readiness to drive us all up river to Hastings, there to find Group-Captain Dodds. It was growing dark as we left in his car and the air was alternately sweet and noisome with the heavy fragrance of what may have been incense trees and the fires, in villages, of burning dung. Something about this combination of the sweet and the acrid very much depressed my spirits. Sunday in time of war, as any serviceman would tell you, was the week's worst day, when families are most missed and most thought of and homesickness sits on the heart like a grey blight. That first drive up the Hooghli on Sunday still lives with me, vivid and gloomy as ever.

Headquarters at Hastings was housed, as I think I am right in saying, in a converted jute-mill. Its personnel consisted, I should say, of ninety per cent American, the rest British. As always, the Americans lacked for nothing: iced beer, drinks of all kinds, a clubhouse, a bar opulently built of bamboo, and girls and all the rest of it. (There is a story telling of how, at one period of the war in New Guinea, the morale of American troops dropped far below zero. The cause of this phenomenon was searched for far and wide. More beer, more hamburgers, more jazz, more women – these and a score of other opiates were investigated and rejected. It was then discovered by chance that what the troops were pining for were the comic supplements to American newspapers. These were duly flown out by the thousand in special aircraft and morale immediately rose like a moon rocket.) Not that we, the poor British, with a beer ration of one can a month, had cause to grouse at American affluence. Though they sometimes behaved with that singular insularity that is one of their less endearing characteristics (I once spent a night sharing a dormitory with seven or eight American officers, not one of whom spoke to me, as if fearing that mere conversational contact with a Limey might prove unpleasantly contagious) they were on the whole generous to their poor relations, conferring on us generous gifts of beer, a drink I am not normally very fond of but which, in Calcutta's sweltering cauldron, was sheer nectar.

It was good to see my old commanding officer again and his dry humour caused my spirits to rise and sweeten. Tomorrow we would meet, lunch, talk, make plans; I must get myself effectively kitted out (I was still wearing my thick RAF uniform and mightily uncomfortable it was) and he would show me where. He also reminded me that another colleague from PR3, an officer named Chadwick, was also in Calcutta, together with one or two others I had known in London, including the journalist Andrew Rice, so that soon there would be no lack of friends. Chadwick was also a member of the Bengal Club, then probably the most exclusive club in the world, so that at least one avenue of civilisation would possibly be open to me. There was also the Swimming Club, a blessed haven as it proved, and Doddie would see that I was made a member of that.

If I have given the impression that Calcutta was wholly and irremediably squalid I must now make some effort to correct it. The east side of Calcutta was, as with so many great cities, its worst; its West End, as with London, Paris and many other cities, was infinitely superior. Here there is a wide park-like space, the Maidan, in which stands Government House, built by Lord Wellesley in 1799 and closely modelled on the great Adam house, Kedleston Hall, in Derbyshire (it must be remembered that Calcutta was once the capital of India, before New Delhi was built, being preferred to its rival Bombay because of the prevalence of plague in Bombay, a disease from which Calcutta, for all the nastiness of its climate, was relatively free). Government House was, when I first saw it, not only a fine Adam-like pile in itself, but more glorious than Solomon himself in its vast brilliant garment of red, salmon and magenta bougainvillaea: an exotic and amazing sight. And as if this vivid lustre were not enough great beds of cannas, six feet or more tall, in scarlet, crimson, yellow, orange and pink, flaunted their trumpets on the emerald, well-watered lawns in front of the great house, like companies of severely drilled soldiery on stiff and solid guard.

Alongside the Maidan runs one of the most famous streets in the world, Chowringee, once a row of palatial mansions, but now more like another Knightsbridge, filled with shops large and fashionable. Behind this were streets of colonial houses and gardens of considerable wealth and charm. Nor, indeed, would it be true to say that all of Calcutta was poor. Its large port ensures that it is a city of great wealth; though, as so often happens, its wealth abides with the few, its poverty with the many.

There is no doubt, however, that the atmosphere of Calcutta was confused, enervating and parochial. Calcutta's sister in the world of jute is Dundee, a fact which meant that a considerable part of the British resident population of the Indian city came from the Scottish one. Some, like Tom Henderson, had been there for the better part of forty years – 'and I'm tellin' ye, mon,' they were fond of saying, 'I still don't know India.'

Here, I realised after less than a couple of weeks' acclimatisation, was my problem. If residents of forty years' occupation didn't know the subcontinent how was I to fare? The problem, I realised, was not wholly unlike that which had confronted me on my first acquaintance with Bomber Command. Now, as then, I found myself in a world totally unfamiliar to me, its idiom strange, its people apparently unapproachable; yet from this difficult and unpromising material it was my job somehow to extract and translate into lucid form articles and stories which would convey to far distant readers a picture of what India, and later Burma, were like in the turmoil of war. What had seemed a task of apparent simplicity – namely that of writing half a dozen short pieces for American consumption – now began to seem of disturbing complexity.

This is precisely what I had felt at Oakington, but there, fortunately, I was living with the battle and with the men who were fighting it. In parochial, steaming Calcutta, in spite of the presence of thousands of servicemen of innumerable nationalities, there was no battle. The war, on its several fronts, was not only far away; it might not have existed. Where, then, was my material coming from? I appeased my conscience a little in that direction by writing what I think was a vivid piece on Calcutta itself which was well enough received, writing it in the comparative cool and quiet of the Swimming Club, in the morning, when the club was virtually deserted. For the rest I knew that I had, as I had done at Oakington, to keep my ears cocked for those stray crumbs of gossip which are so often enough to set the imagination of writers on fire.

Presently one of these crumbs was unwittingly let fall at the Hendersons' flat. Evening after evening there used to appear there a man of perhaps forty or so, clearly of much experience in the

East, apparently hard-bitten and without doubt a hard drinker. He struck me as being very much like a character out of Conrad, a writer on whom in my extreme youth I had been strongly suckled and whose interpretation of the East, both atmospherically and otherwise, had long seemed to me infinitely superior to both that of Kipling, the Imperialist, and Maugham, the pretended cynic who was often a sentimentalist in disguise and whose world was in many ways as narrow as that of Surbiton – as parochial as that of Calcutta itself.

The apparently hard-bitten visitor to the Hendersons' flat belonged neither to the Imperialistic nor suburban world. He generally arrived at the flat about six o'clock, when he would talk civilly and coherently for perhaps half an hour or so, during which time he would ferociously consume a positively fearsome quantity of liquor. As this began to work he became progressively more introspective, maudlin and then almost tearfully truculent, even abusive. I had never seen a man drink so much in so short a time or with less evident enjoyment; here, it seemed to me, was a man setting out either deliberately to destroy himself or to drown some undrownable sorrow or to expiate or try to forget some unforgettable personal disaster – a kind of wartime Lord Jim.

I was so troubled and mystified by all this that I was moved eventually to ask Mrs Henderson what lay behind it all. 'He was a planter in Burma,' she said, 'and he was on the long march to India when the Japs moved in.' Great though the disasters of that march had been, as I knew well enough, they hardly seemed to me to justify a sort of alcoholic death-wish. There must also lie in that distressed mind, it seemed to me, the bitter kernel of some greater, more personal disaster. And so it turned out. His sorrow – and sorrow it was, profound, bitter and unforgettable – rose from the fact that his personal bearer, a mere boy, had died on the journey. The severance of this deep personal bond, born of mutual love and loyalty, had had so great an effect on him that he had been crushed into a state of morbid melancholia.

From this bitter crumb there was eventually to emerge *The Jacaranda Tree*. The birth of that book, however, still lay some years ahead and for the moment all I could do was to let the seed lie dormant, though by no means dead, in the deeper recesses of my mind.

Meanwhile, as Doddie was presently to remind me, Burma itself was very much a reality. Did I feel prepared, he asked, to fly across and have a look-see? A large, formidable map of the country, a jam-like mess of purple and green, secretly told me I was not so prepared. There was in fact a certain chill in my heart. I had a discomforting feeling that I was about to go out into the wilderness and that I might never return. The prospect of such banishment seemed not only harsh; it had the further effect of making even steaming, sordid, insalubrious Calcutta seem like a piece of heaven.

Naturally, however, I said that I was willing and ready to go, and a few days later I was flying out over the Bay of Bengal.

VI

Sometime before this event, however, I had had my one and only quarrel with a fellow officer: nothing more than a flaming, stand-up row with Nickie. Squadron-Leader Nickson was the arch-type of that kind of middle-rank officer who by virtue of that rank sets up his own personal kingdom which he then proceeds to rule by threats, fear and even terror, petrifying all of lesser rank. In Nickie's case Erks, Waafs, Indian clerks, bearers and drivers were all held in terrifying thrall. The king in his kingdom, ruling by shouting, abuse, invective, foul language and often sheer bullying, was a law unto himself, and woe betide any who dared think otherwise.

Among other things Nickie was in charge of PR transport, both in the air and on the ground. Accordingly I went to him to request that I be given a jeep, it having been sensibly recognised at Air Ministry that I should, and must, have my own transport. With this firmly promised arrangement Nickie flatly refused to comply. In vain I pointed out that this was an Air Ministry instruction. 'Jeep? Ye'll have no jeep here. I've no jeep to spare and even if I had ye'd not get it.' Again I protested strongly; again I insisted that these were Air Ministry promises and instructions; again Nickie yelled 'No jeep! I'm tellin' ye for the last time – no jeep.' It was then my turn to yell, livid with lost temper as well as being no little nauseated by the conduct of the petty king-dictator. Presently the air grew flaming hot, then molten, and it was only when it had cooled a little that I saw the virtues of reason and swept coldly out of the office.

Outside, with no hesitation, I commandeered the nearest truck in sight, and promptly ordered its Indian driver to take me to Doddie. He, being the sort of man he was, listened to me with good sense and reason, saw the cogency of my arguments and told me not to worry. He would telephone Nickie. He duly did so and I got my jeep next day.

In the aftermath of this tempestuous atmosphere I now had to approach Nickie again on the question of air transport to Burma. The king-tyrant was again unco-operative, indeed offensive. There were no aircraft, or if there were they were all completely full. A great number of transports were US; others, in case I didn't know it, were being eaten by termites. It would be days and days, perhaps weeks, before anything could be found. I knew all this to be stalling, if not deliberate enmity, but I was both impotent and powerless to do anything and the king-tyrant knew it well. For some days afterwards I turned up every morning at Nickie's office to inquire after my passage, but always with the same result: no aircraft. Finally I got a seat on a Dakota, a Dakota so ancient, so rickety, so tied up with string and, unless I was much mistaken, so eaten by termites that it would surely never, I thought, make the passage from Bengal to the Arakan. Ever since that day I have in fact nurtured the unpleasant thought that Nickie, by that shambles of an aircraft, hoped to kill me.

But reach the Arakan, along the Burma coast, I eventually did. It was mid afternoon when I arrived on the wide dusty airfield, far beyond which, to the north, a range of mountains smouldered in a vast heat haze. On the ground itself, as I stepped thankfully from the aircraft, the searing, blinding sun struck down on me like a blow from a mighty white-hot steam hammer. Never had I felt anything like it; even the heat of Calcutta seemed temperate by comparison.

I was then assailed by a mirage. The dusty, barren airfield seemed suddenly to flower. Then the flower became a woman, a white woman, tall, shapely, elegant, very beautiful. I could only stare and wonder. Such things simply didn't happen on remote, sizzling Asian airfields. Then she moved and walked and I knew that this was no mirage. She was, as it turned out, an actress who had flown in to entertain such few servicemen as were left in Akyab.

My *Encyclopaedia Britannica* describes Akyab as the third largest port in Burma, lying on the coast where three fertile valleys, watered by the rivers Myu, Koladaing and Lemyu, reach the sea in an intricate network of tidal channels, creeks and islands. The hinterland is described as rich with forest, the fertile alluvian valleys yielding inexhaustible supplies of rice.

Alas, when I saw it on that first burning, blinding afternoon, Akyab and its fertile valleys presented only a scene of bitter desolation. No rice had grown there for three years or more; Akyab was a half-swallowed ruin – swallowed by Mother Nature in all her torrid tropical vigour. The jungle ruled and dominated all. Vines, creepers, trees, elephant grass twice as tall as a man, bamboos, palms – fed by tropical suns and watered by monsoons, the once thriving port of Akyab had disappeared under a kind of corruptive natural splendour.

All this had on me an impact as powerful as that of the sun had been; it drove deeply and permanently into my consciousness. At the same time it provoked in me a singular sadness. India seemed a senseless, seething mess; yet I felt that Burma, by contrast, must have been simple, ordered and happy, its people gentle, charming and reserved. Now, like Akyab itself, it was a mere husk, a dusty ghost, its people like trousered and half-broken wanderers in a dream.

Little of apparent significance seemed to happen to me on that first Burma visit. I say 'seemed' advisedly, since once again it was little things that dropped into my mind and lay dormant there, waiting to germinate and flower at some distant, even far distant, date. A large, rambling temple outside which young Burmese boys were pouring a cement-like mixture into small moulds which when baked hard by the powerful sun turned out as miniature Buddhas; a pretty little Burmese girl sitting on the step of a bombed pagoda, playing with a lizard, at first gently, merely teasing it, then with deliberate cruelty, wounding and finally killing it. Little and apparently insignificant episodes, yet the one stuck in the mind as epitomising the futility of religion, the other as an exposure of all the callous futility of war. The second of these episodes haunted me so uneasily that I went immediately back to my small hot tent and tried, before the brilliance of its impact faded, to get it down on paper, I hoped as my first short story of the East. Not a word resulted: for reasons which I shall later set out in detail.

I flew back to India some ten days or so later, to re-enact there the stupid and exhausting merry-go-round I had been through on the first day of my arrival. A young half terrified native truck driver drove me desperately round Calcutta's sleazy suburbs in an attempt to find, in the dingy darkness, the Hendersons' flat. Just as I knew that we were irrevocably lost and he seemed about to go berserk we were stopped by an RAF sergeant M.P. in a jeep, who had the good sense to order the boy back to his unit and then kindly gave me a lift in the right direction in the jeep.

That crazy drive gave me, however, a chance to see another side of Calcutta: Calcutta by night. If I now used words of my own to describe it I might well be accused of biased and deliberate falsification. I will therefore content myself with quoting from a recent article describing not the Calcutta of 1945, but the Calcutta of 1970, a quarter of a century after every wall in India had 'Quit India' scrawled across it and India's millions couldn't wait for the British Raj, the hated Western imperialist, to be driven out. After heading the article 'Oh! Calcutta! World's Greatest Urban Disaster', the writer goes on:

> Millions have the pavements as their home. Miles of streets are strewn with sleeping families at night. But the pavements remain almost as littered during the day. It is evident that thousands of people either lack the energy or the need, being unemployed or unemployable, to move from their gutter-side homes.
>
> Many, clad in filthy rags or nearly naked, loll about obviously starving or half-dead. In the city centre scores of

lepers and cruelly mutilated unfortunates beg unheeded . . .
Roadside stalls sell food openly exposed to dust and flies
which carry cholera germs, Huge garbage dumps remain
uncleared and pavements are strewn with rotting trash.
The gutters are the public lavatories. Dead and dying dogs as
well as humans lie about the footway . . . In the suburbs,
conditions are far worse, with hundreds of thousands
crammed into disease-breeding bustees, hutments built in
foetid areas which lack sewage or running water . . . Diseases
like cholera and plague are endemic. Malaria, once nearly
contained, is spreading again due to failure to spray
mosquito-breeding swamps. Tap water is unsafe to drink
and often runs black. . . Trams built for 75 people carry 200
and hundreds daily risk their lives by hanging on to the
footboards of overloaded buses.

All this and more I saw in 1945. More? Trains loaded with
desperate, yelling, shrieking human cargo, every inch of roof
thick with bodies, every grippable piece of rolling stock precariously clutched by a desperate figure; women crawling on
hands and knees along railway tracks, pathetically searching for a
few walnuts of dropped coal; in the huge central market, a vast
cornucopia of limes, oranges, bananas yellow and red, papayas,
guavas, persimmons, pineapples, watermelons, tomatoes, grapes

and indeed every kind of fruit and vegetable, tropical and temperate alike, fat rats sit with lascivious boldness among the piles of fruit while stall-holders merely laugh at them; the eternal stinking dead cow being stripped by vultures on the roadside, the eternal bloated human body floating down the Hooghli; and every morning, or almost every morning, the sickening report in the newspapers of some young infertile Indian bride being given a can of petrol by her mother-in-law and being told that she knew what she could do with it: another human torch mercifully released from the indignity, the unforgivable sin, of not being productive, as if India's sorrowful sordid millions were not already enough.

By now it was March and India's heat was already comparable to that of a furnace; only in the first couple of hours after breakfast, in some shaded corner at the swimming pool, did I ever feel cool and fit to work. It was therefore with great relief that I met yet another of Calcutta's many Scotsmen, a tea-planter but also a public servant of integrity, a member of the Bengal Assembly, who was kind enough to invite me to spend a weekend on his estate, far to the north, within sight of the Himalayas and the foothills of Bhutan.

Before this visit could be arranged, however, he invited me to do something else: to attend a session of the Bengal Assembly. I duly went and was duly shocked. In revolting contrast to the starving, mutilated and miserable populace on the streets outside the Indian members of the Assembly were fat, oily and well-fed. They were also callous; never, in fact, had I seen the mark of evil and corruption so indelibly bitten into so many human faces at one time. Only the face of my Scottish friend and a few other specimens of the hated British Raj stood out with incorruptible integrity, like good deeds in a very naughty world.

A few days later we entrained for the north, I not having the remotest notion of what other side of India would greet me there.

VII

The scene at the railway station, on the evening of our departure, was exactly as I have already described: crowds of near-hysterical Indian bodies covering the platforms, smothering like clusters of white-winged moths the roofs and buffers and running boards of trains; an almost riotous assembly and altogether a certain air of disordered and almost childish madness. Of all this, however, my friend and I were not obliged to become part. Our first-class compartment was not only reserved but reserved for us alone. Our bearer attended to our baggage, at the same time loading into the compartment vast hampers of food and drink and other comforts.

The railway going northward through Bengal finally ends at Darjeeling, but our destination was some way to the south of the Sikkim border, at a place called Jalpagur. It was, as I remember it, only an hour or so after dawn when we arrived there, in a morning of exquisite freshness totally free of Calcutta's oppressive, sweaty humidity. So far north we could, anyway, be sure that the sun would, at that time of year, never have the implacable power it had in the south. The country air was in fact delicious; the distances were hazy, so that the peaks of the Himalayas were wholly hidden, but the foothills of Bhutan, looking strangely mysterious, brooded almost colourlessly against the northern sky.

We washed, shaved, changed and breakfasted at a club house. Smart army officers, some Indian, were breakfasting too, many of them, as I guessed, going on leave to Darjeeling. On the station platform I had already seen several people clearly coming back

446

from Darjeeling and very refreshing it was to see two young English nurses carrying little baskets made of slender strips of wood and planted with roots of the common primrose in cool, lovely and happy flower.

After breakfast we got into my friend's waiting truck and began to head eastwards, under the foothills. A considerable number of streams flow down here from the great Himalayan range and at that season of the year many of them were totally dry, mere beds of white sun-scalded rock. We crossed these by wooden bridges which, in the eventual monsoon season, would be swept away by torrents of flood water of prodigious power and would in due course have to be built up again.

But at one point we reached a river of considerable size, far too wide to be bridged, and over this we ferried the truck on a precarious arrangement of planks and petrol drums which had to be powerfully handled by numbers of natives with oars and poles in order that it didn't drift helplessly downstream. My recollection is that the men sang loud and vigorous chants, as Indians so often do when doing a job in concert, as they punted and rowed, all looking, in contrast to the miserable bags of bones in Calcutta's foetid streets, as happy as sand-boys enjoying some huge lark.

From the far river bank we eventually bowled and bumped along in a cloud of white dust which gave the impression of rising and sweeping away to the north, there to blanket the foothills in deep haze. This haze however was not of dust but already, in mid-morning, of heat. Not that the day had lost its freshness; on the contrary it had a certain spring-like air, an impression that was much strengthened when we reached my friend's tea estate and bungalow, in the garden of which sweetpeas, marigolds, petunias, sweet williams, stocks and phlox Drummondii were all in delicious flower. In the tea gardens little Indian children were picking some predatory orange-coloured bug off the camellia-like bushes, a task for which they would be paid a few annas a dozen, and occasionally an enormous and brilliant butterfly, more like bird than insect, would fly over with captivating splendour.

The bungalow itself was beautifully furnished, complete with

billiard table, its furniture polished to perfection. Barefooted
Indian servants glided about everywhere, silently, and soon ice
was clinking away in long glasses of gin, tonic water and green
moons of lime. It was all very comfortable, very affluent, very
respectable and very orderly: yet I gained an uneasy impression. It
was that my friend lived a life of great loneliness. He lacked for
nothing; a clap of the hands, the tinkle of a bell, would instantly
bring him all he wanted, and yet the house was, it seemed to me,
haunted by a great emptiness. Some few years later I put all this
into a story called *The Frontier*, but even today I cannot totally rid
myself of that atmosphere of empty loneliness, any more than I
can expunge from my mind the heat-haze on the foothills, the
giant and splendid butterflies or the little Indian children
collecting their bright bugs from the bushes of tea.

That afternoon, being Saturday, my friend set off to the estate
offices to pay his workers, including the little Indian children who
sat outside, cross-legged, with their orange captures of bugs neatly
laid out before them in the dust. My friend didn't claim that his
was an exclusive or even very good brand of tea, certainly nothing
resembling the nectars of Darjeeling; it was his job to produce a
tea that would make 'the good strong cup' so beloved of many
Britishers, whether the housewife struggling with her cooking and
her washing or the truck driver at the 'good pull up for carmen'.
But what he also produced, and which in turn I found fascinating,
was a brand of brick tea made especially for Tibetans. This was
compressed and solidified into black blocks the shape of thick
saucers, some five inches across; they were immensely hard and
heavy and would, if thrown at a man from short range, have
inflicted no little injury. The interesting thing about these iron-
like shapes of brick tea was that they were used by the Tibetans
not only for brewing tea on long treks in wild mountain country
(the tea was not only heavy and durable but almost indestructible)
but also as a form of currency. My friend kindly gave me one of
these formidable slabs but I must confess that I never put it to the
test of boiling water.

Next morning, Sunday, we toured the estate and its environs by car. The air was again delicious, the scent of flowers in the garden tenderly exotic, as in some perfect warm English May.

Again too the foothills were shrouded in heat haze, the Himalayas completely hidden behind them. And now and then, as we drove through narrow jungle roads, the high dry elephant grass on both sides tunnelled by cavernous paths made by rhinoceros, we occasionally passed little groups of trotting Indian men, near-naked and very dark in colour, their bows and arrows slung across their shining backs as they set forth to hunt and kill something for the Sunday pot. They looked totally innocent, totally primitive, totally unsullied by what we are pleased to call civilisation. I found them most attractive and touching.

When we left a couple of days later to entrain for Calcutta I felt no little sense of regret; I would like to have seen more of the foothills, the jungle and its birds, the rivers and the dark trotting little men. Yet I was more than glad to have seen what I had seen and to know that there is a side of India that is lovable and in its own special way as unforgettable as the 'world's greatest urban disaster'. It is in fact not far from the truth to say that for a good twenty years after that visit to the hills and the tea plantation there were few days when I did not think of them and always with affection; and I think of them still.

Perhaps my pleasure at that weekend was the greater because I knew that the road to Calcutta also meant once again the road to Burma, and I have to confess that it was a journey I did not, at that moment, relish very much.

As it turned out it resolved itself more happily.

VIII

Never a lover of Kipling, I have often been puzzled by his lines 'on the road to Mandalay, where the flying fishes play'. It has always seemed to me odd that there should be flying fishes at a Burmese town many hundreds of miles inland from the sea but perhaps, since Mandalay is on the great Irrawaddy, Kipling may have been right after all. It was not, however, to Mandalay that I was going on my second trip to Burma, since the town was still in Japanese hands, but to Monywa, once a pleasant little country town but now a pathetic heap of ruins and overgrown jungle and also on the Irrawaddy.

It was now almost April and as I stepped from the aircraft on to the dusty airstrip the sun once again hit me a vicious, white-hot blow. As quickly as possible I hitched a lift in a jeep, piled my kit into the vehicle and drove off to the RAF camp on the edge of the ruined town. At the encampment I left my belongings on the roadside, leaving a little book of Elizabethan lyrics, bound in white vellum, on the top of them, and then went off to find the camp adjutant and if possible a tent and a bed. The adjutant, when found, was helpful but not hopeful. It might mean, he explained, that I would have to share a tent with at least one other officer if not two. I thanked him and he duly took me off to find the tent. It then turned out that only one other officer was in occupation, although not at home at that moment, and I immediately went off to collect my baggage. When I got back to it the little book of Elizabethan lyrics presented an amazing sight.

The furious heat of the sun, in only a quarter of an hour or so, had had such a powerful effect on the vellum that both covers were completely and tightly curled up, like a brace of white brandy-snaps.

I had scarcely begun to unpack a few things in the tent than my fellow tent-sharer, as if already warned by the swiftest possible message, arrived in a state of what I think is best described as possessive agitation. One of those born fuss-pots with an inordinate passion for tidiness, he was clearly scared stiff that I, the new intruder, would besmirch the sacred precincts of his ordered world.

I, wanting only to be friendly, showed him the strangely transformed book of Elizabethan lyrics, adding something about 'this God-awful heat', in which I was sweating ferociously.

'Heat, old boy? You don't call *this* heat, do you? I mean this is the cool season, the winter. Wait till it really warms up, say June and July – no, old boy, don't put your stuff there if you don't mind. There isn't an awful lot of room for two and I'd rather you didn't clutter things up.'

No tent in the whole of Burma could have looked less cluttered up. My companion, fussy, belly-aching, slightly effeminate, finicky of eye, had carefully seen to that. He had also carefully seen to it that every precautionary bottle of pills, tablets, powders and so on was laid out on his bedside bamboo table in neat order ready to do battle with malaria, the common cold, heat sickness, diarrhoea, lack of salt and all the other ills which a tropical climate may, or may not, inflict on a man.

'I hope you brought your mepacrine, old boy? Terribly important. You need the proper dosage every day. I never miss.'

'Mepacrine? What's it for?'

'Good grief, old boy, you don't know? Malaria, of course. You must take it. Absolutely essential. There are chaps out here who've had malaria a dozen times, even twenty. Might never have happened if they'd been regular with the mepacrine. No, old boy, do you mind not putting your tooth brush into that beaker? It's sort of my preserve, that one.'

Hot though it was, I went outside for air. The hope that I should find it was a vain one, but I felt that if I didn't get out of that tent at once I should suddenly scream. There is no type more liable to drive me crazy than the slightly effeminate male fusspot, especially when the power behind it is the orderly mind. It produces in me a violent sense of impotent frustration.

Another five minutes of 'don't put your stuff there, old boy, do you mind?' and injunctions such as 'it's only fair to both of us, old boy, not to clutter the place up. There's hardly enough room for one as it is, I mean' – once again drove me out of the tent, this time in search of the Mess and a possible cup of tea. This, I thought, might at least refresh my frustrated spirit but to my infinite revulsion all I got from a diminutive Burmese bearer was a cup of what must be the world's most revolting liquid, namely tea made in the pot with sugar, condensed milk and all, the whole looking like pale liquid toffee.

Eventually I splashed about in two inches of water in my canvas field-bath, put on a clean dry shirt, my bush shirt, and a pair of slacks and then went back, in the twilight, to see if the Mess could provide anything stronger than toffee tea.

Fortifying myself with gin, I found myself being addressed by the camp Padre. This too depressed me. My long standing dislike of things parsonic at once put my back up. This, as I presently realised, was another mistake, since the Padre turned out to be neither patronising nor hearty, neither pompous nor obsequious, neither saintly nor, as I had once discovered in another Padre in another Mess, a drunk.

'Are you here for long?' he wanted to know. 'What's your particular field, if you don't mind my asking?'

I told him, explaining about the pieces I had to do for America.

'Very interesting. Perhaps I can help in some way.'

I thanked him and he suddenly said:

'I tell you what. I'm driving out to a Burmese village tomorrow morning. Christian community. Methodists. Care to come? You might find it interesting. We're going to choose the hymns for Easter Sunday.'

'April the first, isn't it?' I said, but he had character enough to ignore the intended joke. 'Well, it's very kind of you. I'll see what it's like in the morning.'

'I can tell you what it'll be like in the morning. Pretty damned hot. Anyway come by all means if you feel like it. I'll come and look you up after breakfast.'

That night I lay awake listening to what must be the world's most grievous, dismal, haunting sound: the wailing of a pack of jackals. The sound is like that of a crowd of imprisoned human souls suffering all the tortures of the damned, wailing in un-appeasable misery, in the depths of hell.

The Padre called for me next morning, in his jeep, about ten o'clock.

'Oh! you've decided to come, have you? Good show. I think you'll find it interesting. They've some astonishing stories to tell, some of these Burmese. Pretty hair-raising too, a lot of them.'

We set off across the wide, empty, dusty, sun-scalded plain. A single-track railway, long since disused, went across it at one point, the red rusting rails ghostly in the burning sun.

I suppose we might have driven for an hour or so across the plain, on which a few white egrets looked like ghosts too, and then at length an oasis of palms, peepul trees, giant bamboos and palm-thatched huts appeared in the yellow glare ahead.

'This is our village,' the Padre said and a minute or two later we were mercifully enveloped in tree shade.

Almost at once there sprang out of the bamboos a shrieking chorus of children's voices, followed by the children themselves, their brown Asiatic faces grinning from ear to ear with explosive delight. How many of them clambered on to the jeep I simply couldn't count. Those who couldn't clamber dropped in the dust, then picked themselves up and, laughing hilariously at the enormity of the joke, ran on behind.

We finally drew up at a compound surrounded by low, palm-thatched houses having shaded verandahs decorated with a few pots of creepers and flowers. Children flopped on their bottoms in the dust as the jeep drew up sharply and the air was joyous with shrieking. This chorus of sound brought three or four Burmese women from one of the houses to shake hands, joyous themselves, with the Padre.

In turn he introduced me to the women, whose reaction was one of polite, sometimes smiling, but mostly grave shyness. Soon we were sitting on the verandah, there to be served with what was, in the rising heat of the morning, absolute nectar: long glasses of fresh lime juice, miraculously cold.

I had been happily sipping at this for perhaps five minutes when I became aware of a vision. A Burmese girl of extraordinary pale skin and very black hair and eyes, her oval face very grave, shy and statuesque, had suddenly glided silently from the house to be among us. She was wearing the simplest of white blouses and

a purple wrapover skirt. She looked every inch a dignified, beautiful, aristocratic goddess.

'This is Dorothy,' the Padre said. 'Dorothy is from the University of Rangoon, or rather she was. But she'll go back there one day, won't you, Dorothy?'

'I shall go back,' she said.

Something about the finality and certainty of these words, spoken in quiet perfect English, was very touching. I did not then know that she, together with the other women and many hundreds of other Burmese, had undergone a journey of sheer hell as they trekked north for hundreds of miles in their escape from Rangoon and the pursuing Japs; nor was there any way of guessing it from that grave and exquisite young face, marvellously full of repose.

Presently, as she refilled my glass with lime juice, the Padre said to me:

'I suppose you're not interested in jewels, are you? Almost all these villagers have stones to sell. Rubies, emeralds, amethysts, zircons, all sorts of things. Some are the genuine thing, some are what they call reconstituted, I think. You have to be careful. But if you'd care to see some Dorothy would take you to one of the houses where you'd get a fair deal.'

I confess I am not very interested in precious stones but out of politeness I said that I should like to see some. Dorothy at once put down the jug of lime juice.

'Very well, I will take you. The house is not far.'

Dorothy and I left the verandah and walked round the compound until we came at last to another house, lived in by a rather elderly Burmese couple, and went in. What struck me at once about the interior of this house was its air of intense, provincial, almost Victorian respectability. It reminded me of the half-sacred front-room parlours of my boyhood: neat antimacassars on chairs, useless trinkets, admonishing Christian texts on the walls, a portrait of the King and Queen of England.

Presently the two Burmese were showing us a few, very small precious stones: rubies, an emerald or two, some amethysts, some

sherry-gold zircons, laying them out on neat white cloths on little trays. I wasn't greatly impressed, or even greatly interested, and presently Dorothy, sensing this, began to make polite apologies for us, so that we might say goodbye.

Outside the house she gave me a quick, grave smile.

'I think the stones were not very good. You didn't want to buy?'

'No. I am sorry. I think they were not very good.'

'The pity is that so many bad ones are sold. The English boys buy them as souvenirs to take home without troubling even to find out if they are genuine or not. It gives us a bad name.'

'You haven't a bad name as far as I am concerned.'

'Thank you. That was very kind of you.'

We walked back to the house of Dorothy's sister. There we talked again, drank more lime juice, and the Padre discussed the hymns for Easter Sunday. My recollection is that I talked little but listened much. 'Little pigs have big ears,' I could hear my grandmother saying and certainly, on that hot April morning I sat listening very much as I used to sit listening on cool rainy days far back in England, in the tool-shed, the hay barn or under the cart-house, listening to my grandfather and his cronies talking politics, cursing governments, arguing, swapping stories, scandal and 'remembrance of things past'. Now, as then, I was the picker-up of unconsidered trifles, scraps of what may well have seemed to the Padre and Dorothy and the other Burmese trivialities of little or no importance but which I hid away, like precious stones themselves, in the recesses of my mind. I cannot now remember if I made any suggestions as to Easter hymns, but it is possible; my long arduous Sunday School training would certainly have stood me in good stead, since even today I can, if necessary, reel off the lines of countless hymns without ever a glance at a hymnal. But it was really not hymns that were in my mind that morning; it was largely the long trek of Burmese going northward from Rangoon and the grave dignified beauty, the courageous calm and the exquisite pallor of the young Dorothy's face.

Readers of *The Purple Plain* will not need to be told, I think, that the incidents recorded above are part of the early fabric of that novel: the drive across the scalding plain, the laughing Burmese children crowding on the jeep, the little Burmese house, the lime juice, Dorothy and her sister, the talk, the precious stones. They will know that in the book the Padre becomes a doctor, that my fuss-pot tent-sharer becomes Blore, that Dorothy becomes Anna, that my place is taken by Forrester, a shattered RAF pilot whose only wish is to die. The little ideas and pictures I gathered up that morning, the unconsidered trifles, were the genesis of the book.

But ideas alone, as I have frequently pointed out before, are of themselves not enough. The single idea that at first seems so good is more often than not sterile; it is a negative needing a positive to fire it into life – or, if you prefer it, an ovary needing to be fertilised before it can produce a living offspring. So, though the incidents and pictures of that morning were pictorially vivid and exciting enough, the truly vital part of it all, the positive agent of fertilisation, was still missing. Nor was I to find it, and then quite by accident, until I got back to the cooler, calmer pastures of England.

IX

I left Calcutta by flying boat, for England, a week later, on 8 April. It is, I think, important to record here what the feeling in both India and Burma was, at that time, about the future of the Burma campaign. It was a bog of pessimism, a hundred miles deep. Not a soul, I think, doubted that the war would last a good ten years longer. Worse than this, and the pessimism it engendered, was an evident sickness of morale. In the Mess tent at Monywa I had heard officers, to my incredulous astonishment, openly talking what I could only tell myself was pure sedition; they were luridly blasphemous about government, higher command, the long futility of the war itself, above all the fact that the people fighting that war seemed to have been brutally forgotten. They were probably saying no more than the German infantryman said in *All Quiet on the Western Front*, what Sassoon and Graves said in *Memoirs of an Infantry Officer* and *Goodbye to All That*, what Wilfred Owen exposed in his poems or what a million soldiers had said or thought in the holocausts of Passchendaele, Ypres, the Somme, Hill Sixty and Verdun, but its effect on me was nevertheless shattering.

This bitterness, the age-old bitterness of the deluded fighting man cursing war's futilities and politicians' duplicities, seemed finally to crystallise in my mind as the big Sunderland flying boat flew westwards over the Hooghli River and the great scarlet steel span of the Willingdon bridge and set course for Karachi over India's deserts, rivers and palms. It crystallised; and then I put it, like some evil thought by which I didn't want to be haunted, aside. Burma, in all its vividness never to be forgotten, suddenly seemed part of an unreal past. Now I was merely glad, indeed near-exultant, to be going home.

The old Sunderland flying boat was a huge comfortable vehicle and that morning there were men and officers of all ranks, many time-expired, on board. There were also wives and children, the children running noisily about the spacious cabin decks, shouting and playing games as in a nursery at home. Officers were segregated by rank, the top brass enjoying the most superior of the boat's comforts, the rank and file herded in the tail. Thanks to this arrangement I found myself sitting next to, and finally making friends with, a young army colonel, a campaign veteran of twenty-five with five years' service in the East, a good example of the swiftness that war offers in the field of promotion. I can best describe him, I think, as the utter antithesis of my tent-sharer at Monywa, the belly-aching fuss-pot, Blore. His character was writ large, the character of a man of action, of a good talker, a good soldier, a lover of life, a bender if not breaker of rules. I liked him very much and we spent a good deal of time together, both in the air and on the ground, on the long journey home. Five years' campaigning had caused him to collect a vast amount of gear, including an enormous amount of tobacco, of which more later. This accumulated tonnage of his made my own modest suitcase, bed-roll and huge stick of still green bananas seem pathetically small. (My younger children had never even seen a banana and I was carrying home that precious green loot – of exactly the same green as the flocks of small shy parrots that I describe in *The Purple Plain* – as something infinitely more precious than all the rubies in Burma.)

In Karachi swallows were nesting under the roofs of houses and even flying about the high open-eaved rooms of our hotel. The town was not unpleasant and the people, so far as one could gather in so short a time, seemed far removed from Bengal, that 'low-lying country occupied by a low-lying people'. It was another side of India I would much like to have seen more of, but *next* morning we were flying on to Bahrein, a narrow-gutted town of mean, narrow streets, much dust and wind, miserable-looking Arabs huddled in what seemed to be white winding sheets, and perfectly hideous food.

This, however, only prepared us the better for Cairo, to which we flew on next day, the flying boat splashing down in brilliant sunshine on the Nile in a great spume of spray among the white scimitar sails of a crowd of Arab dhows. Here again was Mr Groppi's renowned *confiserie*, an El Dorado of cakes, *pâtisseries*, and every kind of sweetmeat from chocolate beans to Turkish Delight. The girls behind the counters were, however, less sweet than the sweets and it wasn't until the colonel and I tried French on them that we got from them the glimmer of a smile. In the evening Cairo glowed in all its incredible brilliance, the chickens turned sizzling on their spits, and the wine glowed in our veins.

We flew on next day to the tip of Sicily, to Augusta, and another dose of contrasts. Unlike Cairo, Italy had not had a cosy war; and though Augusta's streets were brilliant with mimosa and many cherry-red geraniums the air seemed to me dark with blight. As we sat in a café drinking some impossible concoction or other I became aware of a low scurrying, as of mice, at the foot of the doorway. This, we discovered, was the work of three or four ragged Sicilian urchins, fishing for cigarette butts from the floor of the café, their rod and line being a length of wire twisted into a ring at one end, the ring finally hooking the cigarette end and dragging it under the door. The desperate poverty of all this was repeated in doorways and on doorsteps in the streets outside, where mothers were offering their own and their daughters' beds and bodies to all who cared to pay and pick. It was a moment of degradation that I found more sickening even than Calcutta's rancid iniquities.

Next day we flew into Poole Harbour on an afternoon of such exquisite warm brilliance that it might well have been that we had packaged the weather in Cairo and brought it home. An Egyptian on the plane, clearly all-prepared for England's notorious and traditional gloom and fog, simply sat staring in stunned disbelief at a sky that in its deep azure made even Cairo's look pallid by comparison. I confess I could hardly believe it myself and I underwent a small earthquake of emotion.

Continually, on that last section of the flight, my young colonel friend had held discourse on the delicate question of HM Customs and Excise and the equally delicate question of 'knowing the ropes'.

'It's a cinch, old boy. Leave it all to me. I've got the whole ruddy thing taped.'

'You've got rather a lot of tobacco, you said. What about that?'

'Piece o' cake. Nothing to it, old boy. Leave it to me. Had all the gen in a letter from a type who flew home a couple of weeks ago. Loaded with jewels, rugs, silks, tobacco and all the riches of Samarkand and all that and just sailed through like an innocent. Never touched him for a farthing. It's all a question, old boy, of knowing the ropes.'

We were eventually called to the customs' desks in order of rank, so that my colonel friend preceded me, going to a room upstairs. 'Back in a jiff, old boy,' he called and waved a cheery hand. The jiff became ten minutes, then twenty. At this stage I was called for customs' examination and duly declared various bits of silk and clothing and chocolate and sweets, but no tobacco. The duty turned out to be trivial and I was cleared in, I should say, five minutes. At the end of it I looked and waited, in vain, for my friend. His jiff became half an hour, then three quarters. Then slowly a shattered figure came downstairs, pale and haggard, all confidence drained away. Positively groping his way towards me across the customs' hall, he finally halted, shaking his head.

'Wanted thirty-five quid for the tobacco alone, old boy. Sixty-five for the lot. I just hadn't got it. Had to leave the whole bloody lot in bond.'

Fortunately he was able to drown his sorrows on the train. There, to our infinite astonishment, we found a Pullman car – the only Pullman car, as I understood it, still running in wartime England. Several times on the flying-boat journey my colonel friend had wagged his head sagely at me and declared that we were, in his opinion, a couple of ripe old bastards. Now it was obvious that we were a pair of kings, wining and dining at the Ritz. We luxuriated; the steward found us a bottle of wine and even, I think, some brandy.

Thus bathed in refreshment and contentment I gazed out on England, my beloved England. Never, I kept telling myself, had it looked so beautiful. Green meadows, woods rich with golden sallow and white with 'loveliest of trees, the cherry', gardens alight with daffodils and tulips and even, so early in the year, lilacs in pink and white blossom. This was my own, I kept telling myself, my native land, and unashamedly let my eyes fill with tears, so that the countryside slipping by the train windows in the golden glory of evening light became a trembling evanescence of green and blue and gold.

It was late when I arrived home in a night as balmy as in a perfect July. The air was sweet breath on my face, the garden full of scent. I gazed for a few moments on a luxuriant bed of polyanthus that seemed like the very epitome of all that was loveliest in an English spring, then gathered my suitcase, my bed-roll and my bananas from my car.

The kitchen door was unlocked. I dumped my stuff by the stove, then tiptoed upstairs and folded a wakeful Madge in my arms.

X

Old and worn though such clichés as 'living in a dream' and 'walking on air' undoubtedly are, there are times, I think, when even they are permissible. Certain it is that for the next few days, even the next few weeks, I felt myself to be living in a dream, walking on air. Both the dream and the air, of purest April Englishness, were as sweet as spring water after the drought of a desert. I couldn't drink enough of them.

The weather in that still taut-stretched brittle April of 1945 continued to be miraculous. Every day the temperatures, steadily in the eighties, were more like July than April. Dudley Barker, glad to see me back again, I think, and pleased enough with the pieces I had written, generously gave me leave and day after day Madge and I took the children to the sea. The sense of liberation was also miraculous; so that I couldn't have cared a tinker's cuss whether the war ended or not. Certainly, in Europe, it looked like ending, but such hopes had risen before, only for the resilience of the Germans to put us again in jeopardy.

But soon, on a day when the world was half-jubilant, half-ashamed, the first atomic bomb was dropped on Hiroshima and the apparently endless war in Burma was incredibly over, as the war in Europe already was. After that stupendous event a great sense of pointlessness prevailed; an occasional visit to Air Ministry induced nothing but boredom and irritating frustration. There was nothing to do. Nor, I found, could I work at home. Indeed I frequently feared, as writers often do, that I might never write any more, – that the spring waters of imagination had dried up and would never flow again. During the war I had in fact written precious little outside such writing as I had done for the RAF; indeed, all I had to show for the past five years, on my own account, was *The Modern Short Story*, a critical study of the genre and some of its exponents, a novella, the first I had written but by no means the last, called *The Bride Comes to Evensford*, a few reviews and *Fair Stood the Wind for France*: hardly a rich harvest, nor a great source of revenue until *Fair Stood the Wind for France* achieved its welcome success.

Then, towards the latter part of the summer, came my papers for demobilisation. On the appointed day I drove the car up to Air Ministry, there to discover, to my joy, that R. F. Delderfield, already bursting with the phenomenal success of *Worm's Eye View*, together with some others from PR, had forgathered for demobbing too. We all piled into my car and drove jubilantly to Uxbridge. Incredibly, when we reached the RAF Station there, I found myself in the very same room that had been my dormitory on my first day in uniform, a totally unexpected completion of the circle that immediately caused the comedian in me to jump out, as R. F. Delderfield has well described in his *Overture for Beginners*:

It had been a day for new beginnings, or so H. E. Bates declared as he pranced about the Demob Centre in his squadron-leader's uniform, topped by a loud coster-type civvy cap, and looking as incongruous as a pantomime comedian in Ascot rig. Bates and I had been two of the first PR men in the game, scoring heavily on the points system that controlled demobilisation. He was forty and I was thirty-three, with five and a half years' service, so we said our farewells and trundled down the spiral staircase to the lift, schoolboys on the last day of term.

The spiral staircase referred to was at Air Ministry, but before we reached that high point of our jubilations something of much greater significance had occurred. On the way to Uxbridge, before the fooling began, someone casually asked me if I had ever met a certain fighter pilot whose name I have long forgotten. I replied that I didn't think I ever had.

'Remarkable type. Had more gongs than anyone I ever knew. And got them all for trying to kill himself.'

I asked to be enlightened on this unusual situation and was told that the pilot had taken his bride, only a few hours after they were married, to a celebratory dance at a night club in Leicester Square. Suddenly, as they danced, a bomb scored a direct hit on the club, killing scores of people and also blowing the young bride out of the pilot's arms, killing her outright without injuring him. The grievous shock of all this was so great that when he went back to duty it was with the avowed intention of getting himself killed. Instead, by the bitterest of ironies, he merely succeeded in collecting a fabulous number of medals – and remained alive.

In a flash I realised that this was the positive I had been seeking for my Burma negative. This was the key that would wind up the spring that would set the mechanism ticking, so that Blore, the Padre, Dorothy, the Burmese girl killing the lizard, the laughing Burmese children and all the rest could come to life in new identity. My secret jubilation at this was infinitely greater than the jubilation at merely getting out of uniform, so that I could scarcely wait to get my hands on a white virgin ream of paper and begin to set down my version of the Burma scene:

> Shy flocks of small banana-green parrots had begun to come back to the peepul trees about the bombed pagoda. But across the rice-fields, scorched and barren now from the long dry season, only a few white egrets stepped daintily like ghostly cranes about the yellow dust in the heat haze. Nothing else moved across the great plain where for three years no rice had grown.

So for the next three months or more I was in imagination back in Burma, inventing, remembering, re-enacting scenes, incidents, people; nursing Forrester, the pilot, through his grief and cryptic bitterness, redepicting Dorothy as Anna, the salve to the pilot's unhealed wounds, the Padre as the doctor and my insufferable fuss-pot tent-sharer as Blore. Some of the white heat of Burma got into my blood as I wrote, so that the words came out as if driven by a blowtorch. The subsequent book trebled the success of *Fair Stood the Wind for France*, bringing me a vast new readership. It also became a film in which Gregory Peck was wholly admirable as Forrester ('Your damn book nearly killed me,' he told me, referring to his long foot-slog with his shot-down companions, Carrington and Blore, through Burma's pitiless heat;) with a young unknown Burmese girl from Rangoon playing Anna with all the beauty, restraint, withdrawal and gravity so necessary to the part.

Not that the book pleased everybody. Certain of my friends, whose critical acumen I highly esteem, made deep noises of disapproval. They referred me back to such books of mine as *The Poacher* and *The Fallow Land*. 'This,' they lectured me, 'is what we want from you. Not your hot, wretched Burma plain.' Useless for me to try to explain the powerful and almost catastrophic impact the East had had on my sensitivity; hopeless to try to convey the blistering effect of its fatalism, which Conrad had seen and interpreted so well, its callous contempt for life, expressed in the episode of the little girl and the lizard, or the blistering, pulverising heat; pointless to protest that this was an explosive revolution in my life that simply *had* to be set down, or that, God being my helper, I would surely return to depicting 'England's green and pleasant land', which assuredly, in due time, I did.

If I claim nothing else for myself as a writer I will not deny myself versatility. The same hand that writes *My Uncle Silas* also produces *Fair Stood the Wind for France*; the same imagination that produces the Chaucerian farces of the Larkin family is also responsible for the unremitting tragedy of *The Triple Echo*; the same brain that is responsible for *The Poacher* also produces the stories of Flying Officer X. No: if I claim nothing else for myself I will certainly claim that I am versatile.

So it was that within a year or so the hand that had written *The Poacher*, *Uncle Silas*, *The Bride Comes to Evensford*, *The Fallow Land* and the two books into which I have perhaps best distilled my love and feeling for the English countryside, *Through the Woods* and *Down the River*, turned its attention to a second novel of Burma, *The Jacaranda Tree*. This I approached with no little trepidation. For whereas I had seen the terrain and the people of *The Purple Plain* and had absorbed the electrifying atmosphere of central Burma through not only my eyes but the very pores of my skin, I had seen not one inch of the far distant territory over which the long and tragic trek to India had been made in bitter and horrifying circumstances when the Japanese had occupied Singapore and invaded Burma in 1942. I could only imagine what it could be like. But, I asked myself, was imagination enough? Could I possibly recreate the journey that had caused the planter in the Hendersons' flat in Calcutta such alcoholic remorse, and its terrain and atmosphere? I had asked myself very much the same question before writing *Fair Stood the Wind for France*. In that case too I had seen no more than a fraction of the terrain; I was largely unfamiliar with French provincial life even in peacetime let alone in that of war; all, or mostly all, had to be invented. Now I could only hope that, since the earlier novel had achieved the necessary authenticity, my imagination and instinct would again carry me towards the heart of the truth. The surrender of Singapore and the invasion of Burma by the Japanese were two inglorious moments in British imperial history, though certainly no more inglorious than the cataclysm that overtook America at Pearl Harbor, an event which, in my experience, few Americans to this very day care to discuss. Nor were they as great a humiliation as the fall of France in 1940; but let us say that they were in all conscience grim enough. Thus when I came to write *The Jacaranda Tree* I felt I could not, so to speak, overdo its agony. Through the experiences of Patterson, the planter, his boy Tuesday, and other characters, I told myself that, sparing nothing, I must recreate that agony. Again, to this end, as in *The Purple Plain*, I wrote in white-hot heat.

Some few years later I met a lady who asked me, quite simply: 'Were you on the retreat from Burma?'

'No,' I confessed, 'I was not.'

'But I feel you must have been.'

A great foreboding suddenly took hold of me. Had I painted the scene in *The Jacaranda Tree* well or falsely? Had I over-painted it or not?

'You mean,' I said, 'that I have –'

'My sister and I,' she said, 'were in that retreat. If you had exaggerated ten times over what you wrote you would still have been a hundred miles short of the truth. It was truly more ghastly than you could possibly imagine.'

When the book finally appeared it achieved an even greater sale than *The Purple Plain*, again greatly enlarging my readership. But again there were also dissentient voices from friends whose critical judgement I had learned to respect. Yet again it was useless to point out the compulsion of all the circumstances that lay behind the book – the East's unforgettable vividness of scene, the catastrophic nature of the retreat itself, the fatalism, the relentless heat, the provincial pettiness of colonial types such as the Portmans and the devotion to duty and causes as exemplified by Major Brain. Nor would it have profited me to point out that I was by no means the first European, whether writer or painter, to have been so fascinated and seduced by the East as to turn his back on Europe, if only temporarily. Maugham, the young doctor of *Liza of Lambeth*, had found himself under a comparable compulsion to write of Malaya; D. H. Lawrence, brought up on pit-baths in front of kitchen fires in Nottinghamshire, had found himself similarly compelled by Mexico; Gauguin, seemingly content enough to portray the lace-capped peasants of Pont Aven and surrounding Brittany, had suddenly abandoned it all to paint the languorous naked ladies so free with their charms far away in Tahiti.

Nor was it at any time my intention to make my severance with English ties anything but temporary. 'He's finished!' one of these friends cried as he wholeheartedly fell on the two Burma novels, little realising that in many ways the best in me was yet to be, as he himself later readily admitted. Apart from the fact that it was surely singularly unjust to judge a writer on two books alone it was also singularly silly, in my view, not to recognise that so great and explosive an experience as the East had afforded me could by no means be cast aside and forgotten as if it were some trivial summer tea party. The effect of my visit to India and Burma, brief though it may have been, had been almost to give me a disease. Its toxins had somehow to be got out of my system or paralyse me for ever, and writing about it all was, as I saw it, the only cure.

If I had ever felt any conscious compulsion to rehabilitate myself with these dissentient friends – and I certainly never did – I could have pointed to another war book of mine, *The Cruise of the Breadwinner*, which the critic James Agate was good enough, to my intense satisfaction, to compare with Conrad's *Typhoon*. This, the second novella I had attempted, was a sea story that I readily admit had drawn some of its inspiration from Stephen Crane's *Red Badge of Courage*, surely the prime example of the triumph of imagination over observation, for the simple reason that Crane hadn't even been born when the American Civil War of which he wrote with such cauterising brilliance and realism was being fought – a realism and brilliance that had caused ecstatic English critics to compare the young American with Zola and Tolstoy. Truly imagination had carried Crane nearer to the heart of truth than observation could ever have done.

The theme of my long-short story was not wholly dissimilar to his. Whereas his starry-eyed hero goes out, as so many before and after him have done, to seek the glory of war on battlefields, only to suffer the cruellest disillusionment, my similarly starry-eyed hero is a mere boy who goes out to sea in a rickety fishing boat, manned only by a fat skipper and a jaundiced engineer and armed only with an impossibly absurd Lewis gun, to seek his glory and to find his particular disillusionment in the lamplight of the little cabin of the vessel, in a darkening afternoon in the English Channel, as he watches two pilots, one English, one German, die together, indistinguishable in death as enemy or friend but merely representative 'of all the pilots, all the dead pilots, all over the world . . . And there rose up in him a grave exultation. He had been out with men to War and had seen the dead. He was alive and *The Breadwinner* had come home.'

The little story is certainly one of which I am not ashamed and perhaps this is as good a place as any in which to discourse briefly on the fascination the novella has long had for me. I was first drawn to it through Conrad, whose *Youth, Heart of Darkness* and other essays in the form are in classical mould. These had had the greatest possible effect on me in my youth. Later came Tolstoy, with the incomparable *Death of Ivan Ilyitch*, the grave beauty of *Family Happiness* and others. Side by side with them I read such pieces as Chekhov's *The Party*, Maupassant's *Boule de Suif* James Joyce's *The Dead* and later Hemingway's *The Snows of Kilimanjaro*, Sherwood Anderson's *The Triumph of the Egg* and Katherine Anne Porter's *Noon Wine*. These all caused me to reflect what a marvellous achievement it is to pack into a hundred pages what many another writer would spin out diffusely into five hundred and in doing so perhaps achieve an even greater and more memorable impact. To reach this difficult and desirable end requires, without doubt, great technical skill. 'The novella,' a critic wrote recently, 'is a form of notorious difficulty. It must combine the shock or finality of the short story with the psychological complication and density of medium available to the novel.' This is well said; but what is highly astonishing is not how few but how many writers of recent times have been eager to accept the challenge, to the singular enrichment of modern literature. Pushkin, Poe, Chekhov, Maupassant, Kipling, Maugham, Mann, Bunin, Crane, Wells, James, Sherwood Anderson, Knut Hamsen, Hemingway, Conrad, Thornton Wilder, Katherine Anne Porter, Graham Greene, D. H. Lawrence, Oscar Wilde, Joyce – the list of brilliant exponents in the form is as rich as it is seemingly endless.

I now resolved, therefore, to try to add to it myself. The challenge having been taken up I presently produced a volume of four novellas called *The Nature of Love*, only to be warned by my publishers that 'of course it won't sell. You must resign yourself to that.' In fact it did sell and indeed so well that I have ever since been more and more attracted to the form, so that I have now written some twenty novellas, the most recent being *The Triple Echo*, itself a supreme example of the form's 'notorious difficulty'.

The Triple Echo in fact took precisely twenty-five years to write, its genesis having begun in the darker days of the war, in 1943, its completion coming in 1968-shades of the path of art endlessly difficult', of which Edward Garnett had warned me long ago in his preface to *The Two Sisters*, I will not of course mislead the reader by pretending that every day of that twenty-five years was spent in wrestling with that one particular story; it is enough to say that the challenge, the problem and the complexity were always there, constantly kicking away at the womb of the mind, the story apparently unwilling to be born but ever restless in its tireless determination finally to come to life.

Any writer of fiction will tell you that inevitably, from time to time, he finds it necessary to invent a new character to do the work of unravelling his narrative for him. In the case of *The Triple Echo* the exact reverse was true. What had so long inhibited the birth of my story was not the lack of a character but the fact that, as I belatedly discovered, I had one character too many. This superfluous character having been removed, light instantly flooded in on to a canvas that had been so long irremediably dark, and in a mere three weeks the story was extracted from the womb it had apparently been so reluctant to leave. 'The path of art endlessly difficult' indeed.

In 1947, however, *The Triple Echo* was still in the womb and it looked as if nothing less than an operation would ever get it out. Instead of which another crisis in my life occurred.

In the early spring of that year, on a visit to my parents in Northamptonshire, I became aware of a curious lassitude. My arms and legs began to feel as if made of lead; I could scarcely drag myself about. For a time I put this down to the fact that my native town, Rushden, is a town of steep hills and that since I hadn't paid a visit to the town for a considerable time I wasn't at all used to them. But as we drove back to Kent in the car, with snow falling dismally on the Downs, I felt no better. If anything the heavy lassitude seemed worse. Nor did it improve matters to discover, next morning, that my youngest son looked all set for a bout of measles. We accordingly called in the doctor.

When he arrived, however, he scarcely looked at the boy. Instead he asked what was the matter with me, at the same time looking at me seriously and very searchingly. In reply I told him of my extreme lassitude; in fact he didn't need to be told. He had already guessed what was wrong. He murmured something about samples of this and that and that he would call to collect them later. Next morning he telephoned me with the news that he had spoken with a surgeon; the fact was that I had had an internal haemorrhage and the time had come 'to take that little look inside me'.

It was now Easter Sunday, exactly two years after my trip across the Burma plain with the Padre. I do not recall that the news that I was to have an operation, and with all speed at that, in any sense depressed me; I felt rather a sense of blessed relief, glad that at last there might be some chance of ridding myself of the gnawing abdominal pains, with their attendant grey ness of spirit, that had troubled me ever since my teens, I therefore surrendered willingly to hospital and the surgeon next day.

The operation having been completely successful I made the swiftest possible recovery and was home again within ten days. In less than another two weeks I was in Switzerland, convalescing, carrying with me words of great assurance from the surgeon. 'Diet? Fiddlesticks. You don't suppose I've taken away seven-eighths of your stomach so that you can spend the rest of your life on a diet, do you? No, I've done what I have done for precisely the opposite reason.'

From that moment my pains vanished; the greyness of spirit was dissipated; I was a new man.

XI

A great many first novels, as I have remarked before, are auto-biographical, if not wholly so then at least in part. My own first novel, *The Two Sisters*, was a marked exception. Not a single syllable of it is autobiographical; in no sense, physically, emo-tionally or otherwise, can the identity of any of its characters be confused with mine. It is a work, as I have also pointed out, of wild, youthful imagination: an imagination not knowing quite where it is going or what exactly it wants to say. If the result is therefore sometimes confused that is the inevitable fruit of inexperience; I felt much, imagined much but at the age of eighteen and nineteen, simply didn't know enough.

In 1950, however, at the age of forty-five, I at last began to turn my attention, for the first time, to a subject that was auto-biographical. It had been many years since I had seen the figure of a strikingly beautiful young girl in a black cloak lined with scarlet arrive at the station at Rushden in a smart pony-drawn gig in order to catch a train and almost as many since, on a freezing winter night, I had gone on an assignment as a young reporter to Rushden Hall, totally unaware at the time that I was sitting in the same room in which the poet Robert Herrick must have sat, three hundred years before, on his visits to the ever-hospitable Sir Lewis Pember-ton. The two incidents in fact provide another good example of a negative, in this case the unknown young girl, needing a positive, in this case the draughty Elizabethan Hall where I had sat as a nervous young reporter, in order to bring it to life.

Now, at long last, the fusion of these two episodes was complete and I began to feel life flowing from it strongly. The novel I had in mind was to reflect, in part at least, my own youth, its ecstasies and uncertainties, its impatient disposition to judge people (as I had judged my friend the Reverend Bernard Harris) by prejudice, before giving them a chance, its love and love's attendant agonies, its inevitable disillusionments and pain and its final awakening. The theme and spirit of *Love for Lydia* may perhaps be best expressed in a couple of lines taken from the book itself: 'it had not occurred to me that the pain of love might be part of its flowering . . . With inconceivable stupidity I had not given love to her simply out of fear of being hurt by its acceptance; I had not grasped that I might have made her suffer.'

I set this tortured piece of self-examination against my native Nene Valley, where I had skated in winter in meadows of frozen flood water, had wandered in spring and summer with my grandfather, seeing the April unfolding of blackthorn and

hawthorn and kingcup and cowslip, watching kingfishers swoop across the river and pike sunning themselves in smooth waters, and had later so often wandered alone, trying to escape the drabness of my native boot-and-shoe town, wrestling with ideas for my earliest stories, unable to share with another soul the problems they continually created. If certain of my friends had entertained grave doubts about me after *The Purple Plain* and *The Jacaranda Tree* they could certainly find no cause for complaint here; all the distilled essence of the countryside I had so loved as a boy went into *Love for Lydia*, together with the bloom of youth, with all its beauty and tender, tenuous fragility.

Not that the completed book was achieved without much heart-searching. A novel may be autobiographical, either wholly or in part, but this does not at all mean that its execution is merely a question of dipping into memory and fishing out a fact here, an episode there; the birth pains of imaginative creation have still to be endured, the path of art is still endlessly difficult.

Even at the risk of my seeming to be repetitious on the subject of art's difficulties I feel this may nevertheless be a good moment to point out one of the chief sources, indeed perhaps *the* chief source, of these difficulties. It is all too often forgotten, I feel, that all art is ultimately a physical act. Art does not consist of merely dreaming dreams, of hearing the music of the spheres or, as Ibsen was fond of repeating, 'wearing vine leaves in one's hair'. As with love itself the ultimate moment of art's expression is, and must be, physical. This is not merely 'a consummation devoutly to be wished' but one which must at all costs be accomplished. Until the writer puts his pen to paper, the artist his brush or pencil to canvas or paper, the sculptor his chisel to stone or wood, until the composer gives his musicians the opportunity of making music physically possible, there is nothing. This may sound a truism; but it does much to show, I think, that while artistic creation has its own special exhilarations it can also be, and very, very often is, both physically and mentally exhausting. A great amount of self-discipline is needed to accomplish these things and this too increases the tensions and problems constantly facing the artist. Altogether it is a highly complex business and one about which, I often feel, the public knows little or nothing. Perhaps only the artist, struggling to discipline himself, seeking his tortuous way through the maze of thought and imagination and finally arriving at his final moment of exhilarating but exhausting consummation, knows exactly what price art extracts from its executors.

If my world was now achieving ripeness in many directions, some of them totally unexpected, there were still parts of its territory where this had not proved possible. One of these was the theatre. It is true that my first published book was a play, although an extremely short one, in one act, to be followed within a short time by another in one act for radio. It is also true that, nursing fond ambitions, I had as a young man read almost as voraciously of drama as I had of the short story. Ibsen, Chekhov, Turgenev, Bjornsen, Pirandello, Shakespeare, the Elizabethans, Congreve, Sheridan, Shaw, Maugham, O'Neill, Coward, O'Casey: I had swallowed them all, and more, with the keenest appetite. I sought desperately to be a dramatist. On this score Edward Garnett, never forgetting his own disastrous crash with his play *The Breaking Point*, a disaster so remorselessly predicted by Conrad, was for ever trying to turn me away from this course, but I fear I hardly listened. In consequence I wrote other one-act plays, following them up with three-acters, of which I have, I suppose, written seven or eight. Some of these have been performed and are still being performed; the larger part, though attracting the interest and even enthusiasm of an impresario here, an actor-manager there, have not.

The first of these was a piece called *Carrie and Cleopatra*, which was put on, thanks to the tireless interest of that ever-present help in time of trouble, Violet Dean, at the Torch Theatre, one of London's many little theatres of that time, just before the war. Though giving good acting scope to several of the actors, it wasn't very well received. I was not unnaturally disappointed, though undeterred. The result was that on that first memorable assignment to the RAF Bomber Command Station at Oakington it was at first not in the form of short stories that I saw myself expressing the lives and actions of the young pilots there, but in a play. It so happened, however, that before the play could get itself down on paper Terence Rattigan turned up with *Flare Path*, the idea of which wasn't wholly dissimilar to the one I had in mind. I herefore put the idea of the play aside and concentrated, wisely I think, on the stories that were eventually to appear under the pseudonym of Flying Officer X. Not that the idea of the play was dead; on the contrary it continued to be agitated with life and finally became, later in the war, *The Day of Glory*.

Unhappily it proved impossible to produce it until the war was over, a fact that undoubtedly mitigated against any possible commercial success. By that time all fervour for the war had been dissipated and when at last *The Day of Glory* was produced at the Embassy Theatre one could only sense, on the first night, an atmosphere cold and disillusioned. Several parts in the play were also badly miscast, the result being that what I had wanted to say never got put over. The play fared far better on tour, under the auspices of the Arts Council, finding far better acting and far warmer audiences in the provinces than in London, where hard-bitten first night audiences often do as much to kill a play's chances of success as the hostility of critics. *The Day of Glory* is, however, still performed and has even achieved, in Holland, a state of some permanency as an annual event.

I followed this with a dark, Ibsen-like piece called *The Spider Love* (I culled the title from Donne's great lines 'But 0, self-traitor, I do bring / The spider love, which transubstantiates all, / And can convert manna to gall') but its demands on actors are incontestably formidable and it is probably for this reason that it has never been performed. Two other plays have shared the same fate, thus emphasising, if that were necessary, the theatre's eternal uncertainty. The pains and perils of this uncertainty have been well examined and described by my former RAF colleague R. F. Delderfield, who in spite of the phenomenal success of his *Worm's Eye View*, which ran for five and a half years in London, beating even the fantastic pre-war run of *Chu Chin Chow*, finally turned his back on the theatre through sheer disenchantment and settled for the less maddening demands of the novel. I can only say that I wholeheartedly share both his views and his disenchantment, so that I fear the Great Bates Play will not, now, ever be written. Nor will this state of affairs break my heart; the theatre is, I realise at last, not for me.

But in the early fifties I had suffered no such disenchantment with the novel. The considerable success of *Love for Lydia* had on the contrary given me fresh heart to set at least another novel in my native Northamptonshire, in whose soil, although I had by now lived in the idyllic pastures of Kent for exactly the same time as I had lived between the valleys of the Nene and the Ouse, my roots still lay deep.

It is a commonplace in art that writers and painters – painters perhaps the more frequently – are often so fascinated by a theme, a scene or a face that they are unable to resist the temptation to do another and even perhaps yet another and another version of it. This was something of the case with the novel I now planned. As a young man, still only in my twenties, I had written my second novel, *Catherine Foster*, very much under the influence of Flaubert. Its theme concerned a woman of passionate nature and imagination married to a small-town bore who could satisfy neither her passion nor her love of music and her appetite for a warmer, freer life. Like many women before her in similar circumstances she takes a lover, enjoys a spell of excruciating happiness and then eventually goes back 'into that obscurity from which she had once come'.

Since writing that book I had had many successes along with some dismal failures brought about largely by my own obtuse stupidities; of these I have written in *The Blossoming World*. But having learned much from these failures I felt I had now matured enough, both in character and technique, to attempt a bolder version of the earlier theme. *Catherine Foster* had been set in a quiet back street of the little Northamptonshire town of Higham Ferrers, which may fairly be called my spiritual birthplace, since most of the golden days of my childhood had been spent in and about it. The new novel, *The Sleepless Moon*, was to be *set* just round the corner from that quiet street, in the enchanting little chestnut-lined square which to this day is virtually unchanged from the time when I used to go with my grandfather in summer to gather loads of sweet honey pears from the walled garden of a grocer's shop standing in the corner of the square, by the gates of the church, Catherine Foster had been married to a corn merchant; Constance Turner was married to a grocer in the corner shop, 'After all there were no carriages for her wedding. The distance between the church porch and the house on the corner of the square was so short, everyone said, that it was not worth while.'

It was not only carriages, however, that were missing from Constance Turner's marriage; to her bitter surprise the very essence of it was also missing, the very fact of physical love and consummation. To so sensitive a creature such a discovery is little short of tragic; she is driven more and more into herself, imprisoned in solitariness, so that soon she is known as 'the untouchable Mrs T.' Not surprisingly she, too, out of sheer desperation, takes a lover and thereby enjoys a few months of secret idyllic passion. But if the lovers' clandestine meetings are idyllic they are also pierced with pain and the novel moves to its inevitably unhappy climax as surely as any Greek tragedy.

This tragedy of incompatibility is made the more excruciating, I feel, for being set against the calm and serenity of the little town, a town of provincial conventions and gossip, of small intrigues, of church-going on Sundays and fox-hunting in winter: a town in which to such a man as Melford Turner the death of his favourite horse is a greater source of grief than the apparent frigidity of a wife on whom his 'undemonstrative, customary, nightly salutation', a kiss on the forehead, 'a mere brush of dry lips,' has an effect 'as if a great draught of wintry air had solidified inside her, gripping her heart in a freezing neutral shroud.'

All this was far removed from the heat and horrors of *The Purple Plain* and *The Jacaranda Tree*; I was now securely back on my own territory and the result, I confess, did not displease me. It therefore came as a highly discomforting shock to learn that a friend whom I constantly treated as a confidant had reputedly called the novel 'a disgusting book'. This may appear as a criticism both trivial and ludicrous in our contemporary permissive age but at the time it was solemnly and seriously meant. In turn I took it with equal solemnity and seriousness. It was not so much that I was angered; I simply felt crushed by a profound depression; my renewed confidence in myself was suddenly and completely drained away.

When Edward Garnett had lambasted the liver and lights out of me for the *débâcle* I had committed in my early ill-fated novel

The Voyagers I had simply bounced back next day like a jack-in-the-box, eager to atone for my fatuous misdeeds. Not so with *The Sleepless Moon*; suddenly and quite illogically I was ashamed of the book. I deliberately refrained from reading any notices of it; in my heart I disowned it; and worse still I came to a stubborn and depressing decision: I would never, never write another novel.

I did not then know that David Garnett, an old friend for whose judgement I had the deepest respect, had called *The Sleepless Moon* 'a very great novel'; nor was I to know for some years later, when my vow never to write another novel had achieved an obstinate permanency. Perhaps if I had known of David's judgement at the time the course of my creative output, over the next few years, might have been charted very differently. But the fact is that I did not know and it was fortunate that my native buoyancy again came to my rescue. The immediate result of that depressive and ill-conceived judgement on *The Sleepless Moon* was in fact to drive me straight back into the arms of my first love, the short story, and at the same time to induce the novella more and more to share the bed with us. As a consequence I wrote much in both media. The discipline so necessary in the execution of the novella, the form of 'notorious difficulty', was not only highly challenging but highly exciting too. I have rarely enjoyed writing as much as I did in the next decade, when I produced half a dozen volumes of short stories and almost as many of novellas, among them such pieces as *Death of a Huntsman, An Aspidistra in Babylon, The Golden Oriole* and *Where the Cloud Breaks*, all of which I deem to belong to my best work. The judgement on *The Sleepless Moon* may perhaps be left, therefore, to the department of 'it's an ill wind'. Certainly, on reflection, I am not sorry to have been relieved, for a time at any rate, of the exhausting labours of giving birth to novels. I can only say that I greatly enjoyed, and learned much from, my repeated honeymoons with my first and second loves, the short story and the novella.

Moreover these numerous excursions into the shorter fictional forms merely served to prove, if proof were needed, the truth of William Gerhardi's assertion that 'fiction is the natural heir to poetry', a belief shared by Elizabeth Bowen when she claims that 'the short story is at an advantage over the novel and can claim nearer kinship to poetry, because it must be more concentrated, can be more visionary and is not weighted down (as the novel is bound to be) by facts, explanation, or analysis'. Commenting on this Lord David Cecil writes: 'she is right; just because it is as brief as a lyric poem its scope is wider; it can include the visionary and the fantastic as the novel cannot.'

In every sense, then, the aftermath of *The Sleepless Moon* was another phase in my ripening world. Inevitably it led to others, with some of which I shall now proceed to deal.

It is many years now since the short story writer A. E. Coppard first explained to me his contention that we short story writers could learn much from the cinema. I listened with fascination to his discourse on cuts, close-ups, fade-outs and brief swift shots and of how in this way a film was built up to achieve a sharp, pictorial impact. In the same way, Coppard contended, a story should be built up, achieving a comparable visual effect. 'I want to *see* it,' Coppard said. 'I must *see* it.' In other words the short story had to be pictorial rather than discursive or as Miss Bowen rightly says in the passage quoted above 'not weighted down (as the novel is bound to be) by facts, explanation, or analysis'. I was so impressed by the Coppard theory that I instantly resolved to make my writing more and more visual, painting the words rather than writing them, depicting scene and place and people vividly, in pictures, leaving out explanations, letting only essentials do the work. This I have done ever since, thus developing a quality that Edward Garnett had shrewdly detected in *The Two Sisters* – namely that 'the story is implied rather than chronicled'.

It is here worth pointing out that *The Sleepless Moon* is dedicated to David Lean, the film director, who had learned his craft in that graveyard of inessentials, the cutting room. It was not to David Lean, however, that I first owed my association with films, though he was later to buy the rights of several of my stories for that medium. I owed my introduction to films to an American director, Leslie Fenton. It is really wrong, however, to refer to Fenton as an American and I do so only because he had worked solely in America, as a director, for many years. He was in fact English, having steadfastly refused, like Chaplin, to give up his nationality. His devotion to and admiration for England were indeed great, so much so that as soon as the Second World War broke out Fenton immediately shipped himself to England and joined the Royal Navy. In due course he fought in that vicious engagement, the Battle of St Nazaire, where he was badly wounded and finally invalided out.

Even then he remained in London, eager to help England's cause if he could. It was there while contacting the Ministry of Information on some propaganda project or other that he came across the stories of Flying Officer X, for which he at once evinced an enormous admiration. As a result he made it his business to get to know me and then when we met declared, and in no uncertain terms, that the stories were not only admirable in themselves but that unquestionably they ought to be filmed. (That brilliant photographer, Robert Capa, who was later killed in Korea, had already made a similarly emphatic declaration about one of the stories that had come out of Oakington, *The Young Man from Kalgoorlie*, but nothing definite was ever done in that direction). Fenton was more practical. He proposed to make certain of the stories into films himself; if this came about would I write the scripts? I had never attempted a film script in my life and perhaps a little unwisely I said that I would.

One story that had much impressed Fenton was the very first I had ever written at Oakington, *It's Just the Way It Is*, in which the parents of a pilot who had been killed pay a visit to his wing commander, as was the habit of parents, half to satisfy themselves that their son is really dead, half in the touching hope that he may still be alive after all. It was this story that Fenton wanted to film and I not only duly wrote the script for it but even took part in the picture, making my one and only appearance as a film actor in the guise of a dead navigator being carried on a stretcher from a shot-up bomber.

It was during this brief collaboration on the little film that Fenton suggested I must meet Sir Alexander Korda. I knew that Korda and my agent, Laurence Pollinger, had often been in association, and I readily agreed. Accordingly Fenton and I went along one afternoon to Korda's office in Piccadilly, Fenton having explained that Korda was building up a strong pool of writers for a new programme of films and that it was not improbable that he might ask me to be one of them.

But if I had any fond idea that Korda would immediately broach the subject of films and writing for them I was to be swiftly disillusioned. I found Korda a shrewd, cultivated, clever and amusing man and it was utterly in character that afternoon that instead of getting down to the practical business of talking films he immediately launched out on a discourse, hilarious as any Chaplin film, on the subject of farting.

'Ah! you know, Bates,' he said in the strong Hungarian accent he never lost and indeed probably carefully cultivated, 'I adore ze fart. I absolutely adore ze fart. Ze fart is *marvellous*. You know, Bates, what they call it in France? No? *Le piano du pauvre homme.* The poor man's piano. *Marvellous.*'

The eventual result of that inconsequential afternoon was that

Korda put me under contract to him at a salary that looked phenomenal enough on paper until you woke up to the stark fact that, thanks to tax, all you got out of every pound was sixpence. There are, however, other desirable dividends in life rather than money and in this case I eagerly reached out simply in order to profit from a new experience. But one other desirable dividend that in due course presented itself was that I was able to meet, through Korda, David Lean.

David as a film director is dedicated to the proposition, as I also am as a writer, that it is the business of the artist to entertain, not to instruct, to give pleasure, not to preach morals. To this end he was extracting, or was about to extract, every ounce of entertainment from *Oliver Twist* and *Great Expectations*, as he was later to extract even more of it from *The Bridge on the River Kwai* and *Doctor Zhivago*.

David is an intense and dedicated man and we instantly got on well together. He was quick to confess much admiration not only for some of my novels and longer stories such as *Fair Stood the Wind for France*, *The Cruise of the Breadwinner* and *The Purple Plain*, but also for many of the very short ones, the little pictorial sketches in which all is 'implied rather than chronicled', in which there is no time for 'facts, explanation and analysis'. I in turn admired his own methods, a supreme example of which is the dramatic and terrifying cut to the face of the convict in the graveyard in *Great Expectations*, a stroke of arresting shock which tells more in a split second than many a novelist, ambling discursively along, could tell in a page.

Soon David was extending his enthusiasm into more practical form by buying the film rights of *Fair Stood the Wind for France*, *The Cruise of the Breadwinner* and *The Purple Plain*, only one of which, *The Purple Plain*, has ever reached the screen. This fact has never mattered to me; the experience of the association with David was rich enough in itself and the more I saw of him and his methods the more sure I was that Goppard, in his contention that the story writer could learn much from the cinema, was right. This contention obliquely gets the blessing of Lord David Cecil, who in an introduction to a recent anthology of modern short stories has written:

> The 'plot' form is a limited form and one which excludes the work of some of the greatest masters of the *genre*, from Chekhov downwards. Anyway, partly under Chekhov's influence and partly from a general loosening up of fictional form, the old convention gradually lost its grip; and by the turn of the century the short-story writer was free to shape his inspiration into what form he pleased. This is why the twentieth century is the great period for the English short story.

Exactly; nor do I think I am exaggerating when I maintain that the cinema has had some part in the evolution of that greatness.

One day, when David and I were having preparatory discussions as to what sort of boat the *Breadwinner* should be when it came to making the film, he suddenly seemed to go off into a daydream. When he finally emerged from it he surprised me by asking:

'Have you ever been to Tahiti?'

I confessed I never had.

'Would you like to go?'

I replied that I had always wanted to go to Tahiti. The association with Gauguin and his friends had always fascinated me.

'But why,' I said, 'are you asking me?'

In reply he went on to say that an actor friend of his had just come back from the Friendly Islands, bringing with him some excellent photographs, not only of Tahiti itself but more particularly of the island of Moorea, which lies some eighteen or twenty miles away. The photographs, when produced, showed Moorea to be an island looking very much like a piece of the Dolomites turned tropical. It also looked simple, remote and romantic, with palms restful on the shores of a placid lagoon, palm-thatched huts, high tranquil white clouds.

David asked if I didn't think it looked fascinating and I replied that there was no doubt it did.

'Would you like to go?' he said. 'You caught the atmosphere of Burma so well that I thought you might capture something of the Pacific too. I thought if you could wander around and pick up an idea for a story I'd like to make a film of it. What do you say?'

I decided it was an opportunity too good to miss. I agreed to go. This was simple enough; the problem was to know how to get there. It turned out that a boat from Marseilles took a month, a proposition which had no appeal for either Madge or me. The only possible way was by air and this, since the jet age had not begun, meant a series of long hops via New York, San Francisco, Honolulu, Fiji, Samoa, the Cook Islands and then Tahiti – Tahiti being the end of the line, with no communication with the west coast of South America.

The prospect seemed not only inviting but positively exciting and Madge and I immediately began to make preparations to go.

'It looks,' I said to David, as we pored over the photographs again, 'like a proper Lotus Land.' Perhaps I was thinking at that moment of Pierre Loti, the nineteenth century French writer who, like Gauguin, had fallen deeply under the spell of Polynesia. Then, recalling the painful surprise India had had in store for me I said on reflection: 'Well, we shall see.'

Lotus Land? Yes. It all depended, of course, on what you meant by Lotus Land.

Westward from New York to San Francisco, that pleasantest of cities washed by the cold waters of the North Pacific; then a long,

long haul to Honolulu, with a brief call in the middle of the night at Canton Island, an Anglo-US condominium with a signpost in the middle of its white barren expanse of rock and sand proclaiming that everywhere in the world was, as I remember it, 12,000 miles away – a proclamation that induced a lowering of the spirits and a chilling sense of isolation; then eventually to Honolulu, to drive from the airport to the hotel through avenues of little stalls selling *leis* made of flowers in every conceivable brilliance of colour, and seeing on the streets girls of such beauty, many of them a cross between Chinese and Polynesian, that they are surely the prettiest in the world, and then out on the ocean itself a great white spouting of whales; and then presently on to Fiji, with Suva, the capital, full of the scent of frangipani and as hotly steaming as Calcutta itself; and then on to Samoa.

'This,' I had said to Madge as we flew on over bluer and bluer waters, 'is the way to travel. Nothing like a flying boat. Especially the landing. You'll love the landing.'

I began to regret the words as we started to lose height over Samoa and below us the formerly bluest of seas suddenly became an ugly, sinister charge of white horses. A few minutes later we were landing on a sea like a maelstrom, in a twenty-five mile an hour crosswind, very close to peril.

'Landing?' Madge said. 'I'm glad you said landing. Oh! yes, I loved the landing.'

'Any landing,' I reminded her, 'is a good landing.'

Rain fell in warm, steaming torrents. A number of pregnant Polynesian women moaned with fright as the launch took us precariously from flying boat to anchorage and then continued to sit huddled in fear as the bus drove us on our long journey across the flooded island.

But even under rain Samoa looked incomparably beautiful. It is an island of great lushness, of wooded mountains and ravines, of many churches of all sizes and denominations (the work of the London Missionary Society), of delightful village greens, all looking as smooth-shaven and green as any in England, all deliciously embroidered with many flowers, all surrounded by big palm-thatched houses looking like circular seaside bandstands. On one of these greens numbers of small boys were playing cricket, totally oblivious of the torrential rain, using the central rib of a big palm frond as a bat. On another a pretty Samoan girl stood laughingly washing her naked breasts, 'the colour of dark honey', in the rain. All along the seacoast, a short distance from the shore and joined to it by wooden gangways, stood little huts, on the purpose of which I pondered in vain until suddenly I saw the door of one of them open, to reveal a Samoan woman placidly sitting there on the loo, a sight that woke even the fear-struck pregnant women to laughter.

Apia, above which stands Vailima, the former home of Robert Louis Stevenson, looked utterly dismal under the rain, its harbour showing here and there the gaunt bones of wrecks, its waters half-grey, half-red from soil washed down from the mountains. The

493

waterfront itself looked like something out of Somerset Maugham – indeed it was the perfect setting for his story *Rain* – or Conrad: seedy, shabby, the twilit back-end-of-nowhere, inspiring thoughts of beachcombers getting drunk in bars, except that, as we presently discovered as we wound up at our so-called hotel, there was nothing to get drunk on.

My forethought in buying a few miniature bottles of gin on the flying boat helped us through an evening dismal with rain, black hordes of flies on the dinner table and some of the most appalling food I have ever been faced with. All night the rain pelted down and we could only pray it would stop by morning.

It did not stop. At breakfast we knew that, with the wind still raging, we were imprisoned for another day. What on earth could we do with ourselves? The answer came from a pleasant Liberian girl working on the island as a schoolteacher. Perhaps we might care to see the school? She assured us it would be interesting.

More in desperation than anything else we accepted her invitation. At the school a big class of small Samoan children sang lustily for us, the chief items of their repertoire being, as I remember it, 'Rule Britannia' and 'London Bridge is Falling Down'. After this we were invited to the staff mid-morning coffee, during which someone inquired if I too was teaching. When I said 'No, writing,' an essay in detective work began. A few moments later someone deduced that I was the author of *The Purple Plain* and a rumble of curiosity reverberated through the teaching staff. This led to the imperative suggestion that we must of course meet the High Commissioner. A meeting must be arranged forthwith.

That evening we sat in the drawing-room at Vailima, the long white timber house standing on the hills above Apia, then the residence of the High Commissioner, formerly the home of R. L. S., the decaying centre of the strangest of *ménages*, where he lived for the last four years of his life. As we sat there talking with the Commissioner and his wife, two very pleasant people, rain still fell torrentially outside and the air, as in one of Stevenson's own stories, 'smelt strong of wild lime and vanilla'. Throughout the damp, hot evening, in a temperature of ninety degrees or so,

Robert
Louis Stevenson

the scene was dominated by a portrait of the brooding, sickly, Gauguin-like figure of Stevenson himself, hypnotic, compelling, uncomfortable and by no means unsinister as it stared down from the wall: yet another example of the European artist from the cool north who had found it impossible to resist the enchantments of tropical lands and southern seas.

After another day of black hordes of flies and hopelessly bad food – the only other hotel on the waterfront was reputedly nothing but a whorehouse – we flew off at last on the brightest of mornings to the Gook Islands, where big handsome Polynesian girls with long blue-black hair swam in the crystal waters of the calmest of lagoons at Atutaki, or lazed on the brilliant, almost snow-white coral sand.

The fortnightly arrival of the flying boat at Papeete was evidently always an excuse for a near festival: crowds of gay Polynesian girls on the waterfront wearing purple and pink and white and scarlet *leis*, more *leis* for incoming travellers, a general air of care-free excitement. (I use the word carefree advisedly but will qualify it presently.) A good proportion of the girls, I was assured, were waiting for someone to sleep with, regardless of whatever price they might subsequently have to pay. The girls of Tahiti are in fact very free with their favours, to which may be added that they see no stigma of any kind in having children out of wedlock, indeed rather the reverse, since they are very fond of children and also because unions between Polynesian and Polynesian tend to be unfruitful, whereas the Polynesian female tends to become extremely fertile when mated to French, English, American, New Zealand or Australian men or almost any male except their own. The Friendly Islands would seem, indeed, to be aptly named.

Papeete itself turned out to be a scruffy little port, again half like something out of Maugham or Conrad, half like a French provincial town hopelessly gone to seed. Its shops were mostly Chinese; its bars seemed little more than brothels. Its shabby, seedy air was however greatly heightened by many flowers, most exquisite among them that loveliest of vines, the allamanda, whose butter-pure trumpets trailed with prodigal splendour everywhere. On everything there lay a great air of lassitude, of *mañana*, a feeling of 'why today? – tomorrow will do?, so that it took almost all morning to cash a cheque at the old-fashioned French-like bank.

Towards the end of the nineteenth century a great influx of indentured labour, mostly Indian and Chinese, flooded into the Pacific, with remarkable results to be seen everywhere today. In Fiji, for example, Indians already strongly outnumber Fijians. The Melanesians, physically strong and powerful as they are, have been overtaken by Indians with their renowned merchant skills and a religion which continuously teaches and preaches fertility. These Indians today are a magnificent, prosperous people beside whom Calcutta's pavement-dossing hordes look like scum and even many Fijians look sad and heavy with the indolence which has let them become outnumbered. In Tahiti it is the Chinese who have been notably industrious, so that they are now the shop-keepers, the fishermen, the landowners, the market-gardeners.

Hardworking, skilful, thrifty, they leave the Polynesians as far behind as the Indians have left the Melanesians.

The Polynesians are, in fact, a dying race. Their tendency not to reproduce among themselves is naturally largely responsible for this, but with this goes the sad fact that unions between Polynesian women and outsiders are not only highly fruitful but also productive of children who are very often mentally brilliant. This in turn is another melancholy source of frustration, since the outlook for such brilliance in Papeete is highly limited and the Sorbonne is far, far away. A schoolmaster sadly gave us an example of this, swearing that in a school painting competition ninety per cent of the winning entries, all brilliant, came from descendants of Gauguin.

But if Papeete was shabby, seedy, sad and sunk in apathy, the Pacific was certainly not. It is an Everest among oceans: vast, haunting, restless, dominating. Few areas of the world can give off such a powerful impression of being, in the strangest way, the surviving fragment of a mysterious and long-lost world. Over it broods not only that peculiar fatalistic air of coiled-up violence that is an inevitable part of all tropical atmosphere, but a high-charged feeling that at any moment a vast electric spark may leap across it and set its slumbering dramas burning and quivering. You get the same feeling when a shark explodes from the water, a dramatic slash of sinister power, a feeling that anything may happen here.

Soon, in Papeete, we found ourselves in close friendship with a congenial American doctor. We had in fact met him earlier on the flying boat, where he had asked me to look after a wooden box for him. He said something about 'precious cargo' and when I inquired what this might be, replied 'Mosquitoes'. They were in fact a particular brand of giant mosquito apparently having the ability, like fleas on the backs of lesser fleas and so *ad infinitum*, to prey on lesser mosquitoes. The American in fact was engaged in research into the disease filariasis, formerly better known as elephantiasis. Filariasis is perhaps the least aesthetic of many unaesthetic tropical diseases, turning the limbs, even of young girls, into hideous elephantine lumps of swollen flesh that are distressing to behold. The disease is carried by mosquitoes, in a cycle as simple as it is sinister. It begins with a coconut falling from a tree. It continues with a rat gnawing a hole in the coconut, then with rain, which falls with fair frequency in Tahiti, filling up the coconut. In the stagnant rainwater mosquitoes breed, subsequently flying off to bite first of all some sufferer from filariasis and then someone who hasn't got filariasis but soon will have. The lymphatic glands having thus been impregnated, the cycle is all ready to begin again via coconut, rat, rain and all.

It was the American doctor's hope that the resident mosquito population might be much reduced, if not wiped out, by his imported giants. In due course he took us along to his research laboratory to see his mosquito menagerie and then to hospital to see some of the mosquito's distressful victims. He had, however, other weapons in his armoury besides the imported giants. These were largely pills and one afternoon he invited me to tour some parts of the island with him, so that I could see for myself another side of his work.

'But not Madge,' he said.

'No? Why not?'

'I don't think this,' he said, 'is for Madge.'

We motored along the black-sanded shore – the beaches in Tahiti are all of black sand, looking very much like a foundry yard – past the sinister fallen coconuts, past the house reputed to have been lived in by Gauguin, past other houses at which the doctor honked on the car horn in order to give a passing signal to a friend ('No reply. Ah! it's three o'clock. Guess he's in bed with his *vahini*'), until at last we reached a little bay. Some distance inland was a small market-garden growing lettuces, radishes, carrots, watercress and so on. In a wretched hovel, which stank like the sewer it probably was, a Chinaman and his wife were packing and washing vegetables. The Chinaman's method was to wash his feet and the vegetables in the same water, at the same time. The air was odious with stench; and I now understood why this was not for Madge.

Presently the doctor was speaking to the Chinaman. The Chinaman made gestures of innocent protest. The doctor spoke again. The Chinaman pointed towards the sea.

'What,' I said, 'is it all about?'

'The taking of pills. The artful bastards know a thousand and one tricks to make you believe they've taken them when they never have. They hold them under the tongue, in the cheek, anything. This one hasn't taken his because he's going fishing tonight and he says the pills will make him sick and he'll fall overboard. His wife hasn't taken hers because apparently the stars are not right.' 'Pure superstition.'

'Superstition, pure or otherwise, we have always with us.'

The Chinaman paddled his filthy legs and feet in water containing watercress. I retched and was nearly sick.

'The Lotus Land,' I said.

'What was that? What did you say?'

'Nothing much. I was merely thinking,' I said, 'of the Lotus Land.'

XII

The casual nature of life in Tahiti was well illustrated a few days later when we were suddenly told by a man who kept one of the town's better bars:

'Oh! by the way, the Larsens are expecting you for the week-end.'

'The Larsens? Who are the Larsens?'

'American couple. They live on Moorea. Dying to meet you.'

I inquired as to how we got to Moorea.

'Schooner. Goes every morning at 9.30. You're expected Saturday. Be down on the waterfront soon after nine.'

On Saturday morning we duly arrived on the waterfront soon after nine. The front was crowded with the usual throng of Tahitians madly doing nothing but there was, as far as I could see, nothing in sight that could be called a schooner. We idled about for half an hour or so, I with growing impatience, until suddenly Madge drew my attention to what seemed to be a large white ramshackle barrel sawn in half and moored to the quayside. This was being loaded with cargo, bicycles, casks of wine, people and even a horse, the animal being eventually strapped to the side of the deck. This, it turned out, was our schooner.

We went aboard. Several women passengers, as if in anticipation of terrors to come, appeared already to have given up the ghost and lay immobile on deck or on seats with their heads completely covered with shawls. The horse didn't look particularly tranquil either. Of captain and crew there was no sign but more and more cargo, people, wine and bicycles kept coming aboard.

Ten o'clock came and went but still no crew. By this time the morning was already hotting up and the air was thick and sickening with the smell of engine oil. There is invariably a vast swell on the surface of the Pacific and I began to suffer inwardly for Madge, who isn't the best of sailors. Now and then one of the prostrate covered women would give a stifled groan and the horse, growing more restless, would nervously stamp its hooves on the deck.

When eleven o'clock came I was in a mood to disembark and find ourselves a long cool drink somewhere. At this moment a huge, tipsy-looking Tahitian with one eye stumbled aboard, followed by two disreputable characters in no better state, each carrying a bottle of wine. This, I judged, was our captain and crew and my sympathies were now firmly with the moaning, covered women.

Presently one of the crew opened up a hatchway and disappeared into a black hole below decks. The captain took the wheel in one hand and an uncorked bottle of wine in the other and after a sudden shattering explosion from the black hole below decks we were ready to sail into the hot, blinding white light of the great open Pacific. With a certain trepidation I then remembered that although the journey was a mere eighteen miles or so in distance it was to take four hours or more in time.

The swell on the ocean was vast. The barrel perilously rolled, pitched and ducked. Except for an occasional groan or two the covered women might have been dead. The only persons unperturbed were the captain and crew, who swigged with relish and regularity at the wine bottles, at the same time breaking into loud vinous laughter. This gave One-eye an incongruously leering look, as if he were positively enjoying the tribulations of his wretched passengers. By this time we could see Moorea, jagged against the skyline, and the schooner seemed more than ever like a lump of white, drifting flotsam as it pitched and rolled towards the wall of dark rocks.

About this time I discovered that someone had left a Paris newspaper – which one I now forget – on one of the deck seats. Ever anxious to improve my halting French I seized upon it eagerly and spent the next half hour or so reading columns of those fascinating advertisements, always more beguiling in French than in English, in which lonely persons of both sexes proffer their charms and statistics in a yearning search for a mate. By now most of the women were not dead but horrifically and loudly seasick and I have never been so glad of a newspaper in my life.

Soon, to my undisguised relief, I heard the engine cut out and I looked up to realise that we were drifting in towards an anchorage under the high, palm-clad rocks. When we were finally tied up by a jetty there was an eager rush of passengers to lay hands on great frosty chunks of pink and amber watermelon being sold on the quay. While these were being consumed there was a vigorous unloading of cargo and wine-barrels.

We, having no local currency, were unable to buy any watermelon, but presently one of the crew leapt ashore and came back with two delicious amber hunks, into which we buried our faces eagerly, at the same time staring into the depths of crystal-bright water at vast and brilliant shoals of tropical fish in every sort of colour from dazzling electric blue to vivid yellow, an astonishing fishy kaleidoscope flashing this way and that with ordered speed, the whole thing looking as if freshly painted.

This was the first of three stops at similar anchorages along the coastline and at each of them the pattern of watermelon, rolling wine barrels and the kaleidoscope of fish was repeated. We came at last to the entrance to a big lagoon with the inevitable coral reef guarding the entrance and offering a barrier to the Pacific, whose gigantic waves charged it constantly like a massed attack of mad, white-maned fighting horses. There is something fearful about this savage and primeval conflict between ocean wave and coral reef and I never watched it without a certain chill of fright.

After the lash and roar of this ocean conflict the inner reaches of the lagoon were almost deathly quiet. We glided smoothly along between walls of palm and hibiscus and allamanda and frangipani, drifting quietly for perhaps two miles, perhaps more, until we could see at last the head of the lagoon, with houses, a cluster of fishing boats and another anchorage.

As we pulled into this we saw, among the little crowd gathered on the jetty, a middle-aged man and woman waving enthusiastically. Anticipating that these were the Larsens we waved back.

They were indeed the Larsens and soon, on shore, we were being welcomed like long-lost relations, returning prodigals or bosom friends. It was not until some long time later that we learned that the Larsens had not the remotest clue as to our identity. They didn't even know our names. They had simply invited us out of an eager hunger for contact with someone from the world beyond the boundaries of the Lotus Land.

Moorea is one of the most beautiful islands in the world; few places can lay a firmer claim to the word paradise. Not only is this pictorially so but the Larsens, on their estate of 4000 acres, were self-sufficient in everything but wine. From oranges to coffee, bananas to fresh-water shrimps, beef to vanilla, chickens to lemons, timber to fish: theirs could truly be called a land flowing with milk and honey.

Their house was roomy but unpretentious, set in a rambling garden of palms, tree ferns, bananas, hibiscus, frangipani and ginger lilies. We ourselves were assigned to a big bare wooden hut that Madge insists was more like an isolation hospital than a house. My own recollection is that it was hot and uncomfortable and that the constant crowing of jungle cocks kept us awake half the night.

In the morning we breakfasted on coffee so exquisite of flavour and aroma that I was inspired to a chorus of praise for it, even going so far as to say that I felt I was really drinking coffee for the first time in my life. It was purest nectar. The Larsens explained its secret: it came, first of all, from the estate; not a single bean, in the second place, was roasted or ground until it was seven years old – coffee beans apparently having the virtue, like wine or sardines, of improving with age; and last, only the essential quantity needed for each day was roasted and ground at any one time. Certainly, neither before nor since, have I tasted coffee of such ethereal quality.

After breakfast we wandered about the estate. Much of it was hilly, all of it lush. 'The air,' as Stevenson had once written, 'smelt strong of wild lime and vanilla'. This was scarcely surprising, since vanilla, which is an orchid, (*Vanilla planifolia*), was growing everywhere: soft cream lady-slipper flowers of great delicacy giving off their slightly heady scent. During the war synthetic vanilla had largely replaced natural vanilla until it was discovered that the synthetic product might be a possible cause of cancer; as a result natural vanilla was again in demand and that morning on the hillside among giant banana trees petite Chinese women were hand-fertilising vanilla flowers, which are self-sterile, doing the required work with a matchstick, their delicate fingers so swift that they could fertilise a possible two thousand flowers a day. The resulting vanilla pod takes about six months to mature and then resembles a tobacco-brown bean which, incidentally, may be usefully kept with your coffee beans to give them a subtle aromatic flavour.

As we watched the Chinese women deftly engaged among the vanilla flowers it suddenly began to rain torrentially. The air steamed; it was as if we were in a warm sticky bath as we ran for shelter in a little wooden hut. The rain ceased as swiftly as it had begun, leaving the jungle of vines and palms and bananas and tree ferns and bamboo dripping and sparkling. As we walked back down the hillside we stopped to pick oranges from a tree, and to the air that 'smelt strong of wild lime and vanilla' was suddenly added the rich fragrance of the oil of orange peel.

Next morning we walked in an opposite direction, along the shores of the lagoon, on a dry stony track that wound through high palms. We had scarcely started when once again it began to rain torrentially. This time there was no hut in which to shelter and we were obliged to walk on, again as in a warm sticky bath, until we were soaked to the skin. There was nothing to worry about in this. We simply walked on until the rain abruptly stopped and the sun came out, immediately hot and sparkling, the palm fronds dripping a great spattering cascade of silver raindrops. Then we found a stretch of sand on the lagoon shore, in full sun, and there took off our clothes and hung them to dry on a bush while we lay naked in the sun and rolled in the tepid shallow water. This, for an hour or so, was truly the Lotus Land.

The strong attraction which islands have for man is one I find of endless fascination. Men long to possess islands as they long to possess lovers. There are never enough islands, it would seem, to satisfy man's great island appetite. Yet John dos Passos, the American novelist, hit on a singular truth when he described Madeira, his birthplace, as 'very lovely but a prison, a beautiful prison'. What is true of Madeira is even more true of Tahiti and Moorea and as many islands of the Pacific as you care to name. What attracted Stevenson and Loti and Gauguin and his several friends to them? No doubt a means of escape from something – but an escape to what? Dos Passos, it seems to me, had the answer – nothing more than an escape to prison.

The Larsens were another illustration of this. Their beautiful paradise, rich, lush, peaceful, self-sufficient, its infinite natural beauties amazingly and dramatically enhanced every evening by what must be the most spectacular sunsets in the world – it is exactly as if the lid of a giant cauldron is suddenly lifted across the ocean, filling the sky with flame, orange, scarlet, yellow, rose and richest purple until the eyes themselves almost burn too as they try to absorb its powerful intensity – was really a prison which caused one to recall another truth, namely that of Sir John Suckling, who reminded us long ago that 'stone walls do not a prison make, nor iron bars a cage'. No: the paradise of a Lotus lagoon deep in the Pacific can create prison just as successfully – so that when I think of the Larsens it is not so much with a memory of their exquisite coffee, the delicious flavour of fresh-water shrimps or the air strong with 'wild lime and vanilla', as with a picture of them, in the days before flying boats revolutionised communications, sitting down at breakfast every morning and going through the solemn ritual of opening a newspaper that the monthly boat from Marseilles had brought. That the paper was a month old was of no importance. It was an infinitely precious link from prison to the outside world.

Before we left Moorea one other thing seemed to me to symbolise the illusion that here was paradise. We were again walking along the shore of the lagoon when we came upon a tree, a species of hibiscus. This is not the hibiscus which provides the glorious saucers of pink and scarlet and yellow that Polynesian girls wear in their hair but an altogether taller tree whose bark provides the material from which so-called grass skirts are made. An interesting characteristic of this hibiscus is that its flowers, more like bells than saucers, begin the day by being white, then turn creamy-yellow by noon and then a sort of cloudy crimson by sunset, when they at last fall off, their brief daily cycle of blossoming finished. Beautiful and ephemeral, that tree has ever since seemed to me to symbolise the Polynesian malaise.

The weekend being over, we took the schooner back to Papeete and then, a week later, left Papeete too. I wasn't sad to leave the sadness of Tahiti, a sadness made deeper by an incident of a character I later weaved into a story called *Mrs Eglantine*.

'Every morning Mrs Eglantine sat at the round bamboo bar of the New Pacific Hotel and drank her breakfast. This consisted of two quick large brandies, followed by several slower ones. By noon breakfast had become lunch and by two o'clock the pouches under and above Mrs Eglantine's bleared blue eyes had begun to look like large puffed pink prawns.'

'I suppose you know you've got her name wrong?' my friend the doctor said to me. 'It's really Eglinton. What makes you call her Eglantine?'

'She must have been rather sweet at some time.'

'You think so?' he said. 'What has Eglantine got to do with that?'

'The Sweet-briar,' I said, 'or the Vine, or the twisted Eglantine.'

Mrs Eglantine was in fact a piece of alcoholic flotsam such as

Mrs Eglantine

Maugham and Conrad were fond of describing. She at least had
no illusions about the Paradise and the Lotus Land:

> Swindle. The big myth. The great South-sea bubble. The
> great South-sea paradise. Not a decent hotel in the place. All
> the shops owned by Chinks. Everybody bone-lazy. Takes
> you all day to cash a cheque at the bank. Hot and dirty . . .
> You've seen the travel posters, haven't you, dear? Those nice
> white sands and the Polynesian girls with naked bosoms
> climbing the palms. All a myth, dear. All a bloody swindle.
> All taken in the Cook Islands, hundreds of miles away.

Mrs Eglantine had other sources of disillusionment and bitterness. She had come all the way from Australia to marry a
Frenchman in Tahiti only to find, on arrival, that the Admin-
istration had posted him, in her view deliberately, to New
Caledonia. Her dilemma now was that she was either waiting
permission to stay on the island, or deportation – she didn't know
which. She was bitter too with the French, who didn't like the
British, and further embittered by the Governor, who didn't

like her. 'Undesirable type, dear. Divorced and drinks too much. Bad combination.'

Eventually it turned out that Mrs Eglantine was to be deported and it happened that she flew out on the same flying boat as we did. She was much depressed and I bought her customary breakfast for her on the plane. The irony of her going was that she had to be deported to the nearest British possession, which happened to be the Cook Islands, which under a system of partial prohibition were virtually dry. It was hard to know what Mrs Eglantine would have for breakfast.

At Atutaki, after the flying boat had landed on the lagoon and was being refuelled, a group of Polynesian women and girls were singing songs of farewell to a young man about to leave on the plane.

'The songs of Polynesia have a great sadness in them. A few of the women were weeping. Then at the last moment a girl rushed on bare feet along the jetty towards the waking launch, wringing her hands in sorrow, her long hair flying, bitterly weeping final words of goodbye.

'On the scalding white coral beach, under the palms, there was no sign of Mrs Eglantine. And presently, as the launch moved away, I could no longer hear the songs of sad farewell or the haunting voice of the girl who was weeping. But only, running through my head, haunting too:

'"The Sweet-briar, or the Vine, or the twisted Eglantine".'

XIII

During the war and in the years immediately after it I had travelled much and far. I had seen the squalor, the fatalism and the charm of India, the ruin and grace of Burma, the colonial piracy of the Bahamas, something of the West Indies and America, something of the Middle East, from the Pyramids to the great wondrous towers of Baalbek, much of Europe and a glimpse, an unaffectionate glimpse, of the far north. But wherever I went, and however far, I was for ever left with one unbreakable, unshakeable conviction: there was, for me, among the wonders, the paradises, the Lotus Lands and all, no place like England. The more my world enlarged and ripened the more English I became.

At the heart of all this lay an odd paradox. Whenever I began to think in terms of a novel I could conceive of no other background than my native Midlands, the valleys of my childhood which I had left many years before. The powerful knot which bound me to them refused to be broken. Ardent lover of the south country and, in particular Kent, though I had become, consistently maintaining that here was some of the loveliest countryside in the land, I felt no kind of urge to place a novel there. Short stories and novellas, yes, but never a longer work. To complete the paradox I no longer felt impelled to place a shorter work in the county of my childhood.

Somewhere in the mid-fifties, however, I began restlessly nursing a new idea. I had long been fascinated by a rural junk-yard I used to pass two or three times a week. Its crazy mess of old iron, rusting implements, pigs, horses, geese, turkeys, haystacks and use-less junk of every kind sat incongruously next to the most beautiful of bluebell woods, the junk mocking the beauty, the bluebells mocking the junk. Here, it seemed to me, was something that had to be written about. The more I thought about it, however, the farther I seemed to get from any kind of accomplishment.

Here, in fact, was the perfect example of a negative needing a positive to wake it to life. I did not, however, go round consciously searching for a positive; experience teaches that these things happen by accident, unexpectedly. And so it was. One early summer evening Madge and I were driving through a Kentish village twenty-five miles east of us, in apple orchard country, when she suddenly had reason to stop and make a few purchases at the village shop. As I sat waiting for her in the car I noticed, outside the shop, a ramshackle lorry that had been recently painted a violent electric blue. Two or three minutes later there came out of the shop, in high spirits, a remarkable family: father a perky, sprightly character with dark sideburnings, Ma a youngish hand-some woman of enormous girth, wearing a bright salmon jumper and shaking with laughter like a jelly, and six children, the eldest of them a beautiful dark-haired girl of twenty or so. All were sucking at colossal multi-coloured ice creams and at the same time crunching potato crisps. As they piled into the lorry there was an air of gay and uninhibited abandon about it all. Wild laughter rang through the village street and the whole scene might have come out of Merrie England.

This, I suddenly knew, was my positive; here were the inhabitants of my junk-yard. Next morning, in a fever of excitement and laughter, I set the family going in a short story called *The Darling Buds of May*, in which the unconventional natures of Pop, Ma and their children are unashamedly revealed. The eldest and most beautiful girl, unmarried, is revealed as being pregnant, but exactly by whom she doesn't know. Does it matter? Not on your life – 'perfick', says Pop. He, the junkdealer, his pockets stuffed with fat rolls of pound notes, is revealed as never paying income tax. He regards it as sort of immoral even to think of doing so.

The entire family is gargantuan of appetite, unenslaved by conventions, blissfully happy. Pop is further revealed as a passionate lover of the countryside, as ardent a worshipper at the bluebell shrine and its nightingales as he is of Ma's seductive, voluptuous bosoms. He yields to no man in his warm, proud love of England. All is 'perfick'.

Presently it seemed to me a thousand pities to confine such a rich gallery of characters to a short story. In their lusty love of life they cried out for greater space, richer pastures. I accordingly began to expand them into a novel. The Larkin household was then revealed in all its uninhibited glory: two enormous television sets, a Rolls-Royce, a vast glittering cocktail cabinet from which Pop dispenses cocktails of a terrifying potency with such names as Red Bull and Rolls-Royce, a potency that affects Mr Charlton, a visiting taxman, with dire consequences. His seduction by Mariette being at last complete, he finds himself surrendering completely to the Larkins, the Larkin household and above all the Larkin philosophy, which is all *carpe diem* and the very antithesis of the Welfare State. The Larkins' secret is in fact that they live as many of us would like to live if only we had the guts and nerve to flout the conventions. Pop and Ma demonstrate that they have the capacity by indulging deeply in love and champagne before breakfast, passion in the bluebell wood and encouraging their enchanting daughter to a life of wilful seduction. Ma too has a philosophy all her own. It is what she calls 'lending Pop out'. Thoroughly aware of Pop's attraction for the opposite sex, and vice versa, she has no compunction whatever about letting him have an occasional fling with others, whether beautiful or, like the spinster Miss Pilchester, merely hungry and unsatisfied. Result: much Chaucerian fun and infinite happiness.

The Darling Buds of May was instantly a phenomenal success. It went into many languages. Colonials and Americans, having tended to think of the English as cold stuffed-shirts, seized upon its wanton, Chaucerian joys, its flouting of conventions and the Welfare State, with joy and relish. It also became revealed as a healer of the sick, a blower away of the blues. From all quarters came reports of laughter killing depression, of the Larkins working miracles in hospital wards. An American woman wrote to say that one day on looking out of her window she was much startled to see her next-door neighbour writhing on her bed in the throes of apparent agony. On rushing to her aid she found that it was nothing of the kind; she was merely reading *The Darling Buds of May*.

Thus encouraged, I proceeded to a second novel, *A Breath of French Air*, in which the entire Larkin family, new baby and all, set off in the Rolls-Royce for a French holiday, only to suffer certain disillusionments in the matter of French weather, French food ('We shan't get very fat on this') and French sanitary arrangements. The whole thing develops into a wanton Bacchanale. From this I proceeded still further to *When the Green Woods Laugh, Oh! To Be in England* and finally to *A Little of What you Fancy*, not the least distinctive feature of which is the behaviour of Primrose, the beautiful archseductress who is not only capable of thinking, in true Larkin fashion, through the pores of her skin but also proves she is capable of a double act by openly seducing the local curate with her voluptuous body in a mushroom field, having first softened him up with even more voluptuous quotations on the subject of uninhibited love from Blake and Donne.

The Larkins could, if necessary, be read on two planes: purely for the sheer joy of their enviable way of life, but also as a reflection on the revolution that had overtaken post-war England, a revolution that had nowhere been so marked as in the English countryside. In the early thirties not a single farm worker in my village had a car, many not even a bicycle; today many have two cars, many a cottage inhabited by a family displays four, five, even six cars; few village shops sold anything but mouse-trap cheese, fat bacon, candles, paraffin, tart oranges and boiled sweets; today every one has its deep freeze dispensing scampi, smoked salmon, spaghetti bolognese and exotics of every kind. Not that it was either essential or necessary to interpret the books as being in any way a treatise on the revolution; the point was never laboured or forced. The surface delight was no mere coating for a pill; it could be unashamedly enjoyed, as Ma and Pop unashamedly enjoyed their love and champagne and Primrose her seduction by flesh and poetry in the fields, for its own sake.

The comedian in me, which much earlier in my career had produced *My Uncle Silas* and other pieces in lighter vein, is not only capable of laughing at the foibles of others or indulging in the effervescence of comedy; it is also a source of self-criticism; it is a means of preventing myself from taking myself too seriously, of becoming pompous; it even enables me to poke fun at myself and my own shortcomings.

It is not to be denied, moreover, that there is something of myself in Pop Larkin: a passionate Englishman, a profound love of nature, of the sounds and sights of the countryside, of colour, flowers and things sensual; a hatred of pomp, pretension and humbug; a lover of children and family life; an occasional breaker of rules, a flouter of conventions. The only things I don't share with Pop are a business ability to sell junk at a profit of three hundred and more per cent or to avoid the payment of income tax.

Pop is in fact an expression of my own philosophy: the need to go with the stream, never to battle against it. The prolific fruits of this are to be seen in Pop's many children, as they are to be seen in mine. To my four, Ann, Judith, Richard and Jonathan, all now grown up, are now added progeny of their own: Stephen, Jeremy, Andrew, Beverley, Emma, Jonathan, Lydia, Timothy, Catherine and Justin. A handsome cornucopia.

As I write these final words I am looking out over the garden that, forty years ago, was a derelict farmyard; it is now rich in maturity, bright not only with autumn colour but here and there, with a mauve iris or two, a witch-hazel, a viburnum in blossom, with a premature touch of spring. Beyond it stand the great turkey oaks, pure molten gold against the most tranquil of blue November skies in the morning sun. These splendid trees are, to me, something more than trees. They stand for England, my England.

In them, indeed, I see the world in ripeness. *Bon fruit*, the French say, *mûrit tard*, or if you prefer English: 'ripeness is all'.

Also by H. E. Bates

THE PURPLE PLAIN

'This is it, it can't be, after all this time, oh! Christ, it can't be!'

Burma during the Second World War is the setting for this acclaimed story of survival.

Embittered by his young wife's death in the Blitz, Forrester finds renewal and love with the inhabitants of a mission community in Burma. But just as he begins to rediscover life, further tragedy threatens to rob him of it once more.

On a routine flight Forrester's aircraft crashes miles from help in the Burmese wilderness. Forrester and his two companions survive to face a trek in the unforgiving sun to safety. But Carrington, the young navigator, cannot walk; and the frightened Blore disappears . . .

'It haunts you . . . for the mounting suspense and the masterly portraits of the three men' *Sunday Times*

'One of the most vividly evocative writers of English . . . able to conjure up in a handful of words whole landscapes and moods' *Listener*

ISBN 10: 0-413-77597-6

ISBN 13: 978-0-413-77597-9

H. E. Bates

THE JACARANDA TREE

'The idea of running away. That's the most miserable thing in the world.'

As the Japanese invade Burma during the Second World War, Paterson – the manager of a rice mill – organises the evacuation of a small English community. Reluctantly the diverse group, including Paterson's Burmese mistress and her young brother, takes two cars and moves north towards the Indian border in an attempt to reach safety.

Inside the cars, tensions mount as prejudices, grudges and pettiness take hold. On the road outside, desperate refugees battle heat, thirst and disease. Swiftly and inevitably the bonds of English insularity disintengrate, leaving everyone alone to find a way through the tragedy and terror of an insoluble conflict.

'One of the most exciting and perfectly executed pieces of fiction that I have read' *Spectator*

ISBN 10: 0-413-77599-2

ISBN 13: 978-0-413-77599-3

H. E. Bates

THE FEAST OF JULY

'I'll find you some day and I'll kill you.'

Betrayed by her lover, Bella Ford vows revenge and sets out on a journey to find him. Instead, her arduous search brings her to the home of the Wainwright family; the pious and good-natured father, his uncompromising wife, their daughter Nell and their three very different sons – sensitive Matty, quick-tempered Con and sedate Jedd.

Slowly and in their individual ways the Wainwrights restore Bella's trust and, becoming absorbed in their lives, she again finds happiness and love.

Then at the traditional Feast of July, the past makes a sudden reappearance in Bella's life, bringing with it violent and terrible tragedy.

'H. E. Bates can achieve a quality of lytrical intensity that few contemporary novelists can match' *Times Literary Supplement*

ISBN 10: 0-413-77598-4

ISBN 13: 978-0-413-77598-6